ALSO BY MICHAEL POSNER

IN THIS SERIES

Leonard Cohen, Untold Stories: The Early Years, Vol. 1

Leonard Cohen, Untold Stories: From This Broken Hill, Vol. 2

OTHER WORKS

All of Me (with Anne Murray)

The Last Honest Man, Mordecai Richler: An Oral Biography

The Big Picture: What Canadians Think About Almost Everything
(with Allan Gregg)

Canadian Dreams: The Making and Marketing of Independent Films

Money Logic (with Moshe Milevsky)

The Art of Medicine: Healing and the Limits of Technology
(with Dr. Herbert Ho Ping Kong)

LEONARD COHEN

UNTOLD STORIES: That's How the Light Gets In, Volume 3

MICHAEL POSNER

Published by **SIMON & SCHUSTER**
New York London Toronto Sydney New Delhi

SIMON &
SCHUSTER
CANADA

Simon & Schuster Canada
A Division of Simon & Schuster, Inc.
166 King Street East, Suite 300
Toronto, Ontario M5A 1J3

This Simon & Schuster Canada edition November 2022

SIMON & SCHUSTER CANADA and colophon
are trademarks of Simon & Schuster, Inc.

For information about special discounts for bulk purchases,
please contact Simon & Schuster Special Sales at 1-800-268-3216
or CustomerService@simonandschuster.ca.

Manufactured in the United States of America

10 9 8 7 6 5 4 3 2 1

Library and Archives Canada Cataloguing in Publication

Title: Leonard Cohen, untold stories. Volume 3, That's how the light gets in / Michael Posner.
Other titles: That's how the light gets in | That is how the light gets in
Names: Posner, Michael, 1947– author.
Description: Simon & Schuster Canada edition.
Identifiers: Canadiana (print) 20220186774 | Canadiana (ebook) 20220186820 |
ISBN 9781982176921 (hardcover) | ISBN 9781982176938 (ebook)
Subjects: LCSH: Cohen, Leonard, 1934-2016. | LCSH: Cohen, Leonard, 1934-2016—
Friends and associates. | LCSH: Singers—Canada—Biography. |
LCSH: Composers—Canada—Biography. |
LCSH: Poets, Canadian—20th century—Biography. | LCGFT: Biographies.
Classification: LCC PS8505.O22 Z8431 2022 | DDC C811/.54—dc23

ISBN 978-1-9821-7692-1
ISBN 978-1-9821-7693-8 (ebook)

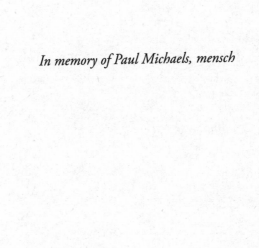

In memory of Paul Michaels, mensch

Contents

Introduction

Oral biography is an imperfect genre. It relies almost entirely on human memory, which is notoriously fallible. On the page, it frequently juxtaposes one confident viewpoint with another, completely contradictory, but no less confident, viewpoint—and then with a third, which might offer an entirely different perspective. The result tends to leave readers a little confused about who to believe, or what version of events to trust. Instead of a convenient, unified, well-argued thesis, it offers no thesis whatsoever, convenient, unified, or otherwise. It thus imposes the tyranny of choice—and some will resist.

On the other hand, memory is always suspect, even in conventional biographies. Moreover, in oral history's typical incarnation—the multidimensional story of important cultural figures or events—the ostensible liabilities may become assets. Readers are exposed to a wider range of opinion than they might encounter in a traditional, authorial narrative. Points of view conflict, but those very conflicts collectively offer a closer approximation of reality, something more nuanced, more faithful to the chiaroscuro complexity of truth. Reconstructing history is not unlike putting a jigsaw puzzle together; the more pieces that are available, the greater the likelihood that a more complete, more accurate picture will emerge.

Oral biography confers another advantage, particularly relevant in the case of Leonard Cohen, the cultural figure who has occupied my attention these last several years: it collates and amalgamates memories and observations before they would be lost forever. Cohen passed away in November 2016 at the age of eighty-two. Inevitably, many of his contemporaries, men and women who knew him best, are—or were—also senior citizens, skiing the perilous downslope of life. Indeed, since I began research on this project, twenty-seven interviewees have also died.

One of these was the late American poet Jack Hirschman, who passed away in August 2021, at the age of eighty-seven. I met him only briefly—a long, delightful conversation in San Francisco's historic Caffe Trieste, his daily breakfast nook. In many respects, he and Cohen were light-years apart. Jack was a committed social activist; Cohen could barely be persuaded to sign an SPCA petition, let only carry a political protest sign. Until his final breath, Jack was an unrepentant socialist, if not a card-carrying Communist; Cohen carried another membership card—the National Rifle Association's—and his own ideological instincts, at least on issues of foreign policy, defence, and security, tilted decidedly to the right, however well he may have concealed them. It should also be said that, aside from the six months that Hirschman and his then wife, Ruth Seymour, spent on Hydra in 1965, he and Cohen were not particularly close. Still, there was an implicit and genuine bond between them, and mutual respect. It was essentially a cultural connection; they were, as Jews say, *lantzmen*.

When Hirschman heard news of Cohen's passing, he wrote a poem, "The 4 Questions Arcane." It's a kind of digest of their relationship, such as it was. The "four questions" allude to a ritual part of the Passover seder—he and Cohen had celebrated the Jewish holiday together on Hydra in 1965. "Arcane," of course, means hidden—Hirschman's recognition that, at the heart of the Leonard Cohen story, lies an unsolved mystery. What was it that lifted Cohen's work so far above virtually all of his fellow workers in song? What secret formula did he have access to? Cohen himself seemed not to know the answer. As he said many times, "If I knew where the good songs came from, I'd go there more often."

Attempting to explain the essential genius of both Cohen and Bob Dylan, music executive Don Was likes to invoke the notion of creative ether—inspirational strands, floating through some imaginary troposphere. "You reach up and pull ideas out," he says. "The best stuff is way up there, and a couple [people] can reach the very top. That's Bob and Leonard."

Jack Hirschman only saw Cohen onstage once, at Oakland's Paramount Theatre in 2013. "I forgave him everything when I saw him perform," he told me, savouring his morning bagel with cream cheese. The "everything" would have pertained to the political gulf between them. A reference to that performance concludes his poem:

> I realized from
> the way you literally
> ran from wings to mic
>
> at center-stage you
> were a great showman able
> to lift your hat like
>
> the tip of a poem,
> your singing Being itself,
> in the beginning, so,
>
> so long, Leonard Cohen,
> your genius voice that set
> a table of poems /
>
> rooted in scripture
> and blues of affirmation
> across the decades
>
> ears will never stop
> feasting on, rest assured,
> dear Label. Yours, Yankel.

The "great showman" represents only one of the incarnations of Leonard Cohen we encounter in this third and final volume of *Untold Stories*. The first book, *The Early Years*, chronicles his childhood, adolescence, and emergence as the golden boy of Canadian letters—effectively, a portrait of the artist as a young man—ending with his ambitious segue from literature to music in 1970. The second book, *From This Broken Hill*, documents Cohen's turbulent middle years—juxtaposing commercial success, especially in Europe, with his creative struggles, his relentless pursuit of women, his immersion in Zen Buddhism, the burdens of fatherhood, his fractured "marriage," and his chronic battle with depression.

In *That's How the Light Gets In*, we accompany Cohen on the roller-coaster ride of his last thirty years. After resurrecting his moribund career in the late 1980s, he nevertheless remains profoundly broken. Sex, alcohol, psychotherapy, hard drugs, pills of every conceivable kind—he tries everything to shake the black dogs gnawing at his psyche. Nothing works. On the cusp of sixty, walking away from an engagement to actress Rebecca De Mornay, he enters the rigorous Rinzai-Ji monastery on Mount Baldy, east of Los Angeles, surrendering to the ministry of his longtime Zen master, Joshu Sasaki Roshi, arguably the single most important relationship of his life. In the end, even submission and asceticism are unavailing. The endless hours of meditation, all the wisdom of Zen, cannot fill the hole inside of him.

Then, miraculously, after exploring the world of Advaita Vedanta Hinduism—six trips to India over five years starting in the late 1990s—light pierces the veritable crack: Cohen begins to notice that his dark incubus is slowly dissolving. Ironically, the lifting of his depression coincides with the discovery that five million dollars, much of his life savings, has also evaporated, allegedly spent by his trusted friend, one-time lover, and personal manager, Kelley Lynch. Ironic on another level as well—the private life of this most private of men unavoidably splashes across newspapers and magazines.

And then the final, more delicious irony. The lurid Lynch saga becomes the catalyst for his hugely successful return to the concert stage—more than three hundred sold-out performances over six years that, in the words of promoter Rob Hallett, replaces all of his financial losses, "and then some. And then a lot some." During this period, Cohen also manages to complete two new albums, and, after illness strikes, yet another—one last, searing confrontation with God, *You Want It Darker*, as well as a book of poetry, *The Flame*, issued posthumously. If there's another artist that has crafted such a productive and illustrious last chapter of his life, I'm not aware of it.

Inevitably, *That's How the Light Gets In* also documents his challenging final years, a decline he bears with characteristic grace, stoic resolve, and sardonic humour. The "old jalopy" is breaking down, he confides to friends, white-knuckling himself through the pain of crushed discs and leukaemia. "Often in the garage for repairs." Knowledge of his condition is closely held; there will be no public display of suffering. When friends come to visit in those final months, they find him in his signature garb (suit, tie, hat), and his first instinct—as always, and sick as he was—is, "What can I get you to eat or drink?" When he eventually shares the grim diagnosis, his friend, Professor Robert Faggen, gulps and says, "That's terminal." To which Cohen replies, "Yes . . . Of course, life is terminal."

Cohen himself disparaged the likelihood of his leaving a meaningful creative legacy. Once, flipping through *The Oxford Book of English Verse*, he noted that such giants as Donne, Milton, and Wordsworth had only merited a few pages—Shakespeare, a mere dozen or so. "I'll be lucky," he told his friend Barrie Wexler, "if I'm a footnote."

I'm not convinced. Poetry no longer commands our attention as it once did. The power of the Word itself, in technological societies increasingly dominated by algorithms, is in serious decline. But music remains as much a universal language as math, and far more accessible. At its summit, where Cohen resides, music connects us more directly with what he liked to call the human predicament. As the late critic George Steiner put it, "Is there a lie, anywhere, in Mozart?" One might ask the same of the Cohenian canon. Indeed, as Leonard himself observed, "The singer must die for the lie in his voice."

Which leaves us with the questions arcane—the abiding mysteries. It's my hope that this book, and the two that preceded it, will begin to provide some additional clues to the life Cohen actually led and, in turn, help chart a course to some deeper understanding of the man and his work. Let the journey begin.

CHAPTER ONE

Back on Boogie Street

I think I was . . . really just born to be his conduit . . . to be an instrument that he played . . . to bring the inner sound of what he did out. That's it. I'm like the waitress. I'm bringing the food. [It] was like walking around an attic, shining a flashlight on unrecognized gems. . . . It said to people, "Have you forgotten what's beautiful?" I'll show you.

—Jennifer Warnes

What was he? He wasn't a pop star, a singer, a poet, a thinker. He was all of those things and more. His temperament was unique. There was always a dimension of irony. He was never not himself for a single second in his whole life. There's nobody like him. Nobody. He's sui generis.

—Leon Wieseltier

It's not precisely clear what tea leaves Jennifer Warnes might have been reading on New Year's Eve 1985 in Los Angeles, when she and Leonard Cohen enjoyed the night together. But the auguries proved auspicious. Both of their languishing careers were about to receive a boost, thanks to Warnes's cover album, *Famous Blue Raincoat: The Songs of Leonard Cohen.* The idea had been hatched seven years earlier when she toured with Cohen and Roscoe Beck.

ROSCOE BECK: We'd perform these songs every night and could hear other possibilities. We said, "Wouldn't it be great to do a record of Leonard's music and present it in a different way?"

SHARON WEISZ: I first heard the idea in 1980. Jennifer had just returned from the tour. She said she was desperate to make an album of Leonard's songs—a pretty obscure prospect at that point.

Indeed, as Warnes later told journalist Bob Mersereau, "It was unsalable, a waste of time and money. We just felt so spiritually called to do it, nobody could talk us out of it."

SHARON WEISZ: Then, in 1986, Craig Sussman was starting Cypress Records. His first project is *Famous Blue Raincoat*. I was hired to launch the project.

ROSCOE BECK: It took seven years of her being laughed at.

Sussman, who had worked in business affairs at CBS Records, had met Cohen at international conventions.

LORI NAFSHUN: Craig had this really interesting idea about marketing to baby boomers—get away from big-money projects and keep it simple. You could sell forty thousand units and still make money. We had a little recording studio in West LA—the Complex.

CRAIG SUSSMAN: I thought, "What if name-brand artists made albums their record companies didn't want them to make, using digitally recorded music?" My wife and I invested our life savings—about $150,000. The 24-track machine alone cost $100,000. I didn't have any creative background. I knew how to make the numbers work, build the team. Jennifer had name recognition and a core audience. I wasn't looking for a home run—just a single. I knew nothing about Cohen's music. I did research and found he had a huge international following. I thought, "Even if it did nothing [in North America], maybe internationally we'd have something special." I had zero creative input. I was smart enough to stay away.

Sussman's production point person was Lori Nafshun.

LORI NAFSHUN: I was twenty-five and really didn't understand who Leonard was. Craig played me his music. I was underwhelmed. But because I didn't know how revered he was, I wasn't shy, as most women were. He had an animal magnetism—it affected men, too—but it didn't affect me. In the studio, he was low-key, wallpaper-esque.

CRAIG SUSSMAN: The record took longer than I'd hoped—and a lot more money than I'd expected. What was difficult [was], artists needed it to be great. This was their comeback record. They weren't going to stop. So it was a process you don't have total control over.

As they added tracks, Warnes and Beck sensed its potential.

JENNIFER WARNES: About halfway through, we looked at each other and said, "Oh-oh, we got something here. This is a marlin!" At that point, we hired better players, started to work midnight to five a.m.—better studio rates. We just went for broke. "Why not a choir? Why not Stevie Ray Vaughan, Billy Payne, Van Dyke Parks?" That wishful thinking permeated the rest of the album.

For the album, Cohen wrote "Ain't No Cure for Love" and sang with Warnes on "Joan of Arc."

LORI NAFSHUN: He wrote ["Cure"] at the Complex. Came in with his little Casio keyboard and played it. I remember thinking, "What is this?"

JENNIFER WARNES: It was a comment [he made] after we both read the *LA Weekly* [story] about AIDS. We took a walk around the block. I said, "Gee, it's getting so people can't even love one another anymore. Just die from it." And he said, "There ain't no cure for love."

In his signature suit, Cohen would arrive at the studio with Courvoisier and pour drinks.

JENNIFER WARNES: We put up "Joan of Arc" and I said, "Do you want to sing that verse?" He said, "Sure." He was slightly drunk. He said I forced him into doing it, but he sang beautifully.

LORI NAFSHUN: Jennifer, Leonard, and Roscoe had creative control. There was only one moment where we made a suggestion, on "First We Take Manhattan"—to bring up Stevie Ray Vaughan's guitar solo in the mix. Our working title was *Jenny Sings Lenny*, but that was for fun. [The album's liner notes, however, included Cohen's drawing of a torch being passed, with the caption "Jenny Sings Lenny."] We were going to release "First We Take Manhattan" as a single, but nobody had any idea of what the song was about. I volunteered to ask him. He very graciously said the song could be about anything I wanted it to be about. Which obviously wasn't helpful. In terms of Leonard and Jennifer, two things were happening, the artistic and the personal. On the artistic level, he said, "I need you to make my songs groove, because I can't."

The Cohen-Warnes romance had long since morphed into a deep friendship, marked by mutual trust and respect. The record itself was released in November 1986 to largely glowing reviews. Soon, Sussman was fielding requests for foreign rights, while domestic sales soared. Of the approximately fifty albums Cypress ultimately produced, *Famous Blue Raincoat* was among the most critically acclaimed and one of its bestsellers.

CRAIG SUSSMAN: Leonard was cordial, warm, a unique soul. When we launched the record, we did a performance in Munich [Park-Café, April 15, 1987]. Leonard introduced Jennifer. Afterwards, on a high, Leonard and I were in a disco. We drank all night long, hard liquor, and he told stories, none of which I remember.

Cohen also promoted the album in LA. After one interview, Sharon Weisz drove him home.

SHARON WEISZ: It was a Friday night. We get to his duplex and he says, "Would you light the Shabbas candles for me?" It was life-changing—because I was embarrassed that I stumbled over the prayers. I give him credit for my [later] joining a synagogue. The candles had been set up to be lit. I was terrified of him because he was such an icon and I felt so inadequate. But then he'd crack a joke and I thought, "He's cool."

When the video for Warnes's "First We Take Manhattan" was shot, Weisz—shooting still photographs—caught Cohen just after he emerged from an elevator holding a half-eaten banana.

SHARON WEISZ: I ordered an eight-by-ten black-and-white and mailed it. A week later, I get a call. "Sharon, I've been looking at the photograph. What would you think if I put it on the cover of my album?" I didn't even know he was making an album. Of course, I said yes.

Cohen later acknowledged that Warnes's album had "resurrected my credentials, certainly in the music industry."

TERESA TUDURY: Jennifer knew the genius, and she redelivered those songs with her lilting, incredible voice. It really pulled him out of that caricature he'd become.

One day, Cohen and Warnes were interviewed on KCRW radio in LA, managed by his friend Ruth Seymour, former wife of poet Jack Hirschman.

RUTH SEYMOUR: He came into the studio with Jenny, and he said, "So, what do you do here, Ruth?" And I had *created* the station. I could see the shock on Jenny's face. It gives you a sense of the place of women in this society—that Leonard, who had known me on Hydra, could not even imagine that I would be the boss. But it wasn't just Leonard. I wasn't the same person. We had all changed.

Inevitably, there was discussion about a follow-up album, but Cohen discouraged Warnes, suggesting that having his songs covered by several artists was wiser. Ultimately, she agreed, saying, "That might have been a really good decision for him."

By October 1986, Cohen was in Spain, to attend a Federico García Lorca festival in Grenada and shoot the video for "Take This Waltz." He visited the house in which Lorca had once resided and, by one account, knelt before a photo of the poet and practiced yoga. Cohen spent the next several months shuttling between Montreal, Paris, New York, and Los Angeles. In New York, he went to see the film *Manhunter,* directed by Michael Mann, about a serial killer.

KELLEY LYNCH: He told me it was his favourite film. He was obsessed with it.

On January 25, 1987, he had dinner with his manager, Marty Machat, and Machat's son, Steve.

STEVE MACHAT: Everyone was close to Leonard, but no one knew him. He had issues and no one could get under his skin. My dad would never get in. I was managing the New Edition, and running the fan club out of 1501 Broadway. I had thirty-five people back there. My dad says, "Leonard's coming in. You can't have this going on. I don't want him to think we're running a circus." So I go [in] and Leonard is there, legs crossed, talking to the kids, helping with the mail, fully engaged, a big shit-eating grin on his face.

Cohen also reconnected with bass player John Miller at the Howard Johnson's on Broadway.

JOHN MILLER: My kind of place. His kind of place. Stayed open 'til the wee hours. He'd call—I'd drop what I was doing and we'd continue where we left off [in 1976]. One time, we got into a cab and the driver, thick Russian accent, says, "Are you Leonard Cohen?" Leonard looks at the license tag and says, "Are you the Russian poet?" He says, "Yes." Leonard says, "How much do you get for the night?" . . . "Two hundred dollars." . . . "Shut the meter. Here's two hundred dollars. Take us to the best place we should all eat and drink." Russian place in Brooklyn. Must have been there 'til five in the morning. Russian music. Great food. It was that type of sensibility.

Another day, Miller dropped by Machat's offices and found Cohen at an Olivetti typewriter.

JOHN MILLER: A stack of papers, two feet high. He's looking at them, crumpling, looking, crumpling, writing, looking, crumpling. I said, "Leonard, what are you doing?" He said, "I'm looking at ten years of my diary and trying to find one sentence that captures the essence of that year." I lean over and see "1966, Marianne paints the kitchen red." Every man can relate to that. It says it all. He was looking for the kernel of truth. Or we'd be driving across the Golden Gate Bridge, and he'd be far more interested in the winos taking a piss under the pier than how beautiful the view was. He was a kindred spirit.

Another day, Cohen's old friend Barrie Wexler dropped by Cohen's suite at the Royalton Hotel.

BARRIE WEXLER: I had a really bad headache. I told him a story about a guru showing Baba Ram Dass how to transfer physical discomfort to a clump of trees. Not to be outdone, Cohen launched into his "Point to your pain" routine, to try to make my headache go away. I joked that his spiritual mumbo jumbo wouldn't work on a confirmed Jewish hypochondriac like me. He shot back that it would if administered by another confirmed Jewish hypochondriac. And it did.

During a visit to Montreal, Cohen spent an evening with his friend Charlie Gurd. He was a client of healer Dawn Bramadat.

DAWN BRAMADAT: Leonard [had] never hit on me, but I had a creepy feeling when Charlie called me at eleven one night and said, "I'm here with Leonard and he wants a session with you, now." I said no. He couldn't believe I'd say no. He honestly expected me to jump up and do this because this was Leonard Cohen. Everybody knew Lenny as somebody who hit on everybody. How long you lasted with him depended on how much you were willing to put aside dignity and integrity, and disillusion yourself about your importance. He came across as somebody unstable, somebody who needed anchoring. Wounded men are very attractive. A lot of women felt they were what was keeping him alive, that in some way, they were responsible for his greatness.

Bramadat was conscious of the powerful effect Cohen had on his entourage.

DAWN BRAMADAT: There was a gurudom. It was known. People devoted to Lenny were totally devoted to Lenny. A lot were also extremely talented artists who maybe hoped his allure would rub off. But they were more than a little under his spell. Around Leonard, people became totally different. On some level, he was the good daddy for them. Some people don't want to talk about him now because of the damage it would do—to bust all these illusions.

By this time, Cohen was hard at work on what would become the *I'm Your Man* album. Its genesis had occurred a few years earlier.

JEFF FISHER: I'd heard [his] name and the song "Suzanne"—that's about all. He saw me performing in Paris with Carole Laure and Lewis Furey. I got a call in Montreal shortly after. He hit me with "First We Take Manhattan"—chords and lyrics. I programmed a drum machine and played all the parts. I arranged it, inadvertently gave it some hooks and riffs. It was Sergio Leone–ish. He asked for no modifications. He sent it to Columbia and got a record deal. I liked him. A nice old guy, pretty cool.

Soon, Cohen brought Fisher more songs to arrange, including "Ain't No Cure." It had already been recorded by Warnes, but Cohen added several new verses.

JEFF FISHER: He went to LA and changed the drums. He had a woman [Anjani Thomas]—I think they were going out at the time. She was very, very good. She pretty well put together the vocal arrangements.

Thomas, a backup singer on Cohen's 1985 concert tour, had been an occasional lover and would become his principal liaison after 2000. After the album was complete, Cohen and Fisher had a falling-out.

KELLEY LYNCH: I thought it came down to money, egos, and proper credit.

JEFF FISHER: Sometimes he thought it was worth it and sometimes he thought I overcharged. He had his ego and was quiet about expressing stuff. I was young and had a lot more ego then. He had hypoglycaemia and sometimes he'd space out. It affected him. On one song, we had some good takes with the rhythm section, but he was quiet about it. In retrospect, he was pissed because he didn't get the take he wanted. But he'd still send me a box of dates at Christmas.

KELLEY LYNCH: That's what I witnessed—a war of silence and Cohen's paranoia over whatever happened. Cohen was very seriously depressed in the mid-eighties. Something awful was going on. He was having a very difficult time with Fisher and other people. He rallied himself for the tours.

A few years later, Cohen sent Fisher a "Let's make up" letter, which Fisher had laminated and hung in his home studio.

JEFF FISHER: This is so Leonard, because we would both disappear into our little bubbles. He writes, "Dear Jeff, you are as crazy as I am. I go into hiding. You go into hiding. I guess this is the price of genius. In any case, why don't we do some more songs together? . . . You will be rewarded handsomely. Let's make that fairly handsomely. Fraternally, Leonard Cohen." That sums it up.

Among the album's most popular tracks was "Everybody Knows," a song for which Sharon Robinson provided the tune. It was not the start of their fruitful collaboration; in a hotel lobby in Israel, in 1980, she played him a melody she'd written. In half an hour or less, he had scripted the lyrics to "Summertime," later recorded by Diana Ross. Cohen told an NPR interviewer that, in "Everybody Knows," "[I was] somebody you couldn't put anything over on. I'm incredibly gullible in my ordinary civilian life." With *I'm Your Man*, Cohen graduated from his original Casio keyboard to more sophisticated Technics models.

JEFF FISHER: He had a whole rack of them in his Montreal home, five or six. He told me, "If I hit a couple notes and it gives me a rhythm section and gives me a song, it's paid for itself."

Cohen bought his first Technics from Montreal dealer George Klaus. He was the right guy to ask about keyboards; he'd been responsible for miniaturizing the B3 organ. For Cohen, the machine was love at first note. "I hit the sustain button on a bass note," he said. "It was exactly what I was looking for. Sustain has always been a very important element to me. I like to sing to a sustained chord, a drone. So I bought it."

GEORGE KLAUS: It had drums, rhythm, backup, accompaniment, all kinds of things, a top-of-the-line machine. It was good for writing. He could experiment. He wanted to learn how to use it better and came a couple of times, in the evening, always in a grey, three-piece, pin-striped suit, no tie. He was very low-key, very friendly, straight to the point.

Cohen saw synthesizers as a critical part of his musical development. "They changed my approach," he later told the BBC. "At a certain point, I couldn't gain the respect of musicians I was working with, because I couldn't get my ideas across. I didn't know the musical vocabulary. . . . With the [keyboard, I was able] to materialize my ideas much more easily."

TOM MCMORRAN: That sound was so perfect. He played one chord with one finger. It all became very endearing. The cheap plastic quality of it, in combination with his low voice and the words, was haunting, completely disarming. It's not how many tools you have in the toolbox. It's do you have the ones you need? He did. But he never considered himself much of a singer. He'd say, "If I want to hear a singer, I'll go to the Met."

BARRIE WEXLER: If Leonard wanted to hear great singing, he'd put on an album of Eastern European cantors, [like] Joseph Rosenblatt or Gershon Sirota. Near his house, you'd sometimes hear a *chazzan* in competition with a neighbour's radio playing *rebetiko*. These were hard-to-find recordings. At one point, he brought a couple of them back to Montreal, where they met an ignoble end—he left them on the car dashboard, and they melted in the summer heat.

BOBBY FURGO: These cheesy-sounding [instruments] really fit what he was up to. I wondered how much of a smile he had inside his soul when he'd play that thing. He loved it. Everyone was forbidden in his family to touch his keyboard. He was furious one time with [his son] Adam, because Adam had the audacity to play it without permission. That was the only thing he was protective over.

In Montreal, Cohen hired Michel Robidoux, co-writer of music for *Passe-Partout*, the Quebec *Sesame Street,* and engineer Roger Guerin to work on three tracks.

MICHEL ROBIDOUX: It was so spontaneous, the way we were with each other, nice and easy does it. It was like we'd known each other a long time. "Let's try this, let's try that," but no questions. Never "Oh, my God, where are we going with that?" We went straight to work on "I'm Your Man," "Everybody Knows," and another one not included on the album. I'm not sure we finished the third song.

ROGER GUERIN: We went to his house—painted white, everywhere. In the living room, no couch, wooden table, two chairs, not much else. No paintings that I recall. No books. Maybe a rug. Kitchen—same thing, super basic.

One line from "Everybody Knows" may have come from a conversation with Gabriela Valenzuela, the Costa Rican model and journalist he'd romanced through most of the early 1980s.

GABRIELA VALENZUELA: We had made love and were having a heated quarrel in bed about fidelity. "You have encounters with other women and I never inquire about them. But you're envious whether I do or don't." He exclaimed, "Ahhh! You may be discreet, but you can't help but meet people without your clothes." And he quickly turned around and scribbled it down on the small pad on his nightstand. The exaggeration bothered me. Especially when I was still attempting to shake my conservative Costa Rican roots and was a devoted lover to him.

LINDA BOOK: "There were so many people you just had to meet without your clothes on." That's a bitter man.

MICHEL ROBIDOUX: This guy could really share everything. He's openhearted. That's a big quality for an artist. One Friday, he had a friend, maybe

Hazel Field, and there was a ceremony with the candles and the little hat [kippah]. He asked me to join—wow. It was already prepared, the food. Always in a three-piece suit with the hat. This is his look, his uniform. What an elegant man.

What Robidoux heard first were Cohen's basic keyboard versions—no arrangements.

MICHEL ROBIDOUX: He sang them for me. I already had an idea of where I was going to go, mostly keyboard. There was no rush. Forget the budget. He made me an offer I couldn't refuse. He asked me if I wanted cash or a percentage of sales. I took the cash because I was broke and the offer was so generous.

In the end, Cohen and Robidoux did the basic tracks at Klaus's studio on Notre-Dame Street in Old Montreal.

GEORGE KLAUS: He didn't want anyone to know he was even there. I put a curtain on the studio window to the hallway.

MICHEL ROBIDOUX: We spent a lot of time together. We went to Greek restaurants—he spoke Greek very well. We talked about everything—life, politics—I found him very knowledgeable, well informed. He was very focused, in the groove, you know? I asked if he'd mind if I stayed for the voice-overs, and he was touched and surprised—nobody had ever asked for that. I encouraged him to be a little more swinging. We changed nothing on the melody, just worked on the arrangement, on the keyboards. I was thinking Beatles—with strings, more British than American.

ROGER GUERIN: He'd pay for lunch, every time. The career was at a low point, but we did not discuss it. He was a fantastic storyteller. I remember only one, about a film director in Germany—he proposed a film and it had been refused, when Hitler was in power. He presented it again and the same person rejected it. He tried again after the war to the same person and it was accepted. The power of persistence. Leonard talked about current events. His politics were humane, more international. We'd be eating and the women would come to the table, well-bred, refined women, and say they appreciated his work. He knew his public needed his presence and would take time for them. He was between lovers. He was not a cheerful, happy-go-lucky guy, but not depressed.

MICHEL ROBIDOUX: There were a few visits by women. I don't know who they were. He's a woman's guy and I don't blame the girls.

Eventually, Cohen cut three cheques for Robidoux, one for each song.

MICHEL ROBIDOUX: When I cashed the second cheque, it bounced. It was drawn on a Bank Laurentian on St.-Lawrence. I told Leonard. He says, "Bring the cheque, please." Very calm. He says somebody was asleep at the switch, a guy who didn't know who Leonard was, and did not check for another account. Anybody [else] would have known to take [funds] from another account, because he had an unlimited budget. That was so funny. If I'd been rich, I'd have had the cheque framed.

ROGER GUERIN: Until the last day, he was humble and appreciative, never raised his voice, no ego. Everything was "It's fine, it's fine." His main interest was his voice. It was the kind of voice you put any microphone to and it sounds great—good, low tone, heavy, raspiness. It can obscure your reference for rhythm and pitch, but it worked for him. He had a good musical memory. He knew what the note should be and how to control his voice.

Some months later, Robidoux bumped into Cohen on the street.

MICHEL ROBIDOUX: He told me he had something to talk about, a new project, but it didn't happen. It was like meeting an old friend. He was a gift I happen to have had from life—just a passage—but these are the most precious gifts.

That fall, Cohen's friend, writer Peter Lindforss, interviewed him by phone for a Swedish radio show. Asked about "First We Take Manhattan," Cohen said,

"I think the song is about looking at every extremist position with irony. . . . It is not about a call to change the state of affairs, but about naming and affirming a certain courage, posed in the status quo. Immutability . . . [It's] about us actually having to do something, but not necessarily within the political landscape. . . . It's about personal training. It is a lifelong task because, like the political landscape, the inner landscape is unstable." Asked to reflect on the turbulent 1960s, Cohen said the era was "a double-edged sword. Many died. . . . Drug use was insane. Personal relationships became very irresponsible. This lack of responsibility in the name of freedom was valuable to some and catastrophic for others. I'm not the least bit nostalgic about that decade."

Cohen decided to do backup vocals and the mixes in LA.

GEORGE KLAUS: Roger was very astute, but a bit too careful as an engineer. Leonard wanted more energy. Roger's levels were probably too low for Leonard's taste and he was a bit frustrated. He told me about halfway through the session. I didn't get involved.

ROGER GUERIN: It was surprising to hear the final mix because the oud was not ours. We had talked about the symbolism we were proposing. It determined a distinct nationality, very Middle Eastern, which gives it another dimension, but went against what we'd talked about. We weren't consulted. Our philosophy was to convince him it was too much folklore, specific to a region that had no connection to the text.

Other album tracks were produced by Roscoe Beck in LA and Jean-Michel Reusser in Paris.

JEAN-MICHEL REUSSER: I remember a phone call in the middle of the night. They were in the studio, adding to "Take This Waltz"—Jennifer Warnes and a violin, which were not on the original. Leonard passed me to the sound engineer, who wanted to know what treatments I'd used on the strings of Jean-Philippe Rykiel's version, because they couldn't duplicate them.

Warnes had invited a friend, singer-songwriter Jude Johnstone, to sing backup.

JUDE JOHNSTONE: I can hear my voice on three or four tracks, but I was only credited for one—typical of the time. It was all done in one day. I really enjoyed working with Leonard, liked the way that he was. He talked to me about his earlier days, when Columbia ignored him. He said, "Listen, this is what it is. These people don't care about you. So don't listen to any of it. Just do what you do, as good as you can do it. It's fun to read the beautiful reviews, but if you're gonna read that, you have to read the other ones that say you've dried up. What I choose to do is keep my head down and do the greatest work I know how, and whether the record company is interested or not, none of that means anything. The gift you have doesn't really matter." That was great advice. None of it is real. I was also reaching for [recognition]. I knew he knew that. It was him who made me [understand there] will always be another beautiful melody, another gorgeous lyric. That was what he taught me. His message was, don't pay attention to any of it. He was wicked funny, super intellectual, a very sensual cat, extremely charismatic, definitely able to get the girls. But he was [also] a gifted philosopher.

At the time, Johnstone, just twenty-two, was a smoker.

JUDE JOHNSTONE: He used to go, "Can I borrow a cigarette?" Like, he was going to give it back to me later. I'd go, "But you said you quit." And he'd go, "I did. . . . Can I borrow a cigarette?" He was a cinematic character. I thought he was a movie star, with his freakin' sharkskin, gorgeous, made-in-Italy suit.

In Paris, Reusser collaborated with Cohen on other songs, which later appeared on *The Future* album, with completely different arrangements.

JEAN-MICHEL REUSSER: I wasn't pissed at all. This is something I understand perfectly from an artist. Some tracks [though] deserved to be released. There was a version of "The Future" which was a total, dark, Pink Floydian version.

Among the songs in Cohen's archive is one he apparently never wanted to release.

JEAN-MICHEL REUSSER: He played it twice when we were demoing—"There's a Light in Jamaica." It would have been a number one hit all over the world. It was a tribute to Bob Marley.

CHARMAINE DUNN: I introduced him to Bob Marley and reggae music. He liked it. He later told me he wrote a song for Marley. I don't know what happened to it.

JEAN-MICHEL REUSSER: Every time we bumped into each other, I said, "Leonard, let's do 'There's a Light in Jamaica.'" His last answer was "I've lost the lyrics," which I absolutely didn't believe. But at some point, you have to stop insisting. Jean-Philippe looked everywhere, as did I. We have thousands and thousands of hours. Maybe it will pop up one day.

JORGE CALDERÓN: I went into a studio in Hollywood with David Lindley and Leonard to record two songs. One of them was definitely reggae. It might have been about Jamaica.

Arguably the album's most unusual track is "Jazz Police." It sprang from his 1979 tour with the fusion band Passenger. "My songs are deliberately made with very simple chords, just triads," Cohen told Matt Zimbel in 1988. "These guys . . . would often try to slip in an augmented chord or a diminished chord, and I'd always call them on it. It became a kind of cat-and-mouse game. I became known as the jazz police. I wanted a song that had the freedom and wit of jazz."

SARAH KRAMER: Anjani Thomas used to tease him that, while he was a great composer, he wasn't an authentic jazz musician. Leonard told her, "I'm Charlie Parker"—that he got jazz in a different way. That conversation is where the song began.

Never entirely happy with the lyric, Cohen did think it captured the mood of the period—"This kind of fragmented absurdity. I was living that." Jeff Fisher provided the melody.

JEFF FISHER: We more or less wrote it on the telephone. Rap was just in its infancy and he said, "Let's do a rap song." That's what it was meant to be. I was coming from the seventies' prog rock mentality. There were five-eight fills and even-eight fills, staggered. Ian Terry [the engineer] had to cut the tape out to make it an even four-four. It ended up sounding nothing like any other Cohen song. He's on record as saying he was not sure he liked it. But he did perform it. It's very tongue-in-cheek. There were other, pseudo-sexual lyrics that didn't make it into the song.

Again, Fisher clashed with Cohen over money.

JEFF FISHER: I wasn't charging a fortune, nothing close, but for him it was—because I had to do overdubs and bring a bunch of equipment, have it shipped, etc. The whole relationship wasn't steady. I'd hear about [things] only after the fact.

GISELA GETTY: "Jazz Police" is ambiguous because one's self contains inner contradictions. Leonard could be very self-ironic, because he knew his own dark side and contradictions, and brought many projections back to himself. Some want clear positions, good [or] bad. But if you show that what we point at as bad is actually yourself, it gets uncomfortable.

Included in the song's lyrics was a reference to J. Paul Getty II; a decade earlier in LA, Cohen had befriended Gisela and her husband, J. Paul Getty III. They had been introduced by folk singer David Blue and met again when both were living at the Chateau Marmont. "For a while, we were almost inseparable," she says. "He wanted me to learn about jazz and took me to little clubs. I took him to new wave music." Cohen, she insists, was "very sweet" with John Paul. "He saw that Paul was very troubled. I think that's why he asked us to take [Joshu Sasaki] Roshi to [see] doctors, so Paul might get a connection to him." Getty also befriended and stayed in touch with Suzanne Elrod.

GISELA GETTY: She left him because she didn't like him anymore. She told me some stories, but these are her stories. She told me he was mean.

In June, taking a break from recording, Cohen and his friend Steve Sanfield attended a Zen retreat at Bodhi Manda in Jemez Springs, New Mexico. One day, they went to visit poet John Brandi in Corrales, an hour away.

JOHN BRANDI: Steve was one of my best friends. We were haiku correspondents. Steve told me Leonard was really fascinated by that whole way of communicating. He had tremendous respect for Leonard. He was very proud and very protective of that relationship. He wrote about him more than he talked about him.

Like others in Cohen's orbit, Sanfield tried to emulate him.

JOHN BRANDI: Steve would buy expensive clothes like Cohen. When Leonard put on sunglasses to go out, Steve would, too. Steve was always on death row because of his health, very fragile. He drank heavily at one point. There was a book coming out—very important to Steve. He wanted cover blurbs by Cohen and Gary Snyder. Cohen was a sure bet—he'd write something for Steve. Gary wouldn't. There were difficulties in their friendship, but Steve always said Leonard came right from the heart. He had a way of communicating with people. He had a trust based on insight and a poet's eye. He was always caught between the Apollonian and the Dionysian, being on the mountain or being with the woman. Given all that, he handled it pretty well.

Cohen's blurb said that Sanfield "writes about the small things which stand for all things."

JOHN BRANDI: That day, a really beautiful day, we prepared a meal outside. Leonard told me about "Take This Waltz." I had published a book containing a translation of Lorca's poem, "Pequeño vals Vienés." Leonard sat on the ground under a huge cottonwood tree and said, "Why don't you read the lines"—Lorca's poem in Spanish—"and I'll play." He didn't actually sing it. He strummed his guitar and said the song as a poem. One line in Spanish from me, then his English version, and maybe five or six lines more. We had this very wonderful moment together, as poets. It gave me a chance to see the seriousness of how he worked. He thought it was a complete honour to translate Lorca into English, because this was the poet that turned him on when he was a teenager. But the point is, Leonard saw something in me that caused him to get that guitar. He had human trust, based on insight.

That same day—"by some karma," as Brandi put it—Buffy Sainte-Marie was at an after-party for a Father's Day concert she had given at the Corrales Community Library.

JOHN BRANDI: When I mentioned it, Leonard said, "Oh, I have a present for her," and wrapped it up. I was instructed to take it to her. She opened it and it was a snakebite kit. Was it a birthday present? Did it relate to some past occasion between them? Some relationship? Then I remembered she had a song "Groundhog" that had [the word] "rattlesnake" in it. I thought the kit was referring to that song. Or did he just grab something he'd packed because he was going to be in New Mexico, where there were rattlesnakes? I loved the whole surreal aspect of that gift.

BUFFY SAINTE-MARIE: I have no recollection of the gift.

Gearing up for the release of *I'm Your Man*, Cohen flew to London to meet Columbia Records' Paul Burger, VP of marketing and sales in Europe.

PAUL BURGER: There was a lot of love for him, but sales were on a downward trajectory. We had lunch—Leonard, myself, my head of promotion, in a Chinese restaurant in Mayfair—our first serious discussion. I told him I'd guarantee him the full backing of the European office. I only wanted one thing in return—to promote the heck out of this record, go on TV and perform, which he'd not done much of before. He looked at me in his inimitable way, and said, "Paul, you seem like an honourable man. I'm inclined to go with your request on one condition." . . . "What's that?" . . . "If it doesn't work, this will be my last record." I think he meant on Columbia. I thought, nothing like dropping a ten-ton bomb. I said, "I'll take your challenge." The rest is history—the record reinvigorated his career. We sold over a million records in Europe, about five times what *Various Positions* had done. He became a superstar in countries as diverse as Poland and Norway. But at that lunch, I felt I was in the presence of greatness. His knowledge, his awareness of so many things in so many spheres, about how the world moved, was spectacular.

The next week, in Paris, Cohen's relationship with Dominique Issermann, long under strain, came to an end—at least temporarily.

JOAN BUCK: He's staying with Dominique, and suddenly he calls. He tells me at my apartment on La rue Guénégaud, then we went to lunch at Chez Benoit [now Ducasse], and his sadness is this solid thing around him. He is devastated—completely devastated. It's the first time we didn't connect because I was high, about to publish my second novel, and he was so sad that he could barely lift his arms to eat. His sadness is overwhelming. Of course, we'd always explored the dark side together, loss and death and despair. We talked of it endlessly, but he was in the middle of it. It was all over him. It was physical. He could hardly walk. He could hardly talk. He wasn't there. He said, "It's over," but he didn't tell me anything about it. I couldn't do anything for him. He was wearing a white shirt, which didn't go at all.

ROBERT FAGGEN: It was a tempestuous relationship with Dominique. She is wicked smart, blunt, and does not suffer fools lightly. She can smell stuff. I got the impression she bounced Leonard on his head. She threw him out.

DON LOWE: Perhaps she was just fed up with women throwing themselves at him.

ANN DIAMOND: I think she got tired of the games.

DIANNE SEGHESIO: Everybody knew that that's who Leonard was, so don't come into the picture thinking that you were going to be the one to change him.

KELLEY LYNCH: Of course, she knew Cohen cheated on her. They broke up over that.

GALE ZOE GARNETT: Fidelity? Not a chance on the longest day you live, even if he is in love with you. If he can walk, he's going to walk with an erection. If there's no longer an erection, he'll think of something. If you don't know that, you are not bright.

CAROLE LAURE: Maybe she broke it off. She's a strong seductive woman, as strong and seductive as he is. But he's a man of women. Like it's written in *Night Magic*, "I want them all." She stayed friends with him. He had a bunch of widows. They all fell deeply in love with him.

ARMELLE BRUSQ: When they met, Dominique was already famous, a powerful and independent woman. She would not be the kind to beg for love. There were two artists, ready to live [at] some distance, with freedom in the relationship. That's maybe why the affair could turn into a deep friendship.

CHRISTOPHE LEBOLD: You read the notebooks for 1986 and 1987, and he's just suffering his heart out. You see where the songs come from. You see how deep he went into exploring and accepting the pain.

CAROL ZEMEL: It's impossible to imagine Leonard bereft, because there was always a coterie, a lineup of women around him.

The precise timing is unclear, but it's possible that, as with Gabriela Valenzuela, who traumatically aborted their daughter in 1986, an abortion may also have factored into the breakup.

SANDRA ZEMOR: Dominique was pregnant from him.

Among Cohen's friends, Issermann had been a favourite.

DON LOWE: Of all [his] women, I liked Dominique the best. She'd come down to Kamini beach to swim. An artist lady, somebody you could spend time with, talk to.

VALERIE LLOYD SIDAWAY: She had a calmness around her, yet was always friendly and chatty. Leonard seemed more relaxed when he was with her. Everyone liked her.

RICHARD COHEN: I met other women he was with, but I always thought she was the best. They really loved each other. They interacted as equals, admired each other, and had great chemistry.

PERLA BATALLA: I always felt Dominique was the love of his life. Rebecca [De Mornay] was charming and fun, but Dominique—their connection was deep, very honest, and always loving. I always felt it when I was with them.

JEAN-MICHEL REUSSER: That was a very strong story, that relationship. But *she* is strong—ooh la, la, la. Completely mad. "Give me more grey—no, it's too grey. Give me more black—no, it's too this." But a great photographer. [The breakup] was very difficult for Dominique.

IRINI MOLFESSI: They were very compatible. I thought she was good for him—straightforward, intelligent. I was hoping he could hold it together. I didn't want him to fall into the attraction of other situations. He needed to be with Dominique, but it was very easy for him to follow something else. I didn't want to be part of the temptation. He was interested. I was, too. I was desperately in love, but I just wanted what I considered was good for him.

KELLEY LYNCH: Leonard used to refer to Dominique as Hitler. She's a business-woman, very controlling, negotiating the money. I witnessed his meltdown over that issue.

BARRIE WEXLER: When things got rough, Cohen sometimes resorted to Hitlerian imagery when it came to women.

GABRIELA VALENZUELA: I had no idea if Dominique and Leonard were in a relationship or having an affair. He would laugh while describing her as a woman like the Gestapo. Her career as a photographer was the only thing he ever praised about her. He was fond of her style, the perfection of her black-and-white photographs, and her distinctive storytelling. I took it for granted that they were working together on a project as a team. Finding out later on in life that she had a liaison with him at the same time I was baffled me. Leonard loved deeply. Reading her depiction of him writing in his underwear on the hotel room floor forced me to believe she was also close with him.

The rupture seems to have catalyzed another descent into depression. Back in LA, Cohen called Tudury.

TERESA TUDURY: I'd never seen him that bad. It was causing him great distress, and he was longing deeply for a connection he didn't really want. The yearning was so cavernous that, had it been filled by someone, I don't think we would have had the art. It was a spiritual malaise—it had nothing to do with the woman. It was an honour that he would let me in—these were late-night calls. "I need help." I was really concerned, but all I had to offer was the *Course in Miracles*. "Maybe you'd like to go to a lecture with me." He said, "I'll think about it." He was seeking deeply. He had to find something or I thought we'd lose him. But there was a real resilience, too. This was his terrain—the crisis, the deep yearning, the insatiable longing, his relentless courage. That's his landscape. This was a guy who never flinched. He's holding that tension between the beauty and the horror, like a fulcrum that he rides. He's reporting from the field.

BARRIE WEXLER: Early on, Leonard told me to think of yourself as a foreign correspondent filing a report, especially when writing in the first person. He was at once a black hole, whose magnetism nothing could escape, and a white hole, where nothing can enter from the outside, though information issues from it. His real home, though, was the artistic tension between the two. The split caught him in the middle of those polarities. Not long after, we had breakfast at the Mayflower Hotel—one of the few times I ever saw him truly brokenhearted.

In his memoir, Eric Lerner confirms that Cohen "was the most ripped apart I'd ever seen him. . . . He said he couldn't, wouldn't, and shouldn't relocate to

Paris for her; she couldn't, wouldn't, and shouldn't relocate to LA for him. He kept using the word 'impossible.' The word took on a special meaning for us, a category of difficulty beyond all others." The women who followed Issermann, Lerner noted, "weren't very kind to him or appreciative."

ERIC LERNER: I forgive them entirely now for their misbehaviour. He made it all too clear that they'd never get what they wanted . . . even as he smothered their objections with his solicitude and generosity . . . I don't think he came clean with any of them.

At the same time, as Cohen told Lerner more than once, "It was hell having dinner alone."

KELLEY LYNCH: Years later, we went to the beach in Malibu. Dominique asked me, "Have you ever had sex with Leonard?" I said, "No, I've never had sex with Leonard." These women were jealous of one another. He liked everyone being jealous. I can't explain how compartmentalized Cohen's life was. He told people what they needed to know and what he wanted them to hear.

That autumn, Cohen celebrated Sasaki Roshi's twenty-fifth anniversary in America at the Biltmore Hotel, underwriting the costs of the evening and a book about Roshi's life. As a boy in Japan, Sasaki Roshi had read about German-American financier Jacob Schiff, who helped finance Japan in the 1904–05 Russo-Japanese War.

MYOSHO GINNY MATTHEWS: Roshi remembered Schiff's name because it sounded like his own family name, something like Shufu. Flying to America, he hoped he'd meet a nice Jewish philanthropist like Schiff.

On January 14, 1988, Cohen underwent knee surgery in Toronto. By one account, he had torn his meniscus—the cartilage under the knee bone—doing a yoga exercise. By another, he had torn both menisci a decade earlier, running across a mountain at night, hitting a stone wall and tripping. Unable to sit in meditation, Cohen had then begun an intense study of Judaism, reading ancient texts, reciting morning prayers, and putting on tefillin.

LARRY SLOMAN: He told me how he almost destroyed his knees [in *sesshin*]. But even doing all this, he never turned his back on Judaism.

CHARMAINE DUNN: I tried to encourage him to practice yoga routinely, in order to sit without pain during meditations. Zen's philosophy is in the mind. My thought was you had to control the body before you could control the mind. We argued this point, numerous times. I failed him once—that knee operation. I said, "I'll get you from the hospital." His answer was he didn't need me to pick him up. Lo and behold, I'm living in Bowmanville [Ontario] without a telephone, and my mother has to drive all the way out and say, "Leonard wants you to get him at the hospital." I wasn't there by the time the message [was relayed]. I saw him later.

Dunn also attempted to introduce Cohen to the customs of Africa's Senufo people.

CHARMAINE DUNN: I'd been at a Senufo initiation ceremony in the Ivory Coast and had this little mahogany flute that fits in the palm of your hand. It's in the shape of a penis. Leonard wouldn't touch it. He said—I remember precisely—it was black magic. And it is black magic, used in that ceremony when they walk on fire to put themselves in a trance. He went to reach for it, brought his hand back, and said, "No." He made a reference to Judaism, in relation to black magic. He wouldn't even touch it.

BARRIE WEXLER: Cohen tended to take creative license with Talmudic prohibitions. The Talmud wouldn't exactly sanction his collection of Greek Orthodox icons and images of Catholic saints. He often cherry-picked the *Kohenic* distance between himself and what he viewed as taboo. But these very contradictions and ironies are part of what made Leonard Leonard, and, artfully juxtaposed, informed the basis of much of his humour and writing.

Cohen didn't need the instrument to make flute sounds—he made his own.

CHARMAINE DUNN: Leonard would put his hands together and make flute noises—like a whistle. He was constantly doing that.

BARRIE WEXLER: He'd cup his hands and blow into the hollow. He had quite a range, at least one octave, maybe more. Once, on Rosh Hashanah, in his kitchen on Hydra, he blew what was the unmistakable *tekiah, shevarim, teruah* sounds you hear in shul.

After knee surgery, Cohen flew to France to shoot a video for "First We Take Manhattan" on the beach in Trouville-sur-Mer, in Normandy. There, he and Issermann—she directed—were reunited as a couple. Many years later, seeing Issermann's videos for the first time, Gabriela Valenzuela noted their "peculiar" similarity to a dream she had recounted to Cohen. Elements of her dream had been incorporated into both the 1985 video for "Dance Me to the End of Love" and the new video.

GABRIELA VALENZUELA: In the dream, I was on a train carrying my mother's old valise. Upon arrival, I find Leonard's corpse in a medical ward. That scene is in the 1985 video. I then began to rush down the hall for an escape. At last, I find a wooden stairway down to the beach. As I run to the shore, more women appear, also toting bags. We are metaphorically experiencing the same thing. I burst into tears. To end this, I let the water take me in. After seeing those videos, I felt conned. Visually speaking, they portray my dream. Did Leonard tell her these details? How else would they get into a video so seamlessly? I wanted to know—were we a creative threesome? Was he harvesting things from our meetings for artistic advantage, revealing my intimacies to Dominique, an outsider?

It did not help that both Susan Hauser—the model cast as the Young Woman in the 1985 video—and the model in the 1988 video, looked remarkably like Valenzuela. And there was another grievance.

GABRIELA VALENZUELA: Leonard often told me he was dedicating the *I'm Your Man* album to me. It was harrowing to read the liner note that said, "D. I. this is for you."

Issermann herself offered a different explanation of the video.

DOMINIQUE ISSERMANN: I imagined a kind of charismatic leader who could lure crowds, as the Pied Piper of Hamelin. He draws them after him. In the end, he leaves them on the beach and they go nowhere, without anything. [Leonard and I] did not talk about this train story at all. I was looking for ideas. But in Trouville, there's a train. I like the station platforms, and I wanted the girl to be on a train at some point. All this is very spontaneous.

On the eve of the album's release, Cohen learned that his manager, Marty Machat, was dying.

MICHAEL MACHAT: I had lunch with my dad in London, December 1987. He had a terrible cough and didn't know what it was. It wouldn't go away. He goes back to New York and they tell him he has [lung] cancer. I didn't think he was going to die in three months.

STEVE MACHAT: They told my father he had a spot on his chest and he didn't deal with it.

SHARON WEISZ: Leonard told me Marty was dying. It was concerning. This was a man who had all of his business affairs in his head.

According to The Judas Trail, a 1998 memoir by Marty Machat's mistress, Avril Giacobbi, Cohen was frequently in touch during Machat's final weeks but was reluctant to visit Machat. Eventually, he flew in from LA to see him—for more than two hours. Afterward, she says, Machat said Cohen had not come to comfort him, but to demand payment of money owed.

KELLEY LYNCH: Leonard [claimed] Marty stole $400,000—his advance on his record deal.

HENRY ZEMEL: I thought it was strange that he turned his money over to Marty. You really have to pay attention and Leonard didn't. There was purposeful neglect.

ROBERT FAGGEN: Marty apparently stole like crazy from Leonard. That's what Leonard said.

RONNIE OPPENHEIMER: Marty was good at the game. He'd been Allen Klein's lawyer, and he picked up stuff from him. When Marty came to London, he stayed at Claridge's or another top hotel. He'd go into stores and charge his clothes to the hotel—all charged up to Leonard. I know because I was paying the bills from the UK account. He was definitely ripping him off.

BOBBY FURGO: After the fact, Leonard says to me, "I wondered where all the money was going. I always had my credit cards paid, but I never had any money left over. Now that Marty has died, I have money." You know what he meant by that.

BARRIE WEXLER: Marty was as much a gonif as anyone else in the business. But he truly loved Leonard. For no other reason, I thought the better angels of his nature might have prevailed.

After Cohen's visit, Machat directed Giacobbi, who had been granted power of attorney, to pay him—$418,000. They went to the bank the next day. According to Kelley Lynch, then still Machat's assistant, "Leonard's cheque had actually been deposited into the Machat & Machat escrow account. It was not stolen. Cohen was paid the full amount."

STEVE MACHAT: Leonard told me he wanted his money. I gave him back his money. I said, "Just give us our commission," and he didn't. When I gave him back his money, Leonard said, "I will take care of you and I will never harm you." I told my then wife, "This guy's about to fuck me."

Allegedly, Marty Machat also told Giacobbi that he never wanted to see Cohen again.

STEVE MACHAT: My dad loved Leonard, loved his ability. Leonard became his private poet. But I once asked my father, "Why do you like this guy? He doesn't look at you." Ultimately, he said, "You're right. Fuck, you're right. Fuck him."

Still, Steve Machat concedes that he wanted his own relationship with Cohen. "I wanted him to be the brother, the uncle I didn't have. And he wasn't capable. [But] I had fun with Leonard. I grew up with Leonard. I discovered my metaphysical existence. Leonard didn't give a shit about anything. He knew what he was doing."

BARRIE WEXLER: Leonard described a really funny scene—himself, Peter Gabriel, and Phil Collins, all clients, surrounding Marty as he was dying, yelling into his almost-deaf ears, "Marty, Marty, where's the money?"

PETER GABRIEL: [The story is] not true for me and, I suspect, for Leonard, though in Avril's book, she says Leonard came to Marty when he was dying, to take back the agreements so his commissions would not fall into the hands of the [Machat] estate.

KELLEY LYNCH: I never heard that Gabriel or Collins were there. Neither were even in New York then. This sounds like pure Cohen. I think I even heard him tell this story. I never heard from [producer Phil] Spector that he felt Marty stole from him. Never heard it from Gabriel. Never heard it from anyone but Cohen.

BARRIE WEXLER: Perhaps it was Phil Collins and another singer. But the anecdote is absolutely what Leonard told me.

STEVE MACHAT: Leonard did not make that story up. Phil Spector stopped talking to my dad around '85. Phil was with me at his death. Phil said, "Protect my money from Avril." Never said I am sorry or sad. Spector, in my vibrational field, is pure darkness. Gabriel got caught up with Avril, went to her witchcraft ceremony by, as he said, mistake, and called to warn me about a spell. I told him I wished he never told me, because he became the messenger of Avril's witchcraft.

Martin J. Machat died on March 19, 1988, age sixty-seven.

STEVE MACHAT: He died the day before I got to New York. Avril let him suffocate on his own phlegm instead of bringing him to the hospital, nine blocks away. We buried him in Connecticut. She took all the limos and left me there without a ride. I went to war with her. When he was dying, there was a liquor store at Madison and Seventy-Ninth—I got a $12,000 bill for vodka. She charged it to me. Leonard had fixed her up with Marty. She was sucking any penis she could get her hands on.

MICHAEL MACHAT: My mom [Roslyn] didn't like Leonard. She blamed him for breaking up their relationship because when Dad got enamoured with Leonard, he went off in a different direction. That's how he met Avril. Leonard knew Avril before my dad did. I was mean to Avril. We all were. Steven was the meanest, but we weren't accepting [the relationship] because my parents never divorced.

KELLEY LYNCH: The shit hit the fan following Marty's death. I wanted to strangle Avril and did not want to attend the funeral, but did so for Marty only. Leonard didn't stay for it. He asked Esther [Cohen, his sister] to attend with me—as his representative. I was on my way to see Marty's casket when an argument between Steven and Avril broke out. I wanted to say goodbye. I lifted up the casket, thought I might get caught, said goodbye, and put the lid down. A man then walked in and flung the casket open, startling the living hell out of me.

Further drama ensued.

KELLEY LYNCH: Cohen's lawyer, Herschel Weinberg, sent a letter demanding that Machat & Machat release his files. Marty had said, "Let him take whatever he wants." Cohen called a locksmith and took files from Marty's office. Some materials were delivered to my apartment.

Another complication surrounded Machat's wills. There were two—one signed March 2, 1988, and another, two days later. That made the Machats suspicious, as did Avril Giacobbi's alleged refusal to let the family—except his daughter, Cheryl—visit their father. However, Machat's second will actually increased the allotment to his children from 30 to 50 percent.

KELLEY LYNCH: The drama surrounding Marty's death was surreal. The DA even called me in to ask if I thought Avril murdered Marty, using vanilla extract.

Indeed, detectives did ask Giacobbi why she kept vanilla essence in the apartment; it can be used to hide evidence of arsenic. Machat's body was subsequently exhumed, but tests showed that he had died of lung cancer, not poisoning.

KELLEY LYNCH: Marty changed his will and personally asked me to witness it. I think he knew the estate would be a mess and that Steven would ultimately sort it all out.

STEVE MACHAT: Avril got rid of me with a fake will. The whole thing was fucked-up. She had my dad on morphine, and the will is signed "Marty Machat." My dad was never Marty, always Martin. She requested fifty death certificates. I said to her, "I don't know what game you're playing, but guess what? Game's over. I'm taking the game board."

MICHAEL MACHAT: My dad's [death] was so unexpected that there were no arrangements for what to do next. Leonard came to the office afterward, because the Rolodex disappeared. We figured the only one who would have taken it was Kelley.

KELLEY LYNCH: I think Cohen gave it to me with instructions to give it to Peter Shukat [the lawyer], who represented Cohen and Steven. Did Peter give it to Cohen? That's entirely possible.

MICHAEL MACHAT: I went into [Marty's] Fifth Avenue apartment looking for papers, the will. There was some nice artwork there. I don't know what happened to it. I guess Avril took it. There was a bunch of money in the Channel Islands, but the trustees of the Jersey trust never divulged what was in there.

Subsequent legal proceedings disclosed that, not including his Connecticut house and his art collection, Machat left assets of about $1 million. His estranged wife eventually sued to annul their 1984 separation agreement and moved, with her children, to deny probate of the will. The case dragged through the courts for more than three years, pitting the Machat family against Giacobbi. Later, they became allies against the US government's attempt to recover unpaid estate taxes.

MICHAEL MACHAT: The estate became a huge protracted litigation. The lawyers made a lot of money. But Avril ended up with a big tax bill because when the IRS got involved, it sued us all. We got out of it because our money came from a [separate] malpractice suit.

KELLEY LYNCH: Avril had a fifty percent claim per the will, but New York is a community property state, and Roslyn and Marty were still married at the time of his death, posing major issues. I don't think Steven wanted Avril to have five cents. Her conduct during Marty's illness and death was appalling.

Giacobbi's memoir was reissued after Cohen's death in 2016. Steve Machat maintains that Giacobbi's son, John, an intellectual property lawyer in London, published it; Giacobbi herself, he insists, had died. Others claim she is hiding from the IRS.

TONY BRAMWELL: I'm still in touch with her. She's alive and ticking, living in France.

TONY PALMER: According to a mutual friend—not Bramwell—she's alive.

There was also an issue about unregistered bearer bonds—effectively, paper money often used to conceal ownership and, with it, tax liabilities.

KELLEY LYNCH: Mark Cristini [a lawyer who rented space in Machat's offices] advised Steven that bearer bonds were in Marty's office before his death. Steven was questioning their whereabouts.

STEVE MACHAT: The next day they disappeared. Cohen denied any knowledge of these bonds. I was unsure if they existed or were part of my father's schemes, cooked up to conceal Leonard's money. But my father was not that stupid. There's no way he'd have an open-ended bearer bond. He'd put it in his name in a heartbeat. Why would you leave it blank? There may have been bonds to R&M Productions—[my mother] Roz and Marty. That's not the same thing.

MICHAEL MACHAT: I looked for them, but never saw them. Steven insisted they existed, but the whole concept seemed absurd. Why would anyone buy bearer bonds?

Sixteen years later, Lynch claims, she flipped open a file in Cohen's LA flat; inside was a bearer bond made payable to R&M Productions, the company that received publishing royalties. The estate was entitled to those royalties because when Marty Machat set up Cohen's publishing company, Stranger Music, in 1970, he had retained a 15 percent equity stake. Both Lynch and Steve Machat claim Cohen never paid the royalties owed.

KELLEY LYNCH: Cohen stole their share of Stranger Music, and was fearful Steven would sue him.

STEVE MACHAT: He owed me fifteen percent. He walked away with it. Because everyone stole. Everyone steals. Everyone wants their candy. It's really fucked-up, the world we live in. I didn't give a shit because I don't live in the past.

Steve Machat declined to pursue Cohen for another reason: any royalties he received would have to have been shared with Giacobbi.

STEVE MACHAT: There was a problem—Avril. Leonard used to get his rocks off inside her occasionally. I protected Leonard because I couldn't stand Avril. I found her beneath any decency. I was not going to fight Cohen to give Avril money. He knew I would never sue him—he knew it better than me. Most people think—how can you walk away from fifteen percent of Stranger? But what's the cost to keep it and who else is going to be attached? Avril claimed it. She claimed she owned my father. I thought, "Dad, what the fuck did you do to me?"

For Cohen, the timing of Machat's death could scarcely have been worse. *I'm Your Man* had just been released, and he was about to commence a fifty-nine-concert European tour that required negotiations with various promoters. There were already problems with Danish promoter Flemming Schmidt.

STEVE MACHAT: Cohen claimed Flemming extorted $100,000 from him, asking for a twenty percent managerial commission, in addition to promoter's fees. Cohen said Schmidt thought he was doing extra work.

KELLEY LYNCH: Schmidt believed his role was not simply limited to promotion, so Cohen paid him an additional $100K. Schmidt drove the record company insane.

STEVE MACHAT: Everyone rips everyone off, but you know something—everyone works. Leonard's view was that if you weren't doing it for nothing, you were ripping him off. Did he mean it in a bad way? No.

ROB HALLETT: I don't like talking ill of the dead [Schmidt died in 2013], but Lorca [Cohen] showed me the contracts. They were seventy to thirty in favour of Leonard, but Marty made Flemming the European [tour] manager, and he took twenty percent of the seventy percent as a manager fee, and thirty percent as a promoter's fee. I went, "What? That's thievery." It's one of the reasons Leonard stopped being interested in touring. He said, "I've toured all my life and never made a penny." I wouldn't be surprised if there had been some financial arrangements between the two gentlemen [Machat and Schmidt]. Leonard woke up and realized that he wasn't as wealthy as he should have been. Leonard never paid attention.

ALBERT INSINGER: Leonard had a naiveté about anything to do with money. He wanted to disassociate himself from the material world so he could get as close as possible to the spiritual.

More urgently, Cohen needed a new manager. Realistically, he had three possible choices: Machat's son, Steven; Kelley Lynch; or someone completely new.

KELLEY LYNCH: Steven later informed me that [Marty's daughter] Cheryl [Dorskind] was upset because she wanted to manage Cohen. Cheryl was never a candidate and never discussed this with Cohen. Cheryl apparently thought she and I would manage Cohen, although we never discussed that. It would have been fine with me.

Dorskind's candidacy, if such it was, may have been clouded by an incident that allegedly occurred years earlier.

KELLEY LYNCH: What Cheryl explained was [she was] a teenager and was showering at Cohen's [house] or hotel. She walked out of the shower naked into Cohen's room. I believe she said they had sex. Cheryl told me she was in therapy for years.

Steve Machat insists he had no interest in managing Cohen, and it's not clear he was ever asked. In the end, without much discussion, Cohen chose Lynch as his personal manager.

KELLEY LYNCH: It wasn't conditional. We never thought we'd need a formal agreement. Later, the Shukat law firm began preparing a personal management agreement. It was far too complicated. Our agreement was simply the standard fifteen percent commission on all income and royalties, paid in perpetuity for all products including artwork, book publishing, etc.

Many people thought Cohen had made a terrible mistake.

MICHAEL MACHAT: I knew Kelley before I knew Leonard. She was wild. I didn't think it was a good idea that my dad had hired her, because I didn't trust her. I do think she slept with Leonard while my dad was alive.

STEVE MACHAT: He stole my secretary [Lynch], straight up. I said, "What are you doing? Listen to me. She will fuck you. I promise you." He took her anyway. Why did I say that? Because that's what she does. She's a spider. She makes a web. She gets you in there. She is what she is. He got everything he deserved physically, and metaphysically everything he earned. He knew what she was.

BARRIE WEXLER: When I asked Leonard what made him go with Kelley, he said something flip, about her knowing where Marty kept the files. Leonard wasn't naive, but he had a romantic streak he couldn't shake or didn't want to, even when it came to things that had nothing to do with sentiment, such as business. I advised him to go with a seasoned management firm. But he didn't listen until after the whole thing with Kelley imploded.

GALE ZOE GARNETT: Kelley was the person you called to find out where Leonard was. She called him "our little man." "Our little man is with Roshi. Our little man is in Vienna."

RACHEL TERRY: I told him, "I don't like this woman." She was afraid of me, I think, and always cold to me. I don't understand what he found in these characters—Kelley, Roshi.

MOSES ZNAIMER: She was a nutbar of the highest order and a drinker, and became a whole other person under that influence. She was deep into Tibetan Buddhism and would go on and on about the lineages.

AVIVA LAYTON: My husband, Leon [Whiteson], took one look at Kelley and said, "I wouldn't trust her as far as I could throw her. There's something absolutely wrong." He just sniffed it.

ROBERT FAGGEN: This is a woman of demonic intelligence, with ferocious energy and a steel-trap mind. Armed and dangerous, very cunning, and absolutely relentless. Kelley was like a nasty Irish grifter, with overlays of Tibetan mumbo jumbo. Leonard told me she had learned the Tibetan language and it impressed him. But he liked that edge in her. He was kind of turned on. He thought if he was going to have a business manager, he should have a shark, which is what he had in Marty. He liked Kelley because she was a shark. But Rebecca De Mornay never liked Kelley, and she has pretty good intuitions about people. Kelley probably knew she was not liked.

GABRIELA VALENZUELA: She had been Marty's secretary, performing duties beyond the usual secretarial tasks, from getting coffee to being a legal clerk.

She had an edge—commanding attention with her strong voice, though always attentive, professional, efficient, respectful. She always treated me well.

STEVE MEADOR: Kelley was very attractive and she knew it, but very manipulative.

BOBBY FURGO: Kelley, none of us liked. Leonard always had management that was wrong. He was the good guy and he'd always have a hatchet person. He probably felt he needed that. There was such a yin and yang to him.

LARRY SLOMAN: Kelley wasn't a manager. He shtupped her and then he gave her a job.

Amid the chaos that followed Marty Machat's death, and the appointment of Kelley Lynch, Cohen prepared for his European tour. It must have been a very welcome distraction.

CHAPTER TWO

Lift Up a Stone

I don't think he ever called me Linda. He always called me "darling."
He called everyone "darling," probably because he had so many
women he couldn't remember their names.

—Linda Clark

Did you know there was an app that when you opened it, it said,
"Hello, darling" in a Leonard Cohen voice?

—Sarah Kramer

To help assemble his 1988 band, Cohen tapped bass guitarist Roscoe Beck,
with whom he had toured in 1979–80. One of Beck's first calls was to Julie
Christensen. When she arrived for her audition at Cohen's Tremaine Avenue
home in LA, they were rehearsing "Suzanne." Leonard said, "We're in the
middle of lowering the keys, darling, because I've been smoking again."

JULIE CHRISTENSEN: Roscoe handed me the guitar and I had not played the
guitar since college. I thought, "Jesus, I'm sunk now." So I start and of
course I sing, "Takes you down to her place by the river," instead of "near
the river." And the way I play chords is not anything like the way Leonard
plays chords. About four bars in, Leonard goes, "That's wrong, darling, but
let's go have lunch." We all went to Mel's Drive-In [on North Highland] and

had a grilled cheese sandwich. He must have been charmed or something. He was really twinkly. Everyone thinks you hand out razor blades and he's morose, but he's really quite elfin, sweet and charming and funny. But he levelled a look over our sandwich and said, "This is going to be a gruelling tour, darling. Four or five nights a week in different towns, moving every night." I'd just come off the road with my punk band, changing clothes in gas stations. I said, "How hard can it be?" So we shook hands, him having heard me sing four bars of "Suzanne."

Christensen, in turn, recommended Perla Batalla.

PERLA BATALLA: Roscoe said, "Don't prepare anything. It's more [about] what Leonard feels." I'd bought his CDs, but he auditioned us on *I'm Your Man.* I couldn't even get [the album]. I sang "Ain't No Cure for Love" and had to sing the high C. My vision of what to wear was all white. Leonard was in all black. He said, "Darling, this is a match made in heaven." Roscoe winked and said, "I could tell he loved you." I got home and got the call. Rehearsals started the next day. I quit my job at Princess Cruises. And my life changed forever.

Christensen also arranged an audition for her then boyfriend, keyboard player Tom McMorran. Until then, he had only a vague idea of who Leonard Cohen was.

TOM MCMORRAN: Being a jazzer, I wasn't really excited about playing three chords for the next couple of years. Bill Ginn was supposed to do the tour, but he was having substance-abuse issues.

STEVE ZIRKEL: Roscoe says, "You wanna go on tour with Leonard Cohen?" I say, "Who's that?" I didn't even know who he was. I was playing Latin jazz, Weather Report, Jaco Pastorius. Mitch Watkins told me, "You're going to learn to play burning half notes, how to play with space." I met Leonard third day of rehearsal—droll. I'd heard enough of his music to know he wasn't a Chatty Cathy.

The final band included McMorran on keyboards, Zirkel on trumpet, keyboards, and bass. Bobby Furgo on violin, Bob Metzger on guitar and pedal steel, and John Bilezikjian on oud. One day, the band had an unexpected treat.

STEVE ZIRKEL: This tall, thin woman in a black pantsuit, broadband Spanish hat, and a cigarette holder walks in. Leonard says, "Let's take five and we'll come back and play for my friend Joni." [Among] my peers, Joni [Mitchell] is one of the four gods in the pantheon. She's sitting there, ice-cold, and we have to pass her to go to the washroom and then play for her. Terrifying.

It took time for the musicians to get a read on Cohen.

PERLA BATALLA: [Leonard] had a sense of how he wanted certain things to sound, and he didn't always put that into words. He'd just say, "No, it's not happening" and become angry. That was a powerful, frightening thing. The energy changes and he becomes very dark. A wall comes at you. Maybe he could not find a way musically to relate it to us. But I also believe he wanted it to happen in a very organic, Zen way. We all wanted to do right by him. Some rehearsals were very long. I'd break down in tears afterward—not often, but I remember those moments because they were very painful.

PICO IYER: I remember interviewing Julie and Perla for the first piece I wrote on Leonard. He had reduced band members to tears with his three-hour rehearsals, so anxious was he to get it right. And in the ancient concert halls of Europe, they said, you really felt you had to tell the truth. Singing backup with him was like being pressed against a wall: How are you going to rise to a better self? I recall Julie saying, "I can't begin to explain it because if I did, it would mean I am bigger than it. And it was so much bigger than I am." I think he had a rare sense that one's lot in life was beyond explanation.

BOBBY FURGO: He used sexual analogies to explain how he wanted things. He'd say, "Don't come right away." In other words, don't climax too soon.

He'd say, "Play with it, toy with it. If you climax at the end of the show, that might be the perfect time." And channel everything through him. Even if you're doing an instrumental solo, keep your eyes on him. That puts the focus on where it needs to be. If we stood alone and showed off to the audience—that you did not want to do.

Honouring his commitment to Sony, Cohen ran the gauntlet of media interviews to promote the album. Matt Zimbel saw him in Toronto for *Wired,* a music show, and came away believing Cohen had revealed "stuff he'd never said before." Zimbel subsequently learned that the same lines had been used in other interviews.

MATT ZIMBEL: That didn't diminish the experience. I felt we did have a connection as musicians. He was very warm. He wasn't in a hurry to go anywhere. I was impressed with his use of language. A tour is "an enterprise." He spoke very slowly. The lesson Leonard teaches is that when you speak slowly, it gives you time to reflect on what word to use next. It brings people in. People hung on to almost every one of his words.

BARRIE WEXLER: Leonard repeatedly used the same lines with lovers, too, only modifying them over time. I know of at least two former girlfriends of his who ran into each other, compared notes, and walked away somewhat disillusioned.

In the US, Cohen hired Sharon Weisz to do publicity.

SHARON WEISZ: It wasn't as easy as one would think. The critics loved him, but audiences didn't know who he was. Among Columbia's publicity people, I met incredible indifference. He knew it was an uphill battle. I had a list of radio people and we decided Leonard would write a letter on Leonard stationery and introduce his record and suggest they help promote it. And, in case they needed incentive, we put in a crisp one-dollar bill—payola. And we'd say, "There's more where that came from," if they promoted the album. He composed it and hand-signed each one. *Billboard* gave it coverage. We were desperate at that point. That was his humour, acerbic and subversive—the letter was dated April 1. But some recipients sent the money back.

At Cohen's LA home, Larry Sloman interviewed him for a magazine profile. They warmed up TV dinners and watched Morton Downey Jr.'s TV show.

LARRY SLOMAN: Leonard was beyond ecstatic, watching that show, like a pig in shit. Most of the time, we talked about spirituality. We talked about Jesus, because of Bob [Dylan's conversion to Christianity]. He told me how he loved the Sermon on the Mount, the greatest single piece of writing. He was emphatic that this is it—this life. Nothing after. This is it. He told me how obsessed with sex he was. Walking down the street, all he'd see would be breasts and asses.

Sloman later coined a word for Cohen's legions of female admirers—schtuppies.

LARRY SLOMAN: Of all the guys I've come in contact with, Leonard was the most down-to-earth—a mensch, an amazing, gracious gentleman. That alone was something women would flip over.

Cohen also confessed to Sloman that he had essentially failed in his mission to "spread light and enlighten my world." On the religious road, he noted, stronger, braver, nobler, kinder, more generous men of high achievements had "burnt to a crisp. Once you start dealing with sacred material, you're gonna get creamed."

To prepare for the tour, Cohen once again quit smoking—for about twenty minutes.

KELLEY LYNCH: My father had cancer. Cohen quit smoking immediately after hearing this story. He used to smoke Gauloises and liked to visit the tobacco shop in Beverly Hills. I accompanied him frequently, which is how we ended up at Cartier, and he offered to buy me a $50,000 solid-gold watch. I refused, but agreed, as a Christmas gift, to a lovely $4,000 watch that I wore every day. He also liked Sherman's [Magic Tobacco], and sometimes would buy me artful, gold-filtered cigarettes in a variety of fun colours.

In late March, after a week of rehearsal, the entourage flew to Germany. The tour formally began April 5, 1988.

STEVE ZIRKEL: Leonard had two suits, two pairs of boots, five charcoal-grey T-shirts, and a bunch of underwear. He wore the same damn thing every day. For long flights, we'd wear sweats, but he'd have a suit on. I said, "Why aren't you wearing something comfy?" And he said, "You'll see." We got off the plane in Frankfurt—photographers, everybody—and I realize he has to be Leonard Cohen every minute of every day. He's not going to be caught dead in anything less than what he was wearing on the cover of *I'm Your Man.*

TOM MCMORRAN: We get off the plane in Germany and Leonard whispers to me, "Just don't mention the war." That was Leonard—always something smart and funny to say.

STEVE ZIRKEL: Before the first show [in Mainz], he drank half a bottle of tequila, and was still shaking. Like, "Dude, are you okay?" And he was, "You guys don't understand. I haven't been on a stage in seven years." Not exactly true—it had been three. So he smoked and drank, but told us he only smoked and drank on tour. He called it "going to war."

TOM MCMORRAN: He was drinking and took bennies [Benzedrine, an amphetamine] to stay awake. I did see him angry once, with me. We get to Frankfurt and I still hadn't memorized the music. He said, "How long do you think it'll be before you memorize the book?" I said, "I don't know. I'll put more effort into it." He was right. If you're in a band, you [need] to get inside the songs.

BOBBY FURGO: There were a couple weeks I'm sure I was disappointing him, because I didn't sound like [his previous violinist], Raffi [Hakopian]. I became an open target for everyone to tell me how to play. Finally, I decided to open up and jam the way I like to play and he said, "That's it, that's it!"

STEVE ZIRKEL: I saw Leonard not in a suit two times in my life, once at breakfast in LA in 1989, and once when we went to swim in Stuttgart. That's the single most important thing on a tour—trying to stay in shape. He swam and then we took a sauna. Leonard said what my mom said—exercise is the only cure. We had played a show the night before [at the Kongresszentrum Liederhalle] and, man, we just sank in the sauna. He was sitting cross-legged, doing the Buddhist thing.

TOM McMORRAN: I realized it was going to be like a chamber orchestra thing, where we all tried to be very supportive of Leonard. I learned so much from playing with him. That low, resonant, gorgeous-sounding voice—I loved it. That's when I realized what a genius lyric writer he was. I thought "Hallelujah" was the best song ever written. It's universal, the perfect hymn song. We'd sing it a capella in these European concert halls and the sound would bounce off the back of the room.

PERLA BATALLA: Leonard and I both liked to walk at this crazy-fast speed. We took many walks, just the two of us, and had a lot of talks. He loved to tease. He'd want to know what my boyfriends were like. I never gave him the time of day. "I'm not talking with you about this." He thought that was very funny.

In Antwerp, an order of nuns briefly joined the tour.

STEVE MEADOR: Four or five of them would stand in the dressing room, off to the side. Leonard said it was okay. They were there just to let us tell them what to do. Like, "I need a hot towel." We played this gig and I said, "I'm craving peanut butter and jelly and milk." I told them what kind and they showed up with a jar of peanut butter, a gallon of milk, and grape jelly. Me, Perla, and Julie went to Leonard's room and had peanut butter and jelly.

On April 20, during a night off in Aarhus, Denmark, Christensen asked Cohen if he wanted to attend a poetry reading.

JULIE CHRISTENSEN: He said, "I don't really like poetry, darling. I just got into it to get girls." I'd ask him what some song was about, and he'd say, "They're all about sex, darling." He had a charming way of putting that and still being the consummate gentleman.

STEVE ZIRKEL: He actually said, "I hate poetry."

TOM MCMORRAN: In Aarhus, I'm having problems with my sinuses. Julie gave me capsules, but neglected to tell me they were cayenne pepper, a potent purgative. One of the first songs was "Who by Fire." Leonard's doing one of those long intros where he strums his guitar and raps with the audience, but it's one chord on the keyboard. I had to go to the restroom like you wouldn't believe, and knew I wouldn't make it [until the end of the song]. So I duct-taped my sustain pedal to the floor so the note would hold out, and told Meador if I wasn't back by the time the tune was to start, to rip off the tape. Fortunately, I made it back, seconds before we started playing.

After his appearance in Gothenburg, a critic called Cohen "a sad old priest." The next night, in Stockholm, Cohen demurred. "That's not true," he said. "I'm a sad, middle-aged priest." In Amsterdam, recalls Furgo, "We walked by a homeless guy and Leonard said, 'Excuse me, friends,' walked into a McDonald's, and bought him a meal. He wouldn't take limos and didn't want special treatment. We stayed at high-end places like the Ritz or the Four Seasons, each with private rooms." Frank Mutter, who had met Cohen on Hydra, reconnected with him in Amsterdam.

FRANK MUTTER: I was working at their hotel. His telephone bill was astronomical. Maybe a thousand guilders—a lot. We went to McDonald's and he took everyone's order, all the band members and the bus driver, and he served them. If someone had a name on a badge, he'd always address them by their name. I walked with him to the concert hall. He gave money to a busker who didn't even know who he was. He said, "I get money from music, so I give money for music."

STEVE ZIRKEL: The cool thing was, whatever he did for the band, he did for the crew. There was no one excluded. If he bought us jackets, he bought the crew jackets—beautiful bespoke jackets made of remnants of different leathers. He bought Swiss Army Knives for everyone. Thirty years later, I use that thing almost every day. Best present I ever got.

STEVE MEADOR: The knives were in Paris at the airport. He bought thirty of them, a hundred bucks apiece.

ANDY CHARD: I was the truck driver and hit it off with Leonard from the start. One of his favourite tricks was when a local promoter asked him out for dinner, he'd bring the whole band and crew, which sometimes came as a surprise.

The morning after the Amsterdam show, Zirkel met Cohen for coffee.

STEVE ZIRKEL: A beautiful spring morning, sixty degrees. Amsterdam is a convention of models. One of every three was a stunning knockout. Every race, nationality, all fucking gorgeous, walking by in sundresses. We're reading the *Wall Street Journal* and the *New York Times*. After a while, I look at Leonard and he's not reading his paper, either, and he says, "Zirkel, I want them all."

TOM MCMORRAN: In every city, Leonard would have at least one dinner with the group. It was always a blast because he was the perfect host. He knew all the best restaurants, with the prettiest girls working there. At one point, we had a chef travelling with us. I can't think of another person who asked me more questions about myself, my parents, my family. He was a naturally interested person.

STEVE ZIRKEL: People ask me, "What was it like touring with Leonard?" He really was nervous. He was shy. On off-nights, he'd take us all for dinner.

He'd make reservations months in advance. Sometimes, he'd reserve the whole café and order for us. We loved talking to Leonard—about sports, politics, food, women—anything other than music. It was amazing just to hang out with someone who had so much command of the language.

One day, Zirkel arrived at sound check, fresh out of the shower, his long hair gelled and slicked back.

STEVE ZIRKEL: I looked like a California surfer drug dealer, in a suit. Leonard says, "Zirkel, that's a good look for you. Changes your whole thing from granola to pimp." Wow, reduced to one-word stereotypes by the master. Another day, the monitor man asked Leonard, "How's the mix?" Leonard said, "Poisonous." What? Poisonous? Another time he said, "It doesn't hurt that bad right now, but in the course of a three-hour concert, it will be a long, slow painful death." We all pulled out our notebooks and wrote it down.

PERLA BATALLA: He always spoke of Lorca [the poet] ruining his life. I always felt he ruined mine. I was twenty—first time touring, first time in Europe. The tour set my standards, basically, working with this poet of the highest degree, singing music that is really beautiful and so deep. There's a rebirth every time I sing it.

Cohen himself, Zirkel recalls, tended to be most down when the band was up.

STEVE ZIRKEL: There were two shows and he comes backstage after the first one and says, "You're the best band ever. Awesome." The next day we had off, and we're rested, more cocky. Leonard came backstage after the second show. We had played every note exactly the same way. But he could feel our energy wasn't focused through him. He'd say, "I don't think you people were behind me." It wasn't the notes. It was where your heart and your mind was.

In Helsinki, Cohen renewed his acquaintance with writer-translator Seppo Pietikäinen. He had first seen Cohen perform in Stockholm in 1972—after taking a boat for twelve hours. They had met during Cohen's 1985 tour.

SEPPO PIETIKÄINEN: I was then translating *Book of Mercy* into Finnish and struggling. I showed him the puzzling sentences and he said, "I know it means something, but I don't know what." I was amazed by him—he can make you feel like you are the most important person in the world. That night, we drank Aquavit in the bar and ate Danish sandwiches, then went to his room and had a bottle of whiskey, and cigars he said Fidel Castro had sent to him. It must have been three or four a.m. when I left. In 1988, I'd brought my daughter to the concert and had to go meet her, and he stopped me and said, "Wait," and found paper and wrote a note—"Your father is great." I thought it might be some kind of act, but it wasn't an act. That's the way he was. I was also impressed that he knew the names of all the Finnish hockey players in the NHL. He had a great way of dramatizing things, so you could not always take him at face value—a good thing for a poet.

In Oslo, Cohen had a long talk with an old friend, folk singer Eric Andersen.

ERIC ANDERSEN: Leonard told me he had talked to Bob Dylan in Paris and brought him back into the [Jewish] fold.

STEVE ZIRKEL: After the last Oslo show, we had to get up at five in the morning to take flights, two connections, to Madrid. Bless the Hispanic heart, every fucking flight was late. So instead of eight to eleven in Madrid, [the concert was] ten thirty to one thirty a.m., and then dinner. This is when McMorran was sick.

TOM MCMORRAN: I had a big piece of salmon. It didn't sit well from the beginning.

BOBBY FURGO: I'm not necessarily proud of that evening. I wasn't really enjoying my salmon and Tom said, "I'll take that." Tom was voracious in his appetites. Then I ordered spaghetti Bolognese—Leonard's favourite dish at the time.

TOM MCMORRAN: I got back to my room and everything started running from every place it could. By four a.m., severe nausea and diarrhea, horrible cramps. By five, I could barely walk. I managed to limp onto the bus to catch a flight to Stuttgart. At the airport, they put me in a luggage cart. I've never been so sick in my life. Our flight was delayed, so Leonard asked three SAS flight attendants to look after me. Then he wheeled me through the airport to our gate.

STEVE ZIRKEL: I'll never forget this moment. It's seven thirty in the morning and we're all in the airport waiting room, zonked. We all looked like shit—green. Leonard comes walking by—suit. He says, "You all are starting to look *gooood*. Now you can play my music." At that moment, I was like, "I get it. You want us to be in as much pain as you were when you wrote that song." It was brilliant, the way he handled us.

TOM MCMORRAN: We finally arrived in Stuttgart after eight hours of travelling. I was so sick I could not stand up straight. That's when Leonard pulled out this brown, vile medicine he got from some Indigenous person in the Amazonian basin. He had a glass of water and put the drops in and said, "This will either kill you or cure you." It cured me almost instantly. Within minutes, my legs stopped hurting. I could sit up. Then I realized I was hungry, so I ate a little cracker. Pretty soon, I felt completely normal. All in half an hour.

BARRIE WEXLER: To my knowledge, Cohen had never been anywhere near the Amazon, though it sounds like something he'd say. Or that F. in *Beautiful Losers* would.

Funk rocker Don Was was touring Europe at the same time.

DON WAS: If we were playing to a thousand people, he was playing to five thousand. What the fuck? When did this happen? I bought the record and it was clear why this was happening. He was no longer what he'd been, an eclectic artist. He was a pop artist. He wanted to reach more people, but there was a point he would not go beyond.

STEVE ZIRKEL: [The band] had these little cliques—the smokers and the hippies. Our little tribe was me, Julie, Perla, and Tom. We took turns doing each other's laundry. There was this pair of black socks that ended up in someone's guitar case. They floated around onstage at every concert.

BOBBY FURGO: Cliques happen on every tour. John Bilezikjian was wonderful but odd, and was left alone because he was odd. Old-fashioned. He pictured himself as the maestro. That set him up for failure socially.

TOM MCMORRAN: The money was the best I'd ever been paid—$1,150 a week, plus $425 per diem for expenses. I came home with $6,000.

STEVE ZIRKEL: Leonard said he was paid five thousand a week. But he was down because *Rolling Stone* came out with a great review of *I'm Your Man* and there were, like, five copies in Tower Records in Manhattan. It took them a month to get another five copies [in]. Leonard was like, "What the fuck?"

Onstage, finding the right level of sound for Cohen proved challenging.

STEVE ZIRKEL: I'd say, "Leonard, how am I doing?" He'd say, "Okay, but I'm still waiting for you to take your throne in the kingdom of the bass." Or the biggest Zen comment of all time—he'd say, "Zirkel, I need you to turn down, but I need more support." What does that mean? In Palma de Majorca, [we] rented a 115 speaker and an old Fender Bassman 100. I play one note at sound check, and Leonard goes, "That's the sound." One note. Meador says, "He wants a 1952 Precision Bass with the original strings." In other words, no tone. Of course, it all made sense. He doesn't want to hear the bass cuz he *sings* bass. He wants to feel the bass. That's what Mitch meant by burning half notes. Play the note and get the fuck out of the way.

PERLA BATALLA: It's always good practice to not play loudly because then it just turns into noise. I heard him say that. But never did he say, "It's about my lyrics." He's got too much humility for that. The reason you don't play loudly is so it's not a nightmare for the sound people, and for your audience.

In London, Zirkel injured his back.

STEVE ZIRKEL: I bent over to pick up a tray of food and could not stand up straight for three weeks. Flying to Lisbon, Leonard says, "You're excused from sound check. Go with this guy." They take me to the largest soccer stadium in Europe and I get a massage from the team doctor. I was in so much pain that Leonard later gave me a Demerol and turned me on to his favourite drink, the Red Needle. I started to drink on that tour.

Others went in search of harder stuff.

TOM MCMORRAN: Leonard had a bottle of Dexedrine and told everybody they could have it if they wanted to stay awake. I'm not good around those things. I think if one's good, twenty's better. Pretty soon, they were all gone. He asked everyone, "Who did it?" And I didn't fess up. Later, when I got into [rehab], I had to make amends, so I told him. I think he knew. He had a look, like, "I was wondering how long it would take." Those pills kept me up for three days.

PERLA BATALLA: One of my favourite moments was his terrible keyboard solo on "Tower of Song." He always [pretended] that he'd just learned to play the Casio. A few people would clap and he'd say, "Thank you, music lovers." Cracked me up, night after night. He told so many funny stories on that tour, between songs. It was the last time, really, that he told them, because on his last world tours, he didn't tell stories. I feel really sad for those people.

STEVE ZIRKEL: When I started the tour, I was a vegetarian, hippie, non-drinker, nonsmoker, no drugs, no meat, yogi. I'd been meditating for years, wearing Guatemalan clothes, living with a woman for years. I had my first hamburger in twelve years at the Hard Rock Cafe in Reykjavík [Iceland]. I started eating meat, started drinking, started wearing black.

Mitch [Watkins] warned me, "It's going to be real different when you get back." I came back—my marriage broke up.

Zirkel's relationship wasn't the only one to suffer. During the tour, Cohen's recording engineer Leanne Ungar fell in love with guitarist Bob Metzger.

ALLAN MOYLE: Leanne left me for Metzger. I was still in love with her, even though I was cheating with rub-and-tugs. She cheated on me only after I cheated on her. I didn't blame them, but I was shocked when she showed up and said it was over. And with Leanne, it's not a negotiation. It was definitive—one of the great things about her. There's a set of rules for living at home and a set of rules for living out there. Leanne had fucked Leonard at least once. She told me. He told her she had perfect tits. After fucking, he wanted to meditate. He didn't want to cuddle. He wanted to lie on his back and trip out. Men are pigs, right?

BARRIE WEXLER: Leanne was beautiful, and Allan's description of her is spot-on. It also brought to mind that I never once heard Leonard use the word "fuck."

When the tour ended, Cohen called Moyle.

ALLAN MOYLE: I would never call him, because first of all I was curled up in a foetal position, and second of all I was devastated, for a long minute. He said to me, "You got a good wife. Even I knocked on her door a few times. She didn't floozy around." Eventually, she married [Metzger], a brilliant guitarist, a wonderful guy, super talented. You could cry during his solos. But this is the most gracious thing. Leonard says, "Thirteen years—you had a great run." Now that it's over, I see that. Leonard went right to the soul and he made the effort, right? If he came to your house, he'd always spend what seemed like ten minutes thanking you for your "hospitality." That's a pretty big word for a garden party.

TOM MCMORRAN: It was a recurring theme. Somebody was bound to either get married or leave their [spouse]. Part of it was just being on the road that long, and part of it was that environment. With those lyrics, it was hard not to think about romance, love, and sex. Start talking at three in the morning with someone of the opposite sex and you're likely to end up in the sack.

The McMorran-Christensen relationship also experienced strain.

TOM MCMORRAN: It wasn't going as well as I hoped. I'd knock on Leonard's door at three a.m. and he'd say, "C'mon in." He had red wine and I had a Coke. That's the one thing I learned right away. If you were in the band, you were in the family. He told everybody, "If anybody's lonely or you want to go for a walk, just hang a coat hanger on your door." I took advantage of that several times.

PERLA BATALLA: There was a lot of drama around Julie's [romance]. Leonard loved it. He was always an observer. But he observed everything, even when the drama was his own. I've seen him through many relationships. I don't know if Leonard ever made the choice. I think the women said, "You. I'm going to join you."

STEVE ZIRKEL: He taught us a lot about women—that men have a fascination for women, and women have a fascination for that fascination. Wow—that explains so much. And the second thing, it's always the woman's choice.

After Lisbon, the band played a gig in Huesca, Spain.

STEVE ZIRKEL: A little town, about a hundred miles northwest of Barcelona. High desert. We played in a cotton mill, dirt floor. This is Leonard at his coolest. The local promoter got there at the end of sound check and we're in short sleeves—it was close to ninety degrees. He says, "Spain is playing Denmark tonight in the World Cup. Nobody's coming 'til after the game." Sure enough, eight o'clock—five people show up. Leonard invited those five people backstage, to hang out, drink wine and eat, talk to Leonard. Spain won [3–2] and everyone came at eleven p.m. So we started at eleven thirty. By then, it was about sixty-five degrees. By two in the morning, it was fucking freezing and none of us had sweaters. So the lighting crew lowered the lights 'til they were right above our heads, and the audience was just fucking jubilant. The best concert ever.

After one night in Bilbao, the tour moved to Italy. There, Furgo got a phone call from his wife in the United States; their marriage was over.

BOBBY FURGO: Distraught, I walked to the restaurant at seven in the morning. Leonard was there, by himself. I started to cry. He says, "Dude, you can try to fix it. I'll send you home." I said, "I don't think I can fix this." He says, "You're right. You'll never be able to fix it, because she's expressed an enemy's position to you. You should stay with us, people who love you. But let me warn you about myself." Then he said his yin and yang was really extreme, compared to normal people. He says, "With me, you will experience higher highs and lower lows than with anyone else. It's quite a ride." And then he smiled.

When her schedule permitted, Dominique Issermann joined the tour. At other times, women lined up at the stage door.

STEVE ZIRKEL: It was ridiculous. They were plentiful and lovely. The women would go to our hotel rooms with any of us, just to get close [to him]. He had a signal he worked out with Julie and Perla to indicate if he wasn't interested in a particular woman. We might be walking to the hotel from the concert hall and, on cue, they'd come up behind him and each would slip one arm through his, and go, "Honey, it's time to go." They helped him escape.

TOM MCMORRAN: He didn't need the escort, but he liked the way it felt to have two beauties on his side.

In Paris, Zirkel met Emma Rubio.

STEVE ZIRKEL: The most beautiful Spanish girl. And this is the healing power of his music. She'd been pregnant, her boyfriend had left her. She had a miscarriage and was depressed. Friends took her to the concert. She didn't know who Leonard was. She heard the music, got a vibe from me onstage, and was waiting at the stage door. She ended up travelling with us. I fell in love with her. Leonard fell in love with her. Emma credited me and the band with healing her heart.

TOM MCMORRAN: I was jealous of Zirkel because every time we pulled into a new place, he had two or three that knew him somehow. But nobody could touch Leonard. Leonard was just an upright good guy—not perfect, a human being like the rest of us. A lot of it was from his training as a Buddhist. I don't think he'd ever try to intentionally hurt somebody. It was like being in a family. You can't avoid conflict completely, but you can manage it so people don't get hurt.

Still, playing Cohen's music for months took a toll.

STEVE ZIRKEL: Slit your wrists. Hang me. Because every song, almost, is melancholic. Once, we stayed in a hotel that had a lounge band. So we ask to sit in. Please. "We'll play 'Satin Doll,' 'Girl from Ipanema.' Anything." Our tour manager said, "You guys just want to show off." . . . "No, we just want to play something other than Leonard Cohen music. We love him, but . . ." Roscoe Beck later did it for six years. I would shoot myself. Leonard recognized that. He'd tour and then give everyone a month off.

In Athens, Cohen arranged premium seats for Gale Zoe Garnett for his concert at the Mount Lycabettus amphitheatre. In Greek legend, the hill was the refuge of wolves.

GALE ZOE GARNETT: I went backstage. Leonard was doing his boulevardier thing with Natalie, the daughter of a French actress. "Natalie, you little beauty." Coming on to her. "I've never had her," he told me. "You will," I said.

STEVE ZIRKEL: This was one of my proudest moments. Second show at Lycabettus Hill, sound check at three thirty, outdoors, rickety stage. I'm a pilot and [have] weather training. I see this big-ass thunderstorm [coming] and there was a flag onstage. I said, "We need to pack this shit up because in thirty minutes, max, that flag is going to go limp and then, poof." Sure enough, it goes limp. Fuck it. I didn't ask. I grabbed my shit, started putting it in the truck. It started hailing. It ruined four amps. The girls are screaming. Leonard took a break. They had to cancel the show, 'cause all the seats got wet. Leonard said, "From now on, Zirkel is the official band weatherman."

IRINI MOLFESSI: Backstage, I talked to him and we left and went to his hotel and stayed there. We spent the next day together, just the two of us. People would drop by for interviews at the pool. I had just ended a two-year relationship and he was curious about the details, not in a gossipy way, but in a human way. Those two days with Leonard, talking all day and all night, I found my own level again—what is it I want? What is it I am? The next day, I quit my job. It was one of these encounters that just wake you up.

From Athens, Cohen, Batalla, and Christensen went to Hydra for a day. A BBC film crew was making a documentary. Zirkel missed the boat. "The birthplace of Western civilization. I could see the Acropolis from my hotel room. Yup, there it is. I slept for two fucking days. By choice. This is how fucking tired we were." Then, on to Reykjavík.

PERLA BATALLA: He made a plan and asked us if we approved—that we not go back to the hotel after the gig, [but] go straight to the Blue Lagoon, basically a spa, with beautiful mineral water.

STEVE ZIRKEL: The Blue Lagoon is anything but—smoky, volcanic, milky—but it was awesome. Leonard loved hot tubs, anything related to swimming, hot springs. It was June 21—daylight, all day and all night.

PERLA BATALLA: We get there and Leonard says, "Ladies here, guys over here. Ladies, we'll see you at the lagoon." So Julie and I get our bathing suits on and we see the whole crew, just their heads popping out of the water, so happily. And they say, "Come over here!" And the water is really shallow where we are and we think it must get deep where they are. So we get closer and closer and they all stand up and they're completely naked and we're screaming, and they're laughing hilariously—Leonard louder than anyone.

TOM MCMORRAN: Then we flew into Oslo—110 degrees in the shade, the worst heat wave in thirty years. John Bilezikjian starts freaking out because his oud was held together with animal glue and it started to come apart. We ended up putting him in an air-conditioned tent, with a floor monitor so he could hear what the band was playing. The one time we had an invisible oudist.

Furgo harbours one regret from the tour.

BOBBY FURGO: We were in Oslo doing "I Tried to Leave You." I had this stupid idea—I dramatically unplugged my violin, jumped off the stage into the audience, and finished my solo on the lap of an older lady. Leonard didn't say anything, but Perla said he was furious and thinking of firing me. I never addressed it with him—too embarrassed. But he cooled off and let it go.

In Stockholm, Cohen spent an afternoon in the Strand Hotel bar with writer Peter Lindforss. Over cheese-and-ham salad and red wine, they discussed how depression should be handled. Cohen told him he'd seen a doctor and said, "Listen, I did not come here to talk about my mother. Just give me pills." But he did not get better. He was paralyzed and could not get out of bed. A young woman offered to nurse him, but Cohen said he could not meet anyone. The next day, she came anyway and told him about a dream her father had that night. The father had never met Cohen, but reported to his daughter that, based on the dream, "Leonard does not have to worry. It's his job to lift the stones." Those words, Cohen told Lindforss, "made me want to take my life again." . . . "To ease the burdens of others," Lindforss said, and Cohen nodded. The stone metaphor echoes Christ's words in the Gospel of Thomas, "Lift up a stone and I will be there."

When the European leg ended in early July, the band returned to North America.

SHARON WEISZ: He did two nights in New York, the Ritz and Carnegie Hall. I used to say that if someone had dropped a bomb on Carnegie Hall that night, rock journalism would be over. The *LA Times*, the *Washington Post*, three from the *New York Times*, six from *Rolling Stone*. Columbia was scratching its head—who is this guy?

BRANDON AYRE: I remember meeting him in the greenroom. That was when I jokingly asked him when he was going to get a real job. "You're in the *schmatta* business, Leonard. Let's get real!" He'd been talking to Judy Collins and Suzanne Vega. They definitely didn't get it.

Valenzuela would see Cohen only once more, briefly. Lynch reached out, insisting Cohen wanted her to attend his Carnegie Hall concert. Lynch then sent tickets—choosing the same seats as the first time she met him, centre aisle, third row—and included backstage passes.

GABRIELA VALENZUELA: Kelley came to fetch us and we went backstage. On the stair landing, he was sitting like a king, his arms open, resting each on the back of the couch. When he saw us coming, his face changed; he was captivated. I had wanted him to see what he abandoned. I had on an Azzedine Alaïa black dress, black heels, and I looked exquisite. I leaned down to say hello and kissed him, and introduced my husband. The whole moment was cold and awkward, though he held my left hand and whispered that he approved of my choice of husband. It was his way of having his last word.

Valenzuela never again spoke directly to Cohen, although she arranged for her clothing company to deliver to him a package of black-washed silk clothing. He sent thank-you notes.

Tom McMorran almost didn't make it on the North American tour. He'd booked a gig with Robben Ford.

TOM MCMORRAN: That was stressful. I wanted to do Robben's gig because it challenged me musically. I asked Leonard if it was all right if I trained a sub, and he really got mad. He says, "No, no, you can't break up the band.

It's a family. How am I going to work somebody else in at this point?" I had to call Robben [and back out]. Then Leonard told me the story of the knight and the horse. The horse throws him off and the knight says, "That's one." Then he throws him again, and the knight says, "That's two." Then he throws him a third time and the knight shoots the horse. So, Leonard says, "You get three times."

Zirkel remembers it differently.

STEVE ZIRKEL: In Europe, they told us the dates for Canada and the US. Tom had already booked some gigs and couldn't make the week of rehearsals. Someone ratted on Tom and Leonard said, "Grrr . . . Not cool. We'll maybe have to get Bill Ginn." Julie started defending Tom— "He's a really good player. You're not being fair." He said, "Julie, you don't know who or what you're defending. Yes, Tom's a great player, but this is different." Then it became a mind game. He messed with Julie big-time. She says, "I don't know who ratted on him, but it's like the Gestapo, the Nazis." And Leonard goes, "Oh, you had to bring that up again." And he just milked it for five minutes. He says, "Just turn me into a lampshade." Julie was horrified. She almost started crying because she was buying every second of it. And we're all [guffawing] because he's pulling her chain. He was a master. How can you be a Zen monk and not be a deadpan master?

After the concerts in New York, the tour continued in California. Dining with his entourage before a concert in LA was Jane Motley, an old Hydra friend, and her son, Jay Dover. The latter had just been stricken with an intestinal virus.

JAY DOVER: I dashed to the men's room, but [was too late]. Desperate, I removed my pants, shoes, and socks, and used toilet tank water to rinse everything. Leonard came in after fifteen minutes. I explained what had transpired, and he came back with the car keys and a piece of cardboard to lay on the car seat. He mentioned that he'd been to Mexico and had also had explosive diarrhea. I can't remember who said it, but a comment was made about his celebrity status having impressed the shit out of me. We both laughed, after which I went back to Malibu, showered, changed, then drove back downtown and caught the last of the show. Certainly a great example of his humour and compassion.

After a concert in Berkeley, Cohen took a three-month break. In Montreal, he called Ann Diamond.

ANN DIAMOND: We went out to Bagel Etc. for dinner. He seemed very interested in me again. I was amazed, as it came out of the blue. Two days later, Dominique arrived for a month. I was a foil in his ongoing struggle to keep Dominique guessing. I was angry, but I just let it go.

Travelling principally by bus, the tour resumed in October—twenty-nine shows in thirty-one days.

STEVE ZIRKEL: It was basically play the show, pack up the shit, ride the bus to the next town, shower if we had rooms, play the show, and do it all again. After about a week, Meador says, "Know what I've just realized? The concert is the downtime." And it was. Three hours when I can do fucking nothing.

For Zirkel, Cohen's often glum demeanor was part of his public persona. Riding the tour bus, he saw Cohen unplugged.

STEVE ZIRKEL: After a few glasses of wine, he would literally be on the floor, very much the child. There was none of this star [mentality]. He never separated himself from us. The band was like his best friend—fellow warriors against the world.

Cohen frequently discussed Zen with interested band members but, on one occasion, they introduced him to what Zirkel calls "a fun, philosophical thing."

STEVE ZIRKEL: Our bus had a VCR, so we'd get into our pyjamas and make popcorn. As a band, we had the honour of turning him on to *Spinal Tap* for the first time. He was on the floor laughing and giggling, just as silly as shit. He was a goofball and he loved that he could be a goofball with us, because we didn't care.

While the tour continued, publicist Sharon Weisz was overseeing renovations of his LA home.

SHARON WEISZ: I got estimates for painting, floor refinishing, etc., and he's all cool with it. We'd have arguments on the phone about shades of grey to paint the apartment. I sent him stain samples for the floors—he wanted to paint them like he had on Hydra. I said, "Over my dead body." Gorgeous hardwood throughout. The compromise was we sanded the floors and sealed them, no stain. He had a dining room set with caned wicker chairs, all broken. I had those repaired. When he arrived home, I bought him a coffeemaker as a housewarming gift. But he was stunned. He just loved [the house]. He kept walking around. He invited me over for smoked meat—he'd brought it, vacuum-packed from Montreal. He said, "Come see what I bought"—a combination washer-dryer, front-loaded. He put a chair in front of it and watched it spin. His new toy.

Offstage, Cohen was dealing with financial-support issues for Suzanne Elrod.

KELLEY LYNCH: Cohen wanted to terminate their [separation] agreement. The lawyer did not like the idea that Suzanne was terminating an agreement beneficial to her. So he negotiated Cohen giving her voluntary monthly gifts—$3,500 a month or $3,700, a lot of money for her. In New York, we both lived on the Upper West Side and we started hanging out. Then Cohen gave me an ultimatum—"If you want to be Suzanne's friend, you can't work with me any longer." That hurt her deeply. So we remained privately friendly. He bad-mouthed her relentlessly. He spent his life turning the kids against her. Lorca already had a problem with [Suzanne]. Adam was a holdout.

RICHARD COHEN: There were many times he really could not believe that Suzanne wasn't trying to kill him—not financially. He just said trying to kill him.

BARRIE WEXLER: He had legal custody, not physical custody, which means he had decision-making input into schooling, medical care, etc., but I don't think he exercised it. He would often say he wanted to spend more time with them. He wasn't being disingenuous, but his life didn't change. The kids really didn't get to know him until they were older. Suzanne and Leonard were both absentee parents. They weren't there, even when they were. Later, she said Cohen was always there for them, which was a lie. She also said he turned out not to be the man she thought he was, which was also untrue, because she always had his number.

Back in LA, Cohen saw model-singer Felicity Buirski, with whom he'd conducted a long, intermittent relationship.

BARRIE WEXLER: I never even heard her name. Between Felicity and Gabriela, I'm beginning to think the girls he made a big deal about were a cover for the ones he didn't.

They had met briefly in 1974 in London, at an after-concert party. Their turbulent affair began after an encounter at the Chateau Marmont in LA in 1978. The next day, she wrote a poem for him—"Ode to Leonard Cohen."

FELICITY BUIRSKI: Love brings up everything unlike itself, especially when you're joined at the wound.

A few months later, headed for a modelling assignment in Haiti, she stopped in LA to see him again.

FELICITY BUIRSKI: In New York, en route from London, I'd bought a beautiful honeysuckle-coloured blouse I thought he'd love—and he did—and a perfume to match, Honeysuckle Dew. I sent the poem to Marty Machat in New York because I knew Leonard travelled a lot. The poem ends with the lines "As you lay so close beside me with a gap a million miles long / I wondered if death would bring you peace or just some other song." Strangely, it only reached Leonard the same day I did. I sat in his kitchenette at the Chateau whilst he read it. He seemed to hate it, and I told him I didn't think he had yet understood it. I then proceeded to tell him a bit about my traumatic past whilst I stood by the window gazing out, and then back at the meticulous way he was preparing a sandwich for us. I mentioned his attention to detail and he said that if something is worth doing it is worth doing well. A couple of days later, he rang me to tell me that he loved the poem, and wanted to sing me a song he'd just written, "The Window." I was profoundly moved and told him it was the most beautiful song I had ever heard.

A few years later, on Maui, she wrote "Come to Me Darling" for him. "I wanted to write something as beautiful as 'The Window.' I did my best." In 1988, while Cohen prepared a pasta lunch, she asked him if he'd like to hear her new album, *Repairs & Alterations*, which concludes with "Come to Me Darling."

FELICITY BUIRSKI: He was deeply moved and I think a bit shocked. For a few months, he attempted to get Sony interested in signing me, played my album to associates and friends, including Kelley Lynch. Roscoe Beck asked to meet with me because Leonard had been raving about my work. Also, Leonard had lunch with Stephanie Bennett, who wanted to produce a TV special on him. She told me Leonard had spent the whole lunch talking about me, suggesting she do a special on me instead. Bless him for this and for his belief in my work. She and her husband asked to manage me. At the same time, with a similar ambivalence to my own, Leonard put me off wanting to be famous or to actively promote my work. "I love your work and think you are a genius, but I don't want you involved in the music business. It stinks."

In the end, Buirski did not sign a contract with any major label.

FELICITY BUIRSKI: I'd like to say it was just the record companies' fault, but there was more at play—my energetic ambivalence about fame and exposure. . . . My own infantile rage and sorrow was still locked inside me. I was urging the horse on with my knees, but holding back with the reins, motivated quite considerably by anger. Such a fuel can only last for a time.

In 2019, Buirski released a new album, *Committed to the Fire*. Interviewed for the Blues & Roots Radio network, she said Cohen had been her "mentor, if not tormentor for a while." One song, "Who Will Guard the Dog?" was written after spending a few days with him in 1990, and "realizing the profound trauma that prevented us from transcending—merely touching through the cages of our own reality."

FELICITY BUIRSKI: I reluctantly accepted we were never going to be together. We would never break free from [the] carefully constructed prisons we had erected for safety and survival, as children, at least not in time for me to still have children. My biological clock had caught up with me and was now ticking fast. When Leonard asked to marry me when I was twenty-seven at the Montcalm Hotel in London [in 1980], it was under the proviso that we not have children together. He did not want any more children, he said, and, although I never did have children, sadly, I wanted them. We had been in and out of a relationship for a long time. . . . He was quite feminine—not effeminate—but with a well-developed feminine side. I have quite a well-developed masculine side. It was a wonderful balance. I wrote in "Ode to Leonard Cohen," "Where I can be you and you can be me / I will make you weak and you will make me strong / And together, we'll be apart our whole lives long."

Buirski said she considered Cohen's music "life-saving. . . . Once I heard Leonard's work, I pretty much didn't want to hear anything else." Lyrics from another song, "Collision of Desire," might describe many of Cohen's relationships. "I want love and you want lust . . . You want excitement I want trust . . . You want uncertainty. I want peace of mind. You're sick of the mundane. You want sublime . . . . You want freedom from your pain. So do I, but not by playing this game. You say you love me as you run away."

*   *   *

Cohen's tour resumed that fall—twenty-six concerts in nineteen cities. On October 31, Barbara Dodge—the woman about whom he'd written a poem referencing Halloween two decades earlier—saw him at LA's Wiltern Theatre, and sent a note backstage, with her phone number.

BARBARA DODGE: He called me the next morning and said, "You need to come and see me." So I went. Tremaine. It was not dissimilar from the time I'd met him at Masha's [in 1968]. Still trying [to seduce me], though at the same time, he can lie back and do his Zen thing and analyze you. He made me lunch—pasta, with red rose and white sauce. He was with no one and struck me as very alone in an almost empty space, rather forlorn, almost pathetic. I felt almost like it would be the last time I'd see him. But it wasn't like Montreal. He was deeply burned down. No enthusiasm. I spent five or six hours there, on the back patio. We talked about the old days, about our evolution. Most of the conversation was about him. People who reach that level of stardom are inevitably narcissists. They think they're the most interesting thing going on.

Dodge had, some years earlier, painted a portrait of Cohen.

BARBARA DODGE: He loved that painting. It was the only painting in the house, not on the wall, but sitting on the floor against the wall. I asked him why, and he said it was against his religion.

BARRIE WEXLER: He must have pulled it out for that occasion. It was otherwise in a cupboard, leaning against the Golden Rose he'd won for *I Am a Hotel*. What's interesting is that he did hang a portrait Suzanne did of the two of them, though he said he disliked it and preferred unadorned walls.

Dodge had reservations about how the afternoon unfolded.

BARBARA DODGE: There were things I would never in my right mind have talked about. I was confrontational. "Why were you with Suzanne? Of all the people you could have had. She's always gracious, but there's no depth there." He was upset, but not bitter [about her]. He said, "She could have taken me for a lot more money than she did." He had a little bitterness about Canada—that there is no promotion of really great artists. You die there. "I thought I was going to change things and nothing happens."

For Dodge, Cohen had lost his former lustre.

BARBARA DODGE: He had degenerated so much from the guy I knew in Westmount. Are you kidding me? You still want to grope young girls, still impressed with your sexual prowess, still looking for adulation? I never found Leonard's appeal interesting. I wanted his real heart. He was incapable of abandoning his behaviour, verging on sociopathic. I always saw the game. He deserted his real calling and on some level knew it. That was his misery. Like Narcissus, falling in love with his image or the shadow instead of humbling himself to achieve the real vision.

Another backstage visitor at the Wiltern concert was real estate agent Linda Clark.

LINDA CLARK: I went on the hunt. I knew it would happen, knew it intuitively.

Jennifer Warnes, Joni Mitchell, Bob Dylan, Jackie DeShannon—anybody who was anybody was backstage. Clark hung around until the crowd dispersed, then approached.

LINDA CLARK: He was standing alone, clearly a little inebriated. He gave me the eye a little. I practically walked into his arms. I said, "Happy to meet you, Leonard. I really admire your music. You've turned pop music into Shakespearian poetry." He smiled—knew I was flirting, and flirted back. I did not know then he was a horndog.

Cohen told Clark he'd be back in LA soon, and could be found at Burger King.

LINDA CLARK: I said, "Then I'm going to go to Burger King every night." He says, "In that case, darling, why don't you call me?" And he gave me his number. Jennifer Warnes swept him away but, later, I tapped him on the shoulder and said, "If I call, how will you know who I am?" I hadn't even told him my name. He says, "Just tell me you were the beautiful girl in the red dress." I waited a couple weeks and called. He said, "Well, darling, why don't you come over?"

The ensuing romance lasted off and on for the next few years.

LINDA CLARK: He'd say, "It's too bad I didn't meet you sooner," because he called himself a burnt-out ladies' man, and said, "I'm not interested in a relationship." He wasn't much of a lover. He didn't want to make love. He kept telling me he was beyond that, that he was into meditation and didn't want sex. I'd have to seduce him, come up behind him and start licking his neck. He'd lay back and have me take him on the journey. One day, he said to me, "Linda, you're such a good lover. You should be making love every twenty minutes."

Cohen did, once, express an interest in threesomes.

LINDA CLARK: He suggested that—we never did. Not my thing. It shocked me. Our lovemaking had always been very bonded and intense. But I said, "What do you want—another woman or another man?" And he said, "Oh, I don't care."

BARRIE WEXLER: It was just another line. He would have never gone through with it, though I've heard more than once that people thought we were lovers.

DORIAN MILLER: Leonard liked guys, too. How do I know? You know when someone is getting close to you, with that intention. You do what you have to do to make your gentle escape. Guys and girls were the same to him. It's my conclusion, based on experience.

VIOLET ROSENGARTEN: I have no knowledge, but intuitively I feel it's possible. I do feel both Leonard and [her former husband] Morton [Rosengarten] were possibly bisexual.

AVIVA LAYTON: Leonard may have, just for the fun of it.

In one 1993 interview, with *New Musical Express*, Cohen denied having had a gay relationship, saying, he'd "had intimate relationships with men all my life. . . . I've seen men as beautiful, I've felt sexual stirrings towards men, so I don't think I've missed out."

BARRIE WEXLER: He did say that he thought it was interesting that both of our favourite poets—Lorca and Rimbaud—were gay.

LINDA CLARK: He didn't come on to me at all. You had to stoke it out of him. It just wasn't important. He didn't have anything to prove. He was like a broken man. He could get an erection, but the rest of him—it was like pulling teeth to get him engaged in conversation. He was so self-absorbed, in his own little world. It was too much effort to engage, on whatever terms you wanted to engage.

Cohen's diminished sexual appetite may have been due to Prozac. In an interview with actress Anjelica Huston, he joked that Prozac was indeed a wonder drug—"[It] completely annihilates the sexual drive." Taking it, he said, allowed him to stop "thinking about myself for a minute or two, [but] didn't seem to have any effect whatsoever on my melancholy, my dark vision."

KELLEY LYNCH: He and [a friend] Sean Dixon were reading *Prozac Nation* and would discuss chipping—occasional use of drugs without becoming addicted. One day, he came into my office and appeared flushed, panicked. I said, "Leonard, you have to get off Prozac. You look like an absolutely vacant person."

LINDA CLARK: If I'm brutally honest, he had intimacy or commitment problems. Threesomes would let him be even more removed—you don't have to be emotionally vulnerable. He never called Suzanne his ex. He'd say, "The mother of my children." He was enigmatic—very, very difficult to get to know. I'm an astrologer. I saw that in his chart and I saw that in him.

Clark saw something else in Cohen.

LINDA CLARK: He was typical of a lot of Jewish men [who had] an all-consuming Jewish mother. They often have intimacy issues because, if women get too close, they feel they're being swallowed. Leonard was an over-oedipalized matriarchal man, as Jewish men are—not patriarchal at all, not John Wayne types. He's the soft male, much more emotional, the nice Jewish boy. Show me a Jewish man and I'll show you a mama pleaser. Like the great lion, you have to walk around her delicately. There's almost always a love-hate relationship. There's love and there's resentment because the mother is so invasive.

SUSAN RAY: Milan Kundera has a line. "The poet is a young man whose mother [leads] him to display himself to a world he cannot enter."

One striking aspect of their relationship is that it occurred entirely within the confines of Cohen's apartment.

LINDA CLARK: He wouldn't go out, wouldn't go anywhere. He was a recluse. He'd just get in these really crabby moods. Nobody, but nobody, knew he went out with me. But we used to banter and he liked that, that I could play with him. He'd walk around in his white boxer shorts. You'd think he'd at least have the courtesy to get dressed. He just wanted to hibernate. One day, I grabbed him by the shoulders and said, "Tell the truth. Are you ashamed to be seen with me in public?" He lowered his head and said, "Why, yes, darling, I'm ashamed to be seen with a beautiful woman." But it did occur to me that the reason we never went out was because he was afraid of seeing Rebecca [De Mornay, who he had begun dating], or someone who knew her. If you were going out with Leonard Cohen, you were going out with Leonard friggin' Cohen. You did whatever he wanted.

After one lovemaking session, Cohen started putting on his Zen robes.

LINDA CLARK: I grab him by the arm and go, "Oh, don't leave. We were just getting to know each other." He said, "That's one of the greatest lines I've ever heard." He says, "Now I'm becoming Roshi Cohen or Commander Cohen. I have to go or Roshi will whack me." I said, "You don't need to go to the Zen centre. Stay here. I'll whack you." He loved that, too. Several times, Jennifer Warnes would call when I was there. He had his dick in me and she'd be on the answering machine, all sweet and sexy: "Oh, Leonard, hope you're doing well." He wouldn't answer.

Clark was never permitted to stay overnight.

LINDA CLARK: That was bad. He'd kick me out of bed at three a.m. and I had to drive sixty miles to Redondo Beach. I said, "Can't I just leave in the morning? It's a forty-minute drive." [But] you did what he wanted. He said, "It's too bad you don't live closer. I'd invite you over more often." He never bought me a gift, never even offered to pay for my gas.

Clark later did a deeper reading of Cohen's astrological chart.

LINDA CLARK: He had Venus opposite the moon—the virgin and the whore. It was a real focal point. His chart is pretty blatant. He was so emotionally involved with his mother that it was hard for him to bond with a woman. If I'd ended up with him, I'd have been a maid and a secretary, having to take care of him, kowtow. That's why he went out with twenty-year-olds. They were eye candy. For all his beautiful imagery, he didn't really connect.

Backstage, after his show at the Warner Theatre in Washington, DC, on November 3, 1988, Cohen met twenty-five-year-old Evangelia Papaioannou. Over the next several years, they formed a bond that fundamentally changed her life.

EVANGELIA PAPAIOANNOU: The connection is very precious, like a hidden gem, a treasure deep in my heart. Leonard is the most special person. He's part of my heart, my life. He shaped me. I was just out of college. He was fifty-four. He had an incredible influence.

Cohen invited her to New York, but it was the spring of 1989 before she made the trip. He was staying at the Mayflower Hotel.

EVANGELIA PAPAIOANNOU: I went several times and he came to see me in Maryland. I met his sister, Esther, who became the dearest friend. I'd go to see her in New York. She was totally different—the same genes, but so light and kind. My connection to Leonard was extremely intense, including a physical part, but also a curious teacher-student thing. He took me under his wing and told me things I didn't know about myself, things that marked me, and led me to follow a spiritual path. He became the most important thing in my life.

At the time, Papaioannou was working on her PhD and taking voice lessons.

EVANGELIA PAPAIOANNOU: I was a good singer, [but] he said I should not get involved in the music business. As soon as he said that, I did not insist, because my connection to him was so important, I didn't want him to think I was trying to get anything from him, which I wasn't. I dropped the music.

Papaioannou's journals documented the friendship "in minute detail, every word he said, everywhere we went . . . all the elation and joy and the suffering that a relationship can give you. His voice is ringing in my ears. The exact words, tone, cadence. It's still living with me, for better or worse."

BARRIE WEXLER: Any number of people would go home after being with Leonard and write down everything he'd said.

EVANGELIA PAPAIOANNOU: He became something you hoped to have in your life, and never dreamt was possible. I wouldn't see it that way now, but when you're young and innocent and see a godlike figure—that becomes the most important thing in your life. I knew there were other women, although he was very good at giving you the impression that you were the sole object of his attention. He told me that he loved me. Of course, the very painful part was seeing pictures [of him] with other people on newsstands. The pain was incredible. I did not have to [call him on it]. I got a call from him one night and, before I could say anything, he said, "Why are you so mad with me, darling?" At precisely the moment when I was very upset and thinking, "My God, what am I doing? I'm wrecking my life." I said, "I'm not mad. Really, I'm not." He's like, "You're very mad. Please don't be mad." And he calmed me down. He could read me like an X-ray. I got the gist of the whole thing, but still hoped I could be his cook, his assistant, anything, so at least I could learn from him—this guru, that teacher, that theory. We stayed email and telephone friends until the end. He wanted to meet again and said I was his "heart friend." He knew he could totally trust me because I'd never betray him. There's only one Leonard. Once you experience that, it's very hard for anybody else to measure up.

Cohen frequently spoke to her in Greek.

EVANGELIA PAPAIOANNOU: He had pet names for me in Greek. His Greek was very good. He'd call me "my little heart, my little sparrow" in Greek. That endeared him to me even more. He was one of us, no longer the foreigner. He had a slight accent, but the tone was so Greek, it was like having a Greek man speak to me in my own language. He encouraged me to speak Greek with him. He said, "You're more real, darling, when you speak Greek to me."

In time, Papaioannou saw other, darker aspects of Cohen, that she "was too naive to [comprehend]."

EVANGELIA PAPAIOANNOU: I don't know if the conspiracy theories about him are true, but I know he had incredible power, something unique. I saw things that indicated he was mysteriously well connected.

On one occasion, at the Mayflower Hotel in New York, a courier delivered an envelope to Cohen.

EVANGELIA PAPAIOANNOU: He opened it, read it, and started telling me things about myself. Where did that envelope come from? Today, I'd probably look at things differently. Back then—"Oh, my God, he's here. Shut up and listen." Incredible admiration. Incredible reverence.

Meanwhile, the 1988 tour lurched toward its close. Arriving in Ann Arbor, Michigan, the band was in a prankish mood. In the hotel elevator, they spotted a framed poster advertising an elaborate Sunday brunch.

STEVE MEADOR: We took that off, hauled it back to the room, cut out a bunch of naked women's stuff, substituted it for the lobsters, and stuck it back up.

STEVE ZIRKEL: Hard-core Swedish porn. A butt on top of the cantaloupe, some pubic hair on brussels sprouts, a penis, a couple of them, one nipple with strawberries. For years, I've thought of some couple going up the elevator. "Oh, look, dear, Sunday brunch. Wait. Is that . . . ?" We told Leonard about it and he loved it. We never got caught.

STEVE MEADOR: We rode the elevators the next day just to see the reaction. Some people were like, "Wha?" That's what you do when you're real bored.

BOBBY FURGO: There *was* a little heat on that one. The hotel was pretty angry. Leonard just shook his head and said, "You need to grow up."

But they weren't finished.

STEVE ZIRKEL: It's one a.m., we're a little drunk, and Meador says, "All the doors have a plate with a room number, but there's only two screws holding it in." And at two a.m., we moved every door number over one. We checked out at seven a.m. Nobody's keys were going to work. I have no idea what happened.

At his November 9 Massey Hall performance in Toronto, Deborah Magerman— the twenty-year-old daughter of Cohen's old friends Alfie and Barbara Magerman—sent a note to him backstage, requesting an interview for a university newspaper. Cohen never read the note—he didn't have his reading glasses handy—so he gave it to Zirkel, who invited her backstage.

DEBORAH MAGERMAN: My dad was in the audience—I said that in the note. He didn't want to go backstage and wasn't asked back. They were both not needing more from each other. Backstage, I remember feeling sorry for him because he was drained, yet people lined up to meet him, wanting more. He told me my father had taught him how to play guitar. I wondered about that, because my dad didn't really know how to play and had no sense of rhythm. I remember taking home the band's laundry to do at my mother's house.

Afterward, Magerman joined the tour bus for a weekend.

DEBORAH MAGERMAN: I did not tell my mom [until later] because she was always wary of Leonard and his interest in young women. But there was nothing of that nature that I saw. I got no creepy vibe from him at all. When we crossed the border into Quebec, Leonard made a crack about entering another country, and explained why Montreal was so much better than Toronto. He was funny. On the bus, Leonard was respected, but kinda the odd man out, with everyone else so young. He was host-like.

At Massey Hall, Al Mair, who had distributed Jennifer Warnes's *Famous Blue Raincoat* album in Canada, came backstage to say hello. In 1986, Mair had paid US$5,000 for the Canadian rights and grossed more than $5 million.

AL MAIR: I gave him my card, but it was obvious he didn't make the connection. The next morning, he called and left his Montreal home number. When I called back, he apologized for not making the connection the previous night. He was just calling to thank me for sending publishing royalties—the only artist in twenty-seven years to thank me for paying royalties, though some received much more in royalties than he did.

In Montreal, there were two shows on the same day at the St.-Denis Theatre.

STEVE ZIRKEL: At the late show, some guy starts yelling, "Suzanne!" from the balcony. Leonard says, "We'll get to that." The guy goes, "I have to work in the morning!" Leonard stops everything. "Work? How did you find yourself in that terrible predicament?" Totally pulled the guy's pants down. But the cool thing was, Leonard would pull his own pants down. That cheesy-ball Technics keyboard. He only plays in two keys, right?—C and F sharp minor. There's a toggle switch that goes through all twelve keys. That night, it was a half-step off, but we don't know that.

He starts ["I'm Your Man"]. We play the intro—god-awful, a train wreck. Six bars in, Leonard says, "Stop, stop, stop." The monitor boss hands him a flashlight and a magnifying glass, and they [move] it a quarter of an inch or less. Leonard goes to the mike and says, "Well, you can't win 'em all." The road crew bought him a magnifying glass with a flashlight and put it on his keyboard the next night. Leonard didn't know it was a joke. He loved it.

LESLEY ST. NICHOLAS: I went backstage after, a seedy greenroom, shabby couch. And who is announced but Pierre Trudeau, former prime minister. I have my legs on Leonard's lap, but when I try to jump up to greet Pierre, Leonard, wearing his cheeky smile, grabs my ankles and won't let me up. I tried to get back at him, saying, "What did you say, Leonard? Lesley—meet Pete?" For half an hour, they behaved like high school boys.

Like musicians on his previous tours, the 1988 band was profoundly influenced by Cohen.

TOM MCMORRAN: There's all the other stuff, about how to just be a man in the world and treat people right. People were always so happy to see him—not fans, just people on the street, who knew his poetry. He was so gentle with people. I loved that about him.

Back home, Zirkel started picking out Cohen's "Story of Isaac" on a nylon-string, Spanish guitar.

STEVE ZIRKEL: One night, I'm sitting in the moonlight, depressed because my girlfriend [had] left. I realized—he's not a very good guitar player. Neither am I. Though he played the shit out of that one flamenco chop he had. He's not a very good singer—neither am I. I learned twenty of his songs and I play them to this day. Being able to sing Leonard songs is a great way to seduce women. Twenty years after the tour, I was in a folk music band, sitting around a campfire playing acoustic guitar. He really did change my life in so many ways.

STEVE MEADOR: That happened to a lot of people—Roscoe, Mitch, Zirkel. I'd have to say it's one of the most influential periods of my life—not as a musician, but as a person. You learn what it means to be a classy individual.

That year, Columbia Records conferred on Cohen a new award—the Crystal Globe, given to artists that had sold five million albums in foreign territories.

BUNNY FREIDUS: That was me. I was doing international marketing. I wanted to show that just because you're [not] famous in America, you can have an incredible career outside of the US. Leonard was a prime example.

DON IENNER: Leonard had a lot of time for Bunny.

Receiving the award, Cohen delivered his thanks to CBS with a deadpan dart—"I have always been touched by the modesty of their interest in my work." On another occasion, he offered a more biting critique, acknowledging "a sense of bitterness toward that great, dark building on 6th Avenue, known to many as the Black Rock, but which I prefer to call the Tomb of the Unknown Record."

CHAPTER THREE

The Gracious Chameleon

Leonard was a man of opposites and conflicts and ambiguities, just vague enough to make the person he was with be very alive.

—John Lissauer

He was so smart. He could whip you to death in a sentence.

—Steve Meador

The success of Leonard Cohen's *I'm Your Man* album and tour won him a rare gig on US network television—a February 1989 appearance on *Night Music*, hosted by David Sanborn and Jools Holland. Sharon Weisz arranged it.

SHARON WEISZ: The music booker was Cathy Vasapoli, married to [Canadian keyboard player] Paul Shaffer. That's how Leonard met Hal Willner, the guest producer. It was pivotal to him because Hal became a good friend.

Willner would later produce *Came So Far for Beauty*, an evening of Cohen songs sung by other artists in Brooklyn (2003), Brighton (2004), Sydney (2005), and Dublin (2006). On *Night Music*, Cohen sang "Tower of Song" and at the end exited the stage with Julie Christensen and Perla Batalla.

SONNY ROLLINS: He had quite a reputation [with the ladies]. I thought, "Okay, this is as advertised."

Later, Rollins performed a one-minute improv sax solo intro to Cohen's "Who by Fire."

SONNY ROLLINS: We had no real rehearsal, no opportunity to do anything—minimal. But I'm always for eclecticism. I like the idea of making things work together, so I was not at all daunted. I did not know his music before—interesting stuff and I like it. We had very little in terms of exchanges backstage. There were so many artists, all with entourages. But we did communicate appreciation for what each other was doing while doing it. He was one of those people—what he was doing was so unique, the musical range did not matter.

DON WAS: I met Leonard on that show. I had this image of him as a dark, manic-depressive. He's probably the most charming human being I've met—just a wonderful, sweet, fascinating, really open guy, with this great sense of humour. That was a total shocker. And the way women went nuts for him. I thought, "I'm gonna watch this guy. I gotta learn from him."

ERIC ANDERSEN: Everybody said he was funereal. He was the funniest. He could turn melancholy into wry smiles. The music is laced with witty drollisms. When I get really depressed, I put on my Cohen albums to cheer myself up. Works every time.

Soon after, Cohen and Was started hanging out together in LA. For his own album, Was asked Cohen to sing "Elvis' Rolls Royce," originally written with Barry White in mind.

HARVEY KUBERNIK: A recitative piece, Leonard doing his best Barry White impression. A perfect blend of irony, humour, and gravitas. Flawless.

DAVID WAS: Leonard arrived [at the studio] in a black suit, white shirt, and tie, on a summer day, no less. He asked how long it had taken for me to write the song. I estimated an hour or two, at which point he flattered me, saying, "Not a word nor syllable" was out of place, and that it took him six years, on average, to complete a song.

Soon after, Cohen sent Don Was the lyrics to "Anthem," asking him to write music to it.

DON WAS: That was a big deal. I wrote a different melody, which he did not use. I was trying to think of a way he could make a rock and roll record. I did the vocal. I think he was amused. He said, "I understand what you're doing, but I can't do that."

BARRIE WEXLER: Leonard had tried that with Phil Spector. He had learned his lesson.

Although Was never considered himself a close friend, he was present at two events that eventually became part of Cohenian legend. The first occurred at a birthday party thrown by Bob Dylan for his then girlfriend, Carole Childs.

DON WAS: I watched the dynamic between them. There was tremendous mutual respect and, like two fighters, competition, too. They talked about a certain song. Leonard complimented Bob and Bob said, "I wrote that in fifteen minutes." And Leonard said, "It took me five years to write 'Hallelujah.'"

Was's account was likely a retelling of the original exchange, said to have taken place in Paris in 1984.

DON WAS: Then Leonard said, "You're buddies with Iggy Pop, aren't you? Will you bring him to my house?" Iggy loved Leonard—a big fan. A couple of days later, we walk in. It's genial. We're sitting in the kitchen. And Iggy is like, "So? *Nu?*" And Leonard pulls out this thing. A woman had taken out this classified ad in the *Guardian* in San Francisco. Someone had sent it to Leonard. "Single white female, thirty-ish, nice looking. (At least I think so.) Looking for a man with the benign nobility of Leonard Cohen and the raw severity of Iggy Pop." Leonard decided they should both answer. He was very good with calligraphy. He crafted this beautiful response—they both signed it. My job was to take the Polaroid. Leonard said, "Iggy, put your phone number on there." Iggy says, "I'm married. I'm not gonna get into this." Leonard said, "Give me the pen. I'm putting my number down. I'm gonna fuck this girl." We put it in an envelope and sent it. What are the chances of taking out that ad and getting that response?

Cohen later said he spoke to the woman in question, but never met her. Returning to Montreal in March, he was approached by his cousin, Edgar Cohen.

RUTH COHEN: There was an incident—family shtick. They were selling a property. My husband [Edgar] was in charge, and Victor Cohen [Esther's husband] was a thorn in his side.

The property, jointly owned by twenty or more members of the extended family, was on Craig Street [renamed St.-Antoine Street in the mid-seventies], located in downtown Montreal.

RUTH COHEN: Edgar wanted Leonard to intervene. He said, "I can't do it." He was so gentle. "It's family. [Esther's] the only relative I have left." They did sell it eventually, at a lower price. They didn't understand real estate.

GORDON COHEN: There's two sides to this. The family had owned a lot of land, and had sold most of it. Edgar wasn't the adjudicator—he was the instigator. He made a deal with Leonard's uncle Horace, then old and sick, to buy our share of the property. He under-offered by a large margin. Leonard was a funny guy. He got on with Edgar. He got on with Horace. Horace wasn't a nice man. Horace criticized Leonard, left, right, and centre. What was Leonard doing ass-licking him? I could never understand Leonard in many ways. Anyway, Victor, representing Esther and Leonard, put his foot down—Leonard would never do anything against Esther—and said no deal. Eventually, the property was expropriated by the city.

Among the friends Cohen saw in Montreal was music journalist Elliot Majerczyk. They had met years earlier, at the Rainbow Bar and Grill, where they ended up in a ferocious game of *Pong*.

ELLIOT MAJERCZYK: He wouldn't let me leave. We played for two hours. He kept on feeding quarters. I finally let him win—I wanted to end the game. I never told him.

Majerczyk, the son of Holocaust survivors, joined the long line of young men and women who gravitated into Cohen's orbit. One day, just back from Israel, Majerczyk bumped into him.

ELLIOT MAJERCZYK: I'd gone to Yad Vashem [Israel's Holocaust memorial] and seen this striking photograph. A Shabbas dinner in the Warsaw ghetto. Around the table, staring at the candles, everyone in long black coats except for one man, off to the side, in a double-breasted suit, clean-shaven, wearing the kind of cap Leonard used to wear. Almost a doppelgänger for Leonard. I took a picture of it and, in Montreal, showed it to him. He stared at it for a long time and then asked if I could make a copy. Morton Rosengarten told me Leonard kept it on his piano, and once referred to me as his "interior decorator."

At the time, Majerczyk had a prostate condition for which no drugs had proven effective. Cohen recommended the Insight Meditation Center in Barre, Massachusetts.

ELLIOT MAJERCZYK: He said it was kosher, since it didn't involve chanting or deities, just concentrating on the breath. I did a ten-day silent meditation retreat. Profound experience, and my prostrate issue cleared up. Mind-body connection.

On one occasion, they meditated together at Cohen's home.

ELLIOT MAJERCZYK: He offered to shave my head. He said he'd shaved a lot of Buddhist monks' heads. My vanity wouldn't allow it. I couldn't tell if he was depressed. He was very good at maintaining a cheerful countenance. He was one of these great guys. Extraordinary—twenty years older and infinitely wiser. I just didn't appreciate his depth and wisdom. Extremely compassionate, funnier than he was given credit for, and very insightful.

I'd go to him with issues—personal conflicts. He might say, "Screw 'em, if they can't take a joke." Or, "Friends let friends off the hook." These off-the-cuff remarks still resonate, thirty years later. I wasn't situated in life and he was very supportive, encouraging. Once, discussing cognitive dissonance, I was saying how weighing two contradictory points of view could lead to paralysis of action. He said, "Yeah, it's called fucked-up in hell."

Cohen and Majerczyk went for long walks—often marked by silence—swam at McGill's Allan Memorial pool, shared late-night smoked-meat sandwiches at the Main Deli, and occasionally saw a film.

ELLIOT MAJERCZYK: Once, arriving late, I said, "I'm the type of guy who, if I miss the opening credits, I don't want to see the film." He said, "Elliot, you've obviously confused me with someone who gives a shit." When I was considering giving up broadcasting to study clinical audiology, he said, "Is it good for business?" As in, could I make any money? Once, I used the line "She's got a heart as big as your momma's stove." He said, "Did you write that?" He might have wanted to use it, with my permission. When I told him it was from a Jesse Winchester song, he looked disappointed. Leonard was a gracious chameleon. That's not pejorative. He would not be obsequious, but he was a really astute reader of people. He'd meet you where you were at.

That month, Cohen's friend Adrienne Clarkson—then publisher of McClelland & Stewart—interviewed him for a CBC documentary. Asked about love, he said, "You need a tight connection in your life. They don't . . . have to be around all the time. But it's nice if they're around some of the time." In the film, Cohen retrieves a pad of paper on which he worked while creating "Take This Waltz," and flips through the pages. The images flash only momentarily, but there's a pencil sketch of Cohen, a monkey, and some doodles drawn by Gabriela Valenzuela, and a sketch of Valenzuela by Cohen. One night, Cohen and Clarkson went to dinner at Moishe's Steak House.

ADRIENNE CLARKSON: We ate our dill pickles, our steak. Then he said, "How would you like to see where I'm going to be buried?" I leapt at the chance. As we stood there in the snow, Leonard pointed out where the Cohens are buried. Then he talked about the hereditary priesthood, about what it meant to be descended from Aaron. It was important to him that he be understood in his appropriate lineage, time, and place.

An institution in Montreal, Moishe's, owned by the Lighter family, was one of Cohen's haunts.

LENNY LIGHTER: I knew him for forty years. He'd come with his mom, friends, his kids, never alone. I remember his mom—a tough woman, feisty, intelligent. He'd always say, "They're never going to get us." Lamb chops were his favourite—he called them the "silence of the lamb chops"—though he did eat steak and liked Bordeaux wine. He had a warmth and soulfulness and a certain smile that spoke of his nature. He treated people well—that was his thing. He'd invite me over and we'd have a chat.

Cohen also made a point of seeing journalist Nancy Southam, a companion of former Canadian prime minister Pierre Trudeau.

KELLEY LYNCH: Southam was in the background. He'd see her in Montreal. They talked and emailed. He once called from his bathroom after Nancy was sprayed by a skunk and they filled the tub, or so I was told, with ketchup for her to soak in.

In interviews, Cohen downplayed his Lothario image, insisting he had spent thousands of miserable nights alone. But to Lynch, he boasted of conquests.

KELLEY LYNCH: He told me he'd slept with four thousand women. I'll assume that number is not correct.

BARRIE WEXLER: There's the answer to why he wrote so slowly.

ROBERT FAGGEN: It's amazing that Leonard got anything done in the midst of all his personal meshugas.

Indeed, according to Lynch, Cohen was "a bit of a loafer."

KELLEY LYNCH: He was an obsessive TV watcher. He didn't spend years working on poems/lyrics. He'd go into delivery mode when he needed an advance. I had to set parameters around his loafing. It is amazing he got any work done.

On March 12, Cohen and actress Rebecca De Mornay attended the Juno Awards in Toronto. Nominated in two categories—male vocalist of the year and Canadian entertainer of the year—he won neither.

JOHN GRIERSON: I bumped into him in the washroom. He's got this tux on. He goes, "How do you like the threads?" I go, "Very nice." He went, "Fifty bucks. Hadassah."

The Toronto chapter of Hadassah, a Jewish charity, annually sold clothing at greatly reduced prices.

Cohen had met De Mornay at a Robert Altman party in the mid-eighties and again in September 1987, at a Roy Orbison concert. By then, she was married to scriptwriter Bruce Wagner. Cohen later maintained that he remembered seeing her two decades earlier, in the mid-1960s, when he visited Axel Jensen, Marianne Ihlen's son, at England's Summerhill School; De Mornay was a student there as well. The relationship evolved from friendship to romance, but achieved lift-off after her separation from Wagner. Although they saw each other frequently, Cohen and De Mornay lived apart.

KELLEY LYNCH: He doesn't like to live with another person or stay with them. It was brutal for him. Honestly, he was going to her house, in one of the canyons below Sunset [Boulevard]. He'd leave at two a.m. and go to the Zen centre. This is his way to get out of it.

Despite the new romance, Cohen spent Easter on Hydra with Dominique Issermann and his island cohort—George Lialios, Anthony Kingsmill, Bill Cunliffe, Irini Molfessi, Brian and Valerie Lloyd Sidaway. He attended a party at Henriette and Morry Cohen's (no relation) house. Another day, Valerie spotted him alone at the Pirate Bar.

VALERIE LLOYD SIDAWAY: When he got up to leave, I said, "Hey, Leonard, there's a good movie on tonight." He came back ten minutes later and said, in his deep voice, "Would you like to be my date?" We went to see *Gorillas in the Mist*. I think he enjoyed the undemanding company. He loved movies. It was an easy way of leaving this world for a while.

Soon after, Cohen and Issermann ended their liaison—this time permanently.

EVANGELIA PAPAIOANNOU: Esther told me that when it was the right time for her, it wasn't for him. And when it was for him, it wasn't for her.

Still, a deep friendship remained.

DOMINIQUE ISSERMANN: It is only death that separated us. The more years have passed, the stronger the friendship became.

In fact, later that year, Cohen instructed Kelley Lynch to wire-transfer $100,000 from his account at Holland's AMRO Bank to Issermann. The funds helped her acquire an adjacent Paris apartment.

ROBERT FAGGEN: Leonard was a fantastically generous man. What he gave Dominique was much less than he gave others.

DIANNE SEGHESIO: When his friends died, Leonard would help their children with legal issues, with money. When my 1966 Volkswagen van broke down for the fourth time, Leonard bought me a brand-new, 1998 stick-shift Honda Accord. He knew I was living on the edge.

He was back in New York in April 1989 to meet Don Ienner—at thirty-six, the youngest president in Columbia Records' hundred-year history.

SAM FELDMAN: Ienner was a fast-talking promotion guy, a good guy, a huckster.

DON IENNER: A lot of artists were complaining that they didn't get the kind of attention they thought they deserved. Tony Bennett said, "I want off the label." I said, "Tony, I can't. My mother would kill me." Cohen [also] wanted out. He was selling a huge amount overseas, but Columbia [USA] wasn't geared to selling fifty or a hundred thousand records. I was happy to sell fifty thousand records as a building block, but Leonard was getting older and wanted success. I'm sure other people were talking to him about it. He wanted out, off of the US label. He wanted to stay with the rest of the world. I love Leonard—a wonderful, wonderful, wonderful man. We'd meet for dinner or listen to work in progress. We shared stories about Dylan and had conversations about depression, because my dad was a manic-depressive.

PAUL BURGER: Leonard was upset that the US company never really invested in his career. In Europe, we viewed him as an important artist, perhaps because Europeans focus more on lyrics. Poets and writers are highly regarded. Certainly [Columbia] would have been embarrassed by the massive success we had in Europe. Donny only had responsibility for Columbia USA.

Burger himself had just been named president of CBS Records Canada.

PAUL BURGER: Cohen's contract was with Columbia USA. I wanted to sign him to Columbia Canada. It didn't really suit Leonard—I suspect for tax reasons, more than anything else. Despite all the work I did resurrecting his career with *I'm Your Man* in Europe—his most successful album to that time—he resisted my overtures. But we worked with him as if he were a CBS Canada artist—both A&R–wise [artists and repertoire] and in planning releases and marketing campaigns.

KELLEY LYNCH: For the Ienner meeting, we arrived at the Sony building and stopped at a small kiosk, where Cohen bought candy. He informed me that when he stood up to leave the meeting, I should take the candy [from the conference room table] and leave with him. The candy [gambit] was a premeditated "Fuck you." This is how Cohen planned meetings. At [one] point, Don asked his team to leave. The meeting continued with Ienner, Cohen, and me. Cohen complained about Columbia's treatment.

DON IENNER: He certainly let me know of his unhappiness. He did it in a wonderful way, but he also was strong.

KELLEY LYNCH: Ienner attempted to explain that he was new in his position and was an ally of Cohen's. They were both completely inflamed. I attempted to explain that Cohen was upset by his earlier experiences with [Tommy] Mottola.

DON IENNER: I made a handshake deal—I'd put the might of the company behind the next album, and if he wasn't satisfied, I'd let him go, for the US. And he never left. Everybody had renaissances under our watch—Dylan, Billy Joel, Springsteen, Bennett, and Leonard. Did I think Leonard could sell millions of albums in the US? I didn't think that. But I did think we could get Leonard the kind of notoriety he wanted.

Although the prevailing view was that CBS, unable to fit Cohen's music into the formatted genres of radio, never put serious money behind US promotion. Lynch disagreed.

KELLEY LYNCH: It's not what I witnessed. Cohen was an important artist to them, although as Walter Yetnikoff pointed out, Cohen was not Weird Al Yankovic. Cohen didn't like to promote his records and/or tour. He freaked out when *60 Minutes* wanted to interview him. He became obsessed with the notion that they expose people.

BARRIE WEXLER: He complained bitterly that the label wasn't supporting him in the States. But he also shouldered responsibility, saying he hadn't been touring to support the records, as he did in Europe. The grievances fed on each other. Cohen would ask, "Why should I tour when they won't promote me?" CBS would ask, "Why should we help him if he won't tour?" He had this line about why his albums sold better in Europe—"Because there, they can't understand the words."

DON IENNER: Europeans have better taste. Here, it's very quick, very trendy. It's only gotten worse with social media. Everybody's attention span is that of a gnat. The shape that America and the world is in—where the fuck is Bob Dylan and Bob Marley? I mean, Jesus, God.

PAUL BURGER: Cohen was an important artist. Columbia stuck with him through the lean years prior to *I'm Your Man*. Then they realized they could do very well out of his success in Europe, which made him important commercially as well as artistically.

Back in LA, Cohen scheduled a regular lunch at the Beverly Wilshire with a childhood friend, Bernie Rothman, a successful television writer and producer.

BERNIE ROTHMAN: Three, four hours. What did we talk about? Two topics only—poetry and women. One time, he told me that he got onto an elevator in a hotel and encountered a striking blonde. Instead of getting off at his floor, he followed her to hers, and to her room. He did not emerge for two days. Cohen was marvellous, just marvellous, soulful. He was not just a romantic. He was the definitive romantic. That was his life. We shared a lot. In Montreal, Cohen and I were always very competitive. When we were eighteen, we made a bet on who would be the first to find the perfect woman.

One night, Lesley St. Nicholas dragged him to their old stomping grounds— Imperial Gardens, recently converted to a disco, the Roxbury.

LESLEY ST. NICHOLAS: I had a tape of "Do You Want to Dance All Night?" which I'd persuaded him to drop from his 1979 album. I gave it to the DJ, asked him to play it on my cue. For about forty seconds, I actually got Leonard Cohen on the dance floor. It was hilarious.

Cohen spent many LA hours with another childhood friend, Nancy Bacal.

NANCY BACAL: We sat around that little wooden [kitchen] table and would talk forever. I felt like I was his closest friend. He told me everything—not so much about the women. About women, he'd say things like "I can't do it anymore. No more women. Finished. No more." It was pressing and complicated for him.

Bacal and Cohen had met at Westmount Junior High and, notwithstanding one brief interlude, had been platonic friends. "I realized early on that there were many women vying for him. There was too much competition. I just wanted to be a friend."

NANCY BACAL: At Westmount, he and I used to meet in the common area and talk and talk and talk. We'd walk to school. I was very taken with Leonard, so I'd ride my bicycle down his street. He told me, decades later, that he was peeking through the window to see if I'd drive by. He said [my] flame of red hair would please him. In high school, I was editor of the newspaper and there was a strike by teachers, which I supported editorially. Leonard came to school one day and said, "Well done."

Later, they met at greasy spoons to plot escape from "that suffocating claustrophobic upper-middle-class Jewish community. We couldn't stand it." At university, Bacal was a frequent guest at Cohen's frat house.

NANCY BACAL: One night, the fire was on, crackling. We were sitting on the bed, quite innocently, under a big black umbrella—we were both pretty eccentric—drinking Armagnac. I was not a drinker and, all of a sudden, I threw up. I got home, very late. My mother said, "You were with Leonard, weren't you?" They didn't like him—nooo, they did not. He was a threat to the Westmount culture. He was deviant.

In 1959, she had preceded Cohen to Stella Pullman's boardinghouse in London.

NANCY BACAL: There was an order to living there. You stayed first on the cot in the living room, with Stella's silver collection. Then you graduated to the next floor and eventually to the attic. That story about Stella saying he had to write three pages a day? She actually said two pages. We'd sit on the landing and he'd have me read his two pages. He said, "You're my first reader." Harold Pascal was another tenant—we'd go down to the all-nighter, mostly West Indians, and dance and smoke weed. I brought Leonard down one night and it was a bad night—there was a bust. He was cool. No one was arrested. He worked hard. He used his Olivetti every day.

BARRIE WEXLER: He often said, no matter what a writer's skill, it was one's capacity for work that made the difference.

Later, Bacal visited Cohen on Hydra. "He was absolutely mesmerized by Marianne. He thought she was a goddess. I certainly liked her, but I didn't know what all the fuss was about. She was lovely, a bit lost, a man's woman. I might have been jealous. I never wanted Leonard as a sexual partner, but we'd been so close—any woman around, it was a little difficult."

Cohen spent part of the summer of 1989 in Montreal, but was back in LA by September. One morning, he invited bandmates Steve Zirkel and Mitch Watkins for breakfast.

STEVE ZIRKEL: We pick him up and there's this sleepy blonde with dark glasses—"my friend Rebecca." She has coffee, starts perking up, takes off her sunglasses, and I say, "Did anybody ever tell you, you look just like Rebecca De Mornay?" She says, "Oh, I get that all the time." And Leonard, total deadpan, says, "Oh? Who's that?" Thank God I didn't say something terrible about her talent. I say, "An actress who played in *Risky Business* with Tom Cruise." I look up and they're all grinning, and I say, "I get it. You *are* Rebecca De Mornay." Open mouth, insert foot.

DIANNE SEGHESIO: I'd come for weekends [to Tremaine] and Rebecca would be there. She was very nice, very polite, but I was in her space and I don't think she liked me very much. These people were all so fancy, but he'd just sit at his kitchen table, and we'd talk about politics and poetry. I'm a writer, too. I'd give him my stuff and he'd say, "Oh, I really like this one. I'm keeping it in my bathroom." That was the honour—to have it in his bathroom. He wouldn't say he liked it unless it was going in his bathroom. He didn't believe in reviews, didn't want people to tell him what they thought of his stuff. He didn't want to tell other people about theirs, except that he appreciated their effort. If it gave him joy, he'd say that. He was positive.

BARRIE WEXLER: He kept his favourite books in the bathroom. It was like a sanctuary, a retreat from whomever he was living with.

By the fall, Cohen was immersed in his next album, *The Future.* It wasn't his first flirtation with the prophetic mode. "First We Take Manhattan," from the *I'm Your Man* album, also belonged in that category. "Leonard has a prophetic nature," Jennifer Warnes noted. "He knows ahead of time what's going to happen. I've watched it happen many times." The prophesies were predictably Cohenian, of course—contrarian. For example, he rejected the "general rejoicing" that greeted the 1989 fall of the Berlin Wall and, with it, the end of the Soviet empire. He saw it as a harbinger of trouble.

LEONARD COHEN: I felt it was going to present a tremendous disequilibrium. That's why I say, "Give me back the Berlin Wall / Give me Stalin and St. Paul," because this is not the beginning of a period of liberation. . . . That's what I felt when the wall came down, freedom to murder.

Marianne Ihlen had also believed in Cohen's prophetic gifts.

BARRIE WEXLER: We played "Master Song" in Norway in 1970 and she said, "That's about us." I told her it was impossible, because he'd written it years before we'd met. That didn't faze her. "You know Leonard," she said. "He can see into the future." I protested, but she insisted. "I'm telling you, he foresaw all of this." The conversation was becoming argumentative, so I let it go. I recalled Marianne's conviction about Leonard's prescience when I heard "The Future." I still don't know if she was right.

In the end, Wexler maintains, Cohen was "a better poet than he was prophet."

BARRIE WEXLER: He was wrong about the Berlin Wall. Its fall marked the end of the Cold War, a reunified Germany, and, eventually, a united Europe.

His songs are reflections of the times, not harbingers. Leonard's gift is the opposite of visionary—it's the ability to reflect the times as though from a distance, to encapsulate them as if in retrospect. That's who Leonard was, the voice of the heart for every generation.

Indeed, over time, Cohen abandoned political prophecy for other domains—the realm of the human heart, the eternal tango of Man and Woman, and his ongoing dialogue with God.

BARRIE WEXLER: More like a tango of Man and Woman and Woman. Leonard was involved in enough triangles in those days to equip the percussion section of several orchestras.

Production of *The Future* was a protracted affair, complicated by Cohen's laborious writing process, his unstable private life, his continuing depression, and his son Adam's near-fatal auto accident, which required months of rehabilitation. His domestic arrangements also changed—daughter, Lorca, moved to LA for high school.

KELLEY LYNCH: She was a very disturbed teenager, though very lovely. I felt like a mother. I introduced her to my stepdaughter, Jennifer Lindsey—they were traumatized soul mates. I drove her to school with Leonard frequently.

NANCY BACAL: He knew Lorca had problems. I won't say what he said. It isn't fair.

Indeed, to some friends, he called Lorca "the mood buster."

VALERIE LLOYD SIDAWAY: As a teenager, on Hydra, she was a happy, smiling girl. Later, things changed—rings in her nose and ears. Leonard told me once he was relieved that she had no new rings. Then she pushed out her tongue, with a ring in it.

But Lorca plainly had her father's quick wit. Once, in LA, she ran into journalist Michael Simmons.

MICHAEL SIMMONS: I said, "Your mother and I used to go out." She says, "My mother and I don't talk." Later, she came to say goodbye, and she turns, starts to walk away, and then wheels around, looks me in the eye with this grin, and says one word, "Motherfucker."

HELEN MARDEN: Lorca hasn't spoken to Suzanne since she was eighteen. But Lorca has an amazing, quirky, wonderful mind. Very smart. Sardonic. There's a bitter streak there. I wanted her to make up with Suzanne. I thought it would be easier if she did. Leonard thought so, too. She didn't want to—her choice. But she is very close to Dominique, a mother figure for her.

SANDRA ANDERSON: Suzanne never cared for Lorca, from the time she was born. I heard that from Leonard, so that may be biased. But the housekeeper, Lee Taylor, said Suzanne wouldn't ever change diapers, especially Lorca's. She wouldn't have anything to do with her. Lorca came by her angst naturally.

ANONYMOUS: Lorca looks just like Leonard and, for whatever reason, Suzanne was kinder to Adam and really horrible with Lorca. A terrible mother. Lorca said she was a bitch and never liked her. Suzanne was from Miami, but in Paris put on a fake French accent.

RICHARD COHEN: He talked about his kids, mostly with pain and sorrow. When Lorca moved in, it was going to be temporary. She stayed for the rest of his life. The relationships were complex, difficult at times.

KELLEY LYNCH: Leonard told me Lorca had a meltdown in front of Rebecca. It really upset him. He didn't want her around Rebecca. She hated Rebecca. Do you remember *The Hand That Rocks the Cradle*? Lorca said, "It's not acting. That's who Rebecca is."

In the film, De Mornay plays a psychopathic nanny that stalks a family. At Cohen's behest, Lynch herself had also relocated to LA from New York, with her husband, Douglas Penick. She used the downstairs flat on Tremaine as an office.

KELLEY LYNCH: Lorca eventually moved in, with her ferret. I had to quarantine her room.

Although others nursed doubts about Lynch, her relationship with Cohen then was solid.

KELLEY LYNCH: What Cohen found with me was a friend. I found one with him. We were able to have fun, go to a Greek restaurant or shopping—very familial. We had a similar sense of humour. He liked a sidekick. I was young and cute. I did willingly lie down in [his] bed and watch TV with him. It wasn't awkward. That's how he liked to hang out. It wasn't like he was trying to fuck me then. So while there were times when it was uncomfortable, there was also a very loving side. We travelled together, got along intellectually. He let me see who he was. I didn't view Cohen as a monster for the twenty years I worked with him. When a sliding glass door fell on my head, he spent hours with me. He was quite sweet when I had panic attacks. I viewed him as a close friend and confided in him. He could also take that information and use it as a weapon against you later. He went for the vulnerabilities.

Not long after arriving in LA, Lynch's marriage unravelled. Soon, she was dating Steve Lindsey, who was producing tracks for *The Future* album. His first impression had not been positive.

STEVE LINDSEY: I remember saying, "Who beat you up as a kid?" [But] I'd never met a girl that smart, that funny, that quick, who was about my age. I said, "Do you like Coltrane?" She says, "No," stops for a second and says, "Unless it's Alice." [John Coltrane's second wife]. That she knew that? Could make the joke? Within a week, [we were] dating.

The relationship became a roller coaster.

STEVE LINDSEY: Kelley was great until she started drinking. Two glasses of wine and she's looking for a target. Phil Spector used to call at four a.m.—they used to date. I was a single father—a daughter, about eleven, living with my parents in Malibu because I was working so much. Kelley moved her into her house. She was very controlling. She had had an affair with Leonard before that. During [our relationship]? Who knows? After I left, they were back at it, sleeping together. I mean, the betrayal level. I called Leonard on it—later. He said, "She told me you guys had broken up."

It was recording engineer Leanne Ungar who introduced Lindsey to Cohen.

STEVE LINDSEY: I'd bought one of his records in 1969 to '70 and just didn't like it. I was a musician first and lyricist last. But I immediately liked *him*, a lot. He played me "Be for Real" [written by Frederick Knight], and we cut it within a week or two. I got inside the lyric with him and talked about the intention of the song, and he said, "Okay, you're my producer"—I think because I understood delivery, not just the music.

Throughout this period, Cohen continued to battle depression. Rachel Terry, with whom he kept trying to reignite a romance, witnessed a particularly dark episode.

RACHEL TERRY: I walk in, he's lying on the balcony, in the dust, sleeping. The house was dirty. The energy was like he'd commit suicide. I said, "You have to snap out of it." I took him to my house, made dinner, gave him a shower—he didn't want to shower. He just wanted to sleep. He depressed me, too, because he was carrying the suffering of the world on his shoulders. He was a shy, vulnerable, insecure human being, just like all of us. Some Friday nights, he'd have Shabbas dinner with my mother. She used to send packages of gefilte fish and *kubaneh*, a Yemenite bread he loved.

Terry "was afraid" to resume a relationship with Cohen.

RACHEL TERRY: Partly because of all the women he'd been with—promiscuity and sexual diseases. Partly because of his weird Roshi venture. Partly because of my own fears. I was an effectively divorced mother with two kids. In retrospect, I wish I'd have been strong enough to say yes, and pull him out of his shenanigans, being the fragile, wounded soul that he was or, more accurately, we were.

AVIVA LAYTON: I knew he suffered, but didn't understand until later, how crippling, crippling, those depressions were.

LEON WIESELTIER: We talked about the difficulty of getting off the floor, about melancholy. But we agreed that it conferred certain advantages in understanding life.

MORGANA PRITCHARD: I saw him on Tremaine—with all the bad food and alcohol you could imagine. I remember saying, "No wonder you're depressed."

ARMELLE BRUSQ: It's not, "I'm feeling bad." It's, "How can I go from one second to the next?" Depression really is the basis of his art.

KELLEY LYNCH: I've seen him curled up on the floor in a foetal position. He was catatonic on Prozac—catatonic but walking. He got into tinkering with that and other psych meds. He liked that dark edge. I never witnessed what I would call "depression." He was mentally unhinged at times.

Cohen did, in fact, briefly consult a psychotherapist at Saint John's Health Center in Santa Monica. After describing his state of mind, the therapist reportedly asked, "How can you stand it?" He had told Felicity Buirski about the therapy as well.

FELICITY BUIRSKI: He had gleaned a deeper insight into his "predicament." We had been honest with each other about how our early traumas had led to a psychological position that seemed to prohibit commitment. I always sensed the problem, but now, with great humility, he explained it to me, after his therapist, I believe, explained it to him, the life-threatening suffering that accompanies the terror of commitment to those who did not bond with their mothers. It is not called commitment phobia for nothing. Most famous writers are in what is known as the schizoid position, shooting up into their heads, their intellect, for survival. "I think therefore I am" replaces "I feel loved, safe, and embodied, and therefore I do not have anything to fear—no need for external validation."

BARRIE WEXLER: I don't think he went more than once. He distrusted the therapeutic model, though he admitted it worked for some people, including me. We had a laugh, because he said he preferred pills and alcohol to a shrink's couch, but there I was—no drugs, no drink, the emotional pain of my childhood dissipated—and he was still a manic-depressive mess. He didn't say it in so many words, but what he was afraid of was that therapy would impair his creativity.

LEONARD COHEN: Therapy seems to affirm the idea unconditionally of a self that has to be repaired. My inclination was that it was holding that notion to begin with that was the problem—that there was this self that needed . . . radical adjustment. It didn't appeal to me.

In LA, he reconnected with Gisela Getty. German filmmakers interviewed him for *SnowwhiteRosered*, a documentary about Getty and her twin sister, Jutta Winkelmann.

GISELA GETTY: I was always more interested in the mind and spirit of men than sex. I stopped short before it came to it. I'm also a spiritual seeker. [Our relationship] was mostly in that direction. Leonard and I talked often about fear of death and dying. He said he wasn't [afraid]. We also had a little fight about vegetarianism—I was and he wasn't. We went late at night to this twenty-four-hour diner on Sunset. Perhaps because I was German, he felt understood. We didn't use that word—depression—but we hung out because we felt down. We talked frequently about the Third Reich, my father's anti-Semitic generation, and the Holocaust. Only one generation later, my generation—Hitler's children—[were] making love with each other. Leonard also had fantasies to wear a black uniform and role-play as an SS officer. Of course, a joke, but we all play with our darker sides, our curiosities. It doesn't mean he wanted to be it. He played with the taboo. It's an indication that we all have a Hitler within.

Soon after, Cohen received a call from Suzanne Elrod. She had a startling confession to make: she had slept with Barrie Wexler, in New York.

BARRIE WEXLER: After dinner, I walked her home. She asked if I wanted to come up. One thing led to another. She said, "Sure you want to do this? You're Leonard's close friend." Unfortunately, the one question a man never asks himself when a woman offers to sleep with him is why. Their lives together had been over for more than a decade, but they were still chronically angry with each other. I was foolish not to realize that our night together was intentionally meant to add fuel to the fire. Many years later, he told me he hadn't just been upset with me—he'd also been upset with himself for allowing her to get to him, as he put it, "from the dust of our relationship."

LINDA CLARK: He told me about it. He said Suzanne did it to hurt him, deliberately, a kind of "fuck you." And it did hurt him.

The Suzanne incident precipitated a fifteen-year rift between Cohen and Wexler.

BARRIE WEXLER: For a long time, I didn't know how resentful he was. I wasn't even aware he knew about it, though Suzanne clearly wasted no time in telling him. I should have realized I was handing her an emotional grenade. But I was embarrassed and didn't have the courage or decency to fess up. There was never a confrontation—we just stopped being in touch.

Back in Montreal, in early 1990, Cohen called Ann Diamond. She was still struggling to reconcile the Cohen who claimed he wanted to marry her with the Cohen who allowed his friends to ostracise her.

ANN DIAMOND: He was on the living-room couch, by the front window. He said, "I'm having an anxiety attack. I can't make it from one minute to the next. I can't make it across this room."

He sent her to buy groceries—nori (seaweed), natto (soybean paste), and other items.

ANN DIAMOND: When I got back, I said, "You need to talk to someone, find out the cause of this." He said, "I have a chemical imbalance. They're trying an experimental antidepressant, but it's not working." I said, "There's always a cause." He said, "Only the doctors at the Allan Memorial can help me." As I was leaving, he said, "You're the only one who understands me, but don't tell the others." I turned the corner and bumped into Hazel [Field] and blurted out what he'd told me—I was the only one who understood him. And she starts backing away and yelling. "He does not know you. You've never been in his house. You're crazy. If I believed you, I'd have to believe the man I've known for twenty years is a psychopathic liar and I know he's not, so you must be lying!" That's when I realized I had a problem. Getting close to him was like a trip to hell, because hell was where he dwelled most of the time.

Cohen was still in Montreal when he learned that Adam—then seventeen and working as a roadie for a calypso band—had been injured in a car accident in Guadeloupe. With a broken neck, nine broken ribs, a punctured lung, a crushed abdomen, and fractures to his knees, ankles, and pelvis, he had been lucky to survive. An air ambulance flew him out on the first available flight to Toronto. Suzanne Elrod, then living in Paris, made plans to fly to Toronto.

SANDRA ANDERSON: Leonard sounded devastated. I had the sense that it had been touch and go. Adam had had holes drilled in his forehead above his eyebrows, to fasten on a helmet to hold his head immobile. Leonard was spending all his time at Adam's bedside.

ANONYMOUS: They were not sure he was going to make it. Suzanne was very distraught. Her relationship with Lorca was awful. With Adam, it seemed much better.

A decade later, on Hydra, Cohen invited Valerie Lloyd Sidaway to dinner one night.

VALERIE LLOYD SIDAWAY: Angelica, his maid, had made too much food and he asked me to share it. Then we went to see *Meet Joe Black*. In the opening scene, Joe Black gets hit by a car and dies. I looked at Leonard and he had tears in his eyes. This obviously reminded him of Adam's car accident.

Cohen spent several weeks in Toronto, visiting his son daily. University of Toronto grad student Win Siemerling came to interview him.

WIN SIEMERLING: We met in some really dingy coffee shop in North York, a cafeteria underground. In the middle of it, there was this loud scream and three girls come over, maybe sixteen years old. It was one girl's birthday and she'd been given a Cohen CD, and she pulled it out. He was just charmed. He asked them to sit down, and they stayed about ten minutes.

LEX GORE: My mom [Eva LaPierre] told me that Adam's brush with death had dredged up old trauma for Leonard about his own father passing away when he was so young. They spoke then on the phone. I don't know whether she saw him. Nobody knows. She was very discrete, mysterious. There was something emotional there, at the very least a friendship. Any time she talked about him, she'd get this little smile, like a sphinx, like she was trying not to say something. She always carried him with her in some way. She played his music frequently.

One day, Cohen spent several hours at Incredible Records, run by former Montrealer Jonathon Lipsin. In his youth, Cohen had met Lipsin's grandfather, Alter Palayew, a Yiddish poet.

JONATHON LIPSIN: I fashioned some cardboard to protect his knees. He spent about $1,000. He declared that he had found everything in one place, all the memories he'd had as a kid, his parents' music, things lovers had taken from him, things he'd lost, things he'd heard about. He left and came back ten minutes later—asked for a pen and paper and wrote a note: "This is the greatest record store in the world."

Cohen deputized CBS Records executive Richard Zuckerman as his chauffeur.

RICHARD ZUCKERMAN: He was what I wanted to be—deeply philosophical and wise and just very centred, on a different level to any artist I'd ever worked with. We spent a lot of time together—nice conversations about philosophy, just life. I once asked him what he thought about the Middle

East. He said, "It should just be one big amusement park. Like Disneyland. Jews, Muslims, Catholics—one big theme park. Charge admission. Let everyone get it on together."

PAUL BURGER: That was his solution to the Middle East crisis—create Bible Land. It would work for everybody.

KELLEY LYNCH: That was the only time I ever spent with Leonard and Suzanne—meals, visiting Adam, recovering in hospital. To be honest, it was a lot of fun. Even Cohen seemed to be enjoying himself. He liked to swim, so we often went for swims together.

Eventually, Adam Cohen continued his convalescence in Montreal. Cohen used this time to write and see friends. One afternoon, at the Main Deli, someone showed him a short story by Edward Singer titled "You Can Drag Suzanne Down to That Place by the River, but You Can't Make Her Drink."

EDWARD SINGER: A mixed metaphor that captured the essence of Leonard Cohen. Evidently, he agreed, because he read it, erupted in laughter, and immediately wrote me a note on the back of a place mat, pledging his "abiding love."

Tragic as his son's accident and aftermath was, it gave Cohen an opportunity to adopt an unfamiliar role—full-time father.

SHARON WEISZ: It's then that Leonard forged a relationship with Adam.

TERESA TUDURY: I bumped into him in a health food store on Wilshire and he talked about taking a year off to nurse [Adam]. He was transmitting to me that he was a father—that he had taken that on. He was more proud of that than anything else. I sensed there had been maybe not the greatest history.

BARRIE WEXLER: Leonard had screwed up as a father to that point, and was well aware of it. In a sense, he got lucky with Adam. His son, talented in his own right, wanted to emulate his famous father. It helped to redeem their relationship.

ERIC LERNER: Being a father defined his life. Right to the end, Leonard possessed or was burdened by a unique sense of duty. It did not matter to him whether there was a God to judge him or an eternal reward for his efforts. He knew he could not live with himself if he fucked up as a father, especially after the union with [Suzanne] shattered.

Continuing to assemble album material, Cohen asked Elliot Majerczyk to suggest songs that he might cover.

ELLIOT MAJERCZYK: I gave him everything from Mississippi John Hurt, Ray Charles, Van Morrison, Lou Reed's *Street Hassle*, to "The Golden Rocket" by Hank Snow, which he loved. I came to his house and he'd been playing the tape on a loop all day. But some days he'd say, "I don't want to hear any music because it affects me too much"—in terms of his creativity. He was a big admirer of Van Morrison. I once asked him if he knew *Common One*, one of Morrison's least known records. He loved it as much as I did. Only later did I realize that Henry Lewy, who helped produce that record, also produced Leonard.

Always staying abreast of new technology, Cohen wandered one afternoon into Merrill's Music in Santa Monica and bought another Technics keyboard.

YOAV GOREN: He literally chose the most expensive keyboard. Technics was the Cadillac of home keyboards at the time. He loved the auto accompaniment.

Cohen then hired Goren to set it up.

YOAV GOREN: I went to his house once a week for [several] weeks. I was teaching him Digital Performer, a sequencing composition software, and it was too complicated. He said, "I'm not going to get this, so stop teaching me and just run it for me. I'm working on a new album and we'll work together on it." It was challenging because that keyboard wasn't very advanced in its MIDI protocol, which connects keyboards to computers.

Goren subsequently earned a coproducer credit on the album.

YOAV GOREN: We started working on "Waiting for the Miracle." We spent a lot of time on that. The ritual was, we never went right into work. He'd ask me if I'd eaten—he made me pasta. As I got to know him, I started asking questions and he'd open up. He introduced me to his meditation regimen. We sat together a few times, on pillows in the room adjacent to the studio. Leonard taught me breathing techniques and what your mind should be doing, focusing on *a thing*. That, along with the breath—that's the essence.

Over the next few months, Cohen and Goren had many long talks, about Buddhism, Judaism, politics, relationships, the human smorgasbord.

YOAV GOREN: He was detached, as if he was looking at this marionette play from above. I was almost thirty—passionate, involved, opinions on everything. I don't remember him falling on any specific side of things, even vis-à-vis Israel, although he was a Zionist. I would have thought him more left-leaning, liberal, but he had this detachment, a prescient knowledge of the games political players play, and wasn't terribly interested in being committed to one side or the other.

Goren ultimately contributed to half a dozen songs.

YOAV GOREN: We'd do MIDI at his place and take it to the studio. Rebecca was there a few times. But I definitely remember feeling there was something going on between Leonard and Kelley, romantically. Kelley was a strong, in-your-face personality. I didn't really enjoy interfacing with her. I saw her get angry a couple times. An A type.

Afterward, he only connected with Cohen a few times. Still, "he had such a deep influence on my life—massive, really. Beyond meditation."

YOAV GOREN: We developed a friendship. It was so enriching—like the university of life. He was so anchored. He had a confident wisdom. Very grounded, very set and pleased with the way he saw the world. He knew who he was. Around then is where I became unshackled from my lack of self-esteem. Leonard was a huge part of that. I saw no sign of depression.

On the surface, he had an almost jovial approach to everything. So quick and witty—his mind had such depth that he could come up with something.

Soon after completing work on the album, Goren devoted himself to music full-time. He later became one of the world's leading composers of music for movie trailers. His Cohen experience had been catalytic.

YOAV GOREN: I wanted to emulate him, the way he carried himself, the way he answered questions about the meaning of life, just the way he was, with his kindness. I never saw anything negative. Yes, he was not open to a lot of experimental things musically. But I got that. He was a hero for me and not because he was a celebrity. He was a huge, huge influence—just as a person. The sensei.

Cohen did find time that summer to meditate at Bodhi Manda.

JOHN BRANDI: There were pretty severe sitting practices—seven or ten days long—and he was just wiped out. We had nothing to say. We were very comfortable eating in silence. I remember Steve Sanfield mentioning more than once Cohen's regard for silence. He quoted a poem of Leonard's—"Silence / and a deeper silence / when the crickets / hesitate." One time, Leonard went to the altar to make some offer. There were kids at the ceremony and one said, "He used to be a famous singer." When I mentioned it to Leonard and Steve, they both chuckled. I really miss those chuckles.

Cohen, still polishing "Democracy," later recited it for his Zen dharma brother and friend Harold Roth.

HAROLD ROTH: There was a cowboy bar down the hill from the Zen centre, Los Ojos, where we'd go to drink. He said, "I feel a little uncomfortable about this," and he recited the lyrics. He wanted to know, since I was from the States and he originally wasn't, how it would be perceived when he said "Democracy is coming to the USA." My reaction was, "These are really interesting lyrics, but it has layers I can't quite get from you reciting it."

Of course, it's not only about American democracy—it's something much bigger. "And it's here they got the spiritual thirst . . . the heart has got to open in a fundamental way." That's about spiritual practice, the opening of the heart and mind to deeper levels of experience. Roshi often talked about the deeper levels. It was what drew us to him.

JORGE CALDERÓN: He told me he'd written so many verses for "Democracy" that if he'd recorded them all, it would have taken over the entire [album].

Meanwhile, Cohen's musical reputation received another boost—an eighteen-track tribute cover album, *I'm Your Fan*. Produced by the French magazine *Les Inrockuptibles,* it featured such performers as R.E.M., the Pixies, Nick Cave, and John Cale. Cale initially wanted to cover "Queen Victoria," from Cohen's 1973 *Live Songs* album, but opted for "Hallelujah" after seeing Cohen perform it. Collaborators in song, Cohen and Cale were occasional rivals in romance. At one point, they pursued the same woman in London; at another, according to Jean-Michel Reusser, "John called his girlfriend in LA, and who picked up the phone? Leonard. They shared girlfriends without knowing it." Some critics argued that *I'm Your Fan* did more for Cohen's career than Jennifer Warnes had. Writing for CoverMeSongs.com, Ray Padgett noted that having the coolest young acts cover his songs "marked him as cool again. It set the stage for everything that happened subsequently." Without Cale's version of the song, later re-covered by Jeff Buckley, "you probably wouldn't know 'Hallelujah.'"

In March 1991, at the Juno Awards in Vancouver, Cohen was inducted into the Canadian Music Hall of Fame.

RICHARD ZUCKERMAN: The Canadian Academy of Recording Arts and Sciences was looking for candidates, so I mentioned Cohen. Because, coming to Canada, I'd found a complete void, especially in English Canada. He was not even on the radar. There was a kind of hush in the room.

PAUL BURGER: Sony had this plan to help raise his profile. *I'm Your Man* did okay in Canada, but not as okay as you'd expect for a Canadian and for a record that did that well across Europe.

When Burger arrived in Vancouver, Cohen was waiting in the hotel bar.

PAUL BURGER: We started a conversation and he recited verses from "Democracy." He was very excited about it. We held a dinner in his honour the night before. I made a presentation, reciting the lyrics to "Tower of Song." You can imagine my unbelievable shock the next night at the awards ceremony.

Burger was shocked because Cohen's acceptance speech was largely a recitation of the same lyrics. "I never asked him if I ruined his speech or if he took the idea from me," Burger said. It might not have been Cohen's only appropriation that night. A fan had recently written him a letter.

SHIRLEY SPENCER: "Waiting for the Miracle" made me weep. I was going through infertility treatments—a dark period. After a long night, I penned a letter thanking him for his words and music, told him I had been listening to him while doing the dishes and trying to conceive. Now, that's a pretty personal statement. I almost fell off my chair when I watched his acceptance speech, when he said, "Most urgent on my list of appreciation are those of you who have welcomed my tunes into your lives, into your kitchen while you're doing the dishes, into your bedrooms when you are courting or conceiving." I hadn't told my husband about the letter and had to fess up. Coincidence? I'll never be sure.

BARRIE WEXLER: As likely as not, no coincidence.

Some years later, in a discussion about the US Rock and Roll Hall of Fame, Cohen was reminded that he'd also been inducted into the Canadian equivalent. To which he quipped, "Yes, but it isn't called that. It's called the Vestibule of Fame."

Afterward, Cohen joined De Mornay in Tacoma, Washington, where she was shooting *The Hand That Rocks the Cradle*. Confined to her movie-set trailer, he wrote "Tacoma Trailer," a melancholic, nearly six-minute-long instrumental originally intended for a stage show that was never produced. It appeared as the final track on *The Future*.

Back in the studio, Cohen recorded Irving Berlin's "Always." The entire band was drinking Red Needles, which Cohen had invented: tequila, cranberry juice, soda water, and fruit. "Always" ended up running more than eight minutes. The album's version was actually the shortest; others ran to twenty-five minutes.

LEONARD COHEN: The musicians told me it was the happiest recording session they'd ever been to. Where the solo guitar comes in, in the second verse, that's where I fell down. I couldn't sing anymore. I had to lie down for a few moments.

STEVE LINDSEY: We should have done two stanzas and called it a day—but we were so drunk. About seven minutes in, we found Leonard passed out and took him to the bathroom. He got sick there. Then he asked [for] the janitor, to thank him for such a clean floor. And we did. But he loved the song. Kelley told me they listened to it over and over in a parking lot. But I had to devise a horn arrangement and a background vocal with girls, to hold your interest for eight minutes. We cut in his vocal later and overdubbed the end.

KELLEY LYNCH: We did listen to it over and over. For weeks, we'd drive around and listen to it.

DIANNE SEGHESIO: That was one of his favourite things—listening to music in his car. Roshi was trying to break me into Realization and Leonard would try to save me and bring his George Jones CD—he loved that cold, hard truth thing. We'd listen to the whole CD, then he'd say, "Feel better now?" A true friend. Or I'd drive Roshi to Leonard's house and we'd all sit on the floor in the living room and listen to his album. Nobody would say anything. At the end, Leonard would say, "Thank you, Roshi, for listening to my music." It was so beautiful. Everything Leonard does is so from the heart. I don't know anybody that's got anything bad to say about Leonard. How could you? He's a gentleman, he's thoughtful, he speaks his truth, because he takes his time with his words, trying to find the balance. To this day, I can't listen to his music or look at pictures of him without tearing up.

Lindsey struggled to understand Cohen's attachment to the Technics keyboard.

STEVE LINDSEY: I was so against this horrible keyboard, but he loved it, and I was a young producer. I should have known how to pull the reverb off it and do it as is, but that didn't occur to me. I liked to play with the chemistry set of possible sounds and he said, "Man, it's too many genres." I never forgot that. Leonard was meticulous, but—I don't want to say unfocused, because he was completely focused. It was that you had to understand a different language. That was the trick with him. And he was very emotional. He changed his mind, changed with the wind. That album took two years to make, and it wasn't because recording the music took two years. He kept rewriting the lyrics, so all the vocals had to be rerecorded. The reason it didn't take ten years was because we ran out of money.

BARRIE WEXLER: Leonard didn't put much stock in poetic inspiration, beyond, perhaps, an initial insight. That's what he meant in "Chelsea Hotel" by "workers in song." He always sensed what he was looking for, but he had to go down dead end after dead end, past the common and the predictable, before he got to something he hadn't heard before. That was part of his genius—recognizing the value of the unfamiliar.

Bass player Bob Glaub was recruited for overdubs.

BOB GLAUB: I recollect Leonard gently guiding me through what he wanted it to sound like. It was a dance track, with a beat, very simple. He didn't want a lot from me, and not really do anything that called attention to the bass. My favourite recollection—he asked someone to pick up a *challah* and wine because it was Shabbas. I did the blessing with him. We had a sip of red wine—it wasn't Mogen David kosher wine. Leonard was very soulful. I loved every minute. He asked me to tour, but he wanted a long commitment, so I turned it down. But he was upbeat, kind, charming, witty, and very easy to talk to, with an impish little grin. He seemed pretty at ease with himself.

STEVE LINDSEY: Three or four weeks later, we did a version of "Waiting for the Miracle." As a producer, that was the best record I ever made. Later, it got me a job with Peter Gabriel for the Cohen tribute album [*Tower of Song*]. Leonard initially hated "Miracle." Although when I asked Kelley for a DAT [digital audio tape] to send to Gabriel, she told me Leonard now liked it, and said we should have used that version.

There was another working title for the album—*Guns and Roses Live.*

STEVE LINDSEY: It was Leonard's joke—"I'll never sell any records as Leonard Cohen, but if I call it 'Guns and Roses Live' . . ." At times, Leonard was happy with what I did, at other times, less so. But Leonard did give me the greatest line—"Why do you hate me? Because I never tried to help you." It's like a version of "No good deed goes unpunished."

Rebecca De Mornay earned a producer credit on the album, for "Anthem."

STEVE LINDSEY: I mean, producing—whatever.

STEVE MEADOR: Leonard let her stand up and tell me what to do. Somebody had to do it. It was already recorded. I just went in and replaced whoever had originally done the drums. She's a charming woman, very attractive. It wasn't difficult to follow her instructions.

In a later interview, Cohen said he always thought producer's credit ought to go "to the one who makes it happen. I'd been playing that song for a lot of years and she finally said, 'I think it's finished now. Let's record it.' She has a very good sense of harmony." Journalist Trish Deitch, who attended one session, later wrote that De Mornay had been locked in a windowless recording studio for ten and a half hours with only a bowl of Cheetos, a quart bottle of tequila, and two engineers. Cohen, "an attractively beaky man in a dark, gangster-style suit, [was] near-comatose." He was also interviewed by Canadian journalist Marilyn Beker, who had met him after a 1964 poetry reading at the University of Toronto. Back then, she found him "charming, a wonderful idea of what a poet would be, with a black leather jacket, dark clothes, the hair. I was totally enamoured. He signed a copy of his book 'all good things.'"

MARILYN BEKER: Flash forward to 1992 and I'm commissioned to write a profile. I meet him at the studio and we go to this really greasy Italian restaurant. I made a mistake—I told him about our first encounter and how it meant so much to me. And the rest of the interview, he was the most obnoxious—not forthcoming. He smoked like a chimney, eating the most disgusting food, [a] pulled-pork sandwich. He did this on purpose. He wasn't upset, but he was playing with me, trying to disabuse me of my enamoured view of him. Stop idolizing me. I wrote an article that was not entirely flattering and *Chatelaine* had it rewritten and published a very complimentary article. He wasn't buying any of it [the adulation]. He saw this starstruck person and said, "Naw, not that."

In March, Montreal celebrated Irving Layton's eightieth birthday at the Centaur Theatre. Artistic director Maurice Podbrey organized it.

MAURICE PODBREY: I said to Leonard, "You have to speak." He said, "I don't want to." I said, "You have to." He said, "Okay." Irving was in the front row—pretty deaf. He kept on shouting, "What are they saying?" Leonard told the story of how he'd once been in the *schmatta* business and Irving said, "You teach me how to dress, and I'll teach you how to live forever." Leonard said, "I want to thank Irving for keeping his side of the bargain." He also mentioned the Jewish belief that when the Messiah comes, he'll be recognized because he was born circumcised. "You may not know this about Irving, but he was born circumcised." And Irving is going, "What's he saying? What's he saying?"

Later that year, Elton John's management invited Cohen to participate on the British star's *Duets* album. The song chosen was Ray Charles's "Born to Lose," written by Ted Daffan in 1942.

ELTON JOHN: There was a big microphone. Leonard was on one side, I was on the other, and he started to sing . . . "Born to Lose" . . . I just couldn't stop laughing. He said, "What's so funny?" I said, "Sounds like an ocean liner leaving Long Beach." It was the lowest note I've ever heard.

One day, Cohen brought De Mornay to meditate with him at Mount Baldy.

HAROLD ROTH: The most beautiful woman I've ever seen. He [came] into the sutra hall with Rebecca and she was absolutely gorgeous, radiant. She literally took my breath away. I had a hard time paying attention to Roshi. They were pretty serious about each other. They gave off that vibe.

PINA PEIRCE: He told me, "She's lovely, but one of these days the whole thing will rupture. She'll find out who I really am." At [one] *sesshin*, I helped her learn some rituals. But after, at the dining hall, Rebecca was talking to some German monks—she spoke good German—and Leonard tried to drag me outside and kiss me, right in front of her. He came running over with this wolfish look. I was trying to defuse whatever he was feeling and said, "It was great doing the *sesshin* with you and Rebecca," and gave him a kiss on the cheeks. And he goes, "*Rrrooar.*" I might have been willing to go to bed, but not with Rebecca there. But that was the Leonard I knew.

De Mornay, however, did not share Cohen's enthusiasm for Sasaki Roshi.

ROBERT FAGGEN: Roshi was from a universe antithetical to the modern woman. His whole way of operating—it caused a lot of tension with Rebecca. She really confronted him about Roshi.

YOSHIN DAVID RADIN: I remember driving to LA from Mount Baldy with Leonard and Rebecca and I told this joke that horribly offended her. "What do you call the excess flesh that surrounds the vagina? A woman." She was just seething. Leonard just tried to keep driving. Then I realized, "Oh, shit, what did I say?"

Meanwhile, *Vanity Fair* editor Tina Brown commissioned Leon Wieseltier to write a profile of Cohen—the start of a deep, enduring friendship.

LEON WIESELTIER: I initially said, "I'm not a profile writer." She said, "Is there anyone you really admire?" I said, "Actually, there is." Leonard. I'd loved him since I was sixteen. I flew to LA, stayed at the Chateau Marmont, had Shabbas dinner with him. The first time I was with him, so was Rebecca, who was a pain in the ass. She kept warning him about *Vanity Fair*. She was there to monitor the situation. Leonard couldn't have cared less. With Leonard, it was love at first sight. It could not have been warmer or richer. He played me new songs, including "Anthem." We listened to a lot of music, talked about Cavafy and Lorca and Amichai, and Judaism. We invented a drink. We were talking about Buddhism and needed schnapps. He put in ginger root and we agreed to call this concoction Schnappssana. He showed me his computer—the most sophisticated I'd ever seen. We sat at his kitchen table—he'd prepared chopped liver, salad, matzoh balls from Canter's—and talked and talked and talked. The conversation lasted until he died. He was hilarious. We laughed a ton.

Cohen took Wieseltier to meet Sasaki Roshi. "Apart from Roshi, every single person there was Jewish—Sid and Murray and Harold and Sheldon." Tina Brown later left *Vanity Fair* for the *New Yorker*, which is where the profile "The Prince of Bummers" appeared in July 1993. Later, Cohen sent tapes, drawings, and witty comments on Wieseltier's *New Republic* columns.

On June 26, 1992, McGill University conferred an honorary doctor of laws degree on Cohen. The man presenting the award was none other than his former professor Louis Dudek, who had published Cohen's first book of poetry in 1956. Dudek used the occasion to issue a kind of apology. Twenty-three years earlier, writing in the *McGill Daily*, he had predicted that Cohen, "a fine poet before he gave all that up to take the guitar, would soon be forgotten." Now, introducing his former protégé, Dudek executed a U-turn. He had often wondered, he confessed, whether fame was good for Leonard Cohen. But reading his lyrics, he realized that Cohen was not seeking fame, but "something far more difficult and much finer than personal glory, something beyond price and beyond measure—the things of the mind. . . . Leonard Cohen has been faithful to the truth of the search for his being. . . . He has won through, so far as anyone can win through in this difficult struggle."

Later, Cohen and De Mornay flew to Paris, booking a suite at the Hotel Lutetia.

KELLEY LYNCH: She was demanding he buy her an engagement ring, and he was feeling pressured.

GABRIELA VALENZUELA: I couldn't wrap my head around this guy in a tuxedo, attending Hollywood premieres. Page Six scandals—destroying his hotel room in Paris in a vicious fight with Rebecca, drunk and out of his mind. The Leonard I knew was the humble, graceful Leonard of the Prince of Asturias speech. The other Leonard—I don't know who that is.

KELLEY LYNCH: According to Cohen, they went to look at rings. When they returned, she was given the *New York Times* crossword puzzle I had faxed for her. It made her jealous [that he and I had been in touch]. An argument ensued. Cohen said he destroyed the hotel room—or at least broke a lamp—but he initially said "destroyed." Not sure which version was factual.

EVANGELIA PAPAIOANNOU: The engagement was a big step. He was ambivalent. It was typical Cohen. "Should I do it?" He felt he had to do it.

FELICITY BUIRSKI: When I heard about Leonard's engagement, I sent a letter expressing support. I was sad, but not surprised when I read the engagement had ended, and how he went to live at the Zen centre with his father figure, Roshi. I felt that if Leonard could close the gap with someone, perhaps I could, too.

Lynch claims to have been the cause of "an ongoing argument between them."

KELLEY LYNCH: One day, Rebecca called and spoke to my assistant. She told her I was upstairs [in Cohen's flat]. Cohen then answered her call and told her he was in the bath. She demanded to know if I was in the bathroom with him. I was, because he insisted on discussing business matters with me while he bathed.

ARMELLE BRUSQ: I believe that completely. Imagine [Rebecca], the woman in love with the guy—you get mad. He had sex with Kelley? He didn't?

The story of Leonard is the story of ambiguity. He creates ambiguity about the relationship.

KELLEY LYNCH: Later, according to Cohen, Rebecca demanded that he close the downstairs offices, which we did. This activity [dictating while he bathed] generally, although not completely, ceased after that.

There was no love lost between the women.

RICHARD ZUCKERMAN: Tension between her and Kelley? That would always be present, definitely. I had lunch with him, Kelley, and Rebecca—very informal, as he was. He went out of the room and comes back with this beautiful blue chiffon shawl. Wrapping it around himself, he says to Rebecca, "My dear, I bought this for you because it matches the colour of your eyes."

JOAN BUCK: When I visited, there'd be dinners at Tremaine. At a certain point, curly-haired Kelley [arrives] and dinners are slightly different, weren't relaxed. Because she was anxious. There was somebody at the table who wanted something very specific. I know they had been lovers. Then there was Rebecca *and* Kelley, and it wasn't as much fun. I liked Rebecca. Leonard and I were dedicated smokers, so a lot of the conversation was about giving up smoking. He gave it up for Rebecca, but then he gained weight, so he started smoking again.

NANCY BACAL: I wasn't close to Rebecca. I was jealous of her, too. We were on opposite sides. He was obviously very taken by her. Their engagement seemed inevitable.

With *The Future* about to be released, Cohen began promotional appearances. In October, he joined De Mornay in Toronto—she was shooting Sidney Lumet's *Guilty as Sin*. During his visit, he had lunch with novelist Barbara Gowdy.

BARBARA GOWDY: People came up to him and he'd give them the time of day. He signed napkins and never acted as if he felt interfered with. He looked around a lot. He saw all the women in the coffee shop, for sure. I was trying to impress him, coming up with metaphors, and he acted impressed. I got the sense of being with a lovely, smart, fine mind—charming, curious, interested, courtly. He was flirtatious, but he was with most women. He was fifty-eight and I was forty-two. He seemed old to me. I found the flirtatiousness surprising because he was with Rebecca and thought, "What do you want?" He gave me his addresses and phone numbers in Montreal and in LA. He wrote them on his plane ticket from LA to Toronto—business class. I must have given him my number. [Later], he phoned me at home—maybe midnight—and asked me if I wanted to come to his hotel. [My boyfriend] Chris Dewdney was actually there [with me] when Leonard called. We were having a fight, so I was able to say, "Leonard Cohen wants me to come to his hotel and have a drink. Should I go?" He said, "No." I think I won that argument, thanks to Leonard. Years later, I saw a psychic and asked, "Did Leonard want to see me for conversation or sex?" She said, "Not for conversation." [But] was I, like, tenth on the list? How many phone calls did he make that night? There must have been trouble there or why was he calling me at midnight? I did send him my next book—didn't hear back, but did hear he occasionally asked about me, which was flattering. I never called him. I regret it for sure. I've often imagined what it might have led to. Just lying on the bed. We'd have sung his songs and he'd have been impressed that I knew all the lyrics and harmonies.

Gowdy's intuition was correct. Cohen also called a former lover, Patsy Stewart.

PATSY STEWART: I heard he was coming. So I sent a note to [LA]. He called when he was here and said, "Let's meet." But he was with Rebecca and they were a public couple, and I was living with someone. We didn't meet.

On Halloween, back in LA, Cohen threw a party for about 150 at the Bel Age Hotel to celebrate Sasaki Roshi's thirtieth anniversary in America.

PAUL HUMPHREYS: He paid the entire cost. He spared no expense. He hired a string quartet. He created an insignia for the occasion, lapel pins.

KELLEY LYNCH: I got Cohen carving pumpkins at the event. The hotel and dinner cost approximately $25,000.

HAROLD ROTH: It was an incredible evening. Leonard's band played half a dozen songs. Rebecca was there. Marcia Radin did this very, very graceful Sufi dance. But the hotel turned out to be the launch site for the drag queen parade. In the men's room, Little Bo Peep came up, hiked up her dress, and pulled down her panty hose. Then her sheep came on the other side of me. This was very much in keeping with Leonard's droll sense of humour. He looked so relaxed. He didn't usually project being that happy or at ease.

There was another party for Roshi at the Rinzai-Ji Zen Center.

BOBBY FURGO: Perla and I played. Leonard was birthday-speeching him, while Roshi sat cross-legged, meditating. During his birthday-izing, Leonard says to us, "No need to wake up Roshi."

Then it was back to Toronto to shoot the video for "Closing Time," at the Matador Club, owned by the family of Charmaine Dunn.

LAURIE BROWN: He and Rebecca were drinking wine and so enjoying the process. It was [as if] there was no one else in the room, just the two of them having the most wonderful time. It was pretty intense and lovely.

LEON WIESELTIER: There was an early version of "Closing Time" he played me—not a square dance, a mid-tempo ballad, set in Montreal.

RICHARD ZUCKERMAN: For *The Future*, he calls and says, "I have a great idea. I want to attach a T-shirt to the album." We didn't do it, but he was always coming up with interesting ideas. He was so ahead of the curve. He had an amazing imagination.

In late November, Cohen and Perla Batalla flew to Europe for promotional interviews. In Oslo, journalist Yan Calmeyer Friis met him at the Grand Hotel.

YAN CALMEYER FRIIS: He was in a very good mood. Drinking his wine, missing his cigarettes—he had quit. He asked if he could put his cap on my head, and walk around a bit. He laughed and laughed. He thought I looked like John Lennon. I'd met him before in Oslo with Marianne. They took me to an Italian restaurant. We talked about Kafka, James M. Cain, Dostoyevsky, *McCabe and Mrs. Miller*. He sometimes spoke like poetry. He showed me how to play "So Long, Marianne" and said, "You are supposed to dance to it, until the night swallows you. You should feel it here." He put both his hands to his heart.

PERLA BATALLA: He knows I love good wine and really good food. At the airport, in Sweden, he said, "Darling, wait here. I need to get something, and I'd rather you not be with me when I get it." The next night was Thanksgiving. He said, "Come to my room. We're going to have Thanksgiving dinner." [Which] turned out to be a *ginormous* tin of caviar he'd bought at the airport and champagne. The best Thanksgiving I've had.

At Christmas, Cohen took De Mornay to Hydra. While there, Kelley Lynch and Steve Lindsey welcomed a son, Ray Charles Lindsey. Cohen became the godfather.

VALERIE LLOYD SIDAWAY: It was freezing cold. I wondered why he was bringing a girlfriend at that time of year. To a primitive house with no heating and one bathroom in his basement. They stayed about two weeks. I bumped into her once at the supermarket asking for basil—I guessed for pesto. It must have been quite a challenge for her after the sophistication of LA. Bill Cunliffe asked me to go by Leonard's house and say hello. I declined. They obviously came here to escape.

DON LOWE: She didn't get out of bed. That was Leonard's story. I saw her once. You'd see Leonard alone when she was here. It was strange to see Leonard with a woman like Rebecca. She was different, as far as Leonard's women went.

Back in LA, Cohen took a call one day from his friend Peter Lindforss.

PETER LINDFORSS: I had collapsed again and called to seek consolation from the Apostle of Darkness. "Have you tried the new generation of antidepressants?" asked Leonard. "Have you?" I countered. "Sure, but they do not work on me." . . . "But you think I should try." . . . "Absolutely. I know people who say they've completely changed their lives. For the better." . . . "But I've heard they take away the desire for sex." And now came the inevitable Cohen comment: "That, Peter, is their great blessing."

CHAPTER FOUR

So Here, Never There

Leonard . . . is perhaps the most masculine, yet gentle person I have ever known.

—Roloff Beny

It was always about the work, never about the woman.

—Barrie Wexler

In late January 1993, the latest incarnation of Field Commander Cohen's travelling minstrels assembled at the Complex Studios in West LA for rehearsals. The band, again recruited by Roscoe Beck, mostly comprising veterans of his 1988 tour—Steve Meador, Bob Metzger, Paul Ostermayer, Bobby Furgo, Bill Ginn. Only Jorge Calderón was new.

JORGE CALDERÓN: I get a call saying Cohen is about to go on the road and his bass player, a Frenchman, can't get a visa. I wasn't sure I could do that type of music, but I played with Ostermayer and Meador. They hired me right away. Then Leonard came. I remember [Meador] saying, "Play the stuff exactly like the record." *The Future.* So I [did]. Leonard comes in— he says, "I want you to play what you feel like, what you hear." I was the FNG—the fucking new guy. For a while, I felt out of place, coming into this little family. They saw me as this Hollywood guy, which I'm not. And, since I was a vegetarian, they all made fun of me. But it all smoothed out and they embraced me.

Several promotional gigs were booked, including appearances on *Late Night with David Letterman*; *Friday Night! with Ralph Benmergui*; the Juno Awards show; *The Tonight Show with Jay Leno;* and, before the tour began, a live rehearsal broadcast on National Public Radio.

JORGE CALDERÓN: At the Leno show, we were going to do "The Future." The producer says, "You can't use that anal sex line." So there's Leonard, with his beads, the Buddhist collar. He goes, "That's what I wrote. That's what I mean." But he also didn't want to blow the gig.

Cohen ultimately changed the line from "Give me crack and anal sex," to "Give me speed and careless sex." He had done the same in Canada. In post-performance banter, Cohen told Leno, "It was very gracious of you to invite me to chop this song in half." For the Benmergui show in Toronto, Cohen initially resisted playing with the house band, codirected by Matt Zimbel.

MATT ZIMBEL: I sent him a letter, and examples of the band. A few days later, he agreed. So he shows up with his piano player, three singers, his violin player, and Leanne Ungar, his engineer. Leonard was going to do "The Future" and "Closing Time." I rehearsed the band, and instructed them, when he came in, to ask stupid questions. I wanted him to believe we'd never heard the songs before. Leonard turns to us in rehearsal and says, "Well, friends, should we give this a try?" We start, and the band was like a wall. It was locked, loaded, nothing tentative. Leonard has a look of shock and joy on his face. He'd never heard the record he'd made—with those dinky Casio sounds—rendered by a live band, particularly one that had spent eight hours rehearsing. He said, "We did Letterman last night and they didn't even know the changes." The following month, he wanted us to play on the Junos with him and we did. He was a very thoughtful man, the philosopher-king. He had a message for us. There really was no one like him.

Later, Zimbel went for a drink with Cohen's piano player, Bill Ginn.

MATT ZIMBEL: I asked him—this shows how much the music industry has changed—"How long do you tour for?" He said, "Until Leonard's money runs out." Because at the time, records made money and touring lost money.

Zimbel was struck by Cohen's obvious love for De Mornay.

MATT ZIMBEL: He was so in love. He would send her roses every day—three dozen, every day.

At the Junos, recalls Kate Grant, "Leonard won best male vocalist and said, 'Only in Canada could I win the award for best male vocalist!'"

KATE GRANT: At the after-party, at the King Edward Hotel, the press started to swarm him. You could see him get uncomfortable. So he and Rebecca left. Bobby Furgo and I were standing outside, and Leonard says, "Wow. Look at all these limos. Who do you have to fuck to get a limo, anyway?" Best male vocalist, but nobody gave him a limo. He made a joke of it.

Hailing a taxi, Cohen invited Furgo and Grant to hop in.

KATE GRANT: We go to Fran's [an all-night diner]. It was quite late, so we ended up ordering breakfast. He had baked beans. There was a conversation about how men hit on women and how women react. So Rebecca starts acting and he says, "Hey, baby," and she's snooty, like, "Who are *you*?" It was really funny. A young girl, borderline homeless, came up and, as a gift, gave him a bent penny. She knew who he was and he was very gracious. You could tell he adored women, in the way he spoke of them. Rebecca could be aloof, the way she carried herself, but would open up for a few minutes. She had a great connection with him.

The tour, which began on April 25 in Holstebro, Denmark, consisted of twenty-six concerts in thirteen European countries. Cohen made the assignment clear.

BOBBY FURGO: He said, "I have a very important message to give to everyone. We are missionaries. Don't act like we're part of showbiz. We're presenting messages that are beautiful." He was not religious, but he was very spiritual. He'd say, "If you are Catholic, Jewish, or Presbyterian, just be a good Catholic, Jew, or Presbyterian. Embrace it. But don't look for secret answers—there are no secret answers." From the get-go, we knew we were lucky to be included in something very special, that it would be a lifelong memory. It has been.

JORGE CALDERÓN: Jennifer Warnes warned me. She said, "You're going to a world where some people worship at the Leonard Cohen altar. But you have to understand, he's a totally normal, down-to-earth person." That's what I saw immediately. He was so here—never there. *There* was for other people to bring to the picture.

As they had been in 1988, Julie Christensen and Perla Batalla were his backup singers.

STEVE MEADOR: Leonard does not really make much sense as a singer. He's an interpreter. Having that angelic background is really a great foil for him. He understands that explicitly. The sexual chemistry and the coy onstage play—all part of the show. Everyone understood that.

BOBBY FURGO: Julie and Perla, they never had a bad night. It was his ultimate signature sound—two of the greatest singers of all time, singing with him.

A major feature of the tour's backstage life was red wine.

PAUL OSTERMAYER: He'd have pretty decent wine—thirty-five- or fifty-dollar bottles, expensive in '93. But by the end of the tour, he claimed it wasn't doing it for him, and he bought a case of Château Latour, 1980, a good year, a hundred and fifty dollars a bottle. He shared that with all of us.

BOBBY FURGO: He was not materialistic, in any way. His stove was the cheapest stove you could buy. But he did like Château Latour. You have to put your money in the right places.

The first case arrived via Batalla's husband, Chef Claud Mann, once an award-winning wine steward at Butterfields in LA.

PERLA BATALLA: Leonard said, "Do you think Claud could score some Château Latour?" My husband asked private collectors if they had it in their cellars. He'd buy cases and bring it out to us on the European leg. Quite extravagant.

KELLEY LYNCH: It wasn't just Perla's husband. It was shipped everywhere—Canada, Europe. Then there were custom black leather jackets, custom sweatsuits. This adds up. The US leg killed Cohen financially for many reasons, including his insistence on flying everyone business class, and staying at the Four Seasons. But he made a ton on merchandising.

MITCH WATKINS: [After] a bottle of wine and a couple of shots of Rémy Martin, there was some incredible stream-of-consciousness stuff that went on between songs. Almost like a rant. And this guy's a master of words. It was brilliant, this crazy poetry, like he was writing *Beautiful Losers* on stage.

In Helsinki, Cohen spent time with writer Seppo Pietikäinen.

SEPPO PIETIKÄINEN: He'd drink three bottles of red wine before the show. You never noticed he was drunk, but if you knew he'd been drinking, you could see he was a bit slow. He was one of the few people you can ask stupid questions like, "Do you think God exists?" He took you seriously.

BARRIE WEXLER: I once told him I found it difficult to believe there's a God. He said even if there isn't, it's probably best to act as though there were.

SEPPO PIETIKÄINEN: We talked about women. He asked me if I was married. I'd been married twice. He said, "I could never take women so seriously as to marry them."

PICO IYER: Every time I saw him, he'd ask if I was married, and say, "Marriage is really hard. Being a monk, meditating eighteen hours a day, is easy. Dealing with one-on-one relationships is really tough."

JORGE CALDERÓN: Before going onstage, he'd be, "Guys, have some wine!" I finally started drinking, especially in Paris. It was so good that I kept drinking throughout the show—and I was not drunk. It was this great feeling. Sometimes he'd start [the show] slow, because he'd drunk so much, but it would never total his performance. He'd quit smoking. He was chewing on these licorice sticks, bark from a tree, the real thing. He said it helped him with the craving. He gave me one, which I never used. I still have it—memorabilia.

BOBBY FURGO: He had insomnia. He'd take sleeping pills to sleep and uppers during the day to stay awake. Once or twice, he was just a little fuzzy onstage. He wouldn't go beyond one bottle. The other bottles were the band members helping him.

Again Cohen paid his musicians generously and added liberal per diems.

BOBBY FURGO: I says, "How about you pay me X?" He goes, "No. How about a lot more?" So he gave me that number. He says, "But you gotta pay taxes this time." Because in '88, it had been cash, no taxes. Plus the per diem. You never had to worry about money and the ethics of Leonard in any way.

JORGE CALDERÓN: Leonard said, "I want to pay you this. Is this good enough?" It was a really good offer, fantastic. But after the tour, I got audited by the IRS. I ended up paying $10,000 additional. There was something fishy about that whole thing. But he was extremely generous. He had this Greek side. "C'mon, man, I'll take you to dinner." Almost every night. And the bill—his dime. More wine? More shrimp? More, more, more, more, more. To the point, after a show—"Oh, no, here comes Leonard." We were hiding because we knew we'd end up at a long dinner and we were getting fat.

PAUL OSTERMAYER: In Copenhagen, Rebecca sent him this big tin of expensive caviar, with bread, crackers, and nice things. He got [it] that morning, and he invited me up to his room. He shared the entire can of caviar with me and Bill Ginn. His spirit was generous—you could just feel it.

BARRIE WEXLER: He once quoted from the Talmud. "The only things you truly own are the things you give away." That's how he moved through the world.

STEVE MEADOR: He got a little paranoid about T-shirts, the swag they were selling. He thought they were trying to rip him off. I said, "Leonard, that's the small stuff." Those tours wore on him physically. Three and a half months in Europe, across Canada, East Coast, West Coast, then back to Europe. A pretty exhausting experience.

Cohen later retained LA's Rich Feldstein to oversee accounting and provide business management. Lynch, meanwhile, was trying to cope with the "abject madness" of the tour.

KELLEY LYNCH: It began with insurance and visa problems, rehearsal issues, creating the tour book, negotiating the merchandising deal, talking to disgruntled tour members every day. Later, there was insanity with Jorge Calderón, Cohen making allegations against tour manager Geoff Clennell overspending. It just went on and on and on.

BOBBY FURGO: At the beginning, the band wasn't necessarily clicking. Meador was thinking of replacing a couple of guys—I won't say who. I took one of them on a long walk and tried to steer him in a more positive direction.

JULIE CHRISTENSEN: [When] Bill Ginn was struggling with his demons, drug abuse and alcoholism, Leonard was trying to see if I could help. I said, "That's not in my job description. It's not my job to keep him sober." That also put a strain on us. It probably scared him a little that he couldn't assign that. Perla and I both struggled with members of the band being not [sufficiently] engaged. We'd been musketeers in '88. It wasn't an all-for-one scenario like it was in '88.

Cohen's former lover Céline La Frenière attended his Royal Albert Hall show in London in early May. Seeking to visit backstage, she was rebuffed by his handlers.

CÉLINE LA FRENIÈRE: Leonard wrote a letter of apology—he had got my message late—and gave his contact details, including his solicitor's in New York. He also called my home in Hampstead and left a message. Much as I remembered him fondly, I did not feel the need to get in touch. That was the last time I heard from him.

A few days later, in Ghent, Belgium, a playful Cohen toyed with his interviewer. "I speak fluent Flemish. I'm familiar with your history, your restorations, your dilemmas, your anxieties, your aspirations. I'm just about aware of everything there is." Asked if he opposed racism, his answer was typically contrarian. "Not entirely," he said. "I don't think we should completely abandon the notions of who we are. In fact, if we deeply study who we are, we will feel a lot better about who everyone else is. You encounter racism only when people forget who they are. When things begin to break up and people embrace only a superficial wisdom about who they are, they become anxious about who the others are. A great race affirms all other races."

BARRIE WEXLER: I'm sure Cohen believed at that moment that having pride in one's own race could lay a foundation for tolerance. But I also know that in a different context, time, or place, he was capable of saying the exact opposite, and believing that, too. Leonard was the walking embodiment of cognitive dissonance.

Backstage at the Zenith in Paris the next night, Cohen was visited by Dominique Issermann, Carole Laure, and Albert Insinger. The latter introduced him to Armelle Brusq, who would later make a documentary film about him.

ARMELLE BRUSQ: He'd drunk a little. He said, "I want to marry you." That's the first thing he told me. Typical Leonard. He was surrounded by all these women. I remember Dominique saying, "He's with his widows." She had a trash humour about him. Like, "You can't kid me, sonny." Not at all like a groupie.

In the morning, Cohen had coffee with Calderón.

JORGE CALDERÓN: I knew he was a great writer, but when you're with him, he's such a normal guy that you're talking about this stuff in a nuts-and-bolts way. "Dance Me to the End of Love." He says, "Did you know the Nazis got Jews to play as an orchestra as they were marching prisoners to the ovens?" I was naive. Then I got what the song was all about. It blew my mind—that he had that depth. He told me how hard it was for him to write certain songs. He said, "It's like a little sculpture. Every day I chip away." He did say, "When this is over, we should get together and knock off a few ditties." It never happened. I wasn't a guy to bug people. But the amazing thing is the way his music got to people. Brought them to such a beautiful place.

PAUL OSTERMAYER: The album we toured—those songs were awesome. That's really what his calling card with musicians was. They could see this guy is good. He's got a special talent that I certainly don't have. He worked bloody hard. He'd use his Casio keyboard to listen to different chords and find one that fit into what he was hearing. He had a gift for it. A dozen [songs] at least were great compositions.

Later, Cohen gave Calderón a copy of *The Future* album, inscribed with the words "To Jorge, the father of modern medicine."

JORGE CALDERÓN: I don't know what he meant. He would say jokey things like that.

Arriving in Barcelona, Spain, Cohen seemed unaccountably jittery.

JORGE CALDERÓN: There was something that really bugged him about Spain. Finally, I asked him, "Are you okay?" He says, "Did you know they kicked all the Jews out [in 1492]? I'm dying to get out of here." We finally cross the border and he says, "I feel better now."

Cohen would return to Spain that year, and—through writer and translator Alberto Manzano—meet flamenco singer Enrique Morente. They spent an hour together, in the cafeteria at the Palace Hotel in Madrid. As a sixtieth birthday present for Cohen, Manzano later persuaded Morente to record four Cohen songs in the flamenco style.

In Milan, Furgo took Cohen to buy new shoes.

BOBBY FURGO: We went to my favourite shoe shop and I forced him to buy two pairs, especially a brown pair, which he hated. He bought a black pair and a brown pair. We wrestled in his hotel after, as I pretended to throw his old shoes—he had duct tape on the soles—out the window. He couldn't part with them. He was freaking out, "No, no, no." This from a guy considered an impeccable dresser. Nice to see those inconsistencies.

JORGE CALDERÓN: The thing with Leonard—he was very cheery, full of life and full of stories, funny. He loved to laugh, loved having the family, the band, together. But sometimes he'd be a bit gloomy, moody. It wasn't something that became a problem, or something you wanted to stay away from. There was something going on about him and "Hallelujah." We never sang it. One of the girls asked, "When are we doing 'Hallelujah'?" So he says, "Tomorrow at sound check, we'll try it." The next day, we played it two or three times—we weren't doing it badly. He stopped it. "No, we can't do this. I don't want to do this." And he walked offstage. And we never did that song, before or after.

Christensen's stress was compounded by the fact that she'd left a young child at home.

JORGE CALDERÓN: Julie said, "I could never say no to Leonard."

JULIE CHRISTENSEN: I wouldn't have done that if I hadn't have wrongheadedly thought this would boost my career. I felt bereft. Everybody told Leonard he was absolutely crazy for taking me. I must have been crazy. There was a lot of political stuff going on behind the scenes. I was naive about that. But my husband, an actor, was at home. Somebody had to make the mortgage payments. Leonard very generously gave them a stipend to come see me in London, Madrid, and Toronto.

BOBBY FURGO: There was always conflict with Julie because she was emotional, all over the place, volatile. The tour manager wasn't nice to her, either.

De Mornay's occasional presence added complications.

JULIE CHRISTENSEN: They were trying to cement the relationship and maybe have kids and he already had kids. Their relationship was straining. This was one time when I sat down with Leonard and said, "She's a remarkable person, but I miss you. You forget who you are when she's around." He just looked at me blankly. Our relationship was never the same. I think Rebecca was bucking for my job. She was jealous of the backup singers. In 1988, we'd interacted a lot. In 1993, he was told by Rebecca and perhaps others not to interact with the band as much, just to face the audience. It was very cold and lonely.

BOBBY FURGO: Rebecca was with us on the bus. We'd see her in her underwear sometimes. It wasn't inappropriate. She was okay—not warm or cold. He'd be on the phone with her for hours when she wasn't with him. It was an up-and-down emotional ride for both of them. Intense.

Cohen seemed to get along better with Batalla.

PERLA BATALLA: Often, during performances, Leonard would stand near me and run his fingers up my back—knowing how ticklish I am. It took all my will to not explode in laughter.

On June 8, the band performed at the Ottawa Congress Centre.

DENNIS RUFFO: Leonard did like his red wine. Before he went onstage, he quaffed a bottle. It didn't affect him. After the show, we hung around, drinking wine, swapping stories. We were up 'til about three in the morning. Nicest guy—nothing pretentious about him at all.

Two nights later, Cohen appeared at the Montreal Forum. A friend, Paul Lowenstein, invited him to an after-party at his Westmount home, where the old fraternity brothers planned to gather.

PAUL LOWENSTEIN: I got a positive response, told all the guys, all of whom went to the concert. He never showed up.

NOOKIE GELBER: That was painful. I was in pain for Paul. Why the hell did he not show up? That's the only thing I fault him for.

BARRIE WEXLER: Socially, Leonard lived in the moment. The space he occupied when he accepted invitations was almost always never the one he was in when it was time to go.

Later that month, Cohen performed at New York's Paramount Theatre. He sent Gabriela Valenzuela four tickets and backstage passes. She hoped to see him after the concert, but was unsuccessful. Allen Ginsberg, quite ill at the time, came backstage; Cohen devoted every minute to him.

GABRIELA VALENZUELA: I wanted to see him, not for romantic affection, but for reasons of the heart. Something had been left unfinished between us. No matter how much I tried to adjust my wounded heart, I never found a remedy for the pain. I felt Leonard had stolen my soul.

During the Toronto leg, the band recorded what became the *Cohen Live* album.

BOBBY FURGO: After the first few nights, Leonard was angry, rushed off the stage and locked himself in his room. Perla and I knocked on his door. He was furious with the band for not acknowledging him onstage, [not] going through him. He ranted about it—in our presence. It was the only time I ever saw him angry like that. Our heads were on the chopping block, career-wise. Everyone was shook, big-time. And there was only one more night of recording. Everyone really toed the line and quit jerking off, pared down the notes to efficiency. Most of the record came from that third night. He got what he wanted, but he had to throw a fit to get our attention.

In Hamilton, Cohen still seemed out of sorts.

PAUL OSTERMAYER: He was very emotional. When there weren't a lot of people, the acoustics were not very good. At sound check, the bass was booming. He couldn't really analyze it as a bass reverberating through the room. He would just see it as "poisonous." That sound check, he was very dark. Maybe he drank too much the night before. But the sound was bad. It was usually the bass because it competed with his voice. By '93, his voice had dropped a lot. The later tours, backstage, he was a different person, lighter, more comfortable in his skin. Didn't have that kind of unsettled feeling we saw, when he'd go into these depressive bouts.

Bass player Calderón was the principal focus of Cohen's irritation.

BOBBY FURGO: At sound check, Leonard might say, "Turn the bass down." A couple of times, Jorge would throw his bass down and walk offstage. Jorge's wife was very ill during that tour. He was temperamental. He refused to wear the tour shirts onstage.

JORGE CALDERÓN: I never liked to wear swag onstage because you are the band. One time, he was, "Jorge, I want you to wear the shirt tonight. Kind of like the Hitler Youth." Then he decided that wearing the swag shirt was a bad idea, saying, "We look like the Hitler Youth." I said, "Leonard, you're confusing me." He was a jokester like that.

But Cohen was chiefly upset about Calderón's playing. In Boston, Eric Lerner visited before the show, at the down-at-the-heels Berklee Performance Center. To Lerner, the venue was a sign that Cohen continued to be a tough sell in North America. He found him in a corner of the stage, looking as if he were guarding the Château Latour wine cases beside him.

ERIC LERNER: As we finished the second bottle, he confided, "I'm making a heroic attempt to drink all the profits. At a hundred bucks a bottle, I think I have a shot." He glanced around at his surroundings, raising his chin and eyebrows. The dismal situation required no further commentary. Sony had shafted him again. "For some curious reason," he began, "my bass player is intent on sabotaging my efforts." Leonard believed, or purported to, that [the bass player] was involved in some conspiracy with his drummer. From then on, Leonard and I referred to various acts of knife-in-the-back treachery as "He did an X." Then, in the manner of English nobility, nostrils flared, eyes gazing over the horizon, Cohen said, "They served Château Latour exclusively on the *Titanic*, you know."

JORGE CALDERÓN: It was not as dreadful as Eric makes it sound. Yes, Leonard's voice and any bass live in the same realm. He came to me with his concern and deduced that the stage volume coming from my amp was getting in his way. I turned it down and made it comfortable for him. He preferred getting bass through his vocal monitor than to hear it coming from the backline on stage. No more issues with sound. He never appeared unhappy with me, and we had a lot of fun and worthwhile conversations.

KELLEY LYNCH: He was furious that Sony did not support the US tour in the manner in which he felt they should have. Steve Meador and Jorge were a huge problem. He demonized them.

ERIC LERNER: Mood . . . may have been Leonard's only certainty. . . . Mood is everything and everything else is just speculation. Mood is the actuality of existence, what it feels like in the bone, whether or not the sages, mystics, masters, or even Roshi believed that. We didn't care. We wanted better moods and, the older he got, the less constrained he felt about pursuing a better mood. Backstage at the Berklee that night, Leonard wasn't having any luck with it.

In Victoria, poet Phyllis Webb surprised him backstage. They had last seen each other thirty years earlier.

PHYLLIS WEBB: I plunked myself down and his manager got quite nervous—this strange woman. I said, "You don't remember me, do you?" He said, "Of course I do, darling." I really wondered if he did. [Then] I mentioned Irving [Layton]. I think at that point he clued in.

The next night, at Vancouver's Orpheum theatre, poet Bill Bissett went to meet him.

BILL BISSETT: I was very nervous, almost backed out. He was very sweet and very gracious, probably one of the kindest people I ever met. He said he knew my work. I told him he was my favourite poet. I asked if I could hug him and he said either sure or of course. That was one of the biggest thrills of my life. I'm not sure if I told him I loved him—it may have been obvious. [Later], I couldn't sleep for hours, rolled a joint, went out again and thought, "I hugged Leonard Cohen and he hugged me," and that whole evening and the magic night that followed, when someone took me by the water of English Bay and we let the water answer.

Also backstage was his former lover Eva LaPierre and her fifteen-year-old daughter, then known as Alexandra Gord—"punk rock, death rocker, torn fishnet, green matted hair."

LEX GORE: He was so cordial. He took me around the room and said, "Look what Eva made. Look what Eva made." He was fascinated by me, very attentive. He commented on my barrettes—silver, gothic bats. My mother cocked her head at the word "barrettes." They exchanged a long, meaningful look and he said something along the lines of "I've kept it." Years earlier, Leonard stole a tortoiseshell barrette my mother used to wear. And refused to give it back. It was just a cheap barrette, so she shrugged it off. He told her he took it for sentimental reasons and kept it all those years. You could tell there was a real fondness between them, an intimacy. After, they stole away to one end of the room—the rest of the room just didn't exist. They spoke for a very long time. I got bored and left. I don't know if they got together. It was the last time she saw him.

Later, Gore overheard her mother on the phone telling a friend about Cohen and heard the word "Bulgari."

LEX GORE: When I went in, she was holding this pearl choker that had the circle clasp and the stick—a really beautiful piece. I think he gifted it to her.

Photographer Kate Grant joined the tour for the western leg.

KATE GRANT: On the bus, Leonard would joke around. He said, "There's room in my bunk, if you need." He was just being flirty. He got me into drinking red wine. At one point, he asked me if there was anyone I'd taken a fancy to—maybe he could facilitate a romance. I think he was implying Bobby [Furgo]. I probably blushed a bit and said, "No." And he said, "Yeah, I guess you could handle that yourself."

On July 5 and 6, Cohen played LA's Wiltern Theatre. Actor Harry Dean Stanton and director Robert Altman visited backstage.

TERESA TUDURY: Leonard was really the first world beat guy—oud player, fiddle player, fascinating textures in music. The show was just transportive. I was so proud and so moved. Jenn Warnes and I went backstage and he was so tired. I looked right into his eye and it was like looking into the eye of a whale, a giant force, quiet resignation and peace.

Another former girlfriend, Linda Clark, also came backstage.

LINDA CLARK: He was with Rebecca. Was it awkward? Not for Leonard. I was dressed to kill, honey—really stunning, miniskirt and high boots. She was in a tailored black men's suit—very mannish, plain, hair pulled back, a Marlene Dietrich look. He saw me and was like, *Vavavavoom.* She comes up and he puts his left arm around her and gave me his right arm and there we are, walking, the three of us, no formal introduction. Nobody is saying anything. It was a good moment in his life.

A few days later, the band arrived in Austin.

BOBBY FURGO: *Austin City Limits.* As he introduced "Democracy," he said his heart was breaking for the human condition. It was a real moving moment. He was very sober. Boy, was he a pain that day. He sound-checked us for two hours and was never satisfied or happy with what we were doing. He was going at us.

After several more North American dates, the tour ended in late July.

JORGE CALDERÓN: We were going to go to Australia, but Leonard said, "That's it. I'm hanging it up. This is my swan song." When it ended, he went silent.

STEVE MEADOR: Leonard wasn't one of those guys you call up and say, "How ya doing, man?"

Despite the friction, Calderón regarded the tour as among his best.

JORGE CALDERÓN: I've played with other fantastic people—Ry Cooder, David Lindley, Jackson Browne. But playing with Leonard doesn't have any rivals. What I remember is the kind, jovial, generous, funny gentleman that he was. He taught me a lot—his way of being and how to bring it to the stage.

Cohen did stay in touch with Batalla and Christensen.

JULIE CHRISTENSEN: Leonard and I were always cordial. He always gave to my son's graduations and film projects, and was always part of the family.

When the tour ended, Cohen and De Mornay repaired to Montreal. One rainy afternoon, they were caught in a downpour near the Vogue Hotel.

KAREN KAIN: My husband [Ross Petty] and I darted under the awning. Under the same awning were Rebecca and Leonard. I was tongue-tied because I'd always been a huge fan. My husband introduced us. Leonard was very charming. Rebecca was not that thrilled to have to communicate at that moment.

Another afternoon, Ann Diamond came by, joining Cohen and poet Henry Moscovitch.

ANN DIAMOND: Henry was demonstrating ESP. He said my aura had completely surrounded Leonard. Leonard also had powerful ESP. A thought would come into my head, and he'd say the thing that was in my head. And he played a game with the TV—he'd anticipate one line of dialogue after another, word for word. Ramblin' Jack Elliott rolled up in his RV. So did Elaine [Malus]. In the park, she prostrated herself in front of Leonard. A thing like that can ruin your day.

That fall, Cohen's publishers brought out *Stranger Music*, a collection of poems and song lyrics spanning forty years.

KEN NORRIS: It featured song lyrics as prominently as poems, which struck me as a business decision, not necessarily an aesthetic one. It was a little skimpy on new poems, [and] I didn't think they were particularly well-selected. It's engaging, but presents an unsatisfying shadow of the more fully realized works. [But] Cohen has always been a writer pushing against the idea of a fixed genre, a writer who will not be contained. His very considerable achievement is to expand the resources of the medium in which he is working.

To choose the poems, Cohen had sought help from Nancy Bacal, who encouraged him to select newer, more stripped-down material. When De Mornay saw the collection, she protested, urging him to include older works.

NANCY BACAL: He and I were working full-time. Then I found out he was also working on it with Rebecca. He said, "Rebecca really wants to work on it." I was not happy and I divorced myself. I felt squeezed out.

Cohen's Quebec publisher, Les Éditions de l'Hexagone, asked Michel Garneau to translate the poems into French.

MICHEL GARNEAU: I said no. It's a lot of work and it eats you up. Leonard phoned me and said, "Michel, here's the problem. My French is not that good, but it's good enough to know that translations made in France become ridiculous in Montreal. They don't work. So I want you to do the translation for Quebec." I agreed. I thought it was important—that I could help make him a Quebecois poet. I said, "When I have a first draft, I'll send it to you." He said, "No, no. You know exactly what you're doing. You have my full confidence. I don't want to intervene."

In late November, Cohen was interviewed in New York by Arthur Kurzweil, then editor in chief of the Jewish Book Club. The conversation contains some of Cohen's most revealing thoughts on the dual attraction of Judaism and Zen Buddhism. In many ways, his views echoed sentiments expressed thirty years earlier in Montreal—that the modern practice of Judaism had effectively erased the experience of the Absolute. Although mystical elements certainly existed, they had been relegated to the margins of Jewish thought.

LEONARD COHEN: We have the stuff, but we don't take it seriously. . . . The actual use of the liturgy . . . that idea, of something passionate and not negotiable, that atmosphere, did not touch me at all in my education. . . . You ask why some of our brightest and best have not been able to embrace the tradition. It's because the tradition itself has betrayed itself, because the messianic unfolding and the meditational systems have not been affirmed.

His own attachment to Judaism, he insisted, was inviolable.

LEONARD COHEN: At our best, we inhabit a biblical landscape, and this is where we should situate ourselves, without apology. The burning bush—those are the experiences we have the obligation to manifest. Otherwise, it's really not worth saving or manifesting or redeeming. That's what the Bible celebrates. The victory of experience. So the experience of these things is absolutely necessary . . . these episodes . . . now relegated to the realm of miracles or superstition, or something that can't happen to you.

At that time, Cohen agreed to narrate a National Film Board of Canada documentary on *The Tibetan Book of the Dead*, with a script by Kelley Lynch's ex-husband, Douglas Penick. According to Lynch, "Cohen initially did not want to be involved, but did it as a gift for me." The *Hollywood Reporter*, announcing his participation, expressed surprise that a Zen Buddhist had been chosen to narrate, instead of a Tibetan Buddhist like Richard Gere. Cohen quickly sent a letter of protest saying, "My father and mother, of blessed memory, would have been disturbed by the *Reporter*'s description of me as a Buddhist. I am a Jew. For some time now, I have been intrigued by the indecipherable ramblings of an old Zen monk. Not long ago he said, 'Cohen, I have known you for 23 years and I never tried to give you my religion. I just poured you sake.' Saying that, he filled my cup with sake. I bowed my head and raised my cup to him, crying out, 'Rabbi, you are surely the Light of the Generation.'"

In early December 1993, Cohen received a Governor General's lifetime performing arts award—from the same government agency whose prize, for English-language poetry, he had spurned in 1968.

BRIAN ROBERTSON: We nominated him in 1992, but he wasn't available. So we postponed it. I met him in Toronto and explained it all—a show at the National Arts Centre, a medal presentation at Rideau Hall, a banquet, applause in the House of Commons—a three-day blast. I said, "I need names of people who could introduce you at the NAC event." Eventually, I get six names, including model Linda Evangelista—all babes. None had ever met him. Most were surprised I was even calling. Wednesday, the week of the ceremony, we still had no one. Thursday morning, I called actress Cynthia Dale. She laughed and said, "This may be fun," though she'd never met him, either. They met backstage. I'm sure he hit on her. But he was totally charming—the image we all knew.

En route to the event, Cohen travelled with his daughter, Lorca, and her childhood friend, James Di Salvio, son of Montreal nightclub impresario Bob Di Salvio.

JAMES DI SALVIO: We'd just spent time with my dad at the casino in Montreal. Leonard has a nice suit and cowboy boots, bordering on tacky, but he was doing it on purpose. Gilles Vigneault was also being honoured—he was pleased about that—and Roch Voisine. As the car's about to stop, he gives me that classic Montreal look and goes, "What the fuck is a Roch Voisine?"

Interviewed by the *Gazette* in Montreal, he disclosed that his relationship with De Mornay was officially over.

ROBERT FAGGEN: Leonard probably wasn't playing it straight with Rebecca. There were other women, even with her. When he first brought up Rebecca, I said something like "That would be a pretty attractive place to land for a guy." He called it a healthy relationship. He said she wasn't interested in being with someone playing games. "You're with me or you're not." He had tremendous respect for Rebecca.

Kelley Lynch had another perspective.

KELLEY LYNCH: She was high-maintenance. He didn't want to marry her. He didn't want to be engaged. He was embarrassed [by] all the headlines—the hand that rocked the cradle. They were drunk and fighting a lot, fighting about me. She was jealous of me. He was very careful about breaking up, because of the media. He sent her roses every week. A year later, I said, "You've got to stop. She's dating other guys." He didn't want her to bad-mouth him.

MARCIA RADIN: She wanted children—that was the issue. He said to her, "I can't do it again."

AVIVA LAYTON: He was really serious about Rebecca. She wanted a child and he wasn't ready. He couldn't.

ARMELLE BRUSQ: He was obsessed about not wanting a child.

SUSAN RAY: He was terrified of having more children, that he made clear. Not that he didn't love his kids. From what I saw with Lorca and Adam as adults, he was an attentive and caring father. He was just not a domestic animal. What he told me was that he broke up with Rebecca because Roshi told him to. I have no trouble believing it—either that Roshi told him to or that Leonard obeyed. He'd made the decision to turn himself over to the Old Man, to see what could be done in that way. But there's usually more than one factor behind a major decision like that, isn't there? I can't speak to why Roshi would have asked him to break the engagement, except that he wanted Leonard to give his energy as fully as possible to the practice.

BARRIE WEXLER: Following Roshi's advice—wanting to see where the practice would go—is consistent with how he wrote, taking each line of thought as far as he could before figuring out if it was a blind alley.

ROBERT FAGGEN: She wanted kids, and he didn't—basically. My strong impression is he would have said, "You want kids and I've already done this." She wanted the relationship and marriage and he told her, "We'll have kids, but I won't be there for them. I'll live in my house and you'll live in your house." And she basically said, "What the fuck?" That was very painful for her. He was apparently very up-front about this. Rebecca later said, "You tried. I know you tried." Leonard was complicated. He wanted a family, but was not the marrying guy. He had tremendous guilt about his own kids, that he wasn't around, and Suzanne wasn't much of a mother.

LINDA BOOK: To start out at sixty with a newborn? Oh, please. But it's difficult for narcissistic people to be in a partnership of equality. Ultimately, he disappoints people. You feel there's so much there, but you're not going to get it. It all goes to the art or his own pursuits. He was a person who indulged his own interests, always, always, always. He knew himself in quite a brutal way. Some people couldn't believe that a man so insightful in his songs could be so shut down.

LINDA CLARK: I don't think he could form an intimate bond. He put women on such a pedestal that it would be very easy to fall off that pedestal. Women were muses to him, rather than relationships. He could be friendly, sweet, accommodating, gracious, humble, but if you were in a relationship with him, you'd probably have dried up like a prune, because he'd ignore you. You'd starve to death. For all [the things] he said, it was all an illusion, completely romanticized. He was married to his music. I told him, "Your relationship is with your poetry and song." He was so internalized, so distant and uninvolved. I felt he was very bitter.

In a later court submission, Lynch claimed Cohen once started to dictate his autobiography to her, beginning with a section describing De Mornay "climaxing like a little train picks up steam."

KELLEY LYNCH: That's a direct quote. He must have awoken in a cold sweat, because he asked me to destroy the chapter.

ROBERT FAGGEN: With minor exceptions, Leonard did not talk in a vulgar way about the sexual nuances of a relationship. The orgasm dictation—that just doesn't sound like him. It sounds like him on drugs or him trying to be funny. I don't see him making fun of her that way. He even said once, "Gentlemen don't talk about things like that." It's very unlikely he would have started an autobiography that way and he is mentally incapable of making shit like that up. I knew Dominique, Rebecca, and later Anjani Thomas—not one had a bad word to say about him. Not one. They really cared about him.

GABRIELA VALENZUELA: He rarely spoke about intimate details of past girl-friends. He was discreet about every single thing, and respectful. I never heard him gossip, never. He never trashed anybody. Someone else's feelings were always more important than his. He was never abusive or humiliating or phony.

Early in 1994, director Oliver Stone approached Cohen about licensing his music for a new film, *Natural Born Killers*.

OLIVER STONE: He saw the point of [the film]—that it was chaotic and violent. Not something you'd think he'd respond to, but he did. Then he saw pieces of the film and loved it, and approved all the singles—"The Future," "Anthem," "Waiting for the Miracle." He was a beautiful man, but withdrawn. He lived a strange, austere life. But I liked him very much. A great sense of humour—sardonic. He certainly made a deep impression on me. His poetic sensibility was very powerful. You never know where someone's soul is. I'm not sure he enjoyed this world as much as I do.

Later, according to Lynch, Cohen asked Stone if he would produce a music video for him. Apparently, Stone declined. Stone, then beginning his own exploration of Buddhism, later visited Cohen on Mount Baldy, but found it harsh and chose to follow the Tibetan stream. In May, Cohen donated $1,500 to bring Tibetan master Kusum Lingpa Rinpoche to LA and allowed part of his management office to be used as a Tibetan meditation centre.

OLIVER STONE: It fell apart of its own inertia. Kelley acted erratically and our informal association fell apart, though I never had personal problems with her.

DIANNE SEGHESIO: Kelley had these Tibetans living downstairs. That turned into a bit of a fiasco.

Tibetan Buddhist translator Sangye Khandro met Cohen through this coterie.

SANGYE KHANDRO: Although Leonard was a Zen disciple, he also sat for [Tibetan] teachings and had great respect for the Tibetan master. Leonard preferred not to engage with the visual aspect of meditation, which Tibetan Buddhism uses. He wanted to do nonconceptual meditation. He came almost every day when he was in town. I thought Leonard was an amazing gentleman, smooth, polite, respectful, and soft-spoken, quite humble, a beautiful example of a human being. I didn't like that he and Kelley were always smoking. It was hard being around it. But I have to tell you—I found Leonard to be completely in love with Kelley. That is what I always thought. He *adored* her. I feel he would have given anything to be with her, but that wasn't meant to be. She was with Steve [Lindsey]. They had a volatile relationship. She was chaotic, always tearing around, but you could see he just adored her. I felt it was absolutely the truth—he loved her very much.

In fact, Lynch claims that a jealous Cohen accused her of having a sexual relationship with Oliver Stone.

KELLEY LYNCH: Leonard Cohen was obsessed with me. He went into Steve Lindsey's office and lied that I had sex with Oliver. He routinely threatened my job when I wouldn't have sex with him. It became intolerable. It caused him to go into fits of rage. Cohen had a vicious jealous streak.

OLIVER STONE: I had no affair with Kelley.

One night, Lynch maintains she witnessed a bizarre scene at dinner with Cohen, Stone, and screenwriter Richard Rutowski.

KELLEY LYNCH: Cohen began fondling Richard's arms and talking about Richard's strong arms and saying how masculine he was. Cohen then got down on the floor and began prostrating himself to me, telling Oliver that I was his teacher. I finally asked Cohen to switch seats so he was next to Oliver and I was next to Richard. It was insane. He was an embarrassing drunk.

According to Lynch, Cohen was also jealous of her associations with Al Cafaro, then CEO of A&M Records, and Sony Canada president Paul Burger.

PAUL BURGER: I liked Kelley, for all her idiosyncrasies. We spent a considerable amount of time together. I always found her to be totally in Leonard's corner. Was she the shit-hottest manager I'd ever encountered? Maybe not. But a big part of management is being really committed, really believing, trying to create opportunities.

GABRIELA VALENZUELA: Leonard's jealousy wasn't sexual jealousy. If he was working with someone, he wanted their full attention and loyalty. He was jealous of the time [not spent on him].

* * *

In northern California, Sasaki Roshi had purchased property for a Zen centre and another ten acres for a women's practice centre.

MYOSHO GINNY MATTHEWS: Leonard served on both boards of directors. He was the only one who knew parliamentary procedure, the one keeping us on track. He was generous with his time and with his donations.

DIANNE SEGHESIO: He did multiple *sesshins* and sometimes just came for family picnics. We'd sit on the lawn, pick vegetables, and make food together. He was just there—he wasn't anybody [special]. And he was so thoughtful. He'd make all these prints of his watercolours and say, "What would your sister like?" . . . "She likes horses." And then he'd find a watercolour with a horse, and make all these colour combinations and say, "Here's some for your sister." And he'd sign them. "Here's some for you and some for your mother." You didn't ask, but he was so excited about his projects that he just wanted to share, with everyone. Roshi used to call him "the international gentleman," because no matter who, what, where, he was just a gentleman, polite and honest. And he was hilarious—subtle, dry, very dry.

BARRIE WEXLER: When not overwhelmed with his own demons, Leonard always tried to live by the next man's needs. With me, he was a benefactor, example, mentor, and friend—none of which, except the last, would he have attributed to himself.

That year, Cohen flew to Montreal with Seghesio to oversee the sale of the old family home at 599 Belmont.

DIANNE SEGHESIO: We [did] his final walk-through together. His room had all his childhood stuff in it. A leather-bound book of Longfellow had a signature from his grandfather. The bookcase was full of books. I said, "Leonard, don't you want to give this stuff to your kids?" He said, "I really don't think they'd be interested. We're just not attached." Then he said, "I want you to have this book." I cry a lot with Leonard because he's just so deep. Then, signing papers and handing over the keys, he picked up this lighter and said, "This was my mother's lighter"—a gold Dunhill or a Ronson. He said, "I think my mother would like somebody to have this. I want you to have it." I said, "Thank you so much but, when I'm gone, I'm going to give the book to Adam and the lighter to Lorca." I was really grateful for being there. His sister was there, too. She didn't want anything, either.

In LA that fall, Sasaki Roshi threw Cohen a sixtieth birthday party at the Zen centre.

SUSAN RAY: I made the cake—almond with chocolate icing. Roshi wanted him to have a necklace of flowers, like a lei, and I arranged that. I met Rebecca there. I actually liked her. She struck me as smart. I looked up her astrological chart and thought, "God, these two are really compatible."

Soon after, Cohen drove to Malibu to spend an afternoon with Catherine Ingram, a writer and dharma teacher.

CATHERINE INGRAM: Richard Cohen had told us for years that we should meet. It was an immediate recognition and an enduring friendship from that moment. We were never romantic, just instant best friends. We had lunch and tea on the veranda by the ocean, chatting about the eternities. We talked about everything we could think of. In his company I did not censor my thoughts. It was a flow of consciousness. It was thrilling to be with someone who was irreverent, yet had a sacred appreciation for life, but who could go to the darkness and look at it without any filter or spin.

Ingram came to view Cohen as a life mentor.

CATHERINE INGRAM: We'd often talk at his small kitchen table until the wee hours. When I made a move to leave, he'd bring out a fine port he'd been saving, or show me recent drawings, or regale me with a story of his time in Cuba in the early sixties. He loved engagement and there was no place in conversation he wouldn't go. One time, he came to see me in Portland. We spent an entire afternoon at a restaurant and went through two different servers. They were eating out of his hand. They had no idea who he was. It was not schmaltzy, not unctuous, but he'd make quips and be generous and considerate. He was always like that—empathic. Whether you were his friend or you were the waiter.

After Ingram's brother died, at age thirty-eight, Cohen invited her to one of his Friday night dinners.

CATHERINE INGRAM: I was really shattered by the ordeal, but decided to go. There were other people there, so it wasn't appropriate to discuss my brother, or mope. But all through the night, Leonard put little presents next to me—a beautiful Japanese photo frame, an incense holder and Japanese incense. It was so dear, such a pithy moment. "I want you to feel a moment of blessing, of happiness. Your friend is thinking about you." Without one word.

Ingram was struck by what she called Cohen's heart bravery—"the highest form of courage."

CATHERINE INGRAM: The word "courage" comes from the Latin *coeur*, meaning "heart." Leonard's special genius was his ability to communicate both the sorrow and the beauty of the world, even in the same sentence. He never looked away from either, not even in his final months when pain racked his body. He had a twinkle in one eye and a tear in the other. For you, it's not just the elephant in the room. It's the elephant on fire in the room, and yet you feel you can rarely mention it. But, as Gandhi said, "Even if you are a minority of one, the truth is the truth." I once asked Leonard's advice on how to talk with others about this. He replied, "There are things we don't tell the children." Most people are not ready for this conversation. They may never be ready, just as some people die after a long illness, still in denial that death was at their doorstep. As Leonard said, "It is in love that we are made, in love we disappear."

In 2002, Ingram wrote "Facing Extinction," a Cohen-influenced essay about the perilous condition of humanity and the Earth. In 2006, she wrote a novel, *A Crack in Everything*. For another book, Cohen offered her the use, on the cover, of the burning bush image that later appeared on *The Flame*.

At a reception to honour Raymond Chrétien, Canada's newly appointed ambassador to the United States, Cohen ran into guitarist Liona Boyd at the Canadian consulate in LA.

LIONA BOYD: Lining up, I saw this wizened, hunched over, depressed-looking guy, and I said to [her then husband] Jack [Simon], "Could that be Leonard Cohen?" He said, "I don't think so." But I went up and said, "Leonard?" And suddenly his face brightened. "Oh, Liona!" That's when we started having rendezvous, nothing romantic, though that would have been interesting.

We had lunch a couple times at the Sunset Marquis. I once ate most of his fruit bowl. We often talked about Lorca, the poet. We discussed *The Unfaithful Wife*.

Cohen also reconnected with Linda Clark.

LINDA CLARK: After he broke up with Rebecca, he called. I saw him a couple of times—I guess he was rebounding. He was pretty broken, beaten, very quiet. I never saw him drink. He smoked, but he did not have cigarette breath. I thought that was so unusual. He liked to have me read poetry, even if it was his own. He said he liked the sound of a woman's voice.

His relationship with Clark continued as before—confined entirely to his house.

LINDA CLARK: He did not cook for me. We had toast and tea—not meals. He admitted he was very moody and irascible. He'd pick fights and was short with me. I was never foolish enough to fight. I was, "Oh, sweetie, you're not feeling well. Let's talk later." One night, he picked a fight and asked me to leave, then called five days later and left a message, saying, "Hi, darling, how ya doing? I love you." That was a form of apology. He'd never said that he loved me before. I was guardedly in love with him, but he wasn't capable of reciprocating. Why get emotionally attached to somebody who's beyond that state in their life? He didn't talk about anybody. He was very private and enigmatic. He compartmentalized—that's exactly what he did—and it's in his astrology chart. He compartmentalized women. I bet you even his children did not know him. He did not connect well.

One night, Cohen asked Clark to bring over some of his older albums.

LINDA CLARK: We put on the album with "Dress Rehearsal Rag." I commented on what a good song it was. He said, "I can't stand it. It's hard for me to listen to my early albums. I don't like my voice." But for another song, he sat there with a thoughtful look and said, "Hmm, whoever wrote that, they're a pretty good writer." I said, "Leonard, we have something in common. We both admire you."

Soon after, the relationship ended.

LINDA CLARK: I called a couple times. I kept inviting him to Redondo Beach. He never called back. I should have persevered. I could have helped him.

For Clark, Cohen was the *puer aeternus,* a Peter Pan, a conceit first articulated by Ovid.

LINDA CLARK: Jung called it the eternal child, the little boy who never grows up. Robert Bly called him the flyboy—special, brilliant. They usually end up with an earth mother. Somebody's got to buy the groceries. Suzanne Elrod was submissive like that, tiptoeing around him. You could be a satellite in his universe, but your satellite had to revolve around his sun. Perhaps his creative spirit kept him from committing to a woman. He was incapable of fidelity.

LINDA BOOK: That goes back to mom, a manic-depressive who was likely both binding and rejecting at the same time—really chaotic and confusing. And the abandonment by his father. His father died, but it's still a huge abandonment. So a gifted preadolescent guy with abandonment issues, growing up without a male figure. He just doesn't know how to be a real boy.

FELICITY BUIRSKI: A smothering mother is one thing, but not bonding at all with your mother prevents the ability to ever truly bond with a lover or build a fixed-ego identity. By his late fifties, Leonard had become more conscious of his predicament. Though consciousness is not a cure in itself, it is a first step out of the suffering of a cloud of unknowing.

In late 1994, after moving to Santa Monica, Clark invited Cohen to visit.

LINDA CLARK: He never came. He was so self-absorbed. He never mentioned going to Baldy. He just disappeared. He told me he loved me. I bet he gave that penny to many people. He was one of the great loves of my life, but I could see he was a very broken man. I knew I'd be headed for a heartache, so I wisely did not invest my heart. He was very honest. Why did I love him? How many minds did you know like Leonard Cohen's? Arguably, one of the most brilliant minds on the planet. I don't give a flying fuck if he was in his boxer shorts. He was wonderful to play with.

CHAPTER FIVE

A Suite at Roshi's Hospital

Is Leonard a classic Virgo? No. Leonard's a one-off. You're not going to find somebody who's like him. We have to outgrow binary thinking. He could be very suave and he could be very insecure and uncomfortable in himself.

—Susan Ray

People think Roshi's either a saint or a sinner. He was both. When Roshi got mad, you could literally see steam coming out of him. And when he laughed, the room would shake.

—Dianne Seghesio

He had been mulling the issue for months but, at some point in 1994, Leonard Cohen made a life-altering decision. At least temporarily, he resolved to spend more time with Sasaki Roshi on Mount Baldy, focusing on service, introspection, and healing. "My kids were grown," he explained. "I didn't have real responsibilities. And nothing seemed to be as urgent as studying these matters that Roshi embodied." That wasn't the complete story, however. The 1993 tour had taken an enormous toll. At the end, he said, "You are dumped into the desert and you don't remember where your house is or if you still have a car or a girlfriend or a wife or children. You're just lost." To one interviewer, he used what may have been a more accurate description—"nervous breakdown."

KELLEY LYNCH: He was drinking too much and continued to do meth in prescription form. This continued after the tour. He needed to dry out. He told me the pharmacologist was opposed to his request [for pills] and Cohen asked him, "Are you afraid I'm going to knock off gas stations?"

SUSAN RAY: I don't know about drugs, apart from Wellbutrin. He may have been taking other antidepressants. He smoked pot once. But he was still drinking. When you hung with Roshi, there was a lot of drinking.

PICO IYER: Part of the lure was being away from all the women, not having to be Leonard Cohen, not carrying that weight.

It might seem illogical that an eighty-seven-year-old Zen master who spoke minimal English could exercise such a powerful hold, but Cohen was unequivocal. Pico Iyer once queried: "So if it weren't for the Roshi, you wouldn't be here?" Cohen replied: "If it weren't for the Roshi, I wouldn't be."

RICHARD COHEN: With Roshi, you had the sense that you were naked in a way that you were never naked before. In a way, that was thrilling and, in a way, frightening.

ERIC LERNER: Roshi was the compass of our lives. Due north, though for the longest time we had no fucking idea how to tell north from south. Or east from west for that matter. Even so, it was an impeccable compass. We trusted it implicitly.

TOM MCMORRAN: One thing I know is, he loved Roshi. Love is really too weak a word to describe it. It was more like a spiritual partnership. He'd always talk about it.

GIKO DAVID RUBIN: He'd often say, "My life would not be like a pinch of raccoon shit if it weren't for Sasaki Roshi."

PICO IYER: With Sasaki, Leonard became completely empty and invisible, a silent servant. He would tell me that the great thing about Roshi is that he loves you for who you are. He doesn't expect you to be anything else. He sees past all the disguises.

SEIDO RAY RONCI: Roshi was dedicated like no one I ever met. I'll forever hear him say, "More *sanzen*. Not enough. More deeply." I learned more from him without language than I ever did from a book or a conversation.

Others were mystified.

RACHEL TERRY: Roshi had a spell on him. Leonard once called me to find a house for a Zen centre. It had to have a little stream. I found this beautiful house within walking distance of his house. Roshi is to see it, but we'll have breakfast at Leonard's. Finally, he walks in. What's he bringing? A bottle of Courvoisier. What did he find in this guy that could inspire? I don't know what the allure was. They never bought this house.

Roshi aside, there was a more pragmatic reason for the Baldy sojourn—work.

KELLEY LYNCH: He used it as a work retreat. Sony was demanding he fulfill delivery requirements. The pressure was on. At Baldy and in LA, he put together a live album with two newly recorded songs to appease Sony International. It was a very productive period. Unfortunately, Cohen was on meth again. Watching him meditate was painful.

RICHARD ZUCKERMAN: There was no real pressure. Nobody was really looking for anything. Leonard didn't fit the bill of a normal artist who had to produce an album every year or two.

Cohen was under no illusions about his new digs. He described a Zen centre as "a kind of hospital. We tend to glorify the thing and make it sound like an achievement, but it really is the confession of a failure. . . . They make you so tired that you give up pretending." Later, he told French journalist Gilles Tordjman that, while his Baldy sojourn offered up "certain erotic possibilities," life on the mountain was "so bad that you end up laughing about it. It's so inhuman that it brings out your humanity."

RICHARD COHEN: What you can never really capture is the intense craziness of what went on between Roshi and his students. That was the essence of it. All the rest was trappings. It was not summer camp. The way Zen is portrayed in the culture—meditation, calm, incense, rituals—it's so far from reality. The reality was madness and very difficult. There was nothing pretty about it.

ARMELLE BRUSQ: Everyone is playing a game there, a game in which the rules are not very clear.

DIANNE SEGHESIO: One of the first things Leonard put in his bathroom was an article I wrote for Mount Baldy's newsletter—people [waking] at two a.m., and you have ten minutes to be in the *zendo*, and forty people rushing for the same three toilets. It's a rough, no-bullshit practice. It's not a judgment—it's just what Mount Baldy is.

DON WAS: He told me about these marathons, sitting for a week, ten hours a day. If you didn't keep your spine erect, the guy whacked you with a stick. You go through all your neuroses and, after about three days, you've thought every thought you ever had, and you just get sick of it. That's when the good stuff starts—discovery, a sense of oneness, incredible awareness. But after all of that, he said, you get in the car and by the time you hit the freeway in San Bernadino, you're giving people the finger.

HARVEY KUBERNIK: I saw him just after he went to Baldy. I asked him why he had shaved his head. He said, "For a woman." I said, "What does that mean?" He said, "I hope you don't find out." But he laughed and said, "I'm seeking clarity, not poetry."

BILL DODGE: I saw his interest in spirituality as a protection from fame and its consequences, which he wrestled with because it could destroy his creative force. [He was] keeping his voice as clear as possible.

RICHARD COHEN: Leonard was talented, famous, had money, but he wanted to do that particular, weird thing. It didn't seem that weird to me.

PICO IYER: He wasn't looking for a religion. He wasn't looking for an answer. He was looking for medicine, maybe. He was not a man of shortcuts. Forgetting about shortcuts was what Zen practice was about. I spend much of my adult life around monks, Catholic or Buddhist. I never met a more committed or disciplined monk than Leonard, with the exception of the Dalai Lama. So many young people are looking for answers. Leonard had been through enough of the wars not to expect too much of Roshi.

SUSAN RAY: Leonard was a strong practitioner. He disparaged spirituality in every interview, but he was very serious, very devoted.

Ray herself had gravitated to Rinzai-Ji Zen in the early 1980s, after the death of her husband, film director Nicholas Ray (*Rebel Without a Cause*). She met Cohen in New York in 1986, picking him and Sasaki Roshi up at the airport and driving them to the Mayflower Hotel. He immediately seduced her.

SUSAN RAY: I found him courtly, maybe a bit macho. He was very seductive with women. He liked to make people like him. He wanted to be honest, though like the rest of us, maybe he wasn't always.

In the mid-1990s, they reconnected on Mount Baldy.

SUSAN RAY: We weren't lovers for long. It was certainly a relationship, not a love affair. I would have liked it to be. He was hard not to love. There was something profoundly familiar about Leonard. I was familiar to him as well, not necessarily in a way that made him comfortable. He once said he didn't like complicated women, and Jewish women are often complicated. I'm complicated, certainly. When the two of us were taking care of Roshi, Leonard told me the old man was behaving like a jealous lover. Talk about complications. I knew Leonard could not be a conventional partner. He would always be chasing skirts. I just loved him, loved his vulnerability, his humour, his heart, his genuine humility, his spirituality. It was real. It was learned through a lot of suffering.

Between formal Zen practice, Sasaki Roshi sometimes enjoyed watching movies.

SUSAN RAY: Roshi liked movies on animals. For a change, one afternoon Leonard brought him *Father of the Bride*. Leonard and I roared through that until we were crying.

At Mount Baldy, Cohen was definitely more equal than others. Given a private cabin, he hired Kelley Lynch's father to remodel it, creating a second room with insulation, heating, electricity, a bathroom with a shower, and a private telephone line. That room became a music studio, designed by Steve Lindsey— desk, computer, synthesizer, fax, amps, books, liquor, a coffee machine, etc.

PAUL HUMPHREYS: No one has ever lived at Mount Baldy quite the way Leonard lived there. That's not to gainsay the sacrifice [he made].

BRIAN LESAGE: It was unusual to have your own cabin. He was given special treatment for all kinds of reasons—his age, and he'd been a student of Roshi for such a long time, and they had a personal relationship.

PINA PEIRCE: A lot of people were resentful.

SUSAN RAY: People were ambivalent. Mostly they loved him, because he was disciplined in the practice, courtly, funny, and humble. Young monks looked up to him. All the nuns were at least a little in love with him, though not all would admit it. He didn't get puffed up over his favoured status, but nor did he question it. And on occasion, the Old Man would flatten him, just as he flattened the rest of us. Leonard's position—genuine—was that he was in service to the Roshi. But in a community that was all about hierarchy and proximity to the Old Man, Leonard was sometimes resented. It was a highly competitive, patriarchal community, and the Old Man did plenty to keep it that way.

Cohen's principal role was to serve as Roshi's *inji*—a combination cook, secretary, manservant, chauffeur, and travel agent.

YOSHIN DAVID RADIN: He made meals, did laundry, kept Roshi's robes in order. Roshi had three-month training sessions, winter and summer and, between those, *sesshins* at New Mexico, Ithaca, Puerto Rico, or Vienna, or occasionally a trip to Japan.

At times, Seghesio shared his *inji* duties.

DIANNE SEGHESIO: He claims I taught him how to shop. "Roshi doesn't have this, doesn't have that." Leonard and I would drive down to buy pots and pans, silverware, usually in his car so he could listen to CDs, and do Roshi's banking. He'd [meditate] in the morning and the evening. During the day he'd be with Roshi or writing. He had this really beautiful Joan of Arc night-light—one of his favourite songs was "Joan of Arc." He'd turn it on when writing. He later gave it to me.

Cohen had no compunction, it seems, about leaving his affairs in the hands of Kelley Lynch.

GIKO DAVID RUBIN: He told me once, "Kelley Lynch *is* Leonard Cohen." He trusted her so much.

SUSAN RAY: Roshi asked me, because he knew I loved Leonard, "If you were with Leonard, what would you do about Kelley?" I said, "Nothing. She can take care of his work. I don't want to." I didn't have a good feeling about her from the get-go. There was something a little coarse about her. I didn't see the heart I would have liked to have seen around Leonard. But she seemed to take care of him, so I didn't question it. I felt she was in love with him and assumed they had slept together.

Cohen was concerned, however, about his daughter, Lorca, twenty years old. Studying at Concordia University, she had been living in the annex to Cohen's home.

LARRY SLOMAN: He was worried about her. I'd go to Montreal and stay at the house. He'd say, "Please keep an eye on Lorca for me." I know she was troubled.

KELLEY LYNCH: Generally, Lorca was a mess. She kept in touch by phone. She seemed okay and was enjoying school. She is very good at keeping secrets, very much like Cohen psychologically. Obviously, she wasn't telling us that she was having some type of breakdown. I was unaware of the extent of her heroin problem, but realized she was doing serious drugs.

ANN DIAMOND: It was well known she OD'd on heroin at the house.

KELLEY LYNCH: She had an overdose and almost died. She told me that her friend shot a saline solution directly into her heart. At some point, Cohen demanded that Lorca return to LA. She wasn't in great shape in LA, either. He promised to help her start her business.

While Cohen sat on Mount Baldy, Lynch and David Anderle quarterbacked the A&M tribute album *Tower of Song*, featuring Elton John, Sting, Billy Joel, Peter Gabriel, Bono, and others. It was completed in 1995.

KELLEY LYNCH: That album brought him to the attention of a younger, edgier fan base, although Cohen called fans his "constituents." Don Ienner was livid that Cohen demanded that we take the project from Columbia to A&M. I hired Steve Lindsey as producer. Celine Dion initially agreed to do a cover, but later declined. Bryan Adams declined and Cohen dictated, under my name, a horrifying letter to him and/or his manager. Daniel Lanois submitted a track, and Cohen personally called to say he didn't like it and it wouldn't be part of the project. Cohen was not supposed to be personally involved and his micromanagement was excruciating. He hated what Peter Gabriel had done with "Suzanne" and blamed him for delaying the release.

Celia Hirschman, daughter of Cohen's friend Jack Hirschman, handled marketing for A&M.

CELIA HIRSCHMAN: I had lots of meetings with Kelley. How did I find her? Deeply manipulative. That was evident from the get-go. Leonard really didn't have anything to do with it, per se. Kelley had a lot to do with it, because she helped orchestrate the recording sessions, and approvals for the marketing.

To write liner notes, Lynch approached novelist Tom Robbins—via his literary agent, Phoebe Larmore. He memorably described Cohen's voice as "a voice raked by the claws of Cupid, a voice rubbed raw by the philosopher's stone. A voice marinated in kirschwasser, sulfur, deer musk and snow. . . . A penitent's voice, a rabbinical voice . . . a voice like a carpet in an old hotel, like a bad itch on the hunchback of love . . . a voice meant for pronouncing the names of women—and cataloguing their sometimes hazardous charms. Nobody can say the word 'naked' as nakedly as Cohen." Soon after, Cohen called Larmore.

BARBARA DODGE: I was working there. He wanted to know if she'd represent him. I talked to Phoebe, who simply said, "We're too busy." I had to tell him. He was very quiet. Said nothing. He didn't take rejection well. I suggested Phoebe explain that she was too busy with Margaret Atwood and not able to take on another client, especially of his prolific output. They chatted and I think he was okay. Months later, she asked me to call him to see if she could rent his place in Hydra. He turned her down.

When the album was released, A&M threw a party.

CELIA HIRSCHMAN: Leonard was the main attraction. At one point, he turned to me—and remember, this man was a father figure to me—and said, "I want you, Celia." I looked at him, flattered and horrified at the same time, and said, "Oh, Leonard, you've always had me." I gave a little laugh and turned away, because I really didn't know what to say. He was sixty and I was thirty-six. Par for the course for Leonard but, because he was like family, I was never going to entertain that reality. It was incredibly inappropriate, but I knew it came from a loving place. All I could do was make it a loving rejection, which I did. He was always a sweetheart, even if he came on to me. He was a seductive guy, but he was also a human being. Nothing is more charming than a gentleman who is fallible. And Leonard was most definitely that.

Later that year, Cohen sent Hirschman a lithograph.

CELIA HIRSCHMAN: It's a naked girl, looking in a mirror, breast exposed. It's called *The Mirror*. He signed it, "To Celia, many thanks, Leonard." A strange gift, all things considered. I had it framed and it's in my studio.

During a promotional interview with Bravo TV, Cohen read "Days of Kindness," a poem that voices regret for "the precious ones I overthrew for an education in the world." He said, "There's a lot of things you do for your own survival. Some of them don't seem too pretty at the time, or in retrospect they seem cruel. But you've got to be able to forgive yourself, too, about some of the things you do."

To the artists involved, Cohen sent engraved silver penknives as thank-you gifts. After the album was certified gold in Canada, A&M honoured Cohen in Toronto. The trip led to a bizarre series of events.

KELLEY LYNCH: We were in the car to the airport. I wanted to visit Erik Drew [a Tibetan Buddhist monk] in New York and see my brother. Cohen demanded that he accompany me. I wouldn't hear of it. He was furious that I had told [his friend] Nancy Southam where we were staying. She showed up at the Four Seasons Hotel. After the presentation, [an] A&R guy said, "Leonard asked me to find you." I said, "Tell him you couldn't." He told Cohen what I'd said. Of course, he was livid. Fending him off in his hotel room after I got back was a nightmare.

SANDRA ANDERSON: It makes sense that if Kelley refused to sleep with him, this made her unattainable. I think the reason he stayed around in my life for thirty-five years was that I didn't sleep with him.

Twice in Toronto, and again when she returned to LA, Cohen told Lynch their relationship "was no longer tolerable."

KELLEY LYNCH: If we were to continue together, changes would have to be made. He wanted a woman we shared as a personal assistant fired. This would have caused an upheaval in my life, because she was my son Ray's nanny. He wrote that my mother, who worked for both of us, was not the assistant he felt would be helpful to him. I therefore put my mother on my payroll. I went to the mat over the issue and it was resolved.

More strangeness ensued, this time involving Lynch's husband, Steve Lindsey.

KELLEY LYNCH: Steve and I were on and off at this point. I had moved out. Cohen had told him we'd had an affair at Mount Baldy, which was ridiculous. He understood Cohen was obsessed with me, behaved like a jealous maniac. Later, Steve found this crumpled fax [from Cohen] in my closet, and thought it was a love letter. One night, perhaps two years later, Steve and I were together at an Adam Cohen concert, and Steve would not say hello to Cohen. In the morning, Cohen called to ask why. I had no idea. Steve later came to my office to pick up Ray. Cohen stopped by and Steve lost it. When Steve left, I told Cohen that Steve had found his letter.

Soon after, shopping in Wolfe's Market in Claremont, California, Cohen met Robert Faggen, a professor of English literature at Claremont McKenna College.

ROBERT FAGGEN: I was ordering sliced roast beef, roast turkey. There was a gentleman next to me who seemed to be talking to himself. He had a striking face and a shaved head—a little unusual for Claremont, a staid college town. Not wild—Leonard never looked wild—but there was something striking about him. He was going back and forth, out loud, about whether to get the whole potato salad or the German potato salad, and talking about the virtues of each. His voice was resonant and distracting, so I took another look and it just clicked. "Are you Leonard Cohen?" He said, "Yeah, man." I said, "What are you doing here?" He said, "I live on Mount Baldy." I said, "That's funny. I just moved up there." I said, "I think you should have the whole potato salad." We had a chuckle and exchanged phone numbers.

Faggen, who lived within walking distance of the Zen centre, then came to visit.

ROBERT FAGGEN: He was in his robes. He was still smoking, so we shared cigars and ouzo, which at seven thousand feet can be pretty heady, and we just kept talking. We talked about our literary interests. He was very well read, but I never had the impression that Leonard's preoccupations were primarily literary.

In the years that followed, Faggen would become one of Cohen's closest confidants.

PETER DALE SCOTT: Faggen had done [a book] on Czeslaw Milosz. Milosz and Leonard are so similar in some ways. Milosz called himself an "ecstatic pessimist"—that kind of ambivalence, extracting joy from shit and shit from joy, would work for Leonard. Irving Layton's line about Leonard—"a narcissist who hates himself"—works for both as well. And both had a certain amount of guilt, coming from the upper class.

In time, Cohen and Faggen would make their conversational way through much of the modern canon—Ezra Pound, T. S. Eliot, Robert Frost, Herman Melville, Joseph Brodsky, W. H. Auden, Federico García Lorca.

ROBERT FAGGEN: He was comfortably familiar with it all. But we also talked about St. John of the Cross's "Dark Night of the Soul" [a sixteenth-century poem that limns the soul's journey toward mystical union with God]. That was of great interest to him. We talked a great deal about the Hebrew Bible and the New Testament, about Scripture. And we talked about science. We talked about everything—all the things close friends talk about, including personal relationships.

Cohen had also discussed the Bible with Albert Insinger.

ALBERT INSINGER: On Hydra, we'd sit in his kitchen and go through the *Song of Solomon*, talking about every line. Also the New Testament—the life of Jesus. Matthew, Mark, Luke, John, the Gnostic gospels. Leonard was, for a Jew, struck by Jesus. He actually said, "This is the coolest guy that ever lived." I remember him saying the amazing thing about Jesus was that forty people, after he was crucified, spent the rest of their lives talking about him. Those Gospels were basically a biography. People told what they had witnessed.

ROBERT FAGGEN: I never asked him what he was doing at Baldy, did not press him to explain it. The last thing you want to do with Zen Buddhism is describe it too much. The fact that I got that was helpful. I also did not ask immediately about songwriting. There was always the sense that these things were mysterious and it would not do much good to talk about that directly. Sometimes, we'd just hang out.

Early on, Cohen inquired about music computer programs at the Claremont colleges.

KELLEY LYNCH: Cohen was fearful he was losing his voice—not being able to sing anymore. He thought Faggen could help him develop a program that would create a robotic voice. He also explored this at UC Berkeley.

Eventually, Cohen wrote and recorded "The Great Event," a sixty-nine-second prose poem recited by a woman named Victoria M., whose reading was filtered through a text-to-speech computer program. Steve Lindsey produced the track; studio musician Jim Cox played piano—a backward version of Beethoven's "Moonlight Sonata." It appeared as the final track on the *More Best of Leonard Cohen* album, dedicated to the memory of his brother-in-law, Victor Cohen.

ROBERT FAGGEN: He never spoke to me about his fear of losing his voice. He did have a chronic throat condition—the muscles were becoming lax, and he was having difficulty swallowing. If the conditioned persisted, he stopped talking about it. It did not seem to be an overwhelming concern, though he did tell me that his doctor warned him to stop smoking. He did.

Frequently, Cohen would share chocolates and candy that friends and admirers sent, alluding to the lines in "Everybody Knows"—"Everybody wants a box of chocolates / And a long-stemmed rose."

ROBERT FAGGEN: High-end, artisanal chocolates, each with a descriptor. We both agreed that none were as satisfying as Snickers. We'd go to 7-Eleven for munchies—bags of Cheetos and Snickers. And he preferred basic liquorice, like Fine's. He also thought the descriptors used for wine were extravagant and silly. Hints of floral, this and that. He wasn't interested in tasting notes. He was interested in what the high was like. For Leonard, art was not an end in itself. It was supposed to get you somewhere. Otherwise, it doesn't do anything. Robert Frost once said, "Let's not be too damn literary." Leonard wasn't too damned literary, which doesn't mean he wasn't an artist.

During this period, University of British Columbia professor Ira Nadel began work on a Cohen biography. The project, Cohen told him, was "benignly tolerated," or, as he told Lynch, it was an "authorized unauthorized" account of his life. *Various Positions* was published in 1996. Nadel had written a slimmer version of it three years earlier, without Cohen's blessing: *Leonard Cohen: A Life in Art.*

KELLEY LYNCH: Cohen spent countless hours discussing what Ira would be allowed to write. It's all thought-out and studied. He very, very carefully maintained his image. He knew how to sell himself.

That summer, Cohen had lunch with Montreal film producer Michel Ouellette and Armelle Brusq at his home. Brusq had written a screenplay based on *The Favourite Game* and had sent the script to Cohen. "He loved it," she says. "It was quite close to his book. 'A scar is what happens when the word is made flesh'—that's how the book starts, and the trigger to my adaptation. It was true to the bone, without any syrup." Another film project based on the novel was parked in development limbo in Hollywood, being shepherded by Canadians Norman Snider (cowriter of *Dead Ringers*) and Marc Boyman.

NORMAN SNIDER: Marc bought the rights and I wrote a screenplay, not a very good one.

ARMELLE BRUSQ: Leonard put me in touch with Norman, to see if we could work together. But he wanted more sex and, for me, it was completely wrong to make a film obsessed by sex. I refused. I bet on the fact that there would be no film, but I had to wait two years for their option to expire.

NORMAN SNIDER: Hollywood was never interested. But I got to hang out with Leonard. You were very aware it was a Jewish household—the menorah and all that. We did have herring and black bread and vodka. Leonard being Mr. Chic, it was red pepper vodka. What struck me was how generically writer-like his houses were—not luxurious. There wasn't a single painting on the walls. I asked him why and he said, "It distracts me when I'm writing."

LEONARD COHEN: It wasn't simplicity I was after, it was the opposite, the voluptuous feeling of simplicity. I don't want to get too paradoxical, but that was what was beautiful.

During lunch, Ouellette asked what it would cost to acquire the newly available film rights.

ARMELLE BRUSQ: Leonard said, "How much do you want, darling?" I said, "One hundred thousand." Very cheap. Francs, not euros. He looked at Michel and told him the same. It was so beautiful, this moment, so elegant.

In due course, contracts were signed. Brusq wanted the right to choose the director. She envisaged English singer Ian McCulloch as Cohen—he had agreed—Iggy Pop as Cohen's father, Gena Rowlands as Masha, with Sean Penn directing. What Michel had not disclosed was that he was already associated with director Bernar Hébert. Worse, for Brusq, the contracts did not expressly require Ouellette to use her screenplay.

ARMELLE BRUSQ: There was a [clause] missing. It was horrible. I asked Leonard to intervene, but he said, "It's too much work, darling. I'm not going on a crusade. They won't succeed. It will be bullshit and no one will see it."

Brusq sued successfully for payment of 100,000 francs, insisting her name not be associated with the film. Released in 2003, *The Favourite Game*—like most Canadian films—quickly disappeared from cinemas.

The day after their lunch, Cohen took Brusq to Mount Baldy, where, without any training, she managed to sit *sesshin* for three weeks.

ARMELLE BRUSQ: It was more than hard, but I had to succeed. I wasn't meditating at all. It wasn't spiritual. I was laughing and suffering inside. Leonard was, too.

We sat side by side—Roshi's decision? It was like flirting—by his pure presence, because we couldn't speak. But we spoke and laughed every evening, drinking vodka and cranberry juice. We discussed *The Favourite Game*, his youth. He'd say, "You know my life better than me." I was interested in what remained of that young Leonard in this strange camp. It reminded me of my script. Not only because of his summer camp experiences, but because he was fascinated by discipline, by order. It was a powerful landscape of his inner life, an allegory.

STEVE KRIEGER: Leonard told me, "I like the idea of groups of men toughing things out together."

BARRIE WEXLER: That goes back to the father he lost when he was nine. Nathan had served in World War One. Rigorous discipline was how Leonard vicariously identified with him.

After Brusq flew home to Paris, Cohen invited her to return. Sasaki Roshi seconded the motion.

ARMELLE BRUSQ: Roshi wanted to marry us. The Baldy community thought Leonard had found the right woman. But I didn't want to go as a groupie again. I said, "What about a film, but only on Mount Baldy and LA? No archival footage. Your everyday life." Everyone in Paris told me I was crazy—to do this by myself, no film experience at all. This is the point. The guy who trusted me was Leonard—because of my script, it was like he already knew me, and vice versa. He had faith in me. He was encouraging. Maybe he liked the free way I looked at him.

Meanwhile, Cohen began an unlikely romance with a young Korean disciple, Jung Kim.

DIANNE LAWRENCE: She was totally mysterious and, according to a friend, not very balanced. That was an odd relationship.

KELLEY LYNCH: Jung Kim was charming and intelligent. Cohen was in a serious relationship with Jung for an extended period. He liked her playfulness.

[They] would have water pistol fights. I do not know specifically what happened at the end, but Cohen told me she accused him of stalking her. His quip was, "Stalking her with a $5,000 cheque." One day, as the relationship ended, she came to my office and appeared to be in the midst of a breakdown. She was doing Zen chants frantically, in French.

ARMELLE BRUSQ: She was like a child, small and round, like a little Roshi. She was completely fascinated with Leonard. Something was crazy there. This girl was like a baby, a puppet, a toy, very far from Cohen's presumed style in women. Even Kelley could not have been jealous of this.

SUSAN RAY: She was living with him. She would practice with us. I didn't take her that seriously.

ROBERT FAGGEN: Leonard concluded that she was one of those women who, once she got her claws into you, there was no getting them out. He was allergic to Korean women after that.

Cohen also conducted a brief, intense affair with Anne Marie Crowe, known as Seisen; she appears in a poem in *Book of Longing*. One day, he and Seisen drove into Claremont. Chris Darrow, the Kaleidoscope band member who helped finish the first album, spotted him outside Yiannis, a Greek restaurant.

CHRIS DARROW: They were both in robes, heads shaved, both smoking, both drinking espresso. I said, "Remember me?" He said, "Of course I do. You saved my album." I don't feel I knew him well, yet I feel I knew him really well. There was this vibrational thing between us. We didn't have to explain things.

As they had on Hydra and in Montreal, women turned up at Mount Baldy in pursuit of Cohen.

BRIAN LESAGE: One young woman seemed not completely there. I vaguely remember his graciousness around it, being clear about boundaries, but kind to her. He met her briefly and then she left.

SEIJU BOB MAMMOSER: There were always beautiful women around. Roshi often found many of Leonard's friends attractive.

EVANGELIA PAPAIOANNOU: I said, "When can I meet the Roshi?" He said, "I don't know if that's a good idea." I talked to Esther about it. She said, "Don't ever talk to him about the Roshi. He gets really upset. Even though there's all these rumours." He wanted to protect me from him.

PICO IYER: The most eloquent thing he said, the first time we met, was replaying what he said to one young woman who had come expressly to seduce him. He told her, "If you knew all the thousands of miles and days that I have put in to bringing myself to this place of clarity and peace, away from distraction and temptation, you would honour that." At least at that moment, it expressed how sincere was his wish to be free of everything. I've always thought his line, "I needed so much to have nothing to touch" was the essence of him.

BARRIE WEXLER: There's no more seminal line of Cohen's than, "I tried in my way to be free" from "Bird on the Wire." Free from drugs consumed to hold depression at bay, free from his unquenchable appetite for women, free from himself. A lifelong quest. Those years with Roshi were as close to finding a way there as he could get.

In December 1995, *Los Angeles* magazine commissioned Iyer to write a Cohen profile. For Iyer, Cohen was something of a hero. In 1974, he'd spent three months travelling India carrying only clothes, an acoustic guitar, and a "very worn copy of the *Songs of Leonard Cohen.*"

PICO IYER: I hadn't encountered popular music with such a literary sensibility before. He spoke to the part of me sitting in the classroom and to the part longing to escape. Leonard lived out all the classic romantic myths.

Cohen had given his blessing to the interview but, as late as the morning that Iyer was due on Mount Baldy, was having second thoughts. Iyer ignored the warnings and turned up.

PICO IYER: He really wanted to share the nourishing fruit of Sasaki Roshi's teaching, so he'd wake me at four in the morning to take me to the meditation hall. But the biggest shock was being greeted by this stooped, aged person in the parking lot in a worn cap, wire-rim glasses, and a tattered black robe—nothing like any image of Leonard Cohen I'd ever had. And doubly so when he greeted me with a very deep bow. I never imagined that a global superstar would insist on carrying my bags into the cabin, and cook for me, as if I were the eminence and he was the servant. To meet a celebrity who all but erased himself was startling.

For a time, Iyer wondered if he wasn't being played.

PICO IYER: He was so seductive. I wondered if there was an agenda. I thought it must be a trick. But the more I saw—no, you can't get away with sham [there]. He was shoveling snow, scrubbing floors, sitting for eighteen hours a day of meditation. He'd gone into that place to get away from sham.

SEIJU BOB MAMMOSER: They came to Jemez Springs for a retreat. Leonard slept on the floor in the kitchen.

PICO IYER: I realized in time I was projecting my own uncertainties onto him. He was not attempting to seduce me or anybody. It was the power, sincerity, and genuineness of his presence that compelled. The last thing he was worried about was how he presented himself. In his songs, he's always taking the mickey out of himself, portraying himself as panicked and bewildered, writing only from his wounds, his failures, his sins. There was nothing bad you could tell him that he hadn't told himself. His lack of interest in presenting himself as a wise man made him that much more persuasive.

Iyer had brought along books he thought Cohen might wish to discuss, including works by D. H. Lawrence.

PICO IYER: As soon as I gave them to him, he said, "Would you mind very much if I gave these away?" He really had no interest in reading literature.

All he was hungry for was philosophical stuff, of the most rigorous kind. My father had, years before, brought out an obscure edition of the Bhagavad Gita. As soon as we met, he said, "You're not related to the Iyer who brought out that book?" He'd been through the whole of a book almost no one else had seen.

Inevitably, Cohen frequently talked about Sasaki Roshi.

PICO IYER: I've never heard a man speak with such unembarrassed love and affection about another man. We spoke about music, the world, many things, but he rose to an electric eloquence and intensity when speaking about Sasaki. My sense is that Sasaki was the great love of his life, that Sasaki gave him a grounded, forgiving, unwavering friendship that he almost never found anywhere else. He could never find a woman he wouldn't leave behind. He was wise to Sasaki's failings, but I had the sense that whoever he was, whatever he did, Sasaki would accept him. Sasaki was the one constant, the still point around which his life revolved. He would say Sasaki was basically Rumi, Meister Eckhart, St. John of the Cross—the same voice you get from these classic mystics—and that a Sasaki Roshi comes along only every couple of hundred years.

MYOSHO GINNY MATTHEWS: He said many times, if Sasaki Roshi had been a German professor of physics, he'd learn German. The hook was this guy, and it developed into the most beautiful friendship. That was Roshi's gift—true love, when one is able to go beyond the limits of one's small self. He could help you experience that, and Leonard got that. They just so enjoyed each other, communicating on a nonverbal level.

PICO IYER: Of course, Sasaki said, "It's better not to talk, because talk gets in the way."

ROBERT FAGGEN: What Sasaki offered was real friendship and devotion and steadiness, with no sense of imprisonment—in fact, with the possibility of liberation. That was a power beyond measure for him.

SUSAN RAY: At first I was jealous—that Leonard could be Roshi's friend, and I wasn't. But I also saw Leonard go through some of the misery—as Roshi's student—that we all went through. Roshi had the capacity to put your face in your shit. That was the attraction for all of us. He described himself as a "no Roshi." He denied ego. He was not there to make anyone feel good.

Of course, there were also skeptics.

MATTHEW REMSKI: Roshi's power is embedded in his ambivalence . . . the tension of not knowing whether he will embrace you or castigate you. As a devotee, you need him to reject you as much as he accepts you, or the acceptance will not feel as sweet. . . . [It's] an . . . imbalance that thrives on the teacher seducing through concealment, and the student desperately craving what is hidden, and only occasionally seeing it, and taking any attention at all as a sign of love. Part of me wonders if Cohen fell in love with the type of man he himself was to many of the women past. If I close my eyes I can see . . . silhouettes of two bald men . . . transfixed by their lust and their pain . . . Two premier practitioners of their respective arts recognize each other, are magnetized to each other. . . . Cohen plays the supplicant, Roshi plays master.

From Mount Baldy, Cohen made a long-distance friend—French painter and singer Sandra Zemor.

SANDRA ZEMOR: It was a very intense spiritual friendship—we weren't lovers. When I [first] wrote to him, I was in love, and he was very seductive, always playing on this seductive attitude. Later, we met in Paris several times. Of course, I knew he was with another woman nearly every night. This side, his dark side, frightened me. I was disappointed when he said [we'd] meet again soon, and then he'd meet someone at a bar. But I'd send him my art, my calligraphies, and he admired them, saying they influenced his ink drawings. He was very generous—encouraging me, giving me strength to trust in my work and in myself, a masculine, positive force, even with its dark part. And he had such a fantastic sense of humour. When he died, I saw him as a black Buddha, in a vision. He is still part of my life.

Cohen wrote less cordially to scholar Ruth Wisse. In October 1995, she published an essay in *Commentary* magazine that included an unflattering description of his friend, the late Robert Hershorn. In the piece, "swaddled in appreciation and love," Wisse lamented what Cohen had not become.

RUTH WISSE: He had written that Canadians were "desperate for a Keats." . . . I was desperate for a Cohen. I bet on him as on a racehorse, prayed for him as for an angel . . . certain that he would become the guardian truth-teller of my generation. By "Cohen," I had in mind the Jewish high-priestly caste. . . . [But] the man climbing Mount Baldy was not standing with me at the foot of Mount Sinai. He would follow his muse wherever she led him; if I wanted a poet or writer for the Jewish people, I would have to look elsewhere.

Cohen protested. "I don't know about flower children's brigades," he wrote to her, citing her description of the audiences he was attracting, "but I was with General [Ariel] Sharon . . . in the Sahara desert during the Yom Kippur War. I didn't see too many secular Jewish scholars from Montreal around."

RUTH WISSE: He signed it, "Yr. old friend L.," as if to charge me with a breach of friendship, and followed up with a small carton of books, saying, "I know you will want to write about me again in the near future in order to retract . . . your reckless evaluation of my life and work." [But] much as I regretted having caused him pain, I could not have "retracted" the essay, because nothing that I'd read of him or heard in his songs contradicted my observations.

In fact, Cohen was so incensed that he consulted a lawyer, an old fraternity brother.

NOOKIE GELBER: Leonard was angry like hell because she had bad-mouthed Hershorn. He called me—I should sue. I persuaded him not to do it. It's a free country. She can say whatever she wants. You don't go suing because they call you a *pisher.*

MEL SOLMAN: The Wisse article is a pivotal moment. She's savagely critical, basically saying that he hadn't been the kind of Jewish hero she hoped he'd be. And he resented it. But in a strange way, he [later] did pick up the mantle she challenged him to. There's a growing awareness [in his work] of his responsibility and roots. Remember the concert in Israel [in 2009] where he blesses the audience as a *Kohen?*

Cohen befriended several other monks on Mount Baldy and at Bodhi Manda in New Mexico.

KOSHIN CHRIS CAIN: I always liked Leonard. We'd have a soiree at Roshi's place. He was demure—is that too strong a word? Not a larger-than-life character. He appeared modest. Doing Zen, there are ways to stick out and he didn't. He tagged along. I'd find a reason to knock on his door and he'd unfailingly invite me in for a drink and read me the latest verse of "A Thousand Kisses Deep." We'd go into Claremont and he'd take me to the Greek restaurant. When you're drinking ouzo and retsina, and it's cold up on the mountain—those are some of my fondest moments.

SEIJU BOB MAMMOSER: Leonard was a beautiful man. He wasn't a saint. I remember a blowout party at the end of a training period—champagne and orange juice with breakfast. Leonard got smashed. He could barely get his head off the table. But he was warm, sincere, and humble. He was never the rock star or the star, period. That's what endeared him to the community.

SHINGETSU BILLY WHITE: The one thing I remember him saying was "You're pretty lucky if you just don't care." Care about anything in life. You're free if you don't care. But in meditation, you get a deeper feeling of a person's essence, more than you do with words. His presence was deep. He was immersed in Zen practice.

BARRIE WEXLER: Leonard once told me that indifference was a true state of grace.

JAMES TRUMAN: Mount Baldy was not a compassionate place, and Leonard was who you went to for personal advice and consolation. Rigorous practice and sleep deprivation made everyone vulnerable, as was the intention, but Roshi's approach was unsparingly unsentimental. Leonard provided a balance for that.

GIKO DAVID RUBIN: Leonard brought Chinese food up pretty often—a treat. He seemed to like being around Sasaki Roshi, but he wasn't a devotee. He once gave Roshi a gift, a gold coin, and Roshi made fun of it. He wanted to cash it in right away. Leonard said, "Oh, don't be so grumpy."

When Brian Lesage was ordained in 1996, Cohen paid for the after-party.

BRIAN LESAGE: It's traditional for whoever is ordained to throw a party. I said, "I don't have any money." Leonard said, "Don't worry, man. I'll totally cover it." He bought wine, chicken curry—a few hundred dollars, at least. It's not that he liked Mount Baldy—he thought a lot of things were screwed-up, and they were. But he'd go out of his way to show graciousness. He wasn't interested in disrupting the scene.

At the same time, Lesage recalls, "for some women, some of whom were Roshi's attendants, Leonard's view of women was not the easiest thing to be around. You'd hear it from the women—wanting to be respectful, but not liking the guy talk. I remember some flirtatious comments to the women."

Cohen was generous to others as well.

PETER VAN TOORN: Leonard was a beautiful cat. [Montreal poet] Ken Hertz was dying—Parkinson's—needed round-the-clock care and ran out of money. I called Leonard. He said, "Would a couple of thousand do?" And says, and this is the point, "You know, Peter, I admire your compassion." It's ironic, because *he* was the one being compassionate. That's what you mustn't lose sight of—the human side. It's his way of teaching, almost. Remember, it's a spiritual trip he was on. He was amazingly generous with time and money. A lot of people confuse the inner man with the golden calf of success.

In March, alone with her camera, Armelle Brusq arrived to shoot her documentary—*Spring 96*—a fifty-two-minute film in which Cohen meditates, plays his Technics KN3000 synthesizer, sings an early version of "A Thousand Kisses Deep," and recites three new poems.

BARRIE WEXLER: Leonard called the Latin poet Catullus the first great love poet after Sappho. He had a well-worn paperback translation on St.-Dominique. One of his most famous poems is "Catullus 5" . . . "Give me a thousand kisses, a hundred more, another thousand, and another hundred." I'm not saying it inspired the song, but given Cohen's familiarity with the poet's work, it's possible it was stirring in his subconscious when he wrote the lyric.

Cohen later explained why the lyric refers to one's "invincible defeat."

LEONARD COHEN: The awareness that you don't control anything is the first reminder of the defeat. After that . . . you have to live on as if your life is real, as if you are the director . . . carry on making . . . choices as if they are real choices that we can control. But the deeper understanding is that you don't run the show, but live your life a thousand kisses deep. . . . You have to accept and surrender to the mystery."

In one conversation with Brusq, Cohen acknowledged his suspicion of "charismatic holy men" like Sasaki Roshi. One could seduce someone, he implied—whether for religion or sex—without really caring about them. "It's like hypnotism," he said. "I knew because I was able to do it in my little own way."

ARMELLE BRUSQ: In Vienna with Roshi—fall of '96—I showed him the film. He was very happy with it but said, "You know, darling, this sentence [about charismatic holy men] is too much." I answered, "I think there is no film without this sentence. Because it gave a true light." He said, "Okay." For me, it was so important this should be said. He was in the grip of Roshi because he was amazed by the power he had himself.

In another conversation, Cohen told Brusq something that would likely shock those who saw him as a relentless Casanova—that when he was fourteen or fifteen, he realized that "sex for him was a prison, a concentration camp."

ARMELLE BRUSQ: Not so surprising when you listen to his songs, where sex and desire often appear as a kind of torture or a prison. He said, "Sex is very sweet when you are in love." But if it's not connected with erotic imagination, or wanting to make someone happy, it's limited. If you have to do it, it's a prison. Leonard doesn't speak a lot about sex. He loves women, but for the power he has on them and their beauty. He's more a voyeur.

SUSAN RAY: I'm sure he seduced Armelle. I don't think Leonard could be in the company of a woman halfway attractive without wanting to bed her. You either [accept that] or you make yourself miserable. One does learn something from Zen practice.

ARMELLE BRUSQ: I think to him I was like Dominique—independent and free and French. She had a camera. I had a camera. He let me shoot him freely, just the two of us. It was all about instinct and trust.

At another point in her film (and in Stina Dabrowski's 1997 documentary, also shot on Mount Baldy), Cohen—without prompting—stripped down to his underwear, to change clothes.

ARMELLE BRUSQ: I didn't ask him. He chose to do that, to create ambiguity. He loves that. For example, he was the only one with a private bathroom on Mount Baldy. He'd say, "Do you want to take a bath?" Of course, you say yes. What he would not tell you—just to hint at the games he liked to play—when you come out of the bathroom, [Lorca] and friends from LA would be there. Somebody sees a woman outside the bathroom, with no explanation—"She's a friend from Paris." You can wonder.

At the same time, maintains Ray, "there was a kind of self-exposure Leonard wouldn't do."

STEVE LINDSEY: Adam's in a difficult position. He's Leonard Cohen's son. How are you going to beat that? You're not. Even if you were a better poet, nobody's going to think so. It was a vanity project.

SAM FELDMAN: [Our agency] represented Adam for a minute. It's an awful big shadow [that Leonard cast].

KELLEY LYNCH: During that project, Adam was an outrage. Adam was difficult to manage and thought Steve was trying to control him. Steve set him up with some of the best songwriters in LA and they all became embittered. Sony was in disbelief that one million dollars was spent, unheard of for a new artist.

Cohen was, however, upset about one track—"Sister"—on Adam's album. Part of the lyric reads "I really wanna know your sister, I really kinda like your sister."

SANDRA ANDERSON: I always thought that was meant for Rufus Wainwright [Lorca's friend and future sperm donor]. That Rufus really liked Adam, but was pretending to come on to Lorca. I recall Leonard being upset and thought it was because it implied homosexuality in relation to his son. He told me he hated homosexuals and homosexuality. I was shocked.

ROBERT FAGGEN: Just for the record, whenever the subject came up, Leonard was all in favour of LGBTQ rights.

According to friends, Cohen—until near the end—was very supportive of Adam. He talked frequently about what great talent he had, but voiced concern about the direction of his career. In time, he also became frustrated by his son's expensive tastes, which contrasted sharply with his fondness for ninety-nine-cent stores.

*   *   *

Did Leonard Cohen genuinely believe his career was over when he booked himself into Sasaki Roshi's Zen hospital? In interviews, he intimated as much.

But it seems highly unlikely. After all, he built recording studios there and in a converted garage on Tremaine. He composed songs for albums contractually owed to Sony. And he wrote new poetry. Mount Baldy also served as the backdrop for two documentary films, and countless interviews—not the conduct of an artist seeking to disappear. Still, he had begun to think about his future estate. Apart from real estate, his principal assets then consisted of two entities—Leonard Cohen Stranger Music, a music publishing company that owned copyrights to his song catalogue, and the artist and writer royalty streams connected to his work. In 1994, Eric Kronfeld, CEO of PolyGram, expressed interest in purchasing some musical properties.

KELLEY LYNCH: Cohen was convinced that digital downloading was destroying the music industry. Eric had pursued acquisitions. The discussions never led to actual negotiations.

DAVID PULLMAN: Leonard may have wanted to cash out. Some artists are like that, thinking they are getting older, about death—get the money now. It's a mindset. Remember, Leonard didn't have giant hits. He had artists covering his songs that had hits. He didn't have big tours or merchandising. He was an artist's artist. Setting up trusts in estates—they were planning for it.

KELLEY LYNCH: There were many interested parties. I negotiated the sale, which was miserable, because Cohen called every five seconds. He micromanaged every element.

One potential buyer was David Pullman, the New York banker who helped create the so-called Bowie Bond—an asset-backed security based on David Bowie's twenty-five pre-1990 albums.

DAVID PULLMAN: Cohen's earnings were very consistent. We had a series of meetings in New York with Kelley and Leonard's accountant, Greg McBowman. Leonard was on the phone from [Mount Baldy]. The deal makes sense. It's not expensive, it's not cheap—right down the middle. It's a good investment. They really want to sell it—they're pushing me—and

I want to buy it. I love the catalogue. But they don't want to sell me the songs. They want to sell me [Stranger] the *company* [that owns the songs]. I didn't want to do that because something told me there were problems, that it was going to be aggressive, tax-wise. I want to do the deal, but I can't. I didn't want to expose myself to this [potential] liability. I had no idea what they were doing with the company. The tax attorney was involved. It all seemed so complex. I'd bought thousands of songs for hundreds of millions, so if I'm thinking this [deal] is complex, it must be pretty complex. And they were adamant about not selling the songs. That made me nervous.

KELLEY LYNCH: These negotiations were exceedingly complex, as were the tax/corporate issues. This put off many buyers and limited the playing field.

Cohen did get an offer from BMG, which he leveraged to persuade Sony to exercise its matching rights. It soon did. During this period, Lynch introduced Cohen to investment adviser Neal Greenberg, a founding principal of Agile Group and a Tibetan Buddhist based in Boulder, Colorado.

KELLEY LYNCH: My ex-husband, Douglas Penick, had invested with him. Cohen met Greenberg when he flew into Los Angeles in 1996 to meet Kusum Lingpa, a Tibetan Buddhist teacher. Cohen thought Greenberg was a great investor. Greenberg then introduced him to Richard Westin and Ed Dean, lawyers involved in restructuring Stranger Music in anticipation of the Sony sale.

In October 1996, Westin established three trusts: the Sabbath Day Charitable Remainder Trust, the Cohen Family Charitable Trust, and the Cohen Remainder Trust. The following month, Cohen gifted the Mount Baldy Zen Center with ownership of 4.581 shares of common stock in Stranger Music, with a par value of almost $508,000. The Sony deal closed in 1997; Sony/ATV, music publishing affiliate of Sony Records, bought Stranger Music for $6.3 million. Cohen was the principal shareholder. The IRS later audited the charitable gift of stock. To address the challenge, Cohen hired Steve Lindsey's accountant, Ken Cleveland, who prevailed.

KELLEY LYNCH: Ken told me it was "a miracle." Cohen was beyond paranoid at this time.

Cohen's trusts received proceeds of the sale—about $900,000 to the Remainder Trust; $500,000 to Sabbath Day; and the balance to the Cohen Family Trust. Greenberg managed funds in the Remainder Trust, while another investment firm, Dean Witter, continued to hold the Cohen Family Trust monies. In time, Cohen agreed to let Greenberg manage the family assets as well. According to a court filing, Greenberg estimated that Cohen could receive about $300,000 a year from the trust, without touching the principal. Lynch later claimed that she did not know or trust Greenberg and could not recommend him. Others recall it differently.

PAUL BURGER: Kelley called me saying there's this guy, Greenberg, managing Leonard's things. Amazing guy. You've got to meet him. I spent forty-five minutes with him. I didn't understand one word. I told Kelley, "I may not be the smartest guy, but I'm not the dumbest and if I can't understand them, the problem's not with me." I said, "If I were you, I'd be careful."

With part of the proceeds, Cohen bought his daughter, Lorca, a funky, 3,400-square-foot antiques store (then called Boo Radley, now called The Window) on LA's hip Melrose Avenue.

KELLEY LYNCH: Initially, Cohen was basically her only customer, but he brought attention to it, and people like Johnny Depp began stopping by.

Among those Lorca hired was her friend Julianna Raye.

JULIANNA RAYE: Leonard would come in occasionally. Soon after we met, he invited me to a Friday night dinner with Lorca. I had begun meditating and had reached the stage where I thought I could use a teacher, so it occurred to me to ask Leonard. He brought out a series of cassettes called *The Science of Enlightenment,* by Shinzen Young—Sasaki Roshi's translator. It was the first time that things clicked, that I could see that this mysterious interior process could be logical. Later, I had unique connections with Leonard, around train-ing. He gently, effortlessly, redirected the course of my life in a dramatic way.

In 1996, two Montreal writers got what they thought was a lucky break—a chance to write the screenplay for *Beautiful Losers*. Their prior credentials were two short films—*Spotting Layton* and *Leonard, Light My Cigarette,* an homage to Cohen and Montreal. Cohen had seen the films and was impressed enough to offer film rights to the novel.

TONY BABINSKI: I had just smoked a cheap cigar when I heard the news. I got so excited I threw up.

JACOB POTASHNIK: Leonard says, "Let me get together with Greg" [Gold, husband of Cohen's backup singer Sharon Robinson]. I should have real-ized that Greg wanted to do this film. I was against it. I thought it had to be done by at least a Canadian, preferably a Montrealer, preferably me.

TONY BABINSKI: Jacob's take on this is very tortured. Leonard wanted the project to unfold "in a peaceful, organic manner," [but] right from the start, Jacob was trying to wrest it away from Greg. It was Leonard's intellectual property, and it's common for artists to hand properties over in a hands-off way. It was unseemly to hector him about it.

Gold ultimately signed a deal with Cohen to produce the film, but was unable to generate interest in Hollywood. Potashnik then took the idea to Denise Robert, one of Canada's most successful producers. She had a deal with PolyGram, which allowed her to fund projects, but gave PolyGram a right of first refusal. Robert eventually transferred ownership of the project to PolyGram.

JACOB POTASHNIK: Leonard signed off on [it]. He liked the idea, because Denise's husband, Denys Arcand, was interested in directing.

TONY BABINSKI: Denise had the right to put together a picture, but Greg retained control of the underlying book rights.

Potashnik and Babinski eventually signed a contract for $54,000, plus 20 percent to write the script. The negotiated title was *Leonard Cohen's Beautiful Losers*. Cohen, however, declined to read the script and resisted meeting the writers. It was not until 1998 that Potashnik was invited to Tremaine.

JACOB POTASHNIK: I brought the script and a Levitts salami from Montreal. I said, "I hope it's okay to offer this to you, as a Buddhist." His voice drops an octave and he says, "We are taught to accept gracefully what is offered."

TONY BABINSKI: This is so silly to prosecute, but in fact, Jacob gave me the sausage to give to Leonard when I went to LA the following year. I said, "Can't you get that here?" And he said, "Not like this." It's Rashomon, with a sausage. I also gave him a box of five Cuban cigars.

JACOB POTASHNIK: Leonard said explicitly, "I really don't want to discuss the script. That's a place I've been to. I don't want to go back." I said, "But we've changed things." He says, "Perhaps, but I really don't want to go there."

KELLEY LYNCH: I think Leonard did read it and didn't like it.

JACOB POTASHNIK: I spent a lovely afternoon with him. He made hot dogs. He had a unique way of warming the buns. He'd place the buns open on top of the toaster vents and let the heat rise.

KELLEY LYNCH: Everyone was always impressed with his hot dogs, tuna, and egg salad, but that's what he eats. Cohen made a great, simple egg salad sandwich.

BARRIE WEXLER: His tuna fish sandwich was his pièce de résistance. Everyone talked about it, but no one knew the recipe. Here it is. He mixed tuna, diced shallots, sweet pickle relish, freshly ground pepper, and a few drops of lemon with a secret Worchester-based sauce. It had three ingredients—a dash of garlic, a dollop of Dijon mustard, and the super-duper, top secret, holy-of-holies ingredient, a squirt of chili sauce.

KELLEY LYNCH: They'd come in, in awe of him, groupie journalists—and if he offered them a tuna sandwich or a popsicle, this blew their minds. This religious sage, this intellectual monster eating a popsicle. But he also *did* like popsicles and tuna sandwiches. Then he'd have an expensive bottle of wine and this would confuse them. And he'd do his own dishes. And he *did* do his own dishes. He's a master. He wouldn't talk to most journalists unless he felt he could control [them]. He'd want to control the environment, make sure it was in a restaurant where someone would say hello to him. Somebody once wrote what books he had in his bookcase, so he put up a curtain over the bookcase. He lived his life posthumously—[knowing] he would ultimately be studied.

JACOB POTASHNIK: He opens his fridge and says, "I have stuff from last night. I'm not sure it's still good." He sticks in a fork and gives it to me. "Is it still good?" I say, "If there's a doubt, let's not eat it." His voice drops again. "Good idea," he says. He said again, "I don't want to be involved in the film, day-to-day. I made that clear at the beginning."

ANDRÉE PELLETIER: I can so understand Leonard. They wanted his imprimatur to help sell it—he was no fool.

JACOB POTASHNIK: I said, "I think you're making a mistake, but okay." Denys Arcand had warned me—"Be careful of working with people higher on the ladder." Stars are different. Their regard for regular people takes second place to their own desires. So yes, he was gracious, welcoming, genteel, generous, and open. But he won't read a screenplay that he himself initiated? I knew then something was wrong.

Early in 1999, the sale of PolyGram to Universal put the project at risk. Potashnik put feelers out to other possible producers—nothing materialized. According to Babinski, the project died because Greg Gold would not renew the option. No book rights, no movie. Soon after, Potashnik was hired to line produce a Cohen music video for "In My Secret Life." One day, on the shoot, he ambushed Cohen in the canteen trailer.

JACOB POTASHNIK: It's like that cognitive dissonance where you see somebody where they're not supposed to be. It hasn't registered with him who I am. Finally it clicks—"Jacob?" And he's stumbling for words, totally off-balance. I say, "We haven't heard from anybody for two years." He says, "I don't understand that." I say, "Why not? The project has been dead for two years." He's scrambling, trying to get his grace together. Finally he says, "I'll have to speak to Greg when I get back to LA."

Later, Potashnik asked Cohen directly why he didn't want to be involved.

JACOB POTASHNIK: It had to do with the Indians. "When the book came out," he says, "I got slaughtered by the Native community." I said, "Which Native community?" He says, "Alanis Obomsawin [an Aboriginal film director]." I said, "Isn't she your friend?" "Yes, but there was a lot of criticism." I said, "It's forty years ago. It's been on high school curricula across the country. We're not stupid, Leonard. We know you made up a lot of stuff about the Natives, but we did not use it. If you'd read the screenplay, you'd have known." It's the star mentality: I don't have to do anything you want me to do. Capricious. He goes back to LA, and nothing, zero.

After a failed attempt to see Cohen in LA, Potashnik asked for an email formally declaring the project dead.

JACOB POTASHNIK: I get an email—"Dear Jacob, I appreciate how much work you've put into the project. However, for now, I have to state that I consider the project dead. But the status could change." Again, ambiguity. Again, I ask for something more definitive and finally he writes—"Okay, it's dead." So now I'm pissed. I wrote back, thanking him for finally relieving the pain. And I said something really stupid, "There's more to being a mensch than writing a few verses and seducing a few women." He writes back, "Dear Jacob, I don't want to think you are actively insulting me. Don't you know that our brethren are dying in the streets?" There was at that time an intifada in Israel. "It's rather petty to bring up a failed project." I wrote back, "You're absolutely right. It's petty and, as someone who lost family in the ghettos and camps, I'm sympathetic to this as well." The project was dead on arrival.

Potashnik struggled to make sense of it.

JACOB POTASHNIK: I'm not a doctor, but Leonard was a lifelong depressive. He asks us to write *Beautiful Losers*, and later—"Shit, what have I done?" But it's too late. What can he do? He can have nothing to do with it, refuse to read the screenplay, and all the blame will be on others. A mensch, a moral person, picks up the phone and says, "I'm terribly sorry. Forgive me. I should not have made you the offer." I would have said, "Fine." So everybody loves Leonard, except this chubby fuck, Potashnik, who calls Leonard duplicitous. Well, it's obviously *him*. Not Leonard—him. *He's* the problem.

TONY BABINSKI: Jacob sabotaged the project. Self-immolated in a spectacular act of psychotic self-destruction. Leonard thought it might be cool to have a movie made. Then he changed his mind. Happens all the time.

BARRIE WEXLER: Depression was a key factor. *I Am a Hotel* elicited the same reaction—wanting nothing to do with the project after initiating it. This was his predictable modus operandi. If it hadn't been for our relationship, and my emotionally blackmailing him for saving Adam after he ingested cough syrup as a toddler, the TV special would have suffered the same fate.

SUSAN RAY: I saw him in the throes of it. You could almost see it in his physicality. At one point, he ran out of Wellbutrin and I got him some. It led to an exchange about depression, that it is not just grey—it's bloody.

Cohen would later say that although he tried everything to shake depression— sex, alcohol, religion, meditation, and almost every drug known to mankind— nothing worked.

LINDA BOOK: Only one thing works for most people—connection. And that he couldn't do. He could not make himself vulnerable. No matter how many people he had hanging with him, he could never be filled up.

EVANGELIA PAPAIOANNOU: I tried to help him. I was working as a researcher at NIH, on depression. But Leonard decided not to speak to my boss, and to stay with Xanax or Prozac, maybe both.

Cohen maintained an equally tangential relationship to a second film project then in development, a comedy Eric Lerner had sold to MGM—*Kiss the Sky*. It was about two unhappy middle-aged men who flee conventional lives to build a Shangri-la beside the highest lake in the world. A beautiful woman arrives, along with a monk, a character loosely based on Sasaki Roshi. Lerner ultimately secured a $6 million budget and the use of Cohen's music for the soundtrack. Initially, he planned to hire Cohen's friend Allan Moyle to direct.

ERIC LERNER: I met with Allan. Lovely guy. MGM approved him as director and flew him to our locations in the Philippines. What happened on that scout is perhaps subject to interpretation, but I was told by MGM execs that Allan wouldn't be a good idea to direct. The whys are not worth going into.

ALLAN MOYLE: One of the dozen devastating moments in my life. Leonard got word to me that he was out of it—"Hey, man, don't blame me." But before it collapsed, I went to New York, trying to get him involved. I had a fantastic meeting in a posh hotel—this ancient man [Roshi] smoking and drinking like mad. Roshi steals the interview, telling me he's decided to give up sex at the age of ninety, and [discussing] all his seduction techniques. He's bragging. Leonard is smiling. The old guy is just beaming. Happy to be alive and strong. I'm thinking, "These two guys have got it made. Isn't it beautiful?" It was the finest meeting about a film I've ever had. Leonard is very careful to not promise more than he can give, saying politely, "I can't help you that much." He approved it, but "You guys fuck it up your own way." When the project died, he said, "Don't take it personally."

The movie, eventually made, had exactly one US screening, at an obscure film festival, and then disappeared. Moyle's positive opinion of Cohen never wavered.

ALLAN MOYLE: Apparently, near the end, he got kind of bitchy. I never saw that. He was the most gracious person. I'd always be thinking, "When is the other shoe going to drop?" But it never happened.

Among Cohen's many enthusiasts was Finnish chartered accountant Jarkko Arjatsalo, a fan since the seventies. After Cohen's Helsinki concerts in 1988 and 1993, Arjatsalo began collecting rare recording material, and subsequently founded the *Cohen Newsletter*. When it discontinued in 1994, Arjatsalo decided to make Cohen the subject of his first website. It launched in the fall of 1995.

JARKKO ARJATSALO: I supplied the content. My son, Rauii, took care of technical issues. Soon, we started receiving all kinds of material. Our direct cooperation with Cohen himself began in 1997 when—to my surprise— he contacted me. Mount Baldy had just gotten an internet connection. He offered to contribute unpublished poems, drawings, and computer graphics.

Some twenty-five years later, Arjatsalo's Cohen Forum was still active.

A nearly constant parade of journalists and filmmakers made a pilgrimage in search of Cohen, among them Pico Iyer, the *Globe and Mail*'s James Adams, and the *LA Times*'s Robert Hilburn. Cohen also gave interviews on the road, including with a *New York Times* reporter in October 1995. After it, he bought and placed lilies at the shrine of Kateri Tekakwitha—heroine of Cohen's 1966 novel, *Beautiful Losers*—at St. Patrick's Cathedral. He also turned down a request from Janis Ian, commissioned by *Performing Songwriter*.

JANIS IAN: I sent a letter reminding him that we'd met and how much I admired him. I got back this wonderful letter, the opening lines of which were "Leonard Cohen loves Janis Ian. Leonard Cohen loves Janis Ian's work. Leonard Cohen is on the mountain. Thank you." It was the absolute best turndown I've ever gotten. So sweet, so Leonard-like.

In April 1996, Pico Iyer made a return visit, bringing his Japanese wife, Hiroko Takeuchi, who had been raised among the Zen temples of Kyoto.

PICO IYER: When we went into the meditation hall, she actually thought Leonard was the abbot because his posture was so perfect. She thought he was in a different league [as a Zen disciple] than anyone else. The translation offered was very philosophical, being and nonbeing, but she told me Sasaki Roshi's sermon was mostly about sex. After, Leonard served us green tea in whiskey glasses in his cabin and extended a cigarette pack to her—"Do you smoke?" Twenty-one years later, she still got weak in the knees remembering that. She'd never seen a man carry himself with that degree of cool.

New York editor James Truman came not to interview, but to practice. A few years earlier, as editor of *Details* magazine, he had commissioned a Q and A with Cohen for an issue devoted to sex.

JAMES TRUMAN: He wrote exquisite answers. The one I most clearly remember was his answer to the question, How do you know when you have fallen in love? . . . "When you have dissolved your strategy toward the other."

Later, Truman assigned another journalist to spend time on Mount Baldy. The writer became so enamoured of Zen life that he never left. In 1997, Truman, who was also exploring Zen, went to Mount Baldy, in part to find out what had become of the journalist. Cohen decided to play a joke on Truman.

JAMES TRUMAN: The monastery sent a monk to drive me from LA. The monk seemed vaguely familiar, but had a new name and a shaved head. It wasn't until the end of the journey that he finally came clean—he was the writer I'd last seen four years earlier. A very Zen move: the fragility of identity and the cosmic absurdity of holding on to it are strong tenets of Zen, especially as Roshi taught it.

Sasaki Roshi, Truman found, "was relentless in enforcing a practice that mandated letting go of all stories that stand in the way of experiencing the emptied, or unmediated, self. Zen practice . . . aims to rid oneself of all the baggage of self, not to create a new self." Life on the mountain was as it was billed—rigorous.

JAMES TRUMAN: We were woken at two thirty a.m. for first meditation. The rest of the day was spent between more sitting, work chores, and meals, conducted in silence. The last sitting finished around nine thirty, after which Leonard would often welcome monks to his cabin to drink brandy. Leonard would become quite expansive during these conversations. He once said, "You do realize that we are on a hospital ship here, where all of us are broken, and none will ever get well and the ship is sinking." He paused for a second, and asked: "Was that me, or the brandy talking?" And roared with laughter.

PICO IYER: Partly he's saying, "There are no answers here. This is not salvation, just the opposite. It's about sitting still in a burning house, going up in flames."

Deprivations aside, Zen discipline may have had a practical effect on Cohen's career.

ANDREW SWEENY: I remember sitting with him at one retreat—a very exhausted old man, chanting, "*Gate gate paragate parasamgate bodhi svaha,*" which means "Gone, gone, gone to the other shore." Few people know how that Japanese chanting affected his vocal styling, and how much hard work he did in Zen temples—this was "the secret life" he sang about. Try chanting the heart sutra in Japanese a few times a day, for years. It's bound to give you that deep and monotone voice, but might destroy the upper ranges. It wasn't just whiskey and cigarettes.

Once, driving back to LA, Cohen asked Truman if he'd like to hear some music.

JAMES TRUMAN: I imagined it would be *his* music, but it was a two-minute recording on cassette of Roshi chanting. It was indeed beautiful. Leonard found it more than beautiful. We listened to it perhaps forty times between

Mount Baldy and LA, as he pointed out the majesty of certain phrasings and cadences. Though I don't think you could say Leonard's music was formally influenced by the chanting, I did come to hear Mount Baldy in his work. It has something to do with a sense of spaciousness and movement toward silence that his singing embellishes, but never interrupts. He often told the story of how, when he first played Roshi his music, Roshi observed that his singing was not sad enough. Of course, there's Zen humour in that, since Leonard inspired generations of singer-songwriters to sing with overwhelming sadness. Perhaps it was Zen that helped make Leonard's sadness sound observed and self-knowing, rather than self-indulgent.

CHAPTER SIX

Jikan the Unconvincing

I felt as close to him as anyone and, at the same time, I hardly knew him. He was probably the most extraordinary and the most ordinary person I ever met.

—Yoshin David Radin

Leonard loved being ordinary and often pretended he was. I don't think you could be Leonard Cohen and not know you weren't ordinary. He always knew he was better than others, always saw himself as an elite. He wants to present himself in a positive light. It's a very manipulated picture.

—Linda Book

In December 1996, when Eric Lerner arrived at Mount Baldy for the annual *Rohatsu*, Cohen told him, "It's perfect up here. I don't have to talk to anyone except Roshi . . . Roshi put out the word to leave 'Renard' alone. What can I say? I just can't stand people anymore."

ERIC LERNER: He developed a precise calculus of what he wanted to do, what he ought to do, and what he could not skip out of doing. There were his kids. There was that other thing—it's hell to have dinner alone. There would always be business to attend to. Otherwise, he hoarded his time.

He had no regrets. He was content to be a recluse, balancing as best he could loneliness with his beloved solitude he had cultivated like a garden.

Yes and no. Beneath this facade of contentment, a knot of anxiety was beginning to tighten. A few months later, in a note to Steve Sanfield, Cohen wrote, "Get me THE FUCK out of here." He signed it "Jikan the Unconvincing." A Cohenian jest, of course, but leavened with granular truth. Seeking distractions, he welcomed visitors and pretexts for being away from Mount Baldy. When Swedish broadcaster Stina Dabrowski arrived to shoot another documentary, he confessed to having discovered that he "had no religious aptitude . . . wasn't really a religious man." She said, "You're a failed monk?" To which Cohen responded, "Yeah, thank God."

Another day, Cohen welcomed life coach Michiko Jane Rolek, great-granddaughter of Sokei-an, the founder of the Buddhist Society of America in New York in 1930. He'd been a major influence on Sasaki Roshi. Cohen had written the foreword for Rolek's first book, *Mental Fitness*.

MICHIKO JANE ROLEK: Leonard was reverent, charming, and down-to-earth. There was a sparkle in his eye when we were together. The energy between us felt like an effortless flow, yet there were Zen pauses where the still water reflected the stars. He helped me find my hallelujah voice, and single-handedly helped me deepen my understanding of my illustrious Zen legacy.

Another guest was Brooklyn rabbi Simon Jacobson. Some years earlier, the rabbi had opened his computer one morning to find an email from Cohen—a response to Jacobson's short essay "The Silent Kohen," which addressed the enduring question: How does a just, all-powerful God permit evil in the world?

SIMON JACOBSON: A long commentary on my article, out of the blue. A critique in a way, but very thorough. I wrote back and then he wrote back. So we had a correspondence. Then he wrote that he'd had a dream in which he was being censured for his critique and he apologized—[for] being arrogant. But he had presented a Buddhist take on the issue. It's a fascinating exchange. Then he invited me to visit.

Cohen later explained that his critique had become "a kind of polemic . . . and I felt very inadequate to represent whatever case I was representing. I didn't want to be an apologist for Zen Buddhism, so I imagined Roshi looking over my shoulder . . . and . . . forbidding me to go any further." The imagined tableau was turned into a poem, published in *Book of Longing*. Later that year, Jacobson and a friend arrived.

SIMON JACOBSON: He was in the middle of a [*sesshin*]. They're marching and we thought, "We'll just stand and bow, and if he doesn't want to talk to us, we'll leave." He came out of the line and we went to the cottage and he offered us Turkish cigarettes. He asked me to sing for him—Hasidic melodies, chants, *nigunim*. Sombre, introspective songs. He sat very quietly, eyes closed, absorbing it, in a mode of receiving. We spent 'til three, four in the morning. We talked, very naturally, about spiritual matters. He talked about how his Jewish thinking affects him so much. I said, "So why are you here?" He says, "I'm not here because I'm a Buddhist. I'm a Jew." He made it clear that he was a *Kohen*—"I'm one of them." He was proud of it. He mentioned it a few times. But he was there, he said, "because the Roshi saved my life. He was there when I needed someone most." He could be humorous and sarcastic, but very reserved. He sounded like he was in a very depressed state.

ROBERT FAGGEN: Leonard was reading the Zohar almost every day. He studied it. We went over translations together. I never sensed that his interest in Zen superseded Judaism. He seems to have been an observant Jew until the end of his life.

WILLIE ARON: I gotta tell you, man, he loved Judaism. He loved it with every fibre of his being. I'd be on the bimah at High Holy Day services and he'd be *dukaning* [uttering the priestly blessing]. He knew his shit.

In February 1997, another escape—Cohen and Sanfield spent an afternoon in Claremont with British poet Christopher Logue, a friend of writer Alexander Trocchi, with whom Cohen had used heroin in 1961.

ROBERT FAGGEN: Leonard had a place in his heart for people who did not sell out. He wanted to meet Logue because Logue never sold out, never gave in. We all sat outside my office with a bottle of wine and Leonard told his Trocchi story about licking the bowl [of heroin], and then going blind and falling on the street. Of course, that never stopped him.

Meanwhile, the Rinzai-Ji community was finally beginning to rebel against Sasaki Roshi's sexual predation. Tales of his misconduct were hardly new. As far back as 1980, at Bodhi Manda, a complaint had been filed and corroborated.

SEIJU BOB MAMMOSER: When he was a dharma teacher, he was extraordinary. But when he was a strong-willed Japanese man with unhealthy interests, that's exactly what he was—with incredible will and focus.

LINDSEY MARTIN: It was an open secret—not even secret—that if there were attractive *injis* around, he was probably sleeping with them.

SUSAN RAY: He molested a lot of his women students, myself included. He couldn't be called [on it]. I fought with him about it and eventually left because of it. I loved him dearly as a dharma teacher, and still do. But his attitudes towards women were not so likable.

GIKO DAVID RUBIN: At the beginning, I was in complete denial. When a woman told me Roshi was molesting her, I could not process that. I was twenty-two. I wasn't really conscious of what was going on.

Emerging "from under water," Rubin eventually proposed that a monitor be present in *sanzen*—private sessions with students. "Roshi slammed his teacup on the table so hard, the cup broke. This man I considered . . . a wise elder . . . seemed somewhere close to insane. . . . He said, 'I'm like a doctor. You wouldn't be angry if I touched your wife's breasts or vagina if I were examining her.'"

GIKO DAVID RUBIN: Susan Ray had been Roshi's *inji*, had left Mount Baldy, and was a writer/editor. Roshi convinced Leonard to pay her a lot of money for three months, under the auspices of writing a book. I was the translator and spent three hours every afternoon, just the three of us, not Leonard. But Roshi had no intention of writing a book.

SUSAN RAY: The book wasn't the only pretext. The pretext was that I would take care of Roshi, which I'd done before. And I'd worked with Roshi's texts much earlier. There had been many plans for books, plans the Old Man, sooner or later, kiboshed. It's true Leonard gave money to cover my expenses. The phrase "literary pimp" occurred to me—after the fact—but when it did, it was not a painless situation. But if that was the intention, Leonard's or Roshi's, I was not aware of it. I guess I had the naiveté or vanity to think my spiritual teacher was interested in my spiritual education. Whenever Roshi asked Leonard for money, he said yes. That was his nature.

By December 1997, Rubin had gathered forty-two accounts of predatory practices and persuaded twelve monks to send an unsigned letter of protest to Roshi.

PAUL HUMPHREYS: The letter required that women be made aware that, by walking into the [*sanzen*] room, anything can happen. They were letting Roshi know that he might want to scale back a little. But the board did offer to use a neutral third party to hear complaints, and there were very few takers. Roshi allocated funds for that.

LINDSEY MARTIN: It was amazing the extent to which the community was not holding Roshi accountable. They were furious with David for even bringing it up. The basic feeling was, if that happens, that's his way of teaching you something. It wasn't "Come and tell the staff." That wasn't at all the vibe. I was touched by him once. It was deliberate. I remember thinking, "What's wrong with me? How can I let him touch me?"

BRIAN LESAGE: I signed that letter. We were essentially told, "If you don't like it, leave." That was really heartbreaking.

GIKO DAVID RUBIN: The vast majority rallied around him. After that, though he still had private *sanzen* time and female *injis*, things did change. Some monks no longer denied it, but counseled people on how to deal with it.

Rubin had one long talk about the issue with Cohen.

GIKO DAVID RUBIN: He said the Roshi is like a force of nature. If you try to control him, you're going to lose the good along with getting rid of the bad. He was very against trying to modify his behaviour or check him in any way. We strongly disagreed about that. But Leonard was fun to be around and very gracious. The only time I saw him bristle was when he thought people wanted something from him. He had very acute radar for when people wanted to use him.

A few years later, Cohen discussed the monks' letter with Pico Iyer, over dinner in LA.

PICO IYER: It was one of the times he rose to his fiercest eloquence, describing to me, in this little Greek café, what Sasaki Roshi was doing in the world and what it meant. One of the phrases I remember so vividly was "Here is Sasaki, like a snowball on fire, rolling down the hillside at top speed." Leonard wasn't trying to excuse Sasaki. He wasn't saying people were wrong. He was saying it was somewhat immaterial to Sasaki's teachings. He made a sharp distinction between the teacher and the man, and refused to lead the charge against him. He was unqualified in his affirmation of Sasaki's program.

BARRIE WEXLER: Years later, when I asked Cohen about Roshi's misconduct, he said, "Being a flawed leader is in line with our own Jewish tradition. The really engaging saints aren't without pimples."

Susan Ray weighed in with her own letter, arguing that the Roshi problem was "the problem of every member of the sangha—reflecting it, participation in it, or passive acceptance."

SUSAN RAY: We were all responsible—not just the men, the women, too—for our blind support of a teacher and community that diminished or rejected the feminine, placing optimum value on power and control over others. The culture was encouraged by Roshi. Historical and cultural influences also had their place. But it was we who accepted his modelling as representing the truth of the dharma, at least as a major factor in determining how Rinzai-Ji was run. This dynamic is not unique to Buddhism or spirituality in America but lies at the core of what's killing the Earth and the life she supports.

In the summer, in New Mexico, Cohen reconnected with David and Marcia Radin. Their teenage daughter had become a source of parental anxiety.

MARCIA RADIN: She was very troubled, trying drugs, even heroin. Her boyfriend died of a heroin overdose. Leonard said, "Give me the keys to the car. I want to go see her." He came back and said, "I'll take her." I said, "What do you mean?" He said, "I'll take her to live with me [in LA]. Lorca was like that. She'd be a good mentor for her." I said, "Leonard, you don't know what you're getting into." He said, "Okay, but if she ever needs anything, like a car, I'd love to do it."

In October, to promote Columbia's *More Best of Leonard Cohen* album—thirteen tracks drawn from three albums, plus "Suzanne"—Cohen spent several days at Shutters Hotel in Santa Monica, meeting the world press and posing for photos on the beach. His interviews were liberally sprinkled with his favourite lines. Among them: "The heart goes on cooking, sizzling like shish kebab." . . . "blackening pages" . . . "this vale of tears" . . . "If I knew where the good songs came from, I'd go there more often." In fact, a few years earlier, German writer Christof Graf and goth-rock bandleader Andrew Eldritch, separately interviewing Cohen in Hamburg, conspired to ask him precisely the same question about dark humour in his songs. Cohen answered both with the same words, referencing lyrics from "The Future." Later, they confessed their plot to Cohen, who replied, doubtless with irony, "I'm so pleased to have partisans in persons like you. I'm really touched."

BARRIE WEXLER: Another common tactic was professing a faulty memory—a pose of modesty actually designed to move on to the next question, or away from an issue he didn't want to address. In fact, Cohen's memory was like his boxes of drafts and memorabilia that encased his life in art—he retained everything.

By degrees, Cohen was inching toward another major decision—to leave Mount Baldy, the fierce embrace of Sasaki Roshi, and return to Boogie Street. Sitting in the meditation hall one afternoon, he thought, "This whole scene sucks. I moved from that into cataloguing the various negative feelings I had for the mother of my children. I found myself descending into a bonfire of hatred—that bitch, what she'd done to me, what she left me with, how she wrecked the whole fucking scene. . . . I was in my robes, and the furthest thing from my mind was spiritual advancement. I was consumed with rage."

KELLEY LYNCH: He told me when he meditated, I was the only person he did not have vindictive thoughts about.

Characteristically, Cohen distilled his anger into a poem: "I hated everyone. But I acted generously. And no one found me out." The same sentiment informs the content of "In My Secret Life," also written during this period.

ARMELLE BRUSQ: I wanted him to leave in 1996, wanted him to be free. I didn't wish for him to die with Roshi. Roshi was very hard with him. He was completely under his power. Imagine—he chose as a friend a guy even more manipulative than Leonard himself. He nearly died. Roshi made him a slave at the end. He wanted him to share his cabin. That's why he left. The monks told me how badly Roshi treated him.

DIANNE SEGHESIO: He didn't feel he was getting the final push from Roshi that he needed. He wanted to try a different route. Roshi was fully supportive. Roshi would tell everybody, "Go, find different teachers, round your corners." He didn't care.

YOSHIN DAVID RADIN: Leonard spent three years never separated from Roshi. That's eighteen to twenty *sesshins* a year, and he still didn't get out of his depression. Sometimes meditation reinforces it, because you're immersed and there's no out. That's why he left. Also, the meshugas started to weigh on him.

ERIC LERNER: Leonard ended up a hollow-eyed wreck, sleeping in Roshi's closet. That's where Leonard grasped some deep sense of who he was, what he is and how he is, and what he could and couldn't do.

Meanwhile, in yet another compartment of his secret life, Cohen began a long-distance "romance" with Rifkah Roth, a forty-four-year-old Swiss thera-pist living in Israel. He had answered her personal ad in the *Jerusalem Post* and had placed his own, under the title "Lenny C," including two photos. For three months, almost daily, they communicated by phone and voice messenger service. Roth, a classically trained pianist with no interest in popular music, had never heard of Leonard Cohen.

RIFKAH ROTH: He only confessed to dabbling in poetry and music, but I had no idea who he was. "Lenny C" was simply a jewel of a man to commu-nicate with on a deep level. He told me he was "weaning" himself [off the monastery], couldn't take it anymore. He'd gone there as a rehearsal for *hineni*, the giving up of oneself. He told me about his children, said he had fooled around, had been a ladies' man, and wanted to get married, wanted a deeper connection, but couldn't find the Jewish woman he was looking for. He invited me to come to Montreal and said, "Let's see if we can make a go of it." I said, "Are you crazy? We haven't even met."

It soon became clear they weren't a match. Cohen's smoking habit and pref-erence for city life discouraged her.

RIFKAH ROTH: And I was a divorcée. *Kohens* aren't allowed to marry divorcées. He told me that's why Suzanne [Elrod] was taboo for him. My impression was he couldn't make a lifelong commitment because she wasn't Jewish and he was a *Kohen*.

BARRIE WEXLER: I always thought that Suzanne wasn't Jewish, in the same way her name wasn't Suzanne. And that Leonard sometimes played loose and fast with his own priestly status.

Only years later, hearing him interviewed on the radio, did Roth come to understand that "Lenny Cohen" was *the* Leonard Cohen. "I recognized the voice. That was the shock of my life." Ironically, in conversations, she had been struck by his resonant voice and told him, "You should do something with that." It elicited a belly laugh from Cohen, but no confession. Many times, they "talked" musically, conversing in a singsong fashion with invented melody. Later, they reviewed *Parashat Ha'azinu*, the Torah portion that was read the day after Cohen's birth in 1934. In Jewish tradition, the birth *parashah* foreshadows one's life purpose.

RIFKAH ROTH: He latched onto that. It was a shock for him. Read Deuteronomy and you see the parallels. The temptations he succumbed to, some level of failure. He said, "I didn't pass that test." His sense of being called, obligated to "do something." That was so deep for him. His sense that his messages, like Moses's and God's, were not always well received. And again parallel to Moses, that he was kept from his holy land. He leads the Israelites to the promised land, but is denied entry for himself.

Seemingly resolved to leave Mount Baldy, Cohen packed his bags, climbed into his car, and started driving, but soon pulled over. Low on medications, he reached behind to his valise, grabbed the pills, and threw them out the window. "I said, 'These things really don't even begin to confront my predicament. . . . If I am going to go down, I would rather go down with my eyes wide open.'" He then returned to the Zen centre, determined to finish the *sesshin* clear-minded.

HAROLD ROTH: Leonard got fed up with being *inji*. He was too creative a being to do that for very long. And without a translator, there was only so much you could talk to Roshi about when you weren't serving him. Which would have been, for Leonard, the allure of doing the job in the first place.

ALBERT INSINGER: There's another reason Leonard might have left—he had the ambition to take over from Roshi, and Roshi decided Leonard was not suited to do so.

BARRIE WEXLER: Cohen would have wanted to take over the Zen centre like a hole in the head.

PINA PEIRCE: I do think Leonard entertained the idea of taking over. Roshi never named a successor and seemed to favour different students at different times. He always treated Leonard specially, like a son. Perhaps he thought he might be the anointed one.

MICHELLE MARTIN: Maybe he thought by becoming a monk, Roshi would make him his successor. There were possibilities for people to succeed. Roshi dangled it and never gave it to anybody.

YOSHIN DAVID RADIN: A part of Roshi did not like to empower people. Or you could say he held such a high standard, nobody could reach it. But a teacher should be skillful enough to raise children. He expected people to leap into insanely intense practice and learn to swim. Some didn't. They learned to cope.

Cohen continued to find diversions. In September 1998, he attended the wedding of Aaron Sanfield, son of Steve Sanfield and Jacquie Bellon—by then divorced—in Santa Cruz. The following month, in LA, he turned up for Jackson Browne's fiftieth birthday party. But another, more ambitious journey was beginning to take shape: India. He had already read Ramesh Balsekar's books on Advaita Vedanta Hinduism and attended talks by Wayne Liquorman at his Redondo Beach home.

WAYNE LIQUORMAN: I have no idea how he heard about me, but he started showing up regularly, for about a year. He was silent at first, but after a few visits began to ask questions. The only thing that set him apart [was his] habit of leaving hundred-dollar bills in the donation basket, not the customary amount. Eventually, someone told me who he was. I said to my wife, "This is the saddest person I ever met." He was profoundly, profoundly sad. What I felt he was seeking to resolve was his sense that things shouldn't be the way they were. This was the source of his suffering. There was a profound sense of Should Not Be. The pain he felt as a poet and sensitive human being got hijacked by this secondary sense of how things should be.

Cohen had discussed India with Marcia Radin at Bodhi Manda.

MARCIA RADIN: I was a longtime admirer of Nisargadatta [Maharaj—Balsekar's teacher]. When I found out Leonard had never been to India, I strongly encouraged him to see Balsekar specifically.

SUSAN RAY: Balsekar was a good choice. But Leonard snooped around [spiritual paths] before he met Roshi. The way he put it was, he'd get into whatever the woman's trip was.

Radin claims to have catalyzed Cohen's final break from Roshi.

MARCIA RADIN: I'd broken three bones in my left foot and Leonard was assigned to be my *inji*. He rented a car and we'd go on drives every day. He's a man of ceremony—the same thing at the same time—so we always stopped at this diner and had chocolate milk and tacos, every day. I had really good grass—I used to grow it for the Grateful Dead. Leonard had told me he hadn't smoked in a long time, but would smoke with me. We went to my bedroom and shared a pipe. After I returned home, I sent Leonard a thank-you gift—a bud of the highest quality and a small pipe.

One day, Cohen told her, he went across the river from the Zen centre, sat on a hill, and smoked the grass.

MARCIA RADIN: It was time for him to make Roshi's dinner and he just didn't want to. He smoked the grass, came across the river, and said to Roshi, "I must go." That's when he booked his trip.

Later, Cohen said that when he asked to leave, Roshi "granted permission very reluctantly. We had a formal dinner [Cohen made salmon teriyaki]. . . . I said, 'I'm going to go down and poke around.' He asked, 'How long will you be gone?' I said, 'I don't know.' I left him in the lurch, so to speak. It had the sad character of a breakup. I love him." Arriving in LA, he told Lerner, "I ran away. I couldn't breathe. I'm not going back up. Roshi's pretty angry with me."

MARSHA RADIN: He called me from the airport and said, "Only my kids and my sister know."

Cohen's *Book of Longing* includes a short note to Roshi, asking forgiveness and saying, "I cannot help you now. I met this woman." His drawing accompanying the text shows a bare-breasted Indian dancer.

KELLEY LYNCH: He was basically saying he left one whore for another whore. The woman was a cover story he thought Roshi would buy more easily than if he had said I'm going to India to study with another teacher, a Hindu. He was trying to let the old man down gently.

On another occasion, Cohen told Albert Insinger that "he'd failed as a monk, and was not in good shape mentally, wondering how he had failed."

ALBERT INSINGER: A friend of his later said Roshi took Leonard to meet the Buddhist hierarchy. Leonard [went] to shake hands, and this monk took Leonard's hand and forced him into the kneeling position. This was not to Leonard's liking. In Jewish thinking, you only kneel for God. It was then he decided to leave.

BARRIE WEXLER: He told me the same thing—that bowing to statues of Buddha was a sign of respect, not a form of worship. We bantered about it. I said a nod would be more appropriate, but definitely no kissing.

LEON WIESELTIER: Leonard was strange, in a way. He was fiendishly smart, brilliant—not a word I use lightly. So he could get bored easily and exhaust the teachings of someone over time. For that reason, he was constantly in search of refreshment. Yet I wouldn't call him a seeker, in the bad sense, because he knew who he was. The remarkable thing is that you can find a worldview from the very beginning of his work. India was refreshment, not because he needed a new Torah. He never abandoned the old Torah.

Cohen's departure from Rinzai-Ji was duly noted.

PAUL HUMPHREYS: Anyone who is part of the practice and then leaves accumulates schmutz on the windshield of the way they are perceived.

In early 1999, Cohen made his first visit to Mumbai.

GIKO DAVID RUBIN: I bumped into him at the airport. He said something about going back to the meat market of flesh that he couldn't be away from. I never understood whether he thought, "Is this really okay—the way I've been living my life and having all these relationships?" The sentiment of "Boogie Street" is the sentiment of that conversation.

LEONARD COHEN: Boogie Street to me was that street of work and desire, the ordinary life and also the place we live in most of the time, relieved by the embrace of your children, or the kiss of your beloved, or the peak experience in which you yourself are dissolved. You feel the refreshment when you come back from those moments. As [Roshi] said, "Paradise is a good place to visit, but you can't live there because there are no toilets or restaurants."

Two decades earlier, briefly in Singapore, he actually found a street named Boogie Street. In one shop, which sold bootleg records, he asked if they had any of his albums; they soon produced an entire box of his cassettes—for one dollar apiece.

WAYNE LIQUORMAN: I set him up at the Shalimar Hotel that first time. I saw him on his second day and said, "What do you think of India?" He said, "This place is great, man. It reminds me of my mind!" I saw him again a few days later and asked if he was still liking India, and he said, "Aw, man, this place is great, man. It's the people, man. You give them a little money and they love you, man, they *love* you!"

In fact, although Cohen initially intended to stay only a few weeks, he was so positively struck that he ended up staying several months—and came back for a few more months later that year. He returned to India for shorter visits in the years following. Not long after he arrived, the *Times of India* reporter Khalid Mohamed arranged to meet him.

RATNESH MATHUR: Khalid actually tricks Leonard. He does not tell him he is a journalist. He pretends to be a fan. I got this from Leonard, so there's no ambiguity. It was an ethical breach, but he was not annoyed. He was very benign, radiating peace.

Mathur, a fan, had read the *Times* article. He called Cohen, hoping he'd autograph some books. Cohen agreed, and told him to leave them at the front desk. By chance, just as Mathur was departing, Cohen appeared. After a brief chat, Cohen invited him to his room for tea. The ensuing conversation—at the Kemps Corner Hotel, to which he had moved—stretched over six hours. Mathur's wife, Sangeeta, later joined them—the start of a sixteen-year friendship.

RATNESH MATHUR: I wore my journalist's hat and he humoured me. We talked about Eric Clapton, the blues movement, Woodstock, sex, rock and roll, Jimi Hendrix, Janis Joplin, Jim Morrison, singer-songwriters, new bands. I must have met him thirty-five to forty times over the next few years. Lorca came on one of those trips. He was spending so much time in India—she wondered what he was doing there. She was selling antique furniture [in LA], so father and daughter went to the Jogeshwari market looking for old furniture.

Cohen made other acquaintances as well, among them Deva Premal, a young woman who, with her partner Miten (né Andy Desmond), had just produced a CD, *The Essence*. One morning, she sat down beside a man who looked a lot like Leonard Cohen. "I guess everyone tells you that," she said. With a wry smile, he whispered, "I am Leonard Cohen."

DEVA PREMAL: During *satsang*, I offered Ramesh my CD. He accepted my gift, even though he'd never owned a CD player. During the talks, everyone was completely focused on Ramesh and engaged on an intellectual level. Leonard was the only one who didn't open his eyes. He meditated. Then Ramesh asked me to sing mantras and people sang along—Leonard did not sing along. That afternoon, we all went to the swimming pool at the Breach Candy Club. The following day, Leonard appeared with a brand-new ghetto blaster for the Master. Ramesh said, "I saw it comes with a one-year warranty. Make sure to bring me the receipt." We talked about finding a girlfriend for Leonard, perhaps an Asian woman. There was something in the air, but nothing happened. He was there for himself and to meditate.

Later, journalist Malavika Sangghvi spotted him at the same swim club and struck up a conversation. The next morning, Cohen invited her to meet Balsekar. Later, she visited him in his monk-like room at the Kemps Corner Hotel.

ALBERT INSINGER: They showed me the miserable little room he had stayed in—so miserable, I decided to find another hotel. I still can't believe Leonard lived in this horrible little room for weeks or even months.

MALAVIKA SANGGHVI: Cohen was here to do spiritual work, trying to get stronger. Music was not on his mind. Each morning, he'd walk to his guru's home in a simple *kurta* pyjama, to listen to his spiritual master.

RATNESH MATHUR: He loved that walk. Part of it is along the waterfront, along Warden Road, less than two kilometres.

After the morning *satsang,* Cohen held private audiences with Balsekar, then repaired to a small tea shop for a breakfast of hot tea and idli [rice cake].

RATNESH MATHUR: He befriended the shop owner and would take us for tea, walk to the Breach Candy Club for a swim, then walk back to his hotel, and be on his own, reading and writing, meditating. There were always incense sticks. He had a stack of Indian music people had given him, including Bollywood music, and he was sketching a lot. Some evenings, he returned to Balsekar. Their bonhomie was very, very clear. He took us twice to the club. He liked the sun there. It's as elitist as it comes. In British colonial days, it had a sign outside saying, "Indians and dogs not allowed." We invited him [to our] home, but it was very clear he was avoiding [social] interactions. He even was avoiding the elite of India, including the singer Jasmine Bharucha. Few people recognized him. He liked that anonymity.

On one trip, Cohen, Mathur, and a young Israeli woman, another Balsekar disciple, visited what had been Mahatma Gandhi's house.

RATNESH MATHUR: Leonard wrote something about Gandhi in the register, then we went to a restaurant and had a meal. The Israeli woman had been through something traumatic. This was not a romantic piece at all. It is Mr. Cohen, the spiritual side. I don't believe he had a romantic partner in India.

VALERIE LLOYD SIDAWAY: Leonard did mention a sexual relationship in Mumbai. He dismissed it as a casual affair, not a romance, and even made a disparaging remark regarding the girl, which surprised me. She was young.

RATNESH MATHUR: We discussed India, Indian culture, marriage. He joked about Sangeeta and me finding him a Jewish Indian wife for an arranged marriage. Indian women didn't seem as good-looking to him. He said he thought the African body is more beautiful. Leonard didn't think Indian women cared for his looks. He said, "I wish an Indian woman would say I'm good-looking."

ALBERT INSINGER: I was at this resort in Goa. At the pool, there was an English guy with his Indian wife. We started talking, and Hydra and Leonard came up. They told me their friend, an Indian woman, had become Leonard's girlfriend. They said he was actually thinking of moving to Mumbai.

After one Sunday *satsang*, Mathur led Cohen to the Kala Ghoda Arts Festival, the Keneseth Eliyahoo Synagogue (the oldest in Mumbai), and an exhibition by the late Rudolf von Leyden, a Jewish cartoonist who became a founder of

India's modern art movement. They spent the rest of the day at the Khyber restaurant.

RATNESH MATHUR: At the synagogue, [he] had a good conversation with the rabbi, and put on the [tallit]. They were alone. We discussed the very small Jewish community in Mumbai. I sent emails to Kelley Lynch on his behalf, when his modem wasn't working. I sent one package to a friend of his in France, as well as audio tapes of his sessions with Balsekar to Jarkko [Arjatsalo]. Balsekar used to sell all of his books and tapes. The conversations with Cohen were the most sold.

Cohen stayed in close contact with Lynch as well. Once, after seeing Balsekar, he told her he visualized "himself as Hitler, looking out at the water, deciding where to invade next. Cohen liked to make statements to shock people." His favourite book, he said, was *The Morning of the Magicians* [a compendium of conspiracy theories dealing with Nazism, UFOs, alchemy, and spiritual philosophy]. He also spent time with German photographer Bianca Nixdorf, a student of Balsekar's.

KELLEY LYNCH: He did a lot of artwork, including using stencils he purchased there. He also bought a huge box of saris and sent them to me. I only asked him to pick up four brightly coloured saris, so I could make curtains. Boy, did I have one hell of a selection and collection. Cohen used newspaper to wrap the saris. The ads on the newsprint all related to men seeking women with computer skills.

One of Cohen's early conversations with Balsekar was taped by another devotee, Jane Adams. In it, Cohen explained that on Mount Baldy he had read Balsekar's *The Final Truth,* and found that it illuminated Roshi's discourses, and vice versa.

LEONARD COHEN: On the intellectual level, your model becomes clearer and clearer—your conceptual presentation—and so does [Roshi's]. On the experiential level, I feel the weakening of certain proprietorial feelings about doership. . . . Of course, greed arises. The hunger arises, legitimately, and without my bidding. The greed for peace, for equanimity, for balance, arises spontaneously. But I feel that somehow I don't have any leverage on the apparatus. Somehow, there is a sweetening of the whole experience.

The conversation contains a powerful description of the dogs of depression that gnawed at Cohen. His songwriting, he says, was practiced against "a background of . . . mental anguish that does not seem to respond to any methods that I impose on it. So as that understanding deepens, I try less to impose any methods; and although the . . . activity of the mind continues, it doesn't seem to have its poisonous sting. . . . The chattering of the mind, and the alleged anguish of the mind continues to operate sometimes in degrees of intensity that make one gasp or cry for help. . . . But with this understanding that is dawning, it seems that I am less willing to criticize or impose."

WAYNE LIQUORMAN: This Advaita teaching of non-duality, which spoke to the unity of things, and even to ugliness and pain, was useful for Leonard. He lightened up immeasurably over the next two or three years. The underlying teaching was the same as Zen, but . . . that system reinforced the separation between life and the spirit. Advaita teaching is more integrated with daily life, including the horrors of the world.

ROBERT FAGGEN: Leonard and I spent a lot of time talking about Balsekar. As a philosophy, as a vision of how to think, he's much more incisive than Roshi. As Leonard used to say, "No hocus-pocus."

ERIC LERNER: He described Balsekar's scene as a trauma recovery ward for spiritual seekers burnt out on various practices that had done nothing for them, the implication being that he was one of them.

SHARON BROYDE SHARONE: Years later, in shul, Leonard said [Balsekar] had asked him why he went to Mount Baldy. Leonard said, "Because I never had a night where I wasn't depressed." And the man said, "Are you no longer depressed?" And Leonard said, "No, I'm still depressed." The man said fame and shame are two sides of the same coin. You're not responsible for what you have or what you don't have. There's a certain inevitability to life. We said, "Then what [happened]?" Leonard said, "That night, I felt well for the first time in my life."

RATNESH MATHUR: [In Advaita], every living thing is a programmed object and therefore has no control over anything. Enlightenment will happen when it is supposed to happen.

ERIC LERNER: Leonard . . . was firmly convinced that Balsekar's words alone— since all Balsekar did was talk—had hipped him to the truth.

SUSAN RAY: You could safely say that Roshi loosened the cap to the ketchup bottle.

BARRIE WEXLER: Leonard tried everything—silence, seclusion, supplication, not to mention sex, drugs, and alcohol. The only thing he didn't try was *encerradura*, the ancient Ladino practice of cloistering for a week, eating only chicken broth, while having your face rubbed with the ashes of Jewish saints. In the end, only time worked. He eventually grew out of his depression—only to have his psychic pain sadly replaced by physical ones, soon after.

PICO IYER: Sasaki gave in silence what Balsekar gave in words. The Indian teacher gave Leonard classical philosophical wisdom. Sasaki gave him that sense of comradeship. He was an emotional anchor, as well as an intellectual liberator. His love songs of the last twenty years—they're addressed to Sasaki. He sings on the final album, "You were my ground, my safe and sound." No woman ever gave him that. Sasaki did.

LEON WIESELTIER: Roshi was the most important person in his life. Leonard's great argument is that sin does not disqualify you from redemption, that brokenness was actually a spiritual advantage, the condition of some sort of salvation. You see it in all his songs. He demanded acceptance as the flawed, broken person he always was and never claimed not to be. Roshi was the figure who taught him to get past any Jewish or Western guilt about the way he had lived. There was something deep in Roshi's teaching that enabled him to be proud of his brokenness and learn acceptance.

BARRIE WEXLER: No one word appears more frequently in his body of work than the word "broken."

STEVE KRIEGER: He said—kind of joking—that Roshi wanted to make things difficult, and Ramesh wanted to make things as simple as possible. He laid out the whole schematic—that we're like computers. Our life is programmed, going to unfold in a certain way—there's nothing you can do it about it. What will be, will be. Chill out. That was wafting off of Leonard a lot. He told me that one day the depression lifted and it never came back.

PICO IYER: He would never say he got the better of spiritual suffering, but he was moving towards an entente . . . a truce, at least. As he said in the final album, "We were broken then, but now we're borderline." So no answers, no redemption, but I haven't been destroyed.

BARRIE WEXLER: I later asked him whether he was still battling depression. He quoted the motto of the city of Paris, *Fluctuat nec mergitur*—Tossed but not sunk.

In a 2007 interview with Robert Enright of *Border Crossings*, Cohen said that "by imperceptible degrees," the dark cloud that had haunted him for decades dissipated.

LEONARD COHEN: I said to myself, "This must be what people feel like. I don't feel great, I don't feel bad. . . . It's just an ordinary day. It isn't a struggle. It isn't an ordeal."

Before that, he conceded, he couldn't love, "because I was in it for completely . . . selfish and divergent reasons. So nothing worked. . . . To get from moment to moment was extremely difficult. The sense of anguish was acute. I was skillful socially, so I could put on a decent face and come up with the right excuses. Then the gloom lifted and my relationships improved." Mumbai, he said, had taught him that he "didn't absolutely have to understand. Actually, I couldn't understand."

BARRIE WEXLER: As he put it to me, he realized that seeking answers was in some sense the enemy of the thing you were looking for in the first place.

DIANNE LAWRENCE: Balsekar's main message was "You are not the doer. You're just the vessel." The Bhagavad Gita says the same thing. They all say the same thing, essentially. Like, give it up. You're not in control. While we were discussing [this], Leonard said, "You and I aren't tourists on this journey." It was this recognition that bound our friendship. It's in you—it's just about when you're ready to have it revealed to you. I think it gave him a sense of peace. He could have been a teacher. He had that mantle, though he couldn't have actual students. But I said to him, "You mean if I murder someone, I'm not responsible?" He said, "Are you thinking of murdering someone?"

WAYNE LIQUORMAN: Ramesh used the term "doer," but [meant] "author." It does not absolve you from societal responsibilities. But the sense that you were the source of the action is what brings suffering, because it implies that you have inherent power. The teaching questions that—do you, in fact, have that power? I was aware of the impact of that on Cohen.

YOSHIN DAVID RADIN: "You are not the doer" means that nothing happens without a cause. Things are produced by causes, not ultimately by will. The chain of causation goes back infinitely in all directions, through time and space. For example, if someone was beaten by his father when young, and has anger that he can't release, one contemplation would be that his father was beaten by his father, and therefore his father was a transmitting chain of cause and effect.

Cohen parted company with Balsekar on at least one point—reincarnation. The guru believed that souls were reborn, but without memory of their former lives. Cohen was skeptical. He quoted Sasaki Roshi as calling reincarnation a Tibetan fairy tale. "It's not that he wishes to denigrate . . . that position. It's more like, 'Don't you have anything better to think about? Your position in the cosmos is at stake at this moment.' I tend to feel that way."

Cohen was still in India when Sasaki Roshi celebrated his ninety-second birthday.

KELLEY LYNCH: Cohen sent me to see him with a cheque for $9,200. Roshi felt betrayed.

*   *   *

By the late 1990s, Cohen's informal fan club extended around the world. Among its more unusual members was Robert Bower, a Times Square newsstand dealer. Then in his late forties, he'd attended Cohen concerts for more than twenty years, and had assembled a treasure trove of clippings and reviews, which he planned to donate to Cohen's archive. Once, during his 1993 tour in Europe, Cohen arranged for Bower to join him for an interview on Danish television.

PERLA BATALLA: Robert was a dear friend of Leonard's—a beautiful gentle soul, very delicate, very sweet. He was always checking on Leonard's sister, Esther, after her husband died, taking her out for tea. When his newsstand was shut down—his entire existence—it was Leonard's doing that Bob Dylan hired Robert to take care of the mail room. When Robert was sick, I'd let Leonard know and he'd call and see what he could do.

Bower passed away in 2011. Unfortunately, according to Batalla, the Bower collection of Coheniana was lost or discarded after his passing.

On June 5, now back in LA, Cohen stopped in at a bookstore after lunch at Le Petit Greek in Larchmont Village with screenwriter Tony Babinski and Kelley Lynch.

TONY BABINSKI: I saw Leonard open a book called *The Elements of Judaism*. He then walked over to the poetry section, squatted down, began scouring the shelves, and emerged with a huge pile of books. He said, "I haven't been in a bookstore for two years, and here I am buying five hundred dollars in books." He said, "I like a poem to work at first blush. I'm not the type to try to analyze the minutiae of every line to crack it, like a code. Irving [Layton] and I used to analyze poems together for whole evenings, years ago. But if it works on you at first blush, you let it work on you. Then you can analyze it."

They found themselves in a section displaying novels by E. M. Forster.

TONY BABINSKI: I asked him, "Were you deliberately subverting Forster in *Beautiful Losers*? He said, "What did he say?" . . . Forster said, "Only connect." Leonard, highly amused, said, "And I said, 'Connect Nothing.' Yeah."

When he left, Babinski thanked Cohen for his hospitality and told him how much he and cowriter Jacob Potashnik valued his work.

TONY BABINSKI: Leonard said, "That reminds me of a story. There was once a very old man who decided to marry a voluptuous young woman. His friends asked him if he intended to have sex with her. He said of course. "But sex is an exertion. It makes your heart pound." And he said: "What can I do? If she dies, she dies." In other words, you just have to do these things. If they're good, they're good. If not, you tried your best." I told him Mel Tormé had died that day. The Velvet Fog. "That makes you his successor." He said, "Yeah. The Velvet Mist."

After Babinski departed, Cohen welcomed website master Jarkko Arjatsalo and his family for a weekend. Cohen made vegetable soup, and his Red Needles cocktail, took them to Le Petit Greek with Lorca and Adam, and showed them the manuscript of *Book of Longing*.

KELLEY LYNCH: Jarkko recorded Cohen reciting "Charge of the Light Brigade" for me. One of my favourite poems. I had Cohen recite it quite often.

Cohen also played host for several days to singer-songwriter Cassidy A. Maze (then known as Lizzie West) and photographer Atar Schimmel, daughter of

Israeli poet Harold Schimmel. They had driven from New York expressly to see him, part of a quixotic quest for "the great American authentic poet."

CASSIDY A. MAZE: Leonard really loved my dog, Figaro, and fed him cans of tuna fish. He offered to keep him. We stayed in the [coach house]. He cooked for us, just really kind and generous. He took us to Mount Baldy to meditate. He said to me, "If you're a seeker, you need a teacher. You're not supposed to figure it out yourself, necessarily." That has always resonated. Roshi was jolly and playful. He wore a lady's sun hat. I met Kelley. She wanted to manage me, but—I don't know why—I just didn't trust her.

Maze later sent Cohen an orange tree that he planted in his yard. He, in turn, sent hand-drawn illustrations of Figaro and a StarKist albacore tuna.

On a return visit to Mount Baldy, Cohen attended the wedding of Zen monk Giko David Rubin and Lindsey Martin, gifting the couple a piece of Japanese art, the symbol for om.

LINDSEY MARTIN: At the reception, David asked him if he wanted to sing. He very kindly demurred.

Cohen had told both Babinski and Arjatsalo that he was planning to drive across America, back to Montreal. Instead, he returned to Mumbai to continue studying with Balsekar, and celebrated his sixty-fifth birthday in the company of Ratnesh and Sangeeta Mathur.

RATNESH MATHUR: He chose to smoke a cigarette that day—the only time I saw him smoke. He liked vegetarian, simple, basic food, lentil soup, not spicy. We had conversations about understanding *Beautiful Losers.* He said, "Don't read it." He was critical of his own music. Ray Charles and Edith Piaf had the best vocal cords. He mentioned depression, but it was tangential. He was more of a saint, like a person spiritually awakened. I saw only a spiritual glow.

That fall, Cohen returned to Greece. Writer David Fagan then claimed Hydra's only internet connection—in an office near the Vangelis Rafalias chemist shop. As a favour, Fagan gave Cohen his office keys "so he could come and go at his discretion." One rainy night, Cohen invited Marianne Ihlen to dinner.

MARIANNE IHLEN: We shared a little meal his maid had prepared. Seeing Leonard move . . . slow, he's so into everything he does . . . was like a meditation. He was doing the dishes, and I was looking at what had once been my little kitchen. Nothing was changed in the house we'd lived in together for so long. The same box with a young woman blindfolded playing a harp without any strings. . . . The Christ someone had given him was gone—a beautiful wooden Christ, old and rotten. But the church bell was still there, the one I'd brought when I moved in.

BARRIE WEXLER: The bell was on a kitchen shelf, about ten inches high. It tinkled when you walked in from the terrace. Before Marianne met Leonard, she crewed on a yacht owned by a German whose first name, curiously, was Marian. They became involved, sailing the Cyclades together. On Santorini, she went for a walk and spotted the half-buried bell. It had an imprint of the Madonna and Child. Marianne was superstitious and thought finding it was some kind of omen, but I forget of what.

MARIANNE IHLEN: After I reminded him, Leonard said, "I'm happy that you told me the story because I'd forgotten about the bell." He walked over to the sink and finished the dishes. I felt so calm and so relieved. I had no wish to go back in time. It was a very, very beautiful meeting. Next morning, we met for coffee at Tassos.

Cohen later gave Ihlen the bell. In June 2019, her estate sold it at auction for US $81,250.

BARRIE WEXLER: He also kept a dark needlepoint depiction of Christ on the cross in the master bedroom—a souvenir from the Agia Efpraxia nunnery. They made the journey not long after he and Marianne met. It's 1,500 feet up, not an easy donkey ride. Leonard tried riding it every which way and twice almost fell off. Marianne said when they got back to the port, his hands were as white as marble from clasping the saddle.

Valerie Lloyd Sidaway was Cohen's dinner guest another night.

VALERIE LLOYD SIDAWAY: Leonard had remarkable intuition, a unique insight into a person's being, if he was inclined. He asked if I'd like to be hypnotized. I declined. He sensed I was inhibited and instead told me information about me of a personal nature. He seemed to have a clear perception as to what was bothering me. That night, we spoke about George Lialios's technique of "calming tranquility" or balancing of energies. George could achieve complete relaxation in ten minutes. It would take me at least two hours in meditation. Leonard advised me to ask George for more sessions, saying George needed to continue with them to retain the skill.

One morning, at the Pirate Bar, Cohen suddenly opened up about his depression.

VALERIE LLOYD SIDAWAY: It was very unexpected, the first time I knew of it. He spent a good hour discussing it—the incredible headaches, which played a large part in causing the depression, the drugs he tried, mostly amphetamines. He said the headaches finally stopped on Mount Baldy. When we finished, he asked if there was a place to swim, close by. We went to Hydronetta, where one could have a drink and snack and jump straight into the sea. It was like a cleansing.

Cohen made a new acquaintance that fall, British poet Roger Green, who taught English at Hydra's private language school and was fluent in Greek. His house overlooked Cohen's garden. Green later wrote *Hydra and the Bananas of Leonard Cohen*, a book mostly about Suzanne [Elrod], the Sanfields, and Cohen's housekeeper, Evangelia.

ROGER GREEN: Suzanne was a very difficult person. Everyone agrees on that. We were quite friendly, but when she found out that I'd published things she'd said without asking [permission], I absolutely got the cold shoulder. I had a row with Adam [Cohen] about it. He complained about my using his father's name in the title to make money.

Green's book describes Elrod as a combination of "Eve, Lilith, the Serpent, and a Cherub with a flaming sword." Later, he adds other descriptives, including Alice—from *Through the Looking-Glass*—Kassandra and Susanna, from the folk song. At one point, Green was called on to act as an interpreter during a dispute between Elrod and Evangelia, whom she still blamed for her arrest on drug charges two decades earlier.

ROGER GREEN: Steve Sanfield took the book to Leonard. He was delighted with all the stuff on Suzanne and said, "Your take on Suzanne is my take on Suzanne." He thought she ought to be pleased because I'd made her out to be a mythological figure.

Cohen was still wrestling with lyrics for "Alexandra Leaving," based on Constantine Cavafy's poem, "The God Abandons Antony."

ROGER GREEN: He was working with three different translations. When he found out I knew Greek, he said, "Let's feed in the Greek text as well." We sat down every day, at his house. He really goes into the thing thoroughly and, though the result may not look like the original, he has really studied it.

ALBERT INSINGER: Leonard was the deepest thinker. I never met anyone who went so deep into an issue, would look at it from many different angles. He bought two books by Cavafy with slightly different translations, which made him a little uneasy. One had the original text in Egyptian, opposite the translated English. There was this guy from Egypt hanging out on Hydra and Leonard asked him questions about the original text.

ROGER GREEN: I wouldn't say he improved on the poem, but he made it his own. We had a very friendly relationship for about six weeks. I remember a lot of coffee. I had a near monopoly on Leonard. We had some pretty intimate talks, about difficult times we'd had in our lives. I was impressed by how well-read he was. He knew some minor English poets like Humbert Wolfe [an early twentieth-century poet]. He said, "We're probably the only two people on this island who know about Humbert Wolfe."

Cohen later included Wolfe's poems as part of his essential reading list. Although he didn't formally pay Green for his work, Cohen was generous in other ways.

ROGER GREEN: He did two things. He gave me money to get my poems printed privately in Athens. And he deputized me to make a donation to the Chapel of Aghios Tykhon, which Cohen's garden overlooked. He gave me a lot of money, too much money, to get something suitable. I bought a *manouali* [a round container filled with sand] in Piraeus. That was his gift—anonymous. There's a line in his book *Death of a Lady's Man* about his being a guardian of many things, including that church.

VALERIE LLOYD SIDAWAY: He read me "Alexandra Leaving" after he had just finished writing it. He also showed me his drawings. He was like a youngster discovering he could draw, like it never occurred to him before that this was possible. Very endearing.

One evening, Cohen, Green, and painter Bill Pownall, an accomplished guitarist, convened for a songfest.

BILL POWNALL: Leonard didn't do fantastic technical things on the guitar, but that rolling, arpeggio style is not easy to do. David Gilmour of Pink Floyd told me he tried to do what Leonard does and couldn't.

ROGER GREEN: We sang one song together—"Why Do Fools Fall in Love." Leonard said it was one of his favourite songs.

A few days later, Cohen dined with Pownall and his wife, Francesca, in Kamini. Pownall confided that he was struggling to earn a living.

BILL POWNALL: He said, "What could we do?" Then he says, "I've been meaning to buy a couple of your paintings." So he bought a couple. Didn't come to the studio. Said, "Pick a couple. I trust you." So I picked some. I said, "You don't have to have these ones." He said, "They're great." We're talking about five or six thousand dollars, significant to me. I don't think it was just kindness. I think he recognized here was a creative person and he could do something, and he did something. He did the same for Anthony [Kingsmill]. He'd just finished "Alexandra Leaving." He recited the whole thing, just the lyric. We were the first people to hear it. Leonard had a lot of qualities, but there was always this modesty, which was manifest in his whole being.

The last time Pownall saw Cohen was that autumn.

BILL POWNALL: We were at the Pirate Tavern talking about life, love, and aging, while looking at the beautiful women in the harbour. Leonard said: "Well, Bill, the old are kind, but the young are hot. Love may be blind, but desire is not." We both laughed.

The lines are from "Sorrows of the Elderly," a poem he'd written on Mount Baldy. Cohen also befriended American painter Michael Lawrence, whom he met on the beach at Kamini.

MICHAEL LAWRENCE: He was meditating on one side, I on the other. I thought, "I'll introduce myself." I did and we had a nice conversation. We come from the same cultural heritage, which created an almost automatic connection. He gave me advice. He said, "You should get married. It's a very good experience." I said, "By the way, I'm having an exhibit—would you like to come?" And he came. We both wore the same outfit [white shirts and black pants].

Another night, Cohen was at dinner with George Lialios and his family at Pirofani, in Kamini, when Valerie Lloyd Sidaway turned up.

VALERIE LLOYD SIDAWAY: The tables were full, but the owner arranged a small table with one chair. I was about to leave [when] suddenly, Leonard asked to join me. I got up to fetch another chair, but he said, "Don't worry. I'll share your chair." So we sat, each sitting on half a chair. He had seen me sitting alone and had felt empathy. As I left, I called to him, "Leonard! There's a Rebecca De Mornay film on TV tonight!" He surprised me by saying, "Come to my place and watch it." I demurred, but he insisted. So I watched the movie and he watched Rebecca. He spoke of Hydra not being the same as before, when there were stimulating individuals living on the island or passing through. Now there was no one interesting to talk to. Before he left that year, he asked me if anyone needed any financial help. I didn't know of anyone.

Inevitably, Cohen would drop by Bill's Bar for a drink or two.

DAVID FAGAN: He had a soft spot for Bill Cunliffe and loved the dry humour, clever banter, and wit which always accompanied the regulars. Chuckling wryly on his stool at the end of the bar, giving as good as he got, Leonard in his old hat. He carried himself with quiet, unassuming grace and blended. Once, a Scottish girl with more than a few under her belt suddenly shouted at him, "Oi, you! I nearly committed suicide because of your songs. Twice!" Everybody cracked up, most of all the man himself.

Back in LA, Rabbi Simon Jacobson came to visit.

SIMON JACOBSON: He offered to pick me up from the airport. I said no, but he came to pick me up in Hancock Park—he insisted. Came in his little jalopy, a Sunday morning, took me back to his house, sat at his kitchen dinette. I was going to record my radio show, on loneliness—it was Tisha B'Av [a day of mourning for the destruction of the Temple in Jerusalem], and invited him to be my guest. He said he wished he could, but could not for contractual reasons. But he gave me a poem on loneliness, previously unpublished, to read on the show. I did it from his coach house studio. He didn't talk much about his life, but you could see that he was suffering. It was all very casual, low-key. He sat with me as with a teacher. He almost didn't want to talk. He only spoke when I pushed him. We were talking about the Holocaust and how a good God allows pain. I sang him a song taught by the Lubavitcher rebbe in 1958, about the three stages the soul goes through in life. First, as a free spirit, with wings spread. Then it has to deal with the ailments of the material world, suffering and pain. And finally, the hope that one day we will soar again. He closed his eyes and listened intently. He was visibly moved. He well understood that you don't explain away depression with some philosophy. The song gives us strength, hope, allows us to express grief. It could be his music was the result of his darkness. It was his therapy.

In 2007, Jacobson invited Cohen to his daughter's wedding. Unable to attend, he sent $1,000—a generous gift at any time, but especially so soon after the discovery that his own bank accounts had been pillaged.

ROBERT FAGGEN: Leonard wasn't interested in money. Have you seen where he lived? By most standards, that was a very modest house. He didn't want complications. He had the same car for twenty-five years—the Nissan Pathfinder. For anyone in LA to own a car for twenty years is odd, but he was pretty insistent on it. He was meticulous about dressing well—we never went out even for lunch when he did not dress nicely. And he never wore jeans. But he liked to shop in low-end clothing stores. Clothing was definitely not a passion. I don't think he saw himself as a social crusader or a Marxist, but he was very concerned about how difficult it is to be born poor or be poor. And concerned about what it is to be Black in America—the burden of that was incomprehensible, though he wasn't preachy about it.

BARRIE WEXLER: Leonard told me he admired the way Cary Grant would put on a suit and a tie, "even to go buy a bottle of aspirins."

Even Kelley Lynch conceded that Cohen "didn't gloat about his finances."

KELLEY LYNCH: He was very careful about managing perception. He'd stay at the Four Seasons, but he was modest about talking about his finances or bragging. He wouldn't get into a stretch limo. To him, that was horrifying. He went bananas when Neal Greenberg placed an ad in *Billboard* for a tribute, and said he was his financial adviser. He didn't want "trustee" printed on any of his cheques.

In other ways, Lynch maintains, Cohen spent beyond his means.

KELLEY LYNCH: Huge donations to Zen centres. I'm talking about $20,000 loans to everybody. It wasn't exactly generosity. It came with strings attached. Eric Lerner, Morton Rosengarten—it made them beholden to him. With Rebecca [De Mornay]—he insisted on paying her and her girl-friend's first-class ticket to Spain. He gave half a million dollars to Roshi. Houses for Adam and later Anjani. A million-dollar building for Lorca. He didn't have this kind of money.

In early October, Cohen flew to Montreal to serve as an honorary pallbearer at Pierre Trudeau's funeral, along with Fidel Castro, Jimmy Carter, and the Aga Khan. On two occasions during that visit, he and Musia Schwartz visited Irving Layton, then living in a Jewish retirement home.

DIANNA PALAMAREK: I was one of Irving's caregivers. Irving was still pretty good then, could still carry on a conversation. Irving was smoking his pipe and Leonard was smoking a cigarette. Leonard told him that his mother [Masha] had been offended by the title of Irving's poetry book, *For My Brother Jesus* [1976]. Later, in Irving's room, I shook Leonard's hand, but couldn't speak. I was so awed by his greatness.

Layton asked Cohen if he'd noticed a reduction in his sexual appetite.

LEONARD COHEN: I said, "I have, somewhat." He said, "I'm relieved to hear that, Leonard." I said, "I take it, Irving, that you yourself have noticed some decline in your sexual appetite." He said, "I have." I said, "When did you first begin to notice this?" He said, "Oh, about the age of sixteen or seventeen."

DIANNA PALAMAREK: They came again a few years later and Irving had declined. Leonard and Musia sat in the room an hour and did not speak, not a thing.

AVIVA LAYTON: Leonard hadn't visited for a while, so I warned him that Irving mightn't know who he was. Afterwards, when I asked Leonard how the visit went, he said that Irving was actually sharper than ever. "He pretended the whole time he didn't know me but, by the twinkle in his eyes, I knew he was only making a sly joke." Leonard couldn't accept the fact that the man he loved and was so close to had disappeared into the fog of Alzheimer's.

Musia Schwartz had a different take on why Cohen characterized the meeting as he did.

MUSIA SCHWARTZ: Leonard didn't like to handle things which were deeply disturbing. It wasn't a conscious choice.

Meanwhile, Cohen addressed himself to phase two of his estate planning exercise—the sale of his 127-song catalogue. One possible route was a Bowie Bond. In January 1997, David Pullman had sold $55 million in $1,000-denominated bonds, carrying a 7.9 percent interest rate, to Prudential Life Insurance. Bowie received the money up front; investors enjoyed the musician's royalties—one of the first times that a bond used intellectual property as the underlying collateral. When the bonds liquidated in 2007, the income stream reverted to Bowie.

RICHARD ZUCKERMAN: At the time, it was common for artists—Bowie, Peter Gabriel, others—to do estate planning by taking the money now, by selling their catalogue. Leonard probably thought it was a good idea.

KELLEY LYNCH: The beauty of bond securitization was the ability to maintain ownership after repaying what was essentially a loan with interest over a fixed period. Taxes are paid as royalty income flows through. The IP assets merely served as securitization.

Early in 1999, CAK Universal Credit Corp., a company controlled by music executive Charles A. Koppelman, offered Cohen a $5.8 million loan, secured by his composition rights and royalty streams. Anticipating an agreement, Cohen signed an engagement letter, formed LC Investments (a bankruptcy-proof entity), and paid CAK $75,000 to evaluate his loan. Then Sony raised an objecting hand: the bond deal might restrict its future negotiating leverage. Music labels typically paid artist advances, money that committed performers to deliver contractually obligated albums. With millions derived from a bond deal, Cohen would need no advances. In November 1999, Sony's Stuart Bondell told Lynch it would pay $8 million for the second intellectual property deal.

KELLEY LYNCH: I called Cohen in India. He instructed me to tell Bondell that if Sony made a $1 million, nonrefundable down payment on the $8 million, he'd forfeit the CAK bond accord and sign with Sony. Bondell agreed.

When CAK learned Cohen was negotiating with Sony, it revised its offer—an amendment he seized as grounds for terminating the engagement letter. CAK subsequently sued, alleging breach of contract, and demanded $363,000 in fees and expenses. Cohen eventually settled the dispute out of court. The $1 million advance became the subject of an IRS inquiry.

Cohen later insisted he had been barely involved in these discussions; an email he sent to Lynch in May 2000 from India clearly suggests otherwise. "Losing patience . . . in this deal," he said. "The dragging of feet is deafening. I don't know if it's you, or the lawyers, or Sony, but something is very wrong. I had a good bond deal on the table with [Koppelman] until Sony spoke up, and now I am in litigation with C. K. [Charles Koppelman], and Sony is busy revising the figures downwards. . . . Am I the only one here with a sense of time? . . . I am working on two albums . . . both of which are about to be undervalued. The least I will do is adopt a more leisurely working pace. In fact, I feel like waiting for the seven-year jubilee, and then quietly excusing myself from the whole matter. In other words, Kelley, this is bullshit. Sony destroys my deal with C. K. (so as not to establish any precedent of their artists leaving the fold), dumps me into litigation, then they postpone the closing of their deal for seven months until they can discover that my catalogue sales are lagging, and then they lower the price. . . . It is time to consider other options. I know you're doing your best . . . but the playing field has suddenly tilted to an unacceptable degree."

Whoever the buyer, Cohen needed a corporate vehicle that would minimize taxes and protect his principal. An initial proposal, designed by lawyer Richard Westin, proposed that Blue Mist Touring (BMT, formerly Leonard Cohen Productions), wholly owned by Cohen, acquire and then sell the royalty rights. BMT was subsequently restructured to give Lynch a 15 percent ownership stake.

But Westin concluded that funds received by selling stock in BMT would be taxed, punitively, as ordinary income. A new plan was drafted.

By October 10, 2000, it was envisaged that Cohen would sell his writer's share of royalties for $4.1 million using LC Investments, and record royalties for $8 million through a stock sale of BMT. From the latter, Cohen was to net about $6 million; Lynch would get about $1.1 million. To soften the tax bite, Westin pitched yet another idea—to sell some BMT assets in exchange for a deferred annuity. To keep Cohen largely immune to charges of self-dealing, his children, Adam and Lorca (99 percent), and Lynch (1 percent) would be shareholders of the company issuing the annuity. Cohen demurred, saying he did not want his children embroiled in his affairs, and at risk of future entanglements.

Sony's Paul Burger, for one, thought that the asset sale approach was a mistake.

PAUL BURGER: I remember telling Kelley it was an absolutely ridiculous idea. They wanted to sell it to us—to Sony. I was like, "This is the future. This is the pension. This is what he has. How can you cash that in? It's such a valuable catalogue. How can you possibly consider doing that?" They managed to retain a bit—they didn't sell absolutely everything. I can understand a dad wanting to set up his kids. But I just couldn't imagine someone of the calibre of Leonard selling all the interests in his songs.

Lynch also was opposed, she claims.

KELLEY LYNCH: It was alarming to see that he was willing to give up permanent IP assets, and other valuable rights, when a bond transaction with similar amounts was on the table. Selling the assets outright also caused the assets to be present-day valued and did not reflect their market value. I advised Cohen, as did Greg McBowman, not to sell.

In early December, Westin revised the plan, proposing that Cohen (.5 percent) and Lynch (99.5 percent) would jointly own a new entity, Traditional Holdings (TH), which would acquire Cohen's assets in exchange for a private annuity; payments of about $38,000 a month would start in 2011. The plan, Westin claimed, would save Cohen about $3.5 million in 2001 income tax. Because payment was deferred, tax was deferred. Lynch's equity was to be rolled into a trust that, on his death, would go to his children. Until the annuity started paying out, any funds borrowed from TH would need to be documented as loans. In the interim, his invested funds would presumably grow. In the end, TH received $6.65 million before deductions of professional fees, including Lynch's commission of more than $1 million. It was Lynch's later contention that TH never properly acquired Blue Mist Touring and that, as a consequence, TH effectively sold assets to Sony it did not own. Having prepaid a $1 million advance, Sony closed the transaction in April 2001, paying the remaining $6.3 million. On paper, Leonard Cohen was a rich man—or so it must have seemed.

CHAPTER SEVEN

All That Matters
Here Is the Heart

He had noblesse about him. He was like royalty. He really cared about the peasants in the field. Really, really cared. It would come out—by not being a celebrity. You could see the decades of practice—body movement, how the eyes process, fluidity.

—Shinzen Young

Some people offer their body to science. Leonard, as an artist, offers his soul for people to look at it.

—Armelle Brusq

With his lifelong depression ostensibly in check, sixty-five-year-old Leonard Cohen began the new century with a renewed sense of vigour. An agreement to sell his record catalogue was about to close and deliver him a sizeable cheque. He had assurances from his financial adviser that his funds, safely invested, would yield an annual spending budget of more than $400,000. And he was about to dive into production of his first album of new material in nine years—*Ten New Songs*.

Cowritten, coproduced, and coarranged with Sharon Robinson, it was easily the most collaborative exercise of his career. Fittingly, the album cover featured Cohen and Robinson huddled together—a photograph taken by his computer's built-in camera. Although most of the lyrics were written on Mount Baldy, and the album was dedicated to Joshu Sasaki, the project itself actually had its genesis in the late spring of 1999.

SHARON ROBINSON: He came up to me after my son's piano recital, said he had some new poems and wanted to work together.

Soon, she and sound engineer Leanne Ungar were in his coach house studio every day. Although Cohen was careful in interviews not to commit to a new album, he owed one contractually to Sony.

PAUL BURGER: There was definitely some frustration between us in the period between *The Future* and *Ten New Songs*.

KELLEY LYNCH: He took advances against that—$500,000. So not delivering albums became a financial problem. Burger [unhappy]? How about the entire hierarchy of Sony?

PAUL BURGER: I went to see him—just Leonard and me. He'd put out a hilarious spread—bagels, smoked salmon, caviar, pickled herring, like going to your grandmother's for Sunday lunch. And a bottle of vodka, frozen. We probably drank a bit too much. Eventually, we went to the shed in the garden. Sharon was there and he played me a few songs. I knew he was back on track.

With the minimalist thrust of the album, few musicians were needed. Only Ungar's husband, guitarist Bob Metzger, is credited, though at one point Cohen invited violinist Bobby Furgo to play.

BOBBY FURGO: I just shined him on. I thought it might be difficult to record with his cheesy keyboard and all this computer stuff, almost no live instruments. He was always really stingy on recordings for instruments. You might play one note. So I just ignored him. I was wrong. I should have gone.

Although she shared equal billing, Robinson recognized that Cohen was the principal artist. "Ultimately, I defer to him on everything," she told one interviewer. "It's his voice we are looking to give a platform to, not mine."

DAVID PELOQUIN: The project was a labour of love. Each song is like a Zen dharma talk, exquisitely nuanced in its spiritual sensibilities. It's really almost a duet album. You simply can't listen to Sharon Robinson's sublime singing and file it under "backup vocal by." She was an equal creative force in making this masterpiece.

Once, during this period, Cohen experienced a brief health scare.

KELLEY LYNCH: He blacked out, fell, and cut his head. I took him to Cedars-Sinai [Medical Center]. Sharon Robinson stayed the night with him. He saw Dr. Joshua Trabulus [an internist]. We were referred to him by Rebecca De Mornay. Nothing was revealed at Cedars. Trabulus noted that it appeared to be some type of cardiac activity. I thought it might have something to do with his brain, because Cohen relied heavily on prescription meth.

To avoid ambient noise, Cohen typically recorded in the early morning, as early as 3:00 am. "I had to start singing before the birds, and the traffic on Olympic, and before my daughter's dogs started barking," he told music journalist Eric Rudolph. "It was very relaxed to . . . find the right place to stand or sit, and have the right drink or smoke in your hand, lean back, go back, erase, go forward. It was a very luxurious way to do the vocals." Later, Cohen handed off the mixes to master engineer Bob Ludwig.

DAVID PELOQUIN: Ludwig's . . . secret lies in his golden musical ears, and in the relationship with the artist and [the] vision. The essence of his work is its naturalness, clarity, musicality, and warmth. You're not simply listening to the music. You find yourself inhabiting it, as a soundscape that seems to wash over you. The key artistic participants were all in the room when Ludwig mastered—Cohen, Robinson, and Ungar. This is the ideal mastering session; when everyone is in accord and dedicated to serving the vision.

Cohen's friends noticed the general improvement in Cohen's mood. When Canadian film producer Robert Lantos dropped by for lunch, Cohen played him the album.

ROBERT LANTOS: I said, "The anger is gone."

It was Cohen's habit in those years to host an annual New Year's Eve party, usually at Le Petit Greek in Larchmont Village.

AVIVA LAYTON: For years, he took over the whole restaurant. Lots of people, including Nancy Bacal, Lorca, and Leonard's sister, Esther. It was a fabulous way to spend New Year's Eve, except that Leonard insisted on starting early and marking the turn of the year at midnight, Montreal time, which meant nine p.m. LA time. "We all have to be in bed fast asleep by ten p.m.," he'd say.

One day, Cohen and his friend Bernie Rothman went for a drive with Bob Dylan.

BERNIE ROTHMAN: I was driving, Dylan and Cohen are in the back seat and Dylan is asking—no, *egging*—Cohen to go on the road with him. Cohen says, "That's so kind of you. But people who go to see your concerts go to see you. They would be very disappointed to see me."

In March, attending his son Adam's concert at LA's Largo, Cohen bumped into Julianna Raye.

JULIANNA RAYE: He was standing outside by himself. I went up and said, "That series [of tapes] you gave me [Shinzen Young's *The Science of Enlightenment*] has radically changed my life." He said, "Come to my house at seven a.m. tomorrow." It turned out that Sasaki Roshi was doing a five-day *sesshin* at Rinzai-Ji. I went with Leonard every morning. Afterwards, we'd go to Roshi's room for tea and crackers. Meeting Roshi was like meeting Bruce Springsteen. By the end of the week, I knew I had to train with Roshi and did, until he died. So Leonard introduced me to my two teachers. That set me on a completely different course, a radical improvement. I could have been a chronically miserable pop star. I felt like Leonard was a ghostly third teacher. He encouraged me in the way that was the right direction for me. He did the right thing introducing me to Shinzen before Sasaki Roshi. It would not have worked the other way.

Another day, Cohen read a poem at a ceremony to honour Shinzen Young.

JULIANNA RAYE: I sang "Come Rain or Come Shine," and naively asked Leonard to accompany me. He said, "Oh, I don't do that." I felt embarrassed—I realized how absurd that was. I said, "I just thought I'd throw it out there." And he said, "Oh, do, darling. Throw it out there." Then he asked me to sing for Roshi at Rinzai-Ji. I sang "Every Time We Say Goodbye," a cappella. That meant a lot to me—that he invited me.

Young, another Jew who immersed himself in Japanese culture, had served as Sasaki Roshi's go-to translator for decades. "Interpreting was a challenge," Young says, "because Roshi spoke long sentences, very fast, and mixed all levels of Japanese simultaneously—vulgar colloquial, esoteric poetry, plus Chinese."

SHINZEN YOUNG: Roshi was giving a version of Buddhism I'd never heard of, though I had a PhD. His formulation of the meditative path is one of the most stunningly original creations since the Buddha himself. I'm sure that's part of what attracted Leonard. How he integrates it in a single paradigm—call it, attention training on steroids. Not just the wisdom function, but a sense that everything I've previously experienced was a prison and I did not know it. It's very rare for someone to say something really new in this field. Sasaki did. All this, while you're sitting for hours, your legs on fire with pain, your bladder about to explode.

Young met Cohen in the early 1980s. "We didn't have a lot of contact, but the unspoken connection was deep. I like to say I sang backup to him during retreats." Once, Young stayed with him during a *sesshin* in Montreal.

SHINZEN YOUNG: I came down for breakfast and he was reading the Talmud. And remember, this is in the middle of the retreat. But the Kabbalistic formulation of God as a functional parent is very, very close to what Sasaki taught—all the expansion-contraction, affirmation-negation stuff. I said, "What's up?" He said, "These guys, our people, they were trying to get to what the old man [Roshi] is talking about."

On May 17, 2001, Sony Music Canada president Denise Donlon arrived in LA to hear the new album. Typically, Cohen initially tried to cancel the appointment, but eventually turned up at Donlon's Santa Monica hotel. They played the demo on a cheap CD player screwed to a bedside table. Its sound was inferior to begin with, and the white noise of ocean waves did not help, so Cohen, Donlon, and Sony executive Ian MacKay moved furniture to optimize audio quality and ended up sitting on the floor.

DENISE DONLON: We drank two bottles of Canadian wine, which I'd brought. He was not bothered. He said, "I'm a patriot." I ordered a couple pounds of cheese and we ate and drank it all. It was a ridiculous scenario—listening to a master-class artist at the height of his powers. But we had an amazing conversation about the marketing—maybe the Dalai Lama would do liner notes. He would tour the album in residencies around the world, do an international press tour and a music video. The next day, Kelley called me. Leonard had sobered up. She said, "He's changed his mind." I asked, "On what?" She said, "On everything."

Cohen later agreed to a scaled-down series of promotional events, and to shoot a video of "In My Secret Life" with Canadian director Floria Sigismondi.

FLORIA SIGISMONDI: I'd always been a massive fan. His records were always on the turntable, growing up. We met at the Chateau Marmont. He started [reciting] his lyrics and I thought he was *talking* to me. It was very funny. "I saw you last night . . ." What? You saw me last night? And he has that great voice and he doesn't crack a smile. Oh, of course—you're reciting the lyrics!

DENISE DONLON: That video was a huge gamble. We needed something eye-catching, risky, artful. Floria had been riding high with David Bowie and Marilyn Manson. I sent him some directors' reels and put Floria on those reels. Canadian. Extreme.

Sigismondi's conceit for the video was similar to the theme that had informed *I Am a Hotel* (1983)—"that he was observing the secret lives of people in an apartment building, with a little bit of a surreal feeling." She covered the faces of the people with stylized egg heads so that they, too, were hiding secrets.

FLORIA SIGISMONDI: I was into masking persona, masking our true selves. I saw a picture of Habitat [in Montreal] and was intrigued by what it offered, cubes on top of cubes, everyone segregated in their own compartments. We shot one day there and one day in Toronto. It was an arty idea. I don't know if it sat right with the record company. I wrote to him about that and he wrote back saying, "Listen to everyone, but make it your own."

KELLEY LYNCH: He liked how he was shot, looked, etc. The egg heads really blindsided him. This also happened, to a lesser degree, with [one of the] "Dance Me to the End of Love" [videos]. He was in shock. We used to call it "Dance Me to the End of Boredom."

FLORIA SIGISMONDI: I remember meeting him in Montreal outside his apartment, trying to figure out what buzzer is his. All of a sudden I hear "Floria!" I look up and there he is, shirtless, in his window. And there's a beautiful woman behind him. We had all this stuff for him—a cigarette case, a little pipe pin. He beat us on everything. His sense of style definitely stood out. We went with what he had. He had a very peaceful, calm, confident air about him. Confident isn't a word that truly depicts the feeling—it's more than that.

HAROLD ROTH: There's one song on the album that came directly from Zen practice—"Love Itself." I said, "This is the first great American Zen ballad," though it's probably the only one. He just said, "Thank you—that's an honour." He was very humble. And in "Land of Plenty," an un-Leonard-like emotion is expressed—hopeful, almost idealistic, in a way I didn't perceive him to often be.

SHINZEN YOUNG: "Love Itself" is Leonard's version of the *teisho* (Zen talk) of Sasaki Roshi. [He] had only one talk. There is zero, inherently unstable, because it consists of all of the positive and negative in the universe. Therefore, it breaks apart, into expansion and contraction.

Cohen's lyric actually uses a phrase Sasaki Roshi invoked when students didn't understand him—"I'll try to say a little more."

SHINZEN YOUNG: Then Roshi would say exactly the same thing.

LEON WIESELTIER: One of the greatest gifts I've ever been given is that Leonard called and played "Love Itself" and said, "That's your song. I've dedicated it to you."

That summer, promoting the new album, Cohen gave more than one hundred interviews in Europe. After a brief sojourn in Montreal in August, he returned to Mumbai, just in time for one of the seminal dates of the twenty-first century—9/11.

KELLEY LYNCH: He called me because Lorca was in New York. Lorca was hysterical. Cohen was deadly serious, which was his version of hysteria, generally speaking.

A few days later, Cohen saw Ratnesh Mathur.

RATNESH MATHUR: We talked about the Taliban and [how just before] 9/11, Osama bin Laden had got two Egyptians to kill Ahmad Shah Massoud, the Che Guevara [of Afghanistan]. I was surprised Leonard had seen that connection already. He understood the complexity of Afghan politics.

At one Balsekar *satsang*, Cohen met Irish yoga teacher Brian Ingle. He later called Cohen "the most loving and kind person I have ever met." One evening, celebrating his birthday, Ingle invited Cohen for a drink. It was 7:00 p.m. and Cohen said he was about to retire. "But you're Leonard Cohen," Ingle protested. "Brian," he replied, "that's why I am Leonard Cohen."

CATHERINE INGRAM: He loved being in India. He was staying with a family in a guest room. He'd write in the morning, go to Balsekar, come home for lunch, and go swimming at the Breach Club. He really felt he was in heaven.

Before leaving for India, Cohen made another critical and ultimately disastrous decision—he granted power of attorney to Lynch. He also made her responsible in extreme medical circumstances for deciding whether he should live or die.

KELLEY LYNCH: Cohen asked me to execute two powers of attorney, prepared by Richard Westin. Cohen was purchasing a home for Adam, and the title company required these POAs. One was broad and one was more narrowly tailored to the home purchase.

MOSES ZNAIMER: I wondered about leaving things in her hands. We all adored Leonard and nobody said, . . . "You should be really, really, really, really careful." I didn't realize how much signing authority she really had. He gave her everything.

LEON WIESELTIER: He gave her the keys to the kingdom. But he was fond of her. She amused him. He trusted her. She was zealous on his behalf. And they had had an erotic relationship—why should she be any different? But it was apparent to me she was deeply unbalanced—batshit crazy.

Soon after, aspiring Montreal filmmaker Matt Bissonnette sent Cohen *Looking for Leonard*, a feature film in part inspired by Cohen's work. Later that year, playing pool, he struck up a conversation with a young woman named Lorca.

MATT BISSONNETTE: I said, "You wouldn't be Lorca Cohen, would you?" She was. I said, "That's funny, I just sent a film to your father." She said, "That's funny. He just gave me the film today and I watched it."

A decade later, Bissonnette sought permission to use five songs and a poem in another film he was developing, *Death of a Ladies' Man*. Cohen consented and arranged for Sony, which owned the copyrights, to charge a modest fee. The film, starring Gabriel Byrne, was released in 2021.

Returning from India in early April, Cohen immediately went to Mount Baldy to attend Sasaski Roshi's ninety-fifth birthday party.

CATHERINE INGRAM: That night, putting Roshi to bed, Roshi did something he rarely did—he touched Leonard's hand and said, "You have helped me for many years." And Leonard said, "No, Roshi, you have helped me." It made me cry, that story—the beauty and the recognition of it. Part of Roshi's influence on Leonard was about how to be like a man—not a whiner. Deal with it. He was tough, psychologically and emotionally.

Sony was planning to release a two-disc package of *The Essential Leonard Cohen*. Cohen initially balked at including one of his most beloved songs, "So Long, Marianne." The final master had arrived without it. It wasn't an oversight and, as Lynch told Denise Donlon, Cohen "wasn't about to change his mind." Yet without that song, some countries were unwilling to release the album.

DENISE DONLON: How could we call it an essentials compilation without one of the most essential songs? Leonard himself got on the line and insisted the song was never as good in reality as it was in memory, and his fans would understand. Finally, I had to remind him that we didn't contractually need his permission. At that point, the poet was pissed. I literally had to hold the phone away from my ear. Leonard doesn't actually yell, but he was very angry. I said, "I have no choice." He said, "Denise, if you insist on going against my wishes, go ahead, but you need to know that you will forever hold a much smaller place in my heart." The next afternoon, I got an email . . . "Your place in my heart is as secure as ever. That conversation was just business. I kind of enjoyed it. I rarely get a chance to argue with anyone. I'm sorry if I hurt your feelings and I sincerely apologize. I have to answer to my superiors just as you must answer to yours. 'Master Song' or 'So Long, Marianne'—nothing really hangs on this issue. They are all very tiny matters and have no weight at all in the butcher shop we call the world. All that matters here is the heart. So let's keep ours open. Your old friend, Leonard." Even his apology is poetic.

The *Essentials* album, including "So Long, Marianne," subsequently went gold or platinum in several countries. Later, Donlon and Cohen spoke on the phone.

DENISE DONLON: I said the episode reminded me of that joke about the grandmother whose grandson gets swept away by a giant ocean wave. Distraught, she drops to her knees to pray. "Please, I'll do anything. Bring my grandson back." Suddenly another wave comes and deposits the boy exactly where he'd been. She looks at the boy and then at the sky and says, "He had a hat." We both got off the phone laughing.

In 2016, when Donlon was writing her memoir, *Fearless as Possible,* she emailed her version of the story to Cohen.

DENISE DONLON: He might have seen it as me making him out to be crankier than he preferred. Two hours later, he [answered] . . . "Dear Denise . . . I'd forgotten about that incident, but your rendition of it made me laugh. Yes, please publish it with my blessing. Love, your old friend, Leo." He was so uncompromising. He never seemed to be completely satisfied with what he did. "That's as good as I can make it for now." That's what made him great.

When the *Essentials* album was in development, Cohen asked Pico Iyer to write the liner notes.

PICO IYER: He never touched a word. My only challenge was that songs kept on coming and going. He kept on changing his mind. He sent me a list and I wrote the notes. The next day, the list had changed.

The fickleness, Iyer concluded, reflected the many dimensions of Cohen's personality.

PICO IYER: He once told me he could never go to India because it was too disorderly. Some time later, India was at the centre of his life. When I met him on Mount Baldy, he told me he'd given up music and smoking, and could barely remember his career. Four months later, there was a cigarette in his hand and a synthesizer in his room.

BARRIE WEXLER: Leonard didn't view his conduct as contradictory. Long before he met Roshi, he saw everything as transitory. Among the books in his old Aylmer Street bathroom was a book of paradoxes, which had a chapter on Zeno, a pre-Socratic philosopher. I remember him telling me about Zeno's arrow—a seemingly contradictory proposition that motion doesn't exist, that what seems to be changing really isn't. For change to occur, something must shift position. But an arrow in flight, at each instant, exists in a fixed position. It can't move to where it isn't, because no time has elapsed. And it can't move to where it is, because it's already there. So no change takes place. If everything is motionless at every instant, then change itself is an illusion. Leonard lived that way. No one was more centred in the moment than he was. It's fundamental to understanding him.

In *Beautiful Losers*, Cohen had written: "I change I am the same I change I am the same I change I am the same I change I am the same I change I am the same I change I am the same." He called it "the greatest prayer ever learned, the truest of the sacred formulas."

BARRIE WEXLER: It isn't a coincidence that he put those words in the mouth of the character he said was his favourite, Catherine Tekakwitha's uncle, the Master of the Ceremony—the ceremony being young men and women coupling in a longhouse over which he presided. It precedes a passage in which he wrote, "Every change was a return and every return was a change."

Years earlier, Cohen had scrawled "Change is the only aphrodisiac" on the wall of a Paris hotel room. But that line, too, evidenced his willingness to subvert his own thinking. There is no change, yet change is the only aphrodisiac.

BARRIE WEXLER: For someone who didn't view his positions as contradictory, he was a bundle of contradictions. The only thing he was really married to was a little voice in his head that said, "Make something." That injunction was in response to a deeper obligation he felt, to make something in Torah-like terms. Mitzvah doesn't mean good deed or commandment—it means obligation. That feeling is what ultimately drove Leonard's work.

CÉLINE LA FRENIÈRE: Leonard did change his position on matters, serious and frivolous. My reading of it was that he wanted to reinvent himself, constantly—a sign of someone who might not have been at ease in his own skin. He would have been a great actor. Like a chameleon, he would adapt to different people and circumstances.

By this time, singer Anjani Thomas had reentered Cohen's life. She would remain his principal romantic liaison for the next several years. She was fond of recounting how she came to comprehend Cohen's musical objectives. It dated back to the 1985 tour. Thomas, playing keyboards, wanted to embellish his simple tunes; Cohen objected. One day, he asked her to play "a straight, plain C" chord.

ANJANI THOMAS: Years of training and road chops disallowed me from holding to a banal triad. I was so sure the major seven, the sus four, the augmented, the six/nine were better musical choices. I spent the tour in subtle sabotage of his request. I did not care that he didn't like it. I took it upon myself to educate him by example, refining his rough cuts into polished gems. He never asked me to play C again, so I figured he was learning and liking it.

Ten years later, after a marriage to and divorce from LA lawyer Robert Kory—Cohen's future manager—Thomas looked up from her Texas garden to see a bird on a wire.

ANJANI THOMAS: Immediately, the words to his song came into my mind. For the first time, I was struck by the power, simplicity, and purity of C—alone, whole, stacked neatly a third apart. Brilliant, clean, no more, no less. Of course, it was the chord of Cohen. I finally learned to play just as he meant to teach me.

KELLEY LYNCH: She was in his life briefly and, before I knew it, he was buying her a house [a two-bedroom bungalow at 1123 Longwood Place, one block from Cohen] with corporate assets, as he [later] testified. Plant a garden worth more than $100,000. Buy an $18,000 baby grand piano. That was when it became serious.

The Longwood house was purchased for $387,000 in February 2002. It sold for $585,000 in 2010.

ROBERT FAGGEN: That was the shrewd thing to do—a house nearby, proximity and some safe distance. He effectively bought her two houses. First, a house near him—a modest but very nice house. She sold that house without telling him and bought another house in [Sebastopol] in northern California. She sold that, too.

PIERRE TÉTRAULT: He told me once, "I have a great relationship with Anjani. She has her place. I have mine."

BARRIE WEXLER: Some couples sleep in separate beds, some in separate rooms. Leonard slept in separate houses. That started with Suzanne.

LEON WIESELTIER: Anjani? I loved her to pieces. A wonderful woman. She got into Kabbalah and did a whole album of Kabbalah-inspired music. She's a really fine soul, very strong, great inner resources.

KELLEY LYNCH: I got down on my hands and knees and literally thanked the Lord above for [Thomas's] arrival, although she was an absolute lunatic, highly manipulative and spoiled. Later, Lorca and Esther Cohen were concerned [about it]. And he was concerned [by] her demands that she become his power of attorney, if he became ill. He didn't want her to be, but [my having] medical power of attorney caused problems for Anjani and I was replaced by her. They used each other—a relationship of convenience. They basically lived separate lives. I saw it more as a professional, career-building relationship, though they did have a friendship. She wanted me to manage her and I started having to do everything for her, including water her garden.

ARMELLE BRUSQ: Leonard needed a woman on his arm, a woman in love with him, when he returned to the stage. He used her for image, to appear on TV shows with, and so on. On TV, she says love fell on them, it's magic. And he looks at her blankly. You feel he's not in love at all. It's like marketing. She plays the part of the wife, although they live separately.

ROBERT FAGGEN: That's insightful. I don't know that it's entirely true, but it has a kernel of truth to it.

LINDA BOOK: There's that song "Because Of" where he speaks about being older, and women visit him and cover him "like a baby that is shivering." That's how he experienced his last years—a hole, a loneliness.

In one interview, Thomas maintained that Cohen, far from mellowing with age, had become "sharper, more intense. He has no time to lose and [is] very concentrated on the things he still wants to do." She described their domestic life together as being mostly about work, immediate family, and housecleaning. "We are both cleanliness fanatics. If not everything is sparkling, we cannot work. We are so similar that sometimes it's scary." Cohen, typically, refused to label the relationship or even call it one. "This expression," he told one interviewer, "has a menacing, almost sinister aftertaste. Everyone works on their relationship, constantly discussing it, which can only cause grief. [It's] better than love. Love, too, has fallen into disrepute. What we both have is better—there is no word for it. . . . There are no words ambiguous enough to describe what we have." Or, as he wrote in "Thanks for the Dance," "Stop at the surface / The surface is fine / We don't need to go any deeper."

Cohen continued to visit Sasaki Roshi and friends from the Zen community. Steve Krieger, a future head monk at Mount Baldy, met Cohen that year.

STEVE KRIEGER: He was just back from India. I'd be in the cabin with him and Roshi. With Roshi, he was always light, happy, carefree. A lot of the time they'd just be in silence, Leonard sitting with his legs crossed. The connection was beyond words. They would do koan practice together. We talked a lot about writing. He doesn't talk much, but when he does, he usually has something to say.

Krieger showed Cohen excerpts from a book in progress—*Zen Confidential: Confessions of a Wayward Monk.*

STEVE KRIEGER: He liked them. It was my dream that he'd write a foreword, but couldn't bring myself to ask. I didn't want to sour the relationship with literary ambition. But he was really encouraging and at one point said, "Is there anything I can do for you?" I said, "You could write the foreword." He said, "I was thinking that."

In his foreword, Cohen wrote: "This punk of a monk, who should be tending to his own affairs, has decided to infect the real world with his tall tales, and worse, to let the cat out of the bag. And what a sly, dangerous, beautiful, foul-smelling, heart-warming beast it is."

In December, back in LA, Cohen turned up at the Jewish Studies' Annual Conference for a discussion about Leon Wieseltier's book *Kaddish* at the Century Plaza Hotel. Canadian James Diamond organized the panel, which also included Robert Alter (Berkeley), Jay Harris (Harvard), Elliot Wolfson (UC Santa Barbara) and, in response, Wieseltier.

JAMES DIAMOND: Leonard initially said he didn't think he'd be able to make it, though he sent a nice note, and said, "If I'm around, I'll try to come." The day of the event, in walks Leonard with his daughter and Anjani. He basically told me, "I'll sit in the audience. I don't want any attention drawn to me." After, we sat around for a good couple of hours, talking. He was very familiar with Kabbalah. He'd read Gershom Scholem—anybody who's worked his way through it is okay in my book. I was very impressed with his sophistication, surprised by what he knew and the analogies he was drawing. This wasn't a normal bullshitter. From then on, we had an email correspondence.

LEON WIESELTIER: These guys started treating Leonard like he was a scholar, a Kabbalist, an Orthodox Jew, a heterodox Jew—making him over in their own image. I insisted he had the Jewish tradition, knew a ton, but was not a scholar, a Kabbalist, or a rabbi. He's a lover, a poet, a voluptuary, and a singer. But after the session, all the young scholars congregated around him and Leonard was just so happy—this very formidable group, sitting at his feet, laughing with him, completely joyful. He used to refer to the Zen centre as the yeshiva, which in terms of discussion and study and concentration, it was.

In January 2003, Cohen returned yet again to Mumbai—his sixth visit in five years. One morning, he befriended Victoria Robertson, from Brooklyn. She had enrolled in Balsekar's three-day course on non-duality.

VICTORIA ROBERTSON: At the end of the first session, I'm looking for my shoes and I see this man on his hands and knees looking for *his* shoes. He looks up at me and then looks at me again and says, "Would you like to get a coffee?" Of course, my antenna went up. But it's ten o'clock in the morning—what could happen? I didn't know who he was. I'd never heard of Leonard Cohen. As we were going down the stairs, people were stopping to talk to him, women, men. We could hardly get out. I thought, "What's that about?"

At the coffee shop, Cohen introduced himself only as Leo, a name they used for the duration of their friendship.

VICTORIA ROBERTSON: One of Ramesh's books mentioned a singer named Leonard who attended his sessions, so I asked him, "Are you that singer?" He said, "I don't know." But we just started laughing. He was so much fun—hilarious. Everything was just light. We didn't talk about Ramesh. He took the lead in conversation, asked a lot of questions. Eventually, he asked me why I'd come and I told him I had a decision to make—whether to become a volunteer teacher for a meditation organization. He said, "It doesn't matter if you do it and it doesn't matter if you don't." My initial attitude was, he didn't understand the importance of it. Then young Indian guys started coming to the table and after the third time, I said, "Are you famous?" He said, "I don't know." I said, "I apologize that I don't know who you are." He was old-school—such a gentleman.

Afterward, Cohen led Robertson to the Breach Candy Club, which he referred to as an "upscale YMCA." After a swim, he took her to a cybercafe so that each could check email, then to the Kemps Corner Hotel, where both were staying. "It was a real dump," she says. "So noisy." They saw each other briefly over the next few days and, as she prepared to depart, exchanged business cards. "I still did not know who he was." Robertson and Cohen subsequently conducted a sporadic email exchange and occasionally spoke by phone.

VICTORIA ROBERTSON: This man was really smart. If he thought there was something worthwhile [with Ramesh], I certainly could give it a shot. Leonard was a very great force. It was not overt. He didn't pretend he was a teacher. But to have someone understand your mind, it's a different kind of intimacy. That's what we shared. I really needed that. I was in a real low place. To meet someone like that—life doesn't do that. It could have gone either way. He's a lady's man and he definitely knew the words to say, but he never tried to seduce me. I became that meditation teacher and travelled the world conducting retreats, but it was a role I played. And I remembered what he'd said—"It doesn't matter if you do it and it doesn't matter if you don't." That popped into my mind often. It was like a koan. I realized that with non-duality, I was never an assistant teacher. His saying that and my remembering that—it sparked understanding.

Some years later, Robertson sent Cohen a video of a camp for mentally disabled children her father had established in Virginia. The video included an appeal for donations, but Robertson expressly told Cohen, "This is not a request for a donation. I just want you to see the camp." He nevertheless sent a donation for $500.

On an earlier India trip, Cohen had bumped into Amanda Tétrault, daughter of poet Phil Tétrault and niece of Pierre Tétrault.

PIERRE TÉTRAULT: In a city of eighteen million people, she ran into Leonard. The following year, my mother asked me to do a documentary on Phil—so that families living with schizophrenia would know they were not alone. I agreed and said the soundtrack should be Cohen songs. I asked Phil if Cohen might contribute music. One day, sitting in the park, I say, "Let's see if he's there." And Phil goes over and knocks so loud, Leonard whips open the shutters and shouts, "Phil, you don't have to break down the door." It was like a French farce. Anyway, Phil comes back and says, "Leonard's agreed."

Pierre Tétrault was then preparing to fly to India to interview Phil's daughter.

PIERRE TÉTRAULT: We needed to reach Leonard and couldn't. A production assistant suggested I go see the guru—maybe Cohen would be there. So we're standing outside and somebody says, "Anybody have any questions for Ramesh?" I put up my hand. At that moment, we see Leonard walking up the street. We go in—there's two chairs at the front and one is for me. About twenty-five people, including Leonard, are on the floor. Now the teacher asks for my question. I say, "One of my best friends committed suicide. I can't get rid of the thought that I should have picked up on it." Ramesh asks, "Did you choose your parents?" . . . No . . . "Choose where you were born?" . . . No . . . "Choose your brothers and sisters?" . . . No . . . "Your school?" On and on. "If you had so little control over your own life, how can you think you could have controlled your friend's?" I start sobbing. When I stop, I feel a hundred times better, a kind of catharsis. At the end, they did chanting—Leonard was singing. It was truly blissful. After, I introduce myself to Leonard. He says, "I guess I'm meeting all the Tétraults in India." He invites me for tea, so I sit with him at his guru's house, alone—the guru is having a nap. We talk about Henry Moscovitch and Phil and Phil's daughter. I ask if he'll participate in our documentary and he says, "Absolutely, but Phil is the star. I just want to be support."

Back in Los Angeles, Cohen welcomed Pico Iyer on occasional visits.

PICO IYER: The first time I was there, we took two chairs out to his tiny garden and just sat there, silently, for about twenty minutes. I thought, "Maybe this is a hint," and said, "Maybe I should go." He looked at me beseechingly and said, "Please, don't go." And I realized that, for him, this silence was the deepest form of communion, much more than anything we could share with words. In the context of Leonard and Sasaki, silence was their language, and Leonard used silence more powerfully than anybody I met. He was extremely spare with words—an extraordinarily quiet person. The fewer words exchanged, the happier he was. When we'd go for a meal, often with another person, he'd rejoice in being almost entirely silent the entire meal. For a man who had such a command of words, really, he loved saying nothing. When he played new records, I might say something. He'd reply with one sentence—that seemed enough. His emails were usually one sentence long, gnomic, haiku-like.

Learning that his friend Yafa Lerner was dying of lung cancer, Cohen called Don Guy, her ex-husband, and arranged to see her.

DON GUY: Yafa was in a hospice in Berkeley, wheelchair-bound, wearing oxygen tubes, but as feisty as ever. She came out on the deck. I left them alone to talk. I don't remember her dissecting her feelings about Leonard. Yafa accepted who he was without criticism. Leonard was this and Leonard was that—these were just givens.

NOAH GUY: My mother was tough on friends. She could cut people off. That didn't happen with Leonard. He was more of a core friend. She was very particular about who she'd see, even before she was sick. When she got cancer, she refused to have certain people visit. Leonard, she would see.

Lerner died July 13, 2003.

In October, Cohen was inducted as a Companion into the Order of Canada at Rideau Hall in Ottawa. The award was presented by his friend Adrienne Clarkson, then governor-general. He had already, in 1991, been invested as a Member, a lower rung on the ladder.

ADRIENNE CLARKSON: I got up very early because I knew he'd be up. In the breakfast room, he looked at me solemnly and said, "I've been thinking about you. You come here to do this work, and it's like entering a monastery. They take everything away from you. You have no belongings. You just must serve. And you're just you. And you have to exist. You're doing it very well." No other approval has ever meant as much to me.

That fall, Sarah Kramer, an aspiring musician, came to live with Lorca Cohen on Tremaine. They'd attended summer camp together in the Adirondacks in the mid-eighties.

SARAH KRAMER: Leonard called it Jew Camp. That's when I met him—on visitor's days. Later, when I was struggling in LA, Lorca was very generous. She let me move in with her. I was there about two years.

Cohen undertook to make Kramer more financially secure.

SARAH KRAMER: I was "Personal Assistant," but he told me my official title would more likely be "Grapefruit Girl"—I could pick grapefruits from the backyard and make him juice. He'd send me to the ATM to get cash or bring his old Nissan Pathfinder for repair. When he wanted Jew food, he'd send me to Greenblatt's. Every Friday, challah and white daisies. And he'd invite Anjani and Lorca, Adam and his wife, music friends, a sculptor friend from Montreal [Morton Rosengarten]. He'd do Shabbat every Friday, which was special. After the meal, he'd put on an apron and do all the dishes. He really valued home life and tradition.

One year, on Cohen's birthday, Kramer bought him a shofar, a ram's horn used to trumpet the arrival of the Jewish New Year.

SARAH KRAMER: I was surprised he'd never had one. He was so delighted. I think he did try to blow it.

Some time earlier, Cohen and Lorca had planted a tree in his front yard that never grew properly. He referred to it as the "ugliest tree on the block."

SARAH KRAMER: I wrote him once to thank him for a Friday night dinner and noted that the tree had finally grown some shoots. He wrote back, "The tree spoke highly of you too."

If Cohen had been largely an absentee parent in the seventies and eighties, he made a genuine effort in LA to rebuild relationships with his adult children.

SARAH KRAMER: He really wanted to have that and tried to do it around Shabbat—lighting candles, saying prayers, having a sense of sacred intention, but also fun and inclusive. Trying to create the possibility of a special time, no family squabbles or other petty crap, but something inviting focus, mindfulness, holiness.

ROBERT FAGGEN: Leonard wasn't totally irresponsible. He took his role as father, in later years, very seriously. He tried very hard to get both children to come to Shabbat dinners at Le Petit Greek. One time, Adam and Lorca flew to New York from London and didn't tell him. He went nuts, wondering where they were. But the whole scene was kind of nuts, for a family.

Sometimes, Shabbas observance migrated to Shabu Shabu Ya, a Japanese restaurant on La Brea.

SARAH KRAMER: He called them Shabu Shabbas nights. He'd bring all the supplies.

MOSES ZNAIMER: Leonard arrived with a plastic bag, order food, and, when it arrived, take from the bag a fresh challah, a cup for making kiddush and kosher wine. He'd make kiddush, and then dine on Asian delicacies. A Friday night Shabbas dinner. That's a fond memory. I think that's the last time I saw him.

Cohen's thematic choice in local spas, however, was Korean.

SARAH KRAMER: Once, he was in there scrubbing his skin and these elderly gentlemen were there, also scrubbing, and it felt to him a little competitive—who could scrub the deepest. He had me laughing at the idea of this scrubbing competition. I miss his humour and perspective. Leonard experienced life as stories, well aware of what he was receiving or offering.

*   *   *

In 2001, Ann Diamond had captured Cohen's attention by going public with a shocking innuendo. She published a book-length blog that included mention of a chance meeting, years earlier, with Freda Guttman, Cohen's girlfriend in the 1950s. According to Diamond, Guttman asked "point-blank if I thought Leonard had molested his daughter"—as Lorca had allegedly told friends. "I went home and didn't get out of bed for two days." Cohen, understandably, was deeply troubled by the blog post.

ROBERT FAGGEN: Leonard consulted me at length about the horrible allegations. I was in favour of a full public stomping of the rumours—get out in front of it, don't appear to be hiding anything. Leonard was against that path for a number of reasons, and he was probably right.

GABRIELA VALENZUELA: I was devastated to hear such an accusation, but I refused to accept it. That is not the Leonard I knew. What I witnessed was a father profoundly concerned with the well-being of his children, adjusting everything to make them feel they belonged, assuring them that they were his first priority. That kind of parent would never molest his child, who he adored.

BARRIE WEXLER: Cohen faced the wrath of three women scorned: a teenage daughter, lashing out at her absent father, and two spurned lovers—Ann and later Kelley—trying to get even.

KELLEY LYNCH: The behind-the-scenes situation was dicey. Cohen began drafting emails to Ann. He was concerned the *Montreal Gazette* would pick up the accusation. I asked Van Penick [a Canadian lawyer and Lynch's former brother-in-law], on behalf of Cohen, what options he had. I asked Van to write Ann, explain the pressure on Lorca.

ANN DIAMOND: I received an email from Penick saying Lorca was upset and to take it down, which I did, immediately. I never heard from Cohen.

According to Lynch, the molestation charge reminded Cohen that he had once slept with a fifteen-year-old nanny.

KELLEY LYNCH: He told me he had sex with the nanny on the cover of the Phil Spector LP [Eva LaPierre—*Death of a Ladies' Man*]. He told me he had the threesome with her and Suzanne in Montreal. He actually pulled [the album] out and pointed to the woman on the left. He asked me to approach Van Penick, who told me there are no statute of limitations in Canada regarding sex with a minor. This led Cohen to advise me to never permit any licensing of his poem "15-year-old girls" [in *The Energy of Slaves*]. He even asked me to advise his attorneys at the Shukat firm.

ROBERT FAGGEN: Leonard was concerned that in Canada the statute of limitations didn't exist for that transgression. He discussed that with me. He wasn't excessively proud of having nailed the babysitter.

BARRIE WEXLER: Eva wasn't the nanny he slept with. Eva was born in 1947. She would have been fifteen in 1962, long before Cohen met Suzanne or had kids. The fifteen-year-old was likely a babysitter in the late seventies and was in all probability the cause of their final rupture. She was a loose cannon, going to paid sex parties at hotels.

SANDRA ANDERSON: He used to phone me from all over the world. Then he started to go deaf, and we went to emails. But after Ann's revelations, we stopped communication. In the late seventies and early eighties, he'd talk about relationships with high school girls—I always thought it was a con. When I read her book, things started popping back into my head. What about this time, that time? He'd say, "I gotta go pick up my girlfriend from high school." I didn't believe he had a girlfriend in high school, but in retrospect. . . . Lee Taylor [Cohen's nanny at the time] told me she was probably the first nanny he hadn't charmed, enticed, had sex with.

Through much of 2003, Cohen continued to blacken pages of *Book of Longing*. But he was principally focused on assembling tracks for *Dear Heather*, an album for which he'd been paid a $1 million advance. One song eventually included was a live version of "Tennessee Waltz," part of the set list on his 1985 tour. That meant his 1985 band members were owed royalties.

RON GETMAN: One of us mentioned getting a "new use" payment. I contacted Anjani—she and Mitch Watkins had got one. John Crowder, Richard Crooks, and I hadn't. She said she'd tell Leonard. Before the day was done, Leonard called, apologizing all over himself. It slipped through the cracks. He literally, that afternoon, wrote us personal cheques—about a thousand bucks.

Cohen stayed in regular touch with journalist Larry Sloman, signing his emails with "Old Leonard."

LARRY SLOMAN: My email is Newyorkjew, so he'd write, "Dear New York Jew." He was such a sweet guy. My wife was having a GoFundMe campaign for a play, and I sent out a mass email. "Oh, my God," she says. "Leonard Cohen donated five hundred dollars." I called to thank him and he wrote back, "I'd do anything for the New York Jew."

BARRIE WEXLER: Cohen signed correspondence in various ways—Leonard, Old Leonard, Leo, LC, L, and by his Hebrew name, Eliezer. Completely attuned to how the other person needed to see him, he adopted different identities, effectively compartmentalizing his life. He hated Len and Lenny and almost never used them. Suzanne, though, would occasionally refer to him in his presence as Lenny, just to annoy him, which it did.

In April 2004, Robert Faggen invited Irish poet Paul Muldoon to lecture at Claremont McKenna College, near Mount Baldy.

PAUL MULDOON: I accepted on one condition—that he introduce me to Leonard. I started listening to him as a student in 1969 and was a fan in the strictest sense of the word—a fanatic. Once, in Montreal, my wife and I found a stray cat and brought it back into the States. We named it Leonard.

Faggen told Muldoon that Cohen might be too busy to see him; in fact, he had already arranged a surprise meeting at Starbucks.

ROBERT FAGGEN: I said, "I just want to stop and get some coffee," and Leonard was sitting there, waiting. Paul was very grateful.

PAUL MULDOON: His manners were extraordinary. In a strange way, he could have been perceived perhaps as overly gracious, slightly unctuous, oily. But the fact is, he was just a very attentive, careful, and caring person, very thoughtful and engaged. I didn't know him well, but he made me feel very close to him. The other thing that struck me was the intelligence, of a very high order. It's a strange thing to say, but he was even smarter than one expected him to be, and more humble, but not in a humbler-than-thou way. He seemed to me to be a holy person, but he was quite amusing about his spirituality.

Muldoon later became poetry editor of the *New Yorker* and published several Cohen poems.

PAUL MULDOON: I was bold enough to make a few suggestions along the way. I don't recall if he ever changed anything, though I don't think he was averse to that. I treated him as a master, which is what I thought he was.

In June, Cohen's friend, publisher Jack McClelland, died in Toronto, after a long illness.

MARILYN BIDERMAN: They were in the limo on the way to the funeral. All of a sudden, Leonard gets a hankering for candy. So Ellen Seligman [from McClelland & Stewart] and Leonard Cohen come into Shoppers Drug Mart and Leonard wanted Maltesers. He was getting all worked up, like a kid. He really could be playful and fun. He had to have candy before the funeral.

Cohen spoke at the funeral.

JACK RABINOVITCH: We were sitting together, talking normally. He told me he was going to do a record with a Frank Scott poem in it ["Villanelle for

Our Time"]. Between the time he left me and the time he got up to speak, his voice dropped four octaves.

HENRY ZEMEL: He spoke because they asked him, but he didn't want to speak. It was difficult for him. He had to perform. Most people in his position had the performance down pat. Leonard did not. He thought it was brilliant. Then he went to the bathroom and he's standing over the urinal and a guy says to him, "That was really brilliant, but very short."

Cohen's 2004 *Dear Heather* album, his eleventh, was dedicated to McClelland.

PETER DALE SCOTT: The jacket for the CD has a drawing of my father [F. R. Scott] by my mother. I sold the rights to Sony for that drawing. Leonard said, "There's big money in this for both of us—five figures." Every now and then, we get a cheque for $2.45, though I did get a one-time cheque for $2,000, for the drawing. Later, there was a suit against Sony in Canada and I joined the suit. We won. I got a cheque for two or three hundred dollars.

SARAH KRAMER: I played trumpet on that album. Again, it felt like he was just consciously helping me out—I don't think he really needed the trumpet. He came up with the part and played it on his synthesizer. He absolutely loved it and paid me for it. I think he always knew how big a deal he was, but both of us kept our relationship just very real. He treated me like family.

The album is an eclectic pastiche of poems, adaptations, and original tunes. Leon Wieseltier called it "a miscellany of ideas and moods and observations and diversions—the definitive declaration of Cohen's glad loss of interest in the definitive." One track, "The Faith," borrows its melody from a 160-year-old folk song, "Un Canadien errant." Cohen's austere lyric—of its 162 words, only seven are more than one syllable—succinctly condenses the history of civilization, asking God, "Oh, love, aren't you tired yet?"—tired, that is, of the endless cycle of pain and suffering. Other reviews were less charitable. One writer referenced the lyric "Look at me, Leonard" (from the song "Because Of") by suggesting that "nobody around him feels comfortable saying, 'Look at me, Leonard: that one sucks.'"

Initially, Kelley Lynch maintains, Cohen agreed to tour the album. In late June, he set up Old Ideas LLC, planning to assign future musical, literary, artwork, trademark, and other properties to this entity.

KELLEY LYNCH: First, we had to resolve a very lengthy negotiation over the advance. Cohen wanted a million [dollars]. That requires providing enough product—marketing agreements, touring—to jack the price up, since he already had a contract in place. The advance was paid in August/September 2004. The album was delivered immediately after. The marketing and a tour had to be worked out. Cohen objected to Sony demanding specific tour dates, but the tour was conceptually planned for 2005. The fact that the album wasn't well-received informed Cohen's decision not to tour.

ROBERT FAGGEN: We sat in Leonard's car and listened to *Dear Heather*. He never said anything about taking it on tour. I don't know who Heather is and never asked.

In September, in Montreal with Anjani Thomas, Cohen bumped into the young poet Asa Boxer at Coco Rico, a chicken joint on the Main.

ASA BOXER: His first question was, who's son was I?—my father's [Avi Boxer] previous wife or the second wife? We talked about everything—poetry, geopolitics. I gave him a stack of books, eight or ten, to catch him up on the poetry scene. He got through them in about a week, clearly hungry and happy to engage. One was Dennis Lee's *UN*, which he said was over his head. He didn't give or offer advice, but he did say young men often [sought his] advice about love. I guffawed. Because most of his work expresses bafflement at human relationships and love, and self-criticism. At no point did he claim to know what women wanted. How to get laid? Maybe.

One day, Cohen gave Boxer a documentary film to watch.

ASA BOXER: "Watch this," he said. "It'll blow your mind." It was *Life Without Death*, a film about the late filmmaker Frank Cole, who was murdered by thieves in 2000, while crossing the Sahara desert on a camel.

Another day, Cohen told him a story about visiting his barber to get ready for a date.

ASA BOXER: The barber says to him, "Three fucks—that's all you'll remember in your life." Leonard says, "Only three? It's hard to believe." The barber says, "Three." I don't remember the context, but I was entertained by the story, as a metaphor—that there are only a few moments that stand out at the end of your life. Leonard seemed to validate it by telling it. What you do with it is your problem.

Meanwhile, Pierre Tétrault was finishing his documentary on schizophrenia, to which Cohen had agreed to contribute. While Phil Tétrault read poetry in a bar, Cohen was where he wanted to be—in the background.

GERRY FLAHIVE: At the end, I thanked him and he said one of those gracious things that you don't need to say. "If there's anything else I can do for you guys." I said, "As a matter of fact, we'd love to get you and Phil together on camera. Could you do something with Phil tomorrow?"

They set up the next day in Parc du Portugal.

PIERRE TÉTRAULT: Leonard comes out of his house and says, "Does Phil have a drink?" I say, "I don't want Phil drinking for the interview." Leonard says, "What does Phil think?" Phil says, "I could use a beer." Leonard goes over to the *depanneur* and comes back with a six-pack for Phil. Leonard had V8 juice. He wanted to smoke, but was having some trouble with his lungs. Spontaneously, Leonard brought out a book of poetry Phil had given him and says, "Should I read from it?" . . . "Yeah!" So he does sight-readings, incredible, with so much warmth and beauty. This is the wrap for the film, and I thank Leonard and he says, "We have to celebrate." And he goes back to the *depanneur* and comes back with two cases of beer. It [was] the most extraordinary afternoon.

GERRY FLAHIVE: It was a wonderful sequence because it reveals that they were good friends, that Cohen was familiar with Phil's poetry and was a fan.

It pulls the rug out from the audience's expectations—a [person suffering from mental illness] *can* sustain a relationship with a major literary figure and is seen as a peer. He didn't see Phil as a difficult person. He just saw him as a friend and a poet. That really touched me.

Later, Tétrault considered inserting segments of the park bench conversation into the film.

PIERRE TÉTRAULT: At that moment, I get a phone call—Leonard. "I just wanted to remind you of our deal—Phil's the star and I'm the support." I don't think he has ESP, but what unbelievable timing. So we went back to our original idea, just having Leonard at the end.

By now, it was the autumn of 2004. Cohen and Anjani Thomas were savouring Montreal, a city ablaze in its annual riot of reds and browns, oranges and yellows. One afternoon, the phone rang on Vallieres. It was his daughter, Lorca, in LA. "Dad," she must have said, "apparently, there's a serious problem with your bank accounts. You need to come home."

CHAPTER EIGHT

Have I Got a Story for You

Kelley, for me, was a phenomenon—a symbol. She paid for all the other ones he drove crazy.

—Armelle Brusq

He was allowing of the range of depravity and criminality, to the most exalted states. He understood one human could contain them all, because he did.

—Catherine Ingram

Even before he received Lorca's alarming phone call in the autumn of 2004, Leonard Cohen may have sensed that something in his relationship with Kelley Lynch was amiss.

PICO IYER: Before the scandal broke, I was at his house and Kelley came to get him to sign what looked to be a will. Even then, he intimated, weird things were going on.

BERNIE ROTHMAN: I knew a year before it came out. He told me, "Rothman, they're doing it. They're taking everything I ever made."

The full extent of Cohen's losses would take time to assess, but the immediate reality became clear in LA: his bank accounts had been seriously drained.

The allegation ultimately levelled was that, abetted by the power of attorney conferred on her, Lynch had siphoned more than five million dollars earmarked for his retirement and/or estate. She maintained then—and forever after—that she had stolen nothing. Virtually all the money, she alleged, had been spent by Cohen or spent on his behalf; she was merely the victim of an elaborate tax-evasion scheme. Most people rejected her claim, including her former partner Steve Lindsey. He had been battling his own demon—a gambling addiction.

STEVE LINDSEY: Once I hit bottom, she got rid of me [the couple separated in 1997] and bought a [five-bedroom] house [with a pool, on Mandeville Canyon Road] in Brentwood, right when she made the sale [of Cohen's royalty stream to Sony]. She got her father and mother involved and got them a condo in the Palisades, started a vintage greeting cards company.

KELLEY LYNCH: I never helped buy my parents a home. I started Amazing Card Company, in 1998 to '99. I could no longer take working with Cohen, the harassment, and insanity, so I thought I'd start a business that would make people happy. My cards did. It became successful immediately.

Not so successful, according to Julie Eisenberg, briefly hired to work for Lynch.

JULIE EISENBERG: She said [about the company], "This is for [her son] Rutger. I'm not going to be dependent on Leonard." But she lost so much money. She was flushing money down the toilet. She must have had thousands of different cards and there were no orders. If there were, they were for a few cards. The printer printed boxes and boxes and boxes. She paid her parents to hang around. I was getting $25 an hour for waiting around to tape up a box. I had high hopes for a career. I wound up among a bunch of degenerates.

Lynch's mother, Joan, had actually been on the Cohen payroll since 1992.

STEVE LINDSEY: The father was flying to Switzerland, all with Leonard's money. She was buying Rutger, who was sixteen, $70,000 BMWs that he was wrapping around trees and getting him another one, and having car detailers up [at the house] almost every day.

JULIE EISENBERG: She'd tell me not to mention stuff, like Rutger's new car.

A decade earlier, Lindsey had introduced Lynch to Betsy Superfon, with whom he played high-stakes poker.

STEVE LINDSEY: Betsy was living in Malibu, loving her life. I thought she and Kelley would be great friends—they're both sassy. They hit it off immediately.

BETSY SUPERFON: We became very close friends. We did everything together.

Superfon had her own remarkable story. In the early 1980s, she and Joel Eisenberg—father of Julie—had pioneered the 1-900 telephone sex-line business, based in Seattle. Inevitably, she became known as Superphone.

BETSY SUPERFON: It started with 976 lines, sixty-five US cities, thirty countries, and then went to 1-900 numbers—first recorded voices, then live. We had to keep it secret from the phone company. I retired by 1991, before I was forty. I did very well.

STEVE LINDSEY: Betsy probably walked off with one or two hundred million dollars from the business.

The business collapsed after the IRS and FBI began investigating it for tax evasion. Superfon claims to have witnessed Lynch's spending sprees.

BETSY SUPERFON: She could be charismatic and very endearing, a fun girl, up for anything. We'd hop on a plane and go to Vegas or Hawaii. But I never knew where the money came from. She'd go to Neiman Marcus and spend $250,000 on shoes and clothes. At one time, her [credit] card was so far over the limit she had to use my card for $30,000, and wrote me a cheque the next day. She'd go to my jeweler and buy diamonds. Whenever she bought herself hundreds of thousands, she'd buy me earrings or a ring.

She spent like there was no tomorrow. One Christmas, she bought me a pair of $20,000 earrings. It was horrible.

KELLEY LYNCH: I never dropped six figures on jewelry. She must be talking about herself.

JULIE EISENBERG: Kelley says it wasn't [true], but I saw the money she was spending, too.

STEVE LINDSEY: I get a call from Betsy. She says, "She's got all the big suites at the Grand Hawaiian so the kids could have wristbands, but we're all staying at the Four Seasons in the presidential suite. She's buying the kids 24-karat-gold shark-teeth chains—$2,000 each. She's spending money like you can't believe."

PAUL BURGER: I heard Kelley was at the bar in Hawaii buying drinks for everyone—and didn't know anyone. Where the hell did she get money like that from?

JULIE EISENBERG: Betsy was disgusted. She had so much shit to talk about Kelley, but Kelley had taken a lot of Vicodins by then, lost a lot of weight. Betsy shopped a lot, but she'd always come back with lots of stuff from Kelley and gifts for me from Kelley. It was hard to say no.

BETSY SUPERFON: I asked her a hundred times [where it came from]. She said, "I've saved up. I have plenty of money." Three or four nights a week, I'd be at her house, playing poker online or watching a movie. She'd order in dinner—two hundred dollars a night, never let anyone pay but herself. Both boys were indulged. There was no "No" in their vocabulary. There were always packages [arriving].

STEVE LINDSEY: They come home from Hawaii and I get up there and say, "What the hell is going on? Where are you getting this money?" She kicked me out. She goes, "Go fuck yourself. It's none of your business." Betsy said, "I have a sneaking suspicion she's stealing money. There's no way she's making it." She originally told me she was making $250,000 a year. I was making that as a producer and I couldn't live the way she was living. She spent $40,000 on a purse. She's got to be ripping off Leonard.

JULIE EISENBERG: Kelley was a horrible boss. She was really mean to me, edgy, barking orders, telling me I was not packaging her greeting cards right. Betsy loved intrigue, loved to gossip, down to saying that Leonard pimped Kelley out to the monks. The most outrageous things you could imagine. She'd go on and on about Kelley, while pretending to be her best friend.

BETSY SUPERFON: One day, Julie comes home and says, "Man, she is ripping him off blind," because [Kelley] was doing the books.

JULIE EISENBERG: I never saw anything. Kelley wouldn't let me touch her pencil. I didn't get anywhere near Leonard, except for watering Anjani's plants once. I was never allowed even in Kelley's office. But anyone who knows Leonard knows he drove an old Pathfinder and lived in a duplex and didn't live [high].

At one point, according to Eisenberg, Superfon and Lynch met Cohen's investment manager, Neal Greenberg, in Las Vegas. Wearing furs and diamonds, Superfon pretended to be a billionaire, seeking financial advice. The scheme, allegedly, was to induce Greenberg to agree to camouflage Lynch's profligacy by offering him a carrot—the prospect of landing Superfon's "billions" to invest.

JULIE EISENBERG: Betsy straight told me that Kelley had spent all his money, to the point where she [Betsy] had to pretend to be a billionaire so the investment guy would play along with Kelley and let her take out the loans. "Oh, the money is there. It's just loaned out. It's still an asset." I didn't want to say anything because I was living with Betsy, and she got me the job with Kelley. At the same time, I was afraid to not say anything.

KELLEY LYNCH: Greenberg was attempting to procure Superfon as a client and also had his eyes on friends of hers, such as Don Sterling [owner of the LA Clippers] and his wife.

BETSY SUPERFON: I think [Greenberg and Kelley] split up the money. I'd hear her yelling and screaming at him [on the phone]. I'm sure Greenberg rued the day he got involved with her.

STEVE LINDSEY: It's possible she was in cahoots with this guy. She had borrowed and he must have let her do it. I said to Betsy, "You gotta have [Julie] tell Leonard to look into his finances. If I do it, and Kelley gets wind of it—I have a kid with her, I could be sued [for custody]."

The next day, Superfon called a young man named Dannon Smith.

BETSY SUPERFON: He was like a son to me. His mother had committed suicide. He lived with me, on and off. He and Julie became an item. I told him, "What do you think we should do?" He says, "Give me his address. I'll go over there."

Smith, Eisenberg says, was "a superbad boy."

JULIE EISENBERG: He pretended to be a hit man. I thought I was his girlfriend. Turns out he was the sugar boy of some billionaire in Malibu [Nedra Roney, cofounder of Nu Skin Enterprises]. It was all very LA. But someone needed to tell Leonard.

Smith had been married to Roney's daughter, Tarah, when, allegedly, he became involved with the mother. Soon after, Tarah committed suicide. Roney herself died in 2020.

KELLEY LYNCH: [Dannon] heard that I'd gone to lawyers about Cohen's tax fraud—and what he actually told him is, "You can't retire because of this tax fraud." Leonard [later] told me the informant—he pretended it was Julie—had found a letter on my desk that I wrote to the IRS, July 2004, about some shenanigans.

JULIE EISENBERG: I was afraid of Kelley. I was afraid of Betsy. I didn't want to put myself in that situation. I thought, "Betsy is not going to turn on Dannon, this tough guy she thinks the world of." And Dannon was jealous of Betsy's relationship with Kelley. So he wanted to do something against Kelley, just for the hell of it. He shows up one day in one of Nedra's million-dollar Ferraris, picks me up from work. I said, "Someone should tell [Leonard]." He said he'd do it. I ducked down in the car and Dannon goes up to the house.

BETSY SUPERFON: Lorca answers the door. He goes, "You don't know me. You're not going to believe a word I'm saying, but look into your books, because Kelley Lynch is taking every dollar you have."

The woman who answered the door was not, however, Lorca Cohen. It was Sarah Kramer, who was still living in the downstairs unit.

SARAH KRAMER: Leonard and Anjani were in Montreal and Lorca was at work. I was the only one home. A guy came to the door asking for Leonard. He was just delivering the message. He basically said Leonard was down to forty grand in the bank and it was going fast. To prove it, he could look at his credit card receipts. I called Lorca at her store while the guy was at the door. I handed the phone to him and they talked. Kelley had just charged some fancy jewelry somewhere. He named a few recent purchases. Lorca then called Leonard.

ERIC LERNER: I was visiting him when he got a phone call, *the* phone call, warning him to check his investment account. All of his money was gone.

JULIE EISENBERG: Dannon said he said, "Check your accounts. You're going to find the money's gone." And [Lorca] said, "No, no, that's not true. Can't be. Kelley's like family."

SARAH KRAMER: Kelley seemed like part of the family, a very close friend. I was baffled by the fact that anyone who considered themselves a Buddhist [Lynch] could do this. Leonard said, "Happens all the time."

ROBERT FAGGEN: I wrote and asked him if he was still in Montreal. He said, "I'm back and, boy, have I got a story for you." He definitely believed Kelley and Greenberg were in cahoots. Later, there was an admonition from the judge in Colorado: "If you were in the dark, why didn't you read your mail? One way to get out of the dark is to turn on the light." But what Leonard told me, and what he heard from Lorca, who heard it from a friend, was that there may have been other plots afoot.

BARRIE WEXLER: Leonard was his own murder victim, at least monetarily—a victim of his own sensibilities. After Marty Machat died, he needed a counterweight, to allow him to maintain who he was. Marty may have been a gonif, but he was a qualified, experienced professional, which Kelley wasn't. And he wasn't sleeping with Leonard.

JULIE EISENBERG: Betsy said Kelley had spent all of his money, had just had his will changed. It sounded outrageous, but it seemed like Kelley was coming unhinged. She had hidden from Leonard how much she had slipped. Whenever she saw him, she put on her nice face, pulled it together, told funny stories.

Greenberg himself was later disgraced. In 2010, he was charged with fraud and breach of fiduciary duty related to $174 million in losses suffered in 2008 by more than one hundred of his clients. In 2011, he was ordered by a federal judge to pay $330,000 as part of a settlement with the Securities and Exchange Commission. About half of his client funds had been invested with Tom Petters—sentenced to fifty years in prison for running a $3.65 billion Ponzi scheme. Greenberg also invested indirectly with Bernie Madoff, convicted of running a $36 billion Ponzi scheme. Greenberg ultimately lost 90 percent of his assets under management.

ROBERT FAGGEN: The irony was that Greenberg got caught up in the Madoff scandal, so Leonard would have lost all his money anyway. "One way or the other," he said, "I was screwed."

JULIE EISENBERG: When I told Betsy, I didn't say, "I took all that confidential information you gave me and went to Leonard and ruined your shopping sprees." I said, "Dannon knew what was going on. We were just driving home. Oh, that's Leonard's house. You know Dannon. He decided to be Mr. Good Guy. I couldn't stop him." Betsy was upset, but what could she do? Then we waited for the fallout.

BETSY SUPERFON: Three days later, I got a call from Leonard. I'd never met him before. He was very gracious, grateful, lovely. What could he do for me? Any concert—whatever I wanted. I'd heard so many horrible things about him from Kelley—he was so cheap, he was this, he was that. I remember saying, "Anybody who could write like this could not be the way you describe him." So soft-spoken. Every sentence was a piece of art. He said he'd wanted to retire and couldn't anymore and would have to tour. That's what he was going to do. He said that in the first conversation. We had brunch. He was heartbroken that this woman who he loved as a sister—I know she was his lover at one time. But he had moved on. I think she was always after him. But it bothered him, the moral turpitude of it.

JULIE EISENBERG: I got an email from Leonard—very cryptic. "Can you meet?" We had lunch. He'd heard stories about Dannon. He figured out that it was me. He told me I had saved his life. He was very sweet. I was very flirtatious back then. He didn't pick up on any of that. He told me to find a simple life and said something about it being a curse to be born in interesting times.

SARAH KRAMER: Leonard said the girl [Julie] was a Jew, so he always thought she was good.

BARRIE WEXLER: Greenberg was Jewish, too.

JULIE EISENBERG: Later, I had lunch with Betsy and Leonard and said, "It was Betsy's idea to tell you. She was so worried about you." And Betsy's going, "Aha, aha," nodding. Playing every angle.

Years later, Eisenberg confessed to Lynch that "it was my fault that Leonard found out. . . . I felt bad for [Kelley], because she was getting stabbed in the back." Superfon, however, never disclosed the role she had played in telling Cohen.

BETSY SUPERFON: I never admitted it. I told her I knew nothing. I didn't want her coming to my house and shooting me.

In the days after his return to LA, Cohen met twice with Lynch at Starbucks. By October 21, she had been fired.

KELLEY LYNCH: First time, he was exceedingly upset about Superfon, Smith, and Julie. Wanted info on each. Second meeting, wanted corporate records, mentioned my letter to the IRS and offered me anything I wanted. Was calling me at five a.m., pleading with me to meet with him and [tax lawyer Richard] Westin, who was flying in on October 30. He wanted me to assist with the unraveling of aspects of the transactions. I refused. On October 21, Cohen lost it with me over that issue and I informed him that I would never speak to him again.

In Lynch's narrative, Cohen himself siphoned as much as $8 million from his accounts, labelling them as loans, attempting to hide evidence of tax fraud.

KELLEY LYNCH: Cohen was spending way too much money. [Westin] prepared corporate minutes confirming Cohen's loans were dangerous to the corporate structure and should be repaid. Neal Greenberg was saying, "He's spending too much and he's also taking too many loans." Greenberg even wrote [these funds] could be viewed as disguised income. That's what was going on behind the scenes. It's not as sexy a story as a woman who was "my lover, who had a meltdown, stole five million."

Westin, she maintains, also advised her that if Traditional Holdings LLC was deemed out-of-bounds by the IRS, she—its registered 99.9 percent equity shareholder—could be exposed. A new accountant referred her to tax lawyers who, she alleges, found irregularities in Cohen's tax history. She then contacted the IRS. A California court later declared that any interest assigned to Lynch in TH was "[held] as trustee for Cohen's equitable title." The ruling was not appealed.

BETSY SUPERFON: She stood by the fact that *he* stole from *her*—this was her company. Her name was on it. She knew the truth, but she was in total denial. She wasn't going to admit it to anyone. I think she believed her own lies.

Among Cohen's friends and associates, reaction ran the gamut from shock to sympathy to schadenfreude.

ERIC LERNER: The worst part . . . [was] the destruction of his meticulously fortified bunker of privacy. The elegantly reclusive Leonard Cohen was up to his eyeballs in a tawdry rock-and-roll scandal.

Still, when Lerner visited in 2005, Cohen seemed remarkably resilient, saying, "It's amazing, but I really don't feel too bad about all this. I'm still feeling awful about this, but not the anguish. Most things annoy me, but they don't drag me under water."

ERIC LERNER: By then, he'd made several trips to India. I couldn't deny that some fundamental change had taken place. The old boy was genuinely in a better mood.

LARRY SLOMAN: Kelley always seemed incredibly loyal, until I got this insane message saying they were trying to kidnap her. I wrote Leonard immediately—what should I do? He said, "Don't answer—stay away."

PERLA BATALLA: I always felt there was an abrasive energy in that relationship. I never said anything, but I'd get an earful from his sister. Leonard was very trusting, but I don't always think he had the best taste in the people he chose to surround himself with.

TERESA TUDURY: Leonard had this uncanny ability of pulling in people who betrayed him.

NANCY BACAL: Leonard didn't trust any of his managers. This is too strong a word, but he was a bit of a wimp sometimes. It was hard for him to cut the tie. Leonard made a lot of questionable choices. They all wanted his income.

BARRIE WEXLER: I never understood—and told Leonard this—how he could vest his affairs with Kelley. I never understood their rapport. She wasn't like anyone I'd known that he'd ever been attracted to. She was street-smart, but in terms of experience, had only been Marty Machat's assistant. He prided himself on being a student of human nature, but was eventually blindsided by his own. It's almost as though, unconsciously, he set up a scheme with a fatal flaw. The crack may be how the light gets in—it's also how things eventually fall apart.

ROBERT FAGGEN: Leonard and I joked about how he had stepped into the cliché—the manager robbing from the artist, preoccupied making art. He wanted to trust certain people to take care of things. The problem is, who can you trust and for how long? He probably thought Kelley was a shark who would take care of business but not turn on him. And they had had a relationship. The dynamic of that is too hard to ascertain. I'm sure she cost the estate a million dollars or more. My sense of it is, Machat had robbed from him and Kelley was just taking lessons from the master.

EDWARD SINGER: When I heard the news, I asked Harry Rasky, his friend, "Did he shtup her?" "Edward," he said, "how could you possibly, for even a second, think—" He paused a long beat, then erupted in laughter. "This is Leonard we're talking about. Of course, he was shtupping her!"

ASA BOXER: Leonard suffered from the Prospero syndrome—the desire to set aside fame and fortune to pursue higher immaterial objectives. In the process, one neglects one's worldly responsibilities. Like Prospero, Cohen returned from his spiritual studies to find his fortune—Prospero's kingdom—claimed by another.

DIANNE SEGHESIO: I *loved* Kelley. We were friends. Leonard loved Kelley. I was heartbroken. We all were. And shocked. That was the heartbreak. How could somebody you loved and trusted—I mean, he gave her everything. She was family. How do you explain that?

GORDON COHEN: If you were his friend and he trusted you, he trusted you. That's what happened to Lynch. Trusting means trusting. I have investments with a Canadian bank—I still add things up every few months. Leonard never checked.

JAMES DI SALVIO: I can't blame Leonard for not seeing that one coming, because she dazzled—she did. I liked Kelley. We'd go out for a few Hollywood nights and laughs. Some things you can go, "What the fuck was he thinking?" With her, you can't.

DON IENNER: Kelley was a great ambassador for him. She worked very hard for him. She was a good spokesperson in relation to what he wanted and what his needs were. I was as shocked as anyone to hear she took advantage of that.

OLIVER STONE: It was not a pretty story. I never talked to her about it, but it sounded pretty authentic. He seemed a very honest man. I saw him afterward and he was shocked and quite broke, but not despondent. He was angry with Kelley because he claimed she had mismanaged quite a number of funds.

PICO IYER: Those people who say he was guilty of inattention might well be right. I said to him, "This is what all those years at the monastery were about—training for losing everything." He acknowledged that and said, "If it were just me, I'd let it go. But I worry for my kids and grandkids." That really weighed on him.

CATHERINE INGRAM: He wasn't paying attention because he trusted her. He had this line, "Cath, I now have to spend my days with forensic accountants and lawyers. . . . I haven't been in a bank or a post office in twenty-five years." There was no anger. It was tiring. There was a pain-in-the-ass element to it. Later, when she was harassing him, he had a kind of lightness. This is how humans behave. It doesn't mean there's nothing good about her. He'd even occasionally say nice things about her.

STEVE KRIEGER: He took the situation seriously, but he kind of admired her chutzpah.

ALLAN MOYLE: They had a great run, because he trusted her completely. Afterward, I get all these calls from Kelley, trying to tell me her story. Why tell me? I'm not the judge. She was insane and ranting, meandering. Leonard smiled when we talked about it. He let it go. I'd be angry, wouldn't you?

LEONARD COHEN: My friends were surprised at my rather passive response. It's the oldest story in Hollywood—everybody gets taken. I suppose I wasn't really fundamentally surprised. The emotion I mostly experienced was boredom. I had to spend an enormous amount of time with lawyers [and] forensic accountants. I said to myself, "If God wants to bore me to death, I guess that's the way it's going to be."

SANGYE KHANDRO: I was shocked. I still have a hard time believing all that. I think there's more to it, because my impression was they had a very beautiful, synchronistic relationship. They had fun together. She was close with his children. She seemed to be doing a great job. I think he truly appreciated it. Kelley is such a unique person, incredibly savvy, intensely involved with the Buddhist thing and her work for him. Or you could argue she snowed him over and he had no ability to see what she was actually doing.

DON WAS: She had a breakdown. She was very cool for a long time, devoted to Leonard. And she lost her fucking mind. I saw her getting weird. When I heard about this, I said, "I get it." Until that happened, I had great respect for her. She truly pissed it away.

BARBARA DODGE: I would have blasted her with a gun—I was so angry. Then I thought, "If you're having meetings in the bathtub, like you did with me, trying to entice her to get in, I'm glad she screwed you. You're an idiot. Why would you do that?" That's the part of Leonard I despise. Why lower yourself to this cast of people who play games with their life force? But it was endemic, part of the cultural moment.

STEVE MACHAT: It was one of the most brilliant, Machiavellian moves I've ever seen. He allowed her to steal—it's not a theory. He set Kelley up to rob him and then never paid the IRS the money, because she stole it. He knew she was stealing it. He went away and left her with the kitty.

PETER KATOUNTAS: Gary Young told me Cohen felt guilty about money because he didn't have to work hard to get it. He almost wants to part company with it. It came to him easily and other people had to work. And he was not very protective of his money. Do you just hand over [control of] five million bucks to someone?

DIANNE LAWRENCE: I was surprised he hadn't taken responsibility [for] his money. "You gave her total control? What were you thinking?" . . . "Darling, I wasn't thinking. That's the problem." [Kelley] was nuts, but that relationship, his money woes, are on Leonard. I couldn't talk to him about this. For that kind of information, there was a wall.

MARILYN BIDERMAN: Ellen Seligman had Leonard on speakerphone in her office and he said, "Ellen, I don't have enough money to buy a cup of coffee," which wasn't true. But he was shocked at his own naiveté.

In fact, Cohen was far from impoverished. Although most of his savings were gone, he still owned houses—in LA, on Hydra, and at least three properties in Montreal—collectively worth several million dollars. Moreover, the asset sales to Sony in 1996 and 2001 only included publisher's rights to the catalogue royalties. Cohen had retained the writer's share of these revenue streams.

PAUL BURGER: I couldn't believe these stories. They seemed too fantastical. I heard from Leonard that she had embezzled him. I heard from Kelley that it was all bullshit. She'd been incredibly dedicated to Leonard. Who was the real Kelley? Had I been duped? To this day, I don't know what the reality was. There'd been a personal relationship. Maybe all of this was a reaction to Leonard saying, "It's over and we're not going back there." In our last real conversation, I said, "Maybe I could help mediate." He was like, "You don't understand it." He cut me off after that, one of the saddest things I've ever experienced. I reached out by email. I got one or two fairly terse emails. I tried to phone—didn't succeed. He probably didn't know which side I was on. I guess he felt completely confident that he'd been taken to the cleaners.

DAVID PULLMAN: I couldn't believe this was true. It seemed so unfathomable. There was nothing grandiose about her. I did notice as the emails went on, she seemed to unravel. I sent her to a lawyer I liked, Bert Deixler. He refused to take her case. Didn't believe a word she said.

Cohen had reached out to Pullman, looking to sell another tranche of intellectual property.

DAVID PULLMAN: We meet at the Four Seasons. He did have rights that had not been sold. He was deciding what he might do. And he's got to go back on the road, has to prove he took a loss in order to take a deduction. Which is insane, because now he has to spend more money on legal fees. He's in a black suit with a tie. He tells me he wears the same thing every day because it gives him structure. Made his life easier, in a Zen way. Then he says—he gets it right out of the way—"Yes, I slept with her." Early on, long ago. And he liked her family. Then he tells me the story. She spent the five million. "What do you mean, she spent it? It's not possible. It's not like she bought buildings or invested in stocks and bonds." He says, "She's a big spender. Retail stuff. Birkin bags." But that's only about $5,000. "No, no. They've got better ones. Thirty thousand dollars. Made of ostrich. She was spending up to $250,000 a month at Neiman Marcus." He goes through the whole thing—I'm getting upset just hearing this. And he's so calm. And I say, constraining myself, "Aren't you angry?" To which he immediately says, "What good would that do?" It was unbelievable. His response will stay with me for the rest of my life. Because he was so right. What good would it do?

MARCIA RADIN: I said, "Well, Leonard, if this is what it takes to get you back to writing songs and singing, so be it."

PICO IYER: It was harrowing for him. He told me things that never came out in the press. He felt it was an even more serious event than the one we know about. I can't share [it all], but he was deeply rattled and not by the financial aspect. One thing I remember him saying was "Somebody's next to you for eighteen years, sometimes as your lover, friend, protector, guardian, voice in the world, and suddenly that happens, and you think, 'One of my closest friends in the world—was I duped from the get-go?'" I don't think he could explain it—to himself. I think some of the later songs deal with this Kelley conundrum—what went on? To sit calmly in the face of the inexplicable is one of the gifts he offered.

Reading about the Lynch debacle, Barrie Wexler met Cohen to discuss it at Peet's Coffee on Larchmont—resuming a friendship severed for more than fifteen years. Ironically, they were living only a few blocks from each other.

BARRIE WEXLER: Leonard did pay selective attention to his affairs when something needed a decision—scanning documents, asking questions. But that's a far cry from putting professional oversight in place. The reason he didn't do that was because he trusted his trust of Kelley. His blind spot wasn't his faith in her, per se. It was wrapped up in the notion of trust itself. That was why her betrayal shook him to the core. It made him question his trust in himself.

Somehow, they started talking about the song "Chelsea Hotel."

BARRIE WEXLER: I asked him how he got the line "I can't keep track of each fallen robin," because it seemed heaven-sent. Quick as a wink, he replied, "Rhymes with Joplin."

Despite the reconnection, the Cohen-Wexler relationship was never quite the same.

BARRIE WEXLER: It took a while before we got around to talking about Suzanne. We cleared it, sort of. The conversation wasn't easy. I think he still resented the betrayal.

ARMELLE BRUSQ: [My theory is], Leonard asked Kelley to cheat and she cheated for herself. But she was a very sad woman. She had no chance—completely in love with Leonard, completely jealous of any woman around him, completely destroyed by his attitude towards her. He was still playing with his charm, because he can't help it. He's *le grand manipulateur.* If you read his work, he's completely honest. He's going to cheat on you. He's not good at loving you. She was so bitter. She fell into his trap and he didn't care. It's a kind of game he has with life and women. It's always the same.

BETSY SUPERFON: She did this to get back at Leonard because he didn't want her anymore. She tried to get back with him, and he didn't [want to]. That's what broke up her relationship with Steve [Lindsey]. She was having an affair with Leonard. It was very tangled.

JULIE EISENBERG: Leonard would have been honest, and probably told her what she didn't want to hear, when she needed to hear it most. She resented aspects of his life and his relationships, and these resentments caused her to look elsewhere, to tell herself it meant he didn't actually care. It was easier to hear what Betsy had to say—false flattery, delusional plans—beyond enabling, actually encouraging wrong behaviours, the pills, the lack of accountability. She never saw what was coming.

With the IRS threatening to seize assets for nonpayment of taxes, Cohen turned initially to lawyer Scott Edelman, at Gibson, Dunn & Crutcher, a prominent LA firm.

ROBERT FAGGEN: Leonard joked that they had chairs and carpets worth more than his house. Tens of thousands of dollars were spent and they weren't getting anywhere. He was not happy. His reaction to Kelley was, "Shit, I've got to respond to this because I owe the IRS money, so I have to prove it was stolen in order to explain why they're not getting it." His attitude was "I don't want to be bothered with this." He was well aware of the vulnerability lawsuits can expose you to.

It was through Anjani Thomas that Cohen eventually found his way to Robert Kory, her ex-husband.

ROBERT KORY: Leonard was facing complete financial disaster, a result of the malfeasance of his advisers. By 2005, we had stemmed the bleeding. I managed to deliver a million-dollar tax refund, based on the taxes he had paid on the money that had been stolen.

ROBERT FAGGEN: Kory was good at taxes—Leonard would give him credit for that. The Kelley thing continued to bother him and he was worried about it. There were things he was vulnerable on, and Kory was best positioned to deal with it. Kory's partner, Michelle Rice, worked brilliantly on the Kelley case, and Leonard had real faith in her. She worked her ass off.

Initially, Cohen attempted to solicit Lynch's help in suing Neal Greenberg and his firm, the Agile Group.

STEVE LINDSEY: Leonard wanted to go after [Greenberg] for malpractice. Kelley had nothing left. She was getting crazier and crazier. She calls me at eleven a.m., obviously drunk, screaming, "You fucking asshole. Why can't I play ping-pong with you and Dr. Dre?" I went to lunch with Leonard and his lawyer. They were just trying to give her a walk and get [Greenberg], and she just wouldn't do it. Her whole thing was, Leonard was dragging her into tax fraud.

BETSY SUPERFON: Cohen and Kory went after Greenberg because he had the deepest pockets and insurance. One plus one equals two. I went to a couple meetings with her at Kory's office. But they were not going to get blood from a rock.

KELLEY LYNCH: Around May 2005, Superfon advised me that Cohen was remorseful, I was the love of his life, and he'd give me whatever I wanted to settle. I asked to be paid what I was owed. Kory offered me 50 percent community property, my share of the value of the corporations, commissions, anything I wanted. They were confident I had causes of actions against everyone who represented Cohen and would assist with those claims, if I agreed to mediate. I authorized Superfon to ask Kory to fax the deal they had in mind. He told her it's not the type of deal one can fax. If I was the calculating, money-hungry woman Cohen and company claim, I would have taken the millions offered, all monies due, lied about anyone they asked, and preserved my life. Once they understood I went to the IRS, which was naive, they retaliated. It's that simple.

Lynch alleges that Cohen's lawyers used restraining orders to prevent her from obtaining tax information that would prove Cohen owed her millions of dollars. According to Cohen's subsequent deposition, Lynch told Kory, "Hell will freeze over before you find out what happened to the money. It was my money."

KELLEY LYNCH: I believe I may have said, "Hell will freeze over before that happens," stood up, and left.

A particularly sorry episode occurred on May 25, 2005: a SWAT team descended on Lynch's Mandeville Canyon home, responding to a call from an unidentified party about a hostage-taking —presumably her younger son, Ray Lindsey, whom she had kept home from school. At one point, Lynch—outside in a bikini, with her Akita—quipped to the police, "Who am I supposed to be holding hostage—my dog?" Then she dove into the pool. Handcuffed, she was driven to King/Drew Medical Center, forty miles away, administered antipsychotic drugs, and kept under observation for twenty-four hours. Soon after, Steve Lindsey—Ray's father—filed for custody and ultimately won. Lynch was detained again two weeks later after a minor traffic accident and again hospitalized in a psychiatric ward, this time for a few days. Lynch saw both of these events as being orchestrated by Cohen, Lindsey, and Kory, to discredit her. By December, she had been evicted from her Brentwood home. For a short time, she lived on the beach in Santa Monica.

STEVE LINDSEY: She could have had a deal, could have kept the house, which she let go into foreclosure.

BETSY SUPERFON: I'd take her for a meal or check her into a hotel. The third time, I get a call from the manager—because it was on my card—she's sleeping with half the guys in the hotel. She had a sister in Texas, but they had a contentious relationship. She had no other girlfriends.

By then, Lynch had begun sending hundreds of vitriolic emails to Cohen and leaving angry phone messages.

NANCY BACAL: She harassed him. He'd say, "Listen to this." It was Kelley— squawk, squawk. It was very hard on him.

On August 15, Cohen filed suit in LA Superior Court against Lynch and Richard Westin, alleging fraud, breaches of contract, and fiduciary duty. Forensic accounting by Kevin Prins concluded that Lynch had siphoned more than $5 million from various Cohen corporate entities, trusts, and personal bank accounts. Prins's affidavit documented the full extent of Cohen's losses, including electronic funds transfers from accounts, and shareholder loans made payable to, endorsed by, and deposited in Lynch's account. Neal Greenberg effectively confirmed this narrative in his own complaint, stating that Lynch had withdrawn some $3.5 million in shareholder loans from Traditional Holdings, without Cohen's knowledge or consent. Lynch maintained that "the so-called cheques [were] unauthenticated and taken out of context," and "conceivably represent corporate distributions for corporate taxes, distributions for promissory note repayments, authorized by Cohen." The following May, the court entered a default judgment against Lynch for a total of $7.341 million, after finding that she was not the rightful owner of any Cohen assets. The Westin case was settled by mediation. No money was ever recovered. Thereafter, Lynch mounted a relentless campaign of harassment and vilification, besieging Cohen with irate phone calls and threatening emails, often dozens each day. It was this conduct, not the alleged theft, that eventually put her in jail: On April 17, 2012, she was sentenced to eighteen months in prison and five years probation for what Judge Robert Vanderet called her "unrelenting barrage of harassing behaviour."

*   *   *

In November, Cohen learned that his old friend, poet Henry Moscovitch, had passed.

HOWARD ASTER: Henry was in terrible shape. Abandoned by his family, he'd been living in a halfway house, diagnosed as a paranoid schizophrenic. He was a chimney. His mouth was burned from the smoking. I published his last book [in 1982]. Cohen offered no money, but sent a poem—the first in the book.

BARRIE WEXLER: Henry was Leonard's psychic alter ego. Leonard was fascinated by diseased minds, as though examining what his own mind might be like if he ever completely lost it. But he was too controlled for that.

In the poem, Cohen wrote, "In wilds of poverty and solitude; I thank you for the years you spent alone with nothing to hang onto but a mood of Glory, searching words that Love could not elude."

HOWARD ASTER: The secret about Henry and Cohen is in that poem. The envy went the other way. Cohen envied Henry's brilliance, and it's absolutely legitimate.

Meanwhile, Cohen needed new management—Kory was then only handling the tax issues. Having drinks one day at the Four Seasons, he bumped into Vancouver talent manager Sam Feldman.

SAM FELDMAN: I was well aware of Leonard and pretty much in awe of his work. We met in LA and later in Toronto, and ultimately struck a deal. But part of the terms was that I also manage Anjani. He said, "She's recorded an album of my songs [*Blue Alert*] and it's really important that we make a record deal." I heard it and thought, "Pretty good," So the first order of business was to make a record deal.

Feldman then accompanied Cohen and Thomas to meet Sony executives in New York.

SAM FELDMAN: There's about ten of the top folks there, Donny Ienner on down, and they were concerned. This type of music is not easy to sell. It needs a lot of publicity. Leonard said, "That's not a problem because I'm going on tour pretty soon, and I plan to have Anjani open the show every night. If you can get press—television, print, appearances—I can be part of every interview. These are my songs and they mean a lot to me." [Sony] brightened up and, lo and behold, we made a deal. Then we got in the elevator and Leonard looked at me and said, "Just let them try to find me." I was, "Oh, fuck."

ROBERT FAGGEN: In the version I heard, Sony, in which he had little faith, was enthusiastic about the album. I somehow doubt that Leonard would have acted in complete bad faith about doing publicity, though he hated doing interviews. Joint events with Anjani would have probably been okay.

In fact, Cohen did several tandem interviews to promote the project. To celebrate the deal, they went to dinner at Caviar Russe, on Madison Avenue.

SAM FELDMAN: We're drinking vodka and eating caviar and I said, "C'mon, Leonard, let's break the bank, really celebrate." So we're going for it pretty good and Leonard at one point stopped and said, "The sturgeon general has decreed that excessive consumption of caviar can be hazardous to your wealth." I had to mortgage my house to pay for the dinner. Leonard was a lot of fun, a really down-to-earth guy, apart from his high form of art.

ROBERT FAGGEN: Leonard often used this kind of wordplay to characterize screwups. "Hands in the air mother-stickers, this is a fuck-up!" Of course, caviar was one of his favourite extravagances.

The spanner in the works, Feldman discovered, was Thomas.

SAM FELDMAN: She became a bit diva-esque. She went from demure to pretty aggressive after her record came out. She probably thought she'd become a star. When that didn't happen, she wasn't going to blame herself.

Meanwhile, Feldman was trying to douse fires ignited by Kelley Lynch.

SAM FELDMAN: She was starting to put out terrible publicity about him and he had to respond. He didn't know what to do. I said, "I have ideas, but let's get some serious folks." So we went to New York and got some damage-control people. I'd like to think I did help, to the extent that he [wrote] saying, "You saved my life. You saved my ass."

In managing Cohen himself, Feldman needed to review contracts and the status of his catalogue.

SAM FELDMAN: We were having trouble getting information from [Kory], which put me on alert. And then [Leonard] fired us, because we could not make [Anjani's] record successful. She wasn't doing what she was supposed to do. He wasn't doing any publicity. So it was "This isn't working. That [record] was my whole raison d'être, so I love you, bye." We parted on good terms. He was apologetic, and wanted to remain pals. The penny dropped when I found out Kory became his manager, and had previously been married to Anjani. You can't write this shit. If I had to read between the lines, it felt like Anjani had a fair amount of control over Leonard. But through this whole period, I liked him a lot. I hold no malice. One of the most, if not *the* most, charming people I've ever met, especially around ladies. Women would fall at his feet. I saw it.

The bizarre Kory-Thomas-Cohen triangle at once baffled and troubled Cohen's friends, but he largely deflected their concerns. He was also immersed in a new project—filmmaker Lian Lunson's *Leonard Cohen: I'm Your Man*. A 104-minute documentary, it combined talking heads, including Cohen's, with clips from Hal Willner's tribute concert at the Sydney Opera House in January 2005 (featuring Nick Cave, Rufus Wainwright, Martha Wainwright, and Kate and Anna McGarrigle). Although Cohen was supportive of Lunson's film, such projects made him inherently uncomfortable. Once, at a lunch, someone asked him if he'd seen Tony Palmer's 1972 documentary, *Bird on a Wire*.

PICO IYER: And he just snarled and said, "Why in the world would I want to watch a documentary about myself?" He was so horrified at the idea of watching himself that his absolute grace cracked for a moment. What he might have been saying in that snarl of impatience was "I've worked so hard to demolish the myth of the self, the public persona. Why would

I want to invest in it?" It goes to what his childhood friend Nancy Bacal said, about "leading from behind." He was never the centre of the room. In fact, I always felt he wanted to be the shadow on the wall. The last thing he was interested in was himself as a public figure or eminence.

BARRIE WEXLER: All true. At the same time, Cohen masterfully projected that shadow, like a holograph, from the wall to the centre of the room. After all, he spent forty years promoting his public persona in interviews, photographs, documentaries, biographies. He was deeply invested in those activities, though he'd take the air out of them in conversation.

In fact, of course, Cohen was closely involved in the making of Palmer's film, though his unease at watching himself on celluloid was completely genuine. That sentiment may have played a role in the definitive documentary that film producer Robert Lantos had long lobbied to make.

ROBERT LANTOS: He was not receptive. He said, "I don't have the time, don't want cameras all over me, people harassing me." I said, "What if we limit your involvement to three days? I don't need to make any money. It's all yours. I can get you a big up-front fee." Finally, he said, "Okay, but three days."

Cohen wanted a female director and, after Lantos secured interest from the CBC, that meant a Canadian.

ROBERT LANTOS: I finally picked someone, showed him her film and he liked it.

Lantos's choice was Patricia Rozema, already a fan of Cohen's work. They eventually decided to call the film *How to Be Happy*—the same title of a Cohen poem. Cohen and Rozema met several times over the next several months, both in Toronto and New York.

ROBERT LANTOS: It didn't end well. The director then did everything I promised we would not do. She got his email and his phone number and was all over him like a groupie, constantly, long before the contract was even signed. Finally, he sent me an email—"This is off"—and explained the harassment. I said I would fix it, but he said, "No, it was a bad idea."

BARRIE WEXLER: It was more likely an excuse, made up or not. Leonard routinely got cold feet and retreated from projects. In part, it was instinct about the venture, which his nonconfrontational nature took to the last possible moment to convey. But collaboration also implied loss of control. And he was terrified at seeing his work or, for that matter, his life, in someone else's hands.

New Zealand filmmaker Barbara Sumner and her Montreal-born husband, Tom Burstyn, had secured funding for yet another Cohen doc—about the women in his life.

BARBARA SUMNER: We had more than enough to make the film. Then we got a cease-and-desist notice [from Cohen's management]. This caused the broadcaster in Canada to pull out. We heard Cohen contacted a number of women we had agreements with and they withdrew. No messing with the myth allowed.

Returning to Montreal, Cohen hosted transplant pathologist Kim Solez and two women involved in organizing annual Cohen tribute events in Edmonton.

KIM SOLEZ: He took excellent care of us. We started on a Friday and had a Sabbath meal with green candles and a lot of cheese. He claimed not to remember much from his 1966 Edmonton visit. He said forgetting was convenient—his life would be a complete chaotic mess if he actually remembered everything. I didn't introduce a single subject. It was all him, asking me stuff. He invited us back on the Sunday and went out to buy us chicken.

Back in LA by October 2005, Cohen was interviewed by Norwegian journalist Kari Hesthamar, who was working with Marianne Ihlen on her memoirs.

KARI HESTHAMAR: He was waiting for me outside, in a suit, and had bought cakes. He invited me to join the Friday night dinner with family and friends, and took me to visit his old teacher from Mount Baldy. I played the radio documentary I'd made about Marianne in his living room. He listened to [it] in Norwegian, while reading an English transcript—feet on the table, travelling in his memories. That was a special experience, and kind of brought her into the room. I learned that silence is of great importance in an interview. Out of that arises something [other] than self-presentation. We spent quite a lot of time together saying nothing.

Although many felt that Ihlen never really recovered emotionally from the rupture of the Cohen relationship, Hesthamar thought otherwise.

KARI HESTHAMAR: My impression is that Marianne moved on. She had a long marriage with Jan Stang. At the same time, those years on Hydra were formative. They treasured those years and each other's friendship. They were so young when they met, and youth shapes us and represents something special.

Cohen himself was brutal in his own self-appraisal. But, as with Solez and others, he professed amnesia.

LEONARD COHEN: I don't have any memories. . . . I don't remember the life I was leading before I met Marianne, or after really. . . . A lot of sunlight . . . and then just working. Trying to answer some invitations to make something beautiful or significant or anything, even if it isn't significant or beautiful, just to make something. The inner voice seems to be saying: "Make something!" It's always been like that. So I never had any choices, any real serious decisions. In fact, I don't think I ever made a decision [in] my life. It just unfolded that way. Always responsive to that impulse of blackening a page, or finish a song . . . a consuming, engrossing work. . . . And then there were the other appetites; for women, for beauty, for sunlight, for applause, for fame, for solitude, for spiritual enlightenment. And as they arose . . . I ignored some and heeded others. But it seemed to be all part of the same activity.

BARRIE WEXLER: Leonard remembered everything. Once, talking about a girl we'd both known thirty years earlier, he recalled a small heart-shaped birthmark beneath one of her breasts—though we argued over whether it was below the left or the right.

That same month, Cohen successfully filed suit to recover a veritable treasure trove of notebooks, photographs, correspondence, and business records stored in Lynch's garage—moved there when Cohen's own garage was converted into a studio and apartment.

ROBERT FAGGEN: When he saw his notebooks from her garage covered in bird shit, he was in tears.

In January 2006, Cohen's friend, poet Irving Layton, passed away at age ninety-three. Cohen flew in for the funeral and served as a pallbearer. "Irving would have been very angry if there were this many people here and none of his poems were read," he said in his eulogy. He then read Layton's "The Graveyard," which ends with the lines: "There is no pain in the graveyard, for the voice whispering in the tombstone, rejoice, rejoice." He then added, "Whatever was between Irving and I does not bear repeating. But what does bear repeating and will be repeated endlessly are these poems, which live and will continue to live." Two of Layton's ex-wives were present.

HARRIET BERNSTEIN: Given the love between Irving and Leonard, and given Irving's fury at me, I reckoned it was likely Leonard didn't have a lot of great feelings about me. However, there was a moment when the service was over, and I was struggling to avoid the cameras, and a hand came out of the throng and took hold of my hand, and it was Leonard. He saw what was happening and pulled me back. He helped me get away. That was magical. He was like a saviour at that moment.

ANNA POTTIER: Leonard came up afterward, hugged me really tightly, looked me straight in the eye, and said, "Thank you for all that you've done. I know how happy you made him." There were no recriminations.

After the funeral, Cohen attended the shiva at Bill Goodwin's house [Layton's nephew], where he had "a touchy conversation" with poet David Solway. There was, Solway concedes, "a certain estrangement, not that we were ever close."

DAVID SOLWAY: There were two things I was never sympathetic to. One was his flirtation with Buddhism. I always thought it was absolutely silly. The whole idea of a monotheistic God who created this world and whose angel touched Jacob on the thigh. It's the foundation of the state of Israel—"he who contests with God." It's who we are as a people. I don't see how that fits in with all the nirvana-mongering in Buddhism, this nonexistent power that is not a power, which releases you from the burden of consciousness. The Lord of our faith requires that we are intensely conscious of who He is and what He demands of us, even if we fail. Leonard was in contradiction, it seems to me. It's an intellectual flaw and you're entitled to your own flaws.

BARRIE WEXLER: There was no contradiction between Leonard's Buddhist affiliation and his commitment to Judaism. They have much in common, including how they view the ethics of reciprocity that govern behaviour. It wasn't that he was flirting with Buddhism—it was that in Roshi he found the lifelong partner that he hadn't with a woman.

The other divide was political.

DAVID SOLWAY: Leonard wasn't really left, he wasn't really right, and he wasn't really centre. I found his politics tepid. He wouldn't commit, though as a Buddhist perhaps it's not so easy to commit. He was the high priest, a bit above it all. I don't think we can be above it all. It's nice to play your guitar on the border of Gaza, but we can't be out of it. Judgment is part of the Jewish tradition. People lionized Leonard, a god on earth, placed him on a golden pedestal. My take is not motivated by anger or love or resentment. But I say what I see. Leonard was not dissimilar. He said, "I'm far beyond this travelling pack of poets." I would have liked to respect him more.

Meanwhile, Ellen Seligman, at McClelland & Stewart, was editing Cohen's long-promised volume of poetry *Book of Longing*. Indeed, the book had been so long in gestation that he jokingly referred to it as "Book of Prolonging."

MARILYN BIDERMAN: Leonard never had a literary agent. In effect, M&S was his agent and I, as subsidiary rights manager, was responsible for selling the rights internationally. We spoke and wrote often—he'd often have Bob Dylan on in the background. He was not interested in the business side. His concerns were more about layout, design, translation, covers. Advances, royalties—he wasn't interested. He trusted me and would say, "Whatever you say, Marilyn." But he insisted that the cover for each international edition had to be his drawing. The Spanish put a picture of him smoking on one book and he was furious. He was incredibly humble. When he came to Toronto to promote the book, he sat in the front seat with the driver. What other celebrity does that?

At one point, walking Cohen through a complicated foreign rights offer, she said, "Do you want to write something down?"

MARILYN BIDERMAN: He said, "Actually, Marilyn, I'm in the bath." He knew the power he had over women and he used it. Not in a way I found offensive. He was always a gentleman, so deferential—though Ellen did tell me he once greeted her at his hotel room door in a towel. She just ignored it. They had a very special relationship. But he really was a spirit—a tiny man, very private, very centred.

Dedicated to Layton, *Book of Longing* was finally published in the spring of 2006. In it, he included translations of two Lorca poems he had worked on—"The Faithless Wife" and "Lorca Lives." Gabriela Valenzuela had helped him with the translations in 1986.

GABRIELA VALENZUELA: It's exquisite. I didn't translate the poems, but interpreted them as a story. It was an homage to our favourite Spanish poet. We laboured a long time, trying to understand the architecture of Lorca's work.

We dismantled each word—breaking it, reconstructing it, and underlining it until it shone, forming an X-ray of Arabic-Spanish linguistic culture.

BARRIE WEXLER: Leonard was also impressed by another Spanish poet, Juan Ramón Jiménez, who had taken Lorca under his wing. He once read Ramón's "At First She Came to Me Pure" out loud on Hydra, and said it was everything you needed to know about poetry. He particularly liked the title of the volume, *Diary of a Newlywed Poet.*

Quebec poet Michel Garneau was again asked to do the French translation for Quebec.

MICHEL GARNEAU: We met and took some pictures and there was an incredibly short conversation. I said, "Have you looked at my translations?" He said, "Yes, very satisfying." I laughed and he laughed.

CHAPTER NINE

Standing Room Only

Leonard was a good man with desires, and he had the courage of his desires. The man who seeks forgiveness even as he seeks experience: he is the hero, or the antihero, of all of Leonard's work.

—Leon Wieseltier

His gift was being big in an ordinary way, even more than it was being big in the extraordinary way. The way he was ordinary, he was incredible.

—Sarah Kramer

The extraordinary third act in the life of Leonard Norman Cohen—selling out vast arenas, finding new audiences and, not incidentally, earning millions of dollars—began with an otherwise obscure British concert promoter named Rob Hallett. Everyone else in the pop world had written Cohen off. He was in his early seventies, had not performed for more than a decade, and had never developed more than a cult following in North America. Hallett, however, was convinced he could mount a successful tour. It wasn't just about money. Cohen had been a factor in Hallett's life since his teenage years. He'd read every poem and knew every album, including bootlegs and cover versions. He once attended seven consecutive Cohen concerts.

ROB HALLETT: The man is an artistic god in my eyes. I was doing some of the biggest acts in the world—Prince, Michael Jackson, Backstreet Boys, Beyoncé. I said, "What's the point, if I can't promote my favourite artist? I've got to get Leonard out."

As early as 2004, Hallett had pitched the idea to his bosses at AEG, but got nowhere. Then he got lucky. Hoping to replace the millions drained from his investment accounts, Cohen and Robert Kory were also mulling a comeback tour. Kory called John Meglen, AEG's president of global touring.

ROB HALLETT: Meglen goes, "There's this guy Hallett who's been going on about Cohen." Then Robert calls me and I go, "Finally!"

ELLIOTT LEFKO: Hallett sat down with Robert and Leonard and told him, "You could tour and make a bunch of money. You're undervalued." Leonard was saying, "On the one hand, I never thought I'd tour again. On the other, I could use the money."

ROBERT FAGGEN: Hallett was the orchestrator of Leonard's tour and comeback. He really appreciated Leonard, could quote many of his poems from memory. He wanted the tour to meet Leonard's standards.

ROB HALLETT: The first thing I say to Leonard is "Can we take a picture together? Just in case this is the last time we meet." I told him I'd lived my life by a couplet from one of his poems. "I will not be held like a drunkard under the cold tap of facts / I refuse the universal alibi." That line resonated. Whenever my mom said, "You can't get in the music business," I refused to be held under the cold tap of facts. Dare to dream, basically. He was impressed that I knew his stuff.

ROBERT KORY: Leonard was very reluctant at first. Touring had always been a disaster. He'd say, "Performing is an opportunity for a thousand humiliations."

ROB HALLETT: He said, "You must be joking. What if no one wants to see me? What if I'm no good anymore? I don't know if I can do it."

Others, too, questioned the idea.

JUDY COLLINS: When Kelley Lynch happened, I said to Nancy Bacal, "Do you think he'll go out on the road?" She said, "He doesn't go out of the house. I don't know how he'll go on the road."

DAVID AMRAM: He took me for an osso buco dinner with Anjani, and he was happily retired. She said he only left the house to get a kosher hot dog. He had enjoyed being with the band, but said, "I don't really miss it at all."

BARRIE WEXLER: He did like hot dogs. We once drove to Jeff's Gourmet Sausage Factory for a late-night nosh—spicy all-beef kosher variety.

It would take Hallett two years, and some hoop jumping, to persuade Cohen.

ROB HALLETT: Leonard said, "You're such a good tour guy? Get Anjani a tour. Then we'll see how good you are." So I put together a tour for Anjani. I got her opening for Rod Stewart in Copenhagen. That was one hurdle. Later, I did a NEeMA tour, again at Leonard's behest. It didn't set the world on fire.

NEeMA was Montreal singer-songwriter Nadine Neemeh, a protégé Cohen had met in the 1990s. Out of their initial conversation emerged a relationship—coffee dates, walks in the park. Cohen started to draw her. She shared her writing.

NADINE NEEMEH: A lot of things were very dear to both of us, our deep spiritual quests, the Semitic background. . . . He taught me to dig deeper, to speak from a more personal voice. . . . Sometimes it was, "I don't hear the song here. Your idea is great, but you should just start from scratch." I'd be crushed. Then I'd wake up with a whole new motivation. Sometimes, we'd work on it together or he'd give me some writing assignment. . . . He'd give feedback on instrumentation, voice, everything.

Later, it was Cohen who suggested using the title of his portrait of her as the title of her second album—*Watching You Think.* When her sister died in 2009, Cohen checked in every day.

NADINE NEEMEH: Once, on video chat, he said, "Let's dance." And he started dancing in front of the screen—this seventy-something old man. He always knew the right thing to say. Poetry wasn't just in his work, it was in his life.

She was struck particularly by Cohen's focus.

NADINE NEEMEH: If he's doing the dishes, he's really doing the dishes. If the light bulb needs to be changed, he'll say, "That needs to be attended to." Everything is in its place. Attention is brought to so much of what he does and how he lives.

Meanwhile, Anjani Thomas was completing *Blue Alert*. The album had begun after she stumbled on Cohen's handwritten lyrics—"There's perfume burning in the air / bits of beauty everywhere." Soon after, she wrote the "Blue Alert" melody to go with the lyric. Cohen, impressed, then gave her material for additional songs. Eventually, Cohen called John Lissauer.

JOHN LISSAUER: He says, "Something's wrong with it. We did it so stark, just her, the piano and synthesized bass and drums." I said, "I'd use soft, subtle, sexy drums and a real bass player and some touches." We did some very nice things. He and Anjani were fighting nonstop. There was so much tension between them, part of which—this isn't public knowledge—was that I'd met Anjani in 1982. She'd come to New York to work with me. I'd just gotten divorced. We were getting fairly close. But I had said, "Never another singer, ever." And I kept that rule up. But Leonard said, "Just so you know, Anjani's been in love with you for twenty years. You're the only man in her life." Meantime, she'd married [and divorced] Kory and been with two other guys. I said, "No, we're friends and that's all it will ever be." But she was using that against him. It was a triangle that didn't exist, except in theory, but she was using it, feeling it. So it was tense—"I don't like this . . . I don't like that." They ended up throwing out things. By the time they were done, they were back to the original demo. I ended up on two songs. But she's a great singer, the most sensuous. It ended up sounding like a demo. It wasn't taken seriously. Leonard had this perverse . . . "I love that it's all cheap electronics." I wanted the quality of Norah Jones. "Oh, no. We're gonna keep it stark."

ANJANI THOMAS: We had great hopes for John's arrangements, and the contributions of other musicians, but felt in the end they were not in keeping with the ephemeral spirit we were striving to capture. Leonard and I agreed we should keep the focus on the voice delivering the lyrics. It was nothing personal. We both love[d] John dearly and were sad that he took it so hard. Another way to explain the situation would be to say that we had created a bowl of pearls sitting in the moonlight, and John added so many rubies and emeralds that suddenly the luminescence of the pearls was diminished.

On May 13, 2006, promoting *Book of Longing*, Cohen made his first public performance in thirteen years, singing with Ron Sexsmith and the Barenaked Ladies at Toronto's Indigo Books.

DEB FILLER: He forgot all the words to his own songs. Backstage, I said, "Want to hear a joke?" . . . "Absolutely." He had a real bulldog of a [handler]—she was not happy. All these celebrities dying to talk to him. But he listened to that joke, eyes down. His focus was pretty extraordinary. This is the joke. Weinstein goes to a doctor—everything aches. After tests prove inconclusive, the doctor gives him a jar and tells him to go home and provide a semen sample. He goes home and tries with his right hand— nothing. He tries with his left hand—nothing. His wife tries with the right hand—nothing. Left hand—nothing. She tries with her teeth—nothing. Without her teeth—nothing. He goes back and puts the jar on the desk, empty. "Mr. Weinstein, where's the semen sample?" Weinstein says, "I tried with the right hand—nothing. Left hand—nothing. My wife tried, right hand, left hand, with her teeth, without—nothing. And still we couldn't get the jar open." Lenny grabbed my arm and said, "Thank you, thank you. Can I use it?"

On the same trip, Cohen dropped in to see his book editor, Ellen Seligman.

MARILYN BIDERMAN: He wanted us to hear [Anjani's] album—Ellen, Leonard, and myself. We put the CD into my computer. He stood there with his eyes closed, concentrating on the music. He was, in the most sincere, spiritual way, devoted to the way art could transcend all the ugliness of the Earth.

In June, after Thomas performed at the Montreal Jazz Festival, Cohen invited the backup band to his house.

LOU POMANTI: It was monk-like, almost. It didn't look like anybody had touched the decorating since 1977. Kitchen appliances looked like they were from the fifties.

LEON WIESELTIER: He wanted it to be real, not opulent. Hydra is a humble house. South Tremaine was a very humble house. He didn't like grandiosity. I once bought him a little vessel, from New Mexico, and sent it with a note, "A humble vessel." He never stopped remembering that little note.

Sitting around, Cohen dispatched Pomanti to pick up smoked-meat sandwiches. He soon returned with sandwiches and a brisket for himself, to take home later.

LOU POMANTI: I said, "Leonard, put this in your fridge for me, but don't let me forget it when I leave." So he's drinking red wine and chowing down on a big smoked-meat sandwich. I said, "I thought Buddhist monks didn't drink or eat meat." He said, "I'm a Buddhist monk when it's appropriate." With the band, he could occasionally be a little raunchy, tell an off-colour joke. A normal guy. We must have been there until about four a.m. Sure enough, I leave the brisket. I call from the cab—he says to swing by on my way to the airport. I tell him it'll be early—he says no problem. "I barely sleep." My cab pulls up at six a.m. There's Leonard in his suit and fedora, holding my brisket. A total classic. That's how I'll always remember him.

Cohen's visit coincided with the death of his cousin, Edgar Cohen, with whom he had a close bond. Leonard attended the shiva every evening. The next month, in New York, Cohen joined his sister, Esther, Eric Lerner, and Lerner's daughter, Sara, for dinner at an Italian restaurant.

ERIC LERNER: This was the dismal period between dead broke and vindication. I suggested a bottle of Barolo. . . . By the time she finished her first glass, Esther was transformed before our eyes, shedding years and tears, and cares, widowhood and cancer . . . her eyes full of . . . good mischief. . . . We referred to the occasion forever after as the Barolo Night with Esther.

Back in LA, Cohen and Thomas attended the wedding of record producer Larry Klein and Brazilian singer Luciana Souza, at Ohr HaTorah Synagogue in Venice Beach. At dinner after the ceremony, Cohen was seated next to Rabbi Mordecai Finley, who had officiated.

MORDECAI FINLEY: I didn't know who he was. I didn't know his music. He was clearly a deep, thoughtful guy. He'd been intrigued by my presentation— ten contrarian commandments for a good marriage. Deep stuff, told in a serious way. Anjani loved it. Leonard liked it. He was interested in my brand of Judaism, which I called post-Orthodox-neo-Hasidic. He chuckled at the acronym. I called my wife afterward and asked her if she'd heard of Leonard Cohen. She almost fainted. I felt bad. I'd been in the presence of a great man.

Also at the table were the shul's cantor, Willie Aron, and his wife; playwright David Mamet, and actress/singer Rebecca Pidgeon. Aron and Pidgeon were performing at the Hotel Cafe in Hollywood two days later.

WILLIE ARON: He grabs his little spiral notebook. . . . "Give me the address," not thinking he'd show up in a million years. They both come. He was quite taken with the show.

Finley was no less astounded when, the next Saturday, Cohen and Thomas turned up for Sabbath services.

MORDECAI FINLEY: Anjani wanted to come for the spiritual psychology. She encouraged him to come, knowing he'd connect. They became regulars, attending weekly. Once, at lunch, he asked a group of people if they'd like him to recite a poem, based on a sermon I gave. People expected a brief gem. This poem had maybe twenty stanzas. He wrote that in about a week.

RUTH BROYDE SHARONE: He'd sit in the front row, right. He had his eyes closed, but you knew he wasn't sleeping. When Leonard wasn't there, Rabbi Finley would read his poetry and talk about conversations they'd had.

Sharone had recently torn up the grass outside her Culver City home and built a rock garden.

RUTH BROYDE SHARONE: I had a party and invited everyone to bring a stone and create a peace mandala. Leonard couldn't come, but the following week brought me the most exquisite black stone with oval, concentric rings of different colours. Really gorgeous.

DINAH BERLAND: One day, at lunch, I asked him how he decided whether he was going to write a poem or a song. He said that when he had an idea, he would start to write, and it would tell him whether it would be a lyric or a poem.

When another congregant expressed delight that Cohen had found a place to practice Judaism, he pointed to Finley and said, "It's not because it's Jewish. It's that man that I come for. I'd follow him if he were flipping burgers"—a variation on his oft-used line about Sasaki Roshi. Soon, Cohen and Thomas started attending Finley's classes on *Mussar* [moral discipline], and *Chasidut* [the teachings of Chassidism].

MORDECAI FINLEY: Leonard would sit in the front row, shoes off, cross his legs, close his eyes, and, when I was done, say, "Beautiful teaching, Rabbi. Loved it." I treated him like everybody else. After a few weeks, I asked what was drawing him here and he said two things—that "this place is not uptight," and that I was a healer. Leonard and I became close, but never chummy. He actually was much more comfortable around my wife, whom I think he truly loved.

WILLIE ARON: He loved Mordecai. He loved that he was an ex-military guy [a sergeant in the marines] also deep in matters of the spirit and could discuss great literature, the Upanishads, Kabbalah, intellectually on the same plane.

NANCY BACAL: Finley was very important to Leonard. He really liked him.

MORDECAI FINLEY: In our email correspondence, he called himself Old Priest and I called myself Old Sarge. He never called me by my first name. He called me Reb, and asked me to call him Eliezer.

In time, Aron, too, became Cohen's friend, although there was "always a veil, a certain distance we respected. We emailed constantly, but I never had his phone number and never spoke to him on the phone. At the synagogue, people were respectful of his privacy and his personhood." Cohen's relationship with Finley deepened after Finley's wife and Thomas became friends.

MORDECAI FINLEY: Leonard and I were a little stiff around each other. Our conversations were limited by my teaching. I was his rebbe. He wanted to talk about what I taught, far more than his poetry. [We] only talked about deep stuff. We weren't able to chitchat. I think the authenticity of my Kabbalistic practice and knowledge spoke to him. But when the women became friends, he and Anjani were invited over. The first time was Succoth, with David Mamet and his wife. The men sat on a back porch and sipped whiskey. We talked about where our ideas come from.

Cohen repeated another well-known line, "If I knew where the good songs came from, I'd go there more often."

MORDECAI FINLEY: We all felt we were in the service of the Muse (the *Bat Kol*). We tried to channel her. We had to be careful around her. I remember we all stopped talking at once, agreeing silently that She did not want people talking about Her as if She weren't listening. We stopped and went back to drinking and swapping jokes. Man, I loved his laugh. He would have a visceral experience of pure joy at a punch line. The torment would cease for a moment. That's when he and I thawed.

Finley's approach to Kabbalah stressed its Gnostic and neo-Platonic origins.

MORDECAI FINLEY: If you don't understand the former, you can't understand Kabbalah. Leonard really dug that. It opened up probably our most profound connection—Gnosticism. In his core, he's a Lurianic, Gnostic, quasi-Sabbatian. The Torah is given to refine us intellectually, morally, and spiritually. In the Gnostic perspective, traditional life is more like an impossible box we're disfigured into—a violation of our spirit. In many ways, Leonard believed the world we live in is impossible. Gnosticism is expressed in Lurianic Kabbalah by the breaking of the vessels. [Our] world is one level up from Hell. The vessels break, so the light of God is shattered. The fragments fall and create the lower realm, the Gnostic underworld. The shards of light are hidden by husks, so the world we live in is profoundly inhospitable. Leonard was well-versed, but he became better versed. He had the key books in his library. He'd read Gershom Scholem's classic, *Sabbatai Sevi*, and nearly everything on Kabbalah that I'd read, including Daniel Matt's masterful translation of the *Zohar*. But [he] had never really had a rabbi steeped in it from an academic perspective. The one issue in dispute was, I offered a path of repairing the broken vessels. Leonard could not accept that suture. He said the human condition is mangled into a box into which the broken soul does not fit. We all chafe, terribly.

ROBERT FAGGEN: He liked Finley and would send me his sermons. But we both agreed the pulpit rarely got into things that made people love God. And Leonard wanted to love God. I have no doubt about that. That was a very deep part of him. He once said, "A lot of people talk about God, but how many talk about loving God?" He also talked about God as a bipolar maniac whom it is our task to heal. *Tikkun Hashem* [heal God], not *tikkun olam* [heal the world]. God was fractured.

BARRIE WEXLER: Leonard said something had been lost with each generation of Jews wanting to speak to God. Today, for most Jews, it was enough that they knew the basic story. I asked him what came next and he quipped, "I *heard* there was a story." When we talked about Scholem's books, he said something about finding a way to plug the hole made by the loss of God, without falling through it. He was always looking for a passport to the spiritual source of his Jewish roots.

Cohen with his friend Gisela Getty, backstage at a Hollywood nightclub, late 1970s. (*Courtesy of Gisela Getty*)

Canadian actress Andrée Pelletier, Cohen's lover from 1976 to 1978. (*Courtesy of Andrée Pelletier*)

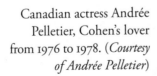

Cohen with his children, Adam and Lorca, mid-eighties. (*Courtesy of Steve Zirkel*)

Cohen with his 1988 touring band. Back row, left to right: Bobby Furgo, Bob Metzger, Julie Christensen, Steve Meador, Steve Zirkel, and Tom McMorran. Front row, left to right: John Bilezikjian, Leonard Cohen, and Perla Batalla. (*Courtesy of Steve Zirkel*)

Cohen with girlfriend Felicity Buirski, circa 1991. (*Courtesy of Felicity Buirski*)

Cohen's girlfriend Linda Clark, circa 1988. (*Courtesy of Linda Clark*)

Cohen's friend Evangelia Papaioannou, whom he met in 1988 and to whom he spoke fluent Greek. (*Courtesy of Evangelia Papaioannou*)

Cohen with members of his 1993 *The Future* touring band. From left to right: Bill Ginn, Paul Ostermayer, Jorge Calderón, Leonard Cohen, and Steve Meador. (*Courtesy of Jorge Calderón*)

Cohen with girlfriend actress Rebecca De Mornay, 1993. (*Courtesy of Jorge Calderón*)

Cohen with his friend Steve Sanfield and Joshu Sasaki Roshi at the Zen master's eighty-fifth birthday party, 1992. (*Photo by Dan Farber*)

Cohen with his friend Professor Robert Faggen. (*Courtesy of Robert Faggen*)

French documentary
filmmaker Armelle Brusq,
circa 1996. (*Courtesy of
Armelle Brusq*)

Cohen with his friend writer Catherine Ingram.
(*Courtesy of Catherine Ingram*)

Cohen with friend Ratnesh Mathur in Mumbai, 1999. (*Courtesy of Ratnesh Mathur*)

Cohen with girlfriend
singer-songwriter Anjani
Thomas, circa 2007.
(*Courtesy of
Dominique Boile*)

Cohen's friend
writer Pico Iyer.
(*Photo by Derek Shapton;
courtesy of Pico Iyer*)

Cohen at his LA office in Larchmont Village with his French biographer, Professor Christophe Lebold (centre) and Zen dharma brother Jack Haubner (aka Steve Krieger). (*Courtesy of Robert Faggen*)

Cohen in concert, circa 2013. (*Courtesy of Paolo Brillo*)

WILLIE ARON: In Kabbalistic terms, he thought it was our collective destiny to repair the broken God, "one customer at a time." But Leonard believed in his own destiny. He often talked about how he knew, from a young age, that he was going to be "a leader of men."

Finley later introduced Cohen to the thinking of Rebbe Yakov Leib HaKohain (né Lawrence Corey), a spiritual descendant of the Dönmeh, a neo-Sabbatian sect of Jews in the Ottoman Empire who converted publicly to Islam, but retained their beliefs. Cohen became his friend and patron.

BARRIE WEXLER: The Sabbatian approach emphasizes redemption through sin. Leonard said for him, unholiness, as a path to the divine, was perfect.

ROBERT FAGGEN: Leonard was very fond of Leib. We discussed his postings and broadcasts often, at great length. I don't think Leonard thought he was too far out. He thought he had the fire. Hour for hour, Leonard was more preoccupied with that kind of thing than he was with a lot of other meshugas. Theologically, the connection with Leib was deeper than his connection with Finley. Leonard distinguished between loving religion and loving God. That distinction was important to him. God was a real presence in his life.

YAKOV LEIB HAKOHAIN: Leonard said, "I've got your back," and he did, for the next eleven or twelve years. My number one friend, my spiritual patron. Without him, I would not be here—literally. He was a great tzaddik himself.

In general, according to Finley, Cohen "had a low tolerance for bullshit."

MORDECAI FINLEY: He saw all through people. He'd say, "Reb, that guy's a real fucker," He could be just lacerating. So he's gracious, genteel, chivalrous, but could not stand a pompous ass. The other thing he liked was my focus on good thinking as a spiritual practice. Because he could not stand lazy thinking. When I gave talks on how to think clearly, he was deliriously happy.

Predictably, Cohen became the shul's top benefactor.

MORDECAI FINLEY: He was incredibly generous—mildly solicited. When he came back from [one] tour, he handed my wife a cheque for $200,000 and said, "This is for you, honey." A one-time gift. Other gifts were smaller, but we couldn't have survived without it. He helped fund our preschool as well. He always handed [us] his cheques in person. On one visit, he spent a full afternoon with the prekindergarten kids—the teachers almost fainted. And he let me borrow a copy of a sefer [a book] his grandfather wrote. A true rabbinic classic—beautifully written.

*   *   *

In the early 1990s, composer Philip Glass had been commissioned to write songs for poems by three Canadians, one of whom was Cohen. In turn, Cohen had attended several Glass concerts. The two men had another, more tenuous, connection; sitarist Ravi Shankar, one of Glass's seminal teachers, had been the lover of Cohen's friend Nancy Bacal. Some years later, in LA, Cohen read to Glass excerpts from his draft manuscript of *Book of Longing*; Glass then proposed creating an evening of poetry and music inspired by it, and Cohen agreed. That idea remained on hold until 2003, when Linda Brumbach and Hal Willner staged *Came So Far for Beauty*, an evening of Cohen songs performed by Anjani, Antony, Laurie Anderson, Perla Batalla, Nick Cave, Julie Christensen, Lou Reed, and others.

LINDA BRUMBACH: I asked Philip, "Is it time now?" He wrote a letter and seventeen minutes later, he heard from Leonard, "Let's do it."

Later, Brumbach, Cohen, and Glass met in New York to discuss the collaboration.

LINDA BRUMBACH: Philip had poems he wanted to write for, and clear ideas—a cello part, violin, oboe, and four singers. It was very clearly mapped out as a song cycle. He asked Leonard to record the poems, so he could listen while composing. What changed in that meeting was that Leonard was doodling, and I asked him what they were. He said he had hundreds of drawings and paintings. We hadn't thought about a visual element, but I asked him to see them. He sent me this insane amount of stunning artwork, really mind-blowing.

With Cohen's consent, Brumbach later hired Montreal-born, Tony Award–winning set designer Christine Jones to incorporate the art into the evening.

CHRISTINE JONES: I wanted to use these drawings as part of the landscape we'd create. They were really part of a meditation for him. He drew every day, as consistent in his practice as one would be doing daily exercises. He took it seriously, despite the fact that the drawings themselves are whimsical and sketch-like. He gave me access to his entire collection. He was curious about using technology to enhance his drawings. The earlier drawings used Xerox machines—he'd make copies and do layers or change the colour. Then he was using a [tablet], digitally drawing with a pen. He had taught himself—he was always exploring and playing with different tools.

For show director Susan Marshall, the Cohen-Glass collaboration was a perfect fit.

SUSAN MARSHALL: It's like they were tickled pink to be in each other's presence. So much respect. They would crack each other up. They had a similar style of giggling, where they just went silent and shook.

LINDA BRUMBACH: It was like they'd been family their whole life. An unbelievable chemistry, so much love on both sides. It was almost like they had this language together for fifty years.

In June 2007, *Book of Longing*—Glass's ninety-minute song cycle—premiered at Toronto's Luminato arts festival, the inaugural show of its inaugural season. The work featured four singers, Cohen's recorded voice reading his poetry, eight instrumentalists, and rear-screen projections of fifteen pieces of Cohen's art. At the dress rehearsal, Cohen went straight to the singers.

SUSAN MARSHALL: He gave them an essay to read, "How to Speak Poetry" [from *Death of a Lady's Man*]. It's a don't-chew-the-furniture essay—say the words, don't emote, don't overdramatize. I was both crushed and grateful, because the singers were [trying] to be simple and elegant, yet allow the songs' dramatic arc to come through. We'd been looking for [a balance] and Leonard comes in—boom—and made it very clear which path we'd take. No more negotiation. The show took a huge jump after that.

Cohen's message—don't embellish, make the words, not yourself, the star— was the same mission statement he had drafted for himself when he started to perform in 1967.

ALISA REGAS: His words were always short, sweet, and to the point—whatever everyone needed. I was looking after press materials and sent them to him. He wrote back, "Sorry, friends, this is just too dull. And besides, they left out my bar mitzvah."

Awaiting opening night, the inevitable question arose: Would the experimental marriage of Glass's music to Cohen's words and art actually work? The show drew a sustained standing ovation. Glass and Cohen came running from the wings to rapturous applause.

LINDA BOOK: Leonard's face was wreathed in a smile from here to here. It was Sally Field's—"You like me, you really like me." He looked like a three-year-old who'd been given his first bubble machine. It was stunning because he's so in control of his presentation. The performances he gives are very orchestrated, with few spontaneous occurrences.

Christine Jones couldn't make the opening; she was giving birth to a son in New York. Cohen thoughtfully sent an email welcoming Ever Reverend Jones into the world. Later, the show played to sold-out houses in Charleston, Chicago, New York, Stanford, London, Cardiff, Groningen, Madrid, and Adelaide.

LINDA BRUMBACH: I've got a hundred emails from him, so sweet. "Are you sure you want me to give a talk, and not have all the focus on Phil? What does Phil prefer?" He wrote that he regarded it as a fraternal collaboration for which he was deeply grateful.

ALISA REGAS: He wrote and said, that a man with Philip Glass's gifts had found his work useful made him feel somewhat useful himself.

The Luminato show coincided with *Drawn to Words: Visual Works from 40 Years*, an exhibition of Cohen's art at Toronto's Drabinsky Gallery. The show was the result of what he called "the incessant prodding" of Manchester art dealer Richard Goodall, who had initially pitched the idea to Kelley Lynch.

RICHARD GOODALL: After extensive correspondence, projections, etc., she invited me to LA. Afterwards, she told me things were progressing and she was discussing it with Leonard. Then nothing. Much later, I got a call from Robert Kory. They found [our] correspondence in a crate seized from Lynch's place, which they had no idea about but looked very interesting. It progressed from there.

Having conferred power of attorney to Lynch, and already in the dark about the Goodall discussion, Cohen might never have seen any serious revenue from his art.

For the Toronto show, gallery director Linda Book and Luminato producer Clyde Wagner flew to LA to choose the art.

LINDA BOOK: I was on *shpilkes* [Yiddish, for nervous] to meet Leonard. We get to the door, and Clyde says, "I have to ask a question. Which one of us gets to sleep with him tonight?" Leonard came with Anjani. The pictures were spread out on a table—originals. He called the work "acceptable decorations." He was very modest about his ability to draw. I share that assessment. If he's not Leonard Cohen, troubadour, the show would never be mounted. They are very good line drawings—the self-portraits are quite brilliant.

STEPHEN LACK: His artistic talent? Unbelievable. Oh, what a line. Hazel [Field] had a drawing he'd done of her dog, Alfie, an Afghan. It was fast, beyond Matisse-like.

LINDA BOOK: As a writer, Cohen squirrelled away stuff, thought about it, pushed in into a sentence, took it out and put it back. He'd polish coal into diamonds, a craftsman beyond anything else. The words were tortured and, at a primal level, so was he. Always troubled, guarded, very good at not answering questions. That's why the drawings were so important— instant gratification. It was what it was. It's why he could give them away to waiters. These were doodles, a way of remembering something, and faster than anything he ever did. He really stood apart, as if he was a bit embarrassed about the whole process.

According to Book, Cohen looked tired, "like someone not as well as he should have been. He was very quiet."

LINDA BOOK: He was being very careful about his health. Stomach issues. Kory brought in food and Leonard had chicken soup. We all sat in chairs— Leonard sat on the floor. When I finished my salad, I said, "Let me take your dishes in." And he stood up and said, "No, let me take yours." I said, "Leonard, you're the talent. The talent doesn't do dishes." He said, "I'm Leonard and I do the dishes." And he picked up everyone's dishes, took them into the kitchen, and washed everything. Our meetings were brief, but so full that I felt I'd met him fully.

BARRIE WEXLER: Leonard had a kind of spiritual—if not quasi-erotic— relationship with dirty dishes. On the other hand, he hated dusting, and preferred not to disturb it.

CLYDE WAGNER: It wasn't that he didn't have an ego, but there was also a humility. He was modest about his work and about who he was. Normally, there's a whole system around such people. With Leonard, there was a stripping away of that, [by] his choice. And it wasn't ticktock, five minutes, in and out. He was very generous with his time. He spoke with that voice that hits you like a wall—calm and powerful at the same time.

LINDA BOOK: I called my sister to say, "Leonard Cohen is washing my dishes." That was the most exciting part, because it was so ordinary. I'm ordinary. But he wasn't. We won't see his like again.

Cohen's line drawings, produced as numbered and signed limited editions, sold at prices ranging from $1,500 to $6,000. Reluctantly, Cohen sold seven originals—priced for rarity, at $40,000. Later, he told *Maclean's* that his work "did very well. I was able to pay a lot of lawyers." To accommodate Luminato, Toronto won the premiere—in association with Goodall's gallery. Subsequent shows were mounted in Manchester, Vancouver, Oslo, Winnipeg, and Montreal. Cohen proved as attentive to art as he was to poetry and song.

LINDA BOOK: Leonard went over every picture with a fine-tooth comb. He adjusted the colour, the contrast—checked everything. He examined the framing. He was meticulous. We had lineups around the block, had to have security. But I've never met anyone like him. He had a way of recognizing you instantly. Not what school did you go to, but who, in your essence, you were. He'd know very quickly if you were a person he would speak to or not. It wasn't "Do they know about opera?" It had to do with an assessment of integrity. He was always looking for that. He could say, "No" like no one I'd seen.

When the show opened, the gallery held a private reception.

LINDA BOOK: Greg Gatenby came—the guy who started the Harbourfront book festival. He had this huge bag, every book Leonard had written. Leonard was hiding out in our project room, with Adrienne Clarkson and publisher Avie Bennett. They had their heads together like a couple of kindergarten kids, a conversation no one was going to interrupt. Greg barged in—"Leonard, would you sign?" Leonard signed three, looked up and said, "I think that will do." Greg stood there like a doe in the headlights. But it was over, no question. He wasn't rude or offensive, but it was such a clear message.

On another occasion, Garth Drabinsky suggested he and Cohen go for lunch.

LINDA BOOK: Leonard squared himself up and said, "I've just received a call from the hotel. Anjani has arrived and I think I'd like to go lie with her."

It was not said in a lascivious way, but in this tender, beautiful, almost poetic way. Leonard was like a puppeteer. He knew exactly what to say to people to shut them down or turn them on.

Busy as he was, Cohen wasn't too busy to help out a friend—Brian Johnson—who was making a short experimental film of Dennis Lee's new poetry book, *Yesno.*

DENNIS LEE: I asked Leonard if he'd read a poem—"Tango." It's a gorgeous reading, recorded in LA. The voice was somewhere down near the soles of his feet by then. The poem is a dance of death for our civilization. I put in the word "merengue," but misspelled it. So there it is—meringue. Leonard wasn't getting revenge, but he reads the poem exactly as written and says "meringue," which makes no sense. The poem itself flirts with sense, so any number of listeners wouldn't even notice. But I thought, "Why the fuck can't he say the name of the dance?" Until somebody gently pointed out my error. It was a gratis exercise.

Even with all these commitments, nothing could have kept Cohen from Roshi's one hundredth birthday party at Rinzai-Ji.

PAUL HUMPHREYS: We set up a banquet inside the *zendo*, thirty to thirty-five people. Roshi made some summary statement about politics, suggesting that ultimately there was no difference between Roosevelt and Hitler. He made it seem as if that was also Leonard's view of things. Someone said, "Jikan, what do you say about that?" After a brief pause, he said, "My politics have been misrepresented." What a lovely, truthful, respectful, almost poetic thing to say.

To promote *Blue Alert,* Elliott Lefko had organized three US concert dates for Anjani Thomas. In LA, Cohen took a nap in the greenroom during her show.

JOEY CARENZA: We went to warn him it was over and he sprung up and greeted her at the door. "Oh, dear, it was a lovely show."

ELLIOTT LEFKO: She then asked him to sing a few songs. He didn't want to, but he sang "Never Got to Love You" and "Whither Thou Goest." And people freaked.

They performed the same songs in New York at Joe's Pub in April.

LEON WIESELTIER: My then wife converted to Judaism and took the name Ruth. She loved that book of the Bible and that speech—"whither thou goest." When we were being married, I asked Leonard if he'd consider recording the song. He said, "Let me think about it." The next thing I know, there arrives a CD—he and Anjani had recorded the song, "a gift for Jennifer from some of Leon's friends."

For the European leg of the Thomas tour, which began July 11 at Paris's New Morning jazz club, Cohen recruited keyboardist Lou Pomanti, Rob Piltch on guitar, and Scott Alexander on bass.

LOU POMANTI: We started with a drummer as well, but Leonard didn't think it worked. It was too much for him. We rehearsed in Toronto for three days and were together for the next month. He's very much like James Taylor, in personality. If a room's noisy, he'll sit there and be quiet. But if it's quiet, he'll come forward. We were in Montreal, at dinner after a show, before we left for Europe, about ten to fifteen people, and everyone's all bubbly and Leonard is sitting there quietly. All of a sudden, the talking subsided and he held court, probably for forty-five minutes. Stories about people he had met.

In Paris, Cohen ran into Eric Andersen.

ERIC ANDERSEN: It was quite funny. He came over, gave me a big hug, and says to Anjani, "You've got to meet Eric Andersen. He's a great songwriter. I know every song he ever wrote, and I'll sing them all for you back at the hotel." She looked perplexed. Then we went to the bar and all Leonard wanted to do was complain about his [former] manager and the $400,000

American Express bill she left him. I said, "Leonard, a $400,000 Amex bill—you're a Buddhist. You're attached to this?" He wouldn't stop talking about it. He was quite alarmed.

In Oslo, the couple appeared on a TV talk show featuring Al Gore and Norway's former prime minister Gro Harlem Brundtland.

LOU POMANTI: In the greenroom—I've never seen anything like it. All these people were like little kids at a campfire when Leonard was talking. Al Gore was completely rapt. Everyone deferred to him.

In one city, the tour manager initially booked Cohen and Thomas into a more luxurious hotel than the band.

LOU POMANTI: Right in front of the road manager, he said, "We're not doing this. Everybody stays at the same place. Either I move or they move."

Thomas, Pomanti says, was "no dummy. She knew how big Leonard was in Europe—in Warsaw, like the Beatles—and she knew he went to shed some light on her." In Poland, Pomanti came down with a cold.

LOU POMANTI: I was at the bar having a cup of tea, and Leonard wanders in. He says, "I've got a remedy." And he asks the bartender for a shot of vodka, straight up. The vodka comes, he says, "I want you to do this," and he takes two fingers, dips them in the vodka, stuffs them up his nose, and sniffs. "Try it." I'm thinking, "That's a little unsanitary." But he's Leonard, my boss, so I stick my fingers in the vodka and up my nose. He says, "Feel better?" I go, "I'm not sure." It was just a very odd little moment.

Pomanti had worked with many famous musicians, including Joni Mitchell, Burton Cummings, Neil Young, k.d. lang. "But the reaction I got from people when I told them I was going to Europe with Leonard Cohen was like nothing I'd ever seen."

Back in Montreal that summer of 2007, Cohen was alone in Parc du Portugal when Andy McClelland, a young musician, approached.

ANDY MCCLELLAND: I thought, "I gotta go talk to him. An auspicious sighting." I sit down, light a cigarette, and say, "Hi, Mr. Cohen, I'm about to go on my first tour across Canada. Any advice?" He says, "Get as much sleep as you possibly can. Those words will be ringing in your ears." Then he says, "There's an old adage in show business that you're not paid to play. You're paid to travel." We then started talking about our favourite Christian saints. He said, "A good one for touring is St. Jude, the patron saint of hopeless causes." We laughed about that. We talked about radical theologian Ivan Illich—his ideas of Christianity being at heart about relinquishing all forms of power.

Suddenly, an attractive young woman said in French, "Would you participate in a survey about how construction has affected businesses on Boulevard St.-Laurent?"

ANDY MCCLELLAND: We sat there stunned. I said, "Sure." So she proceeds to ask us questions. Do we shop on St.-Laurent? Which businesses? Cohen mentions Bagel Etc. and the grocery store. Ten minutes. When it's wrapping up, Leonard excuses himself, wishes me good luck, and walks away. I said to her, "Do you know who that was?" . . . "No." . . . "That was Leonard Cohen." . . . "Really? That old guy?"

Meanwhile, having mounted the Anjani Thomas tour, promoter Rob Hallett redoubled his campaign to put Cohen himself back on the road.

ROB HALLETT: Finally, I said, "Here's the deal. Go into a rehearsal room and audition musicians and, if you don't feel comfortable, or don't think you're any good, or you can't do it, for whatever reason, walk away. I'll pick up the tab, and we'll leave as friends. At least we tried." He said, "Sounds fair enough."

Taking up Hallett's offer, Cohen decided to test the waters for a possible tour.

ELLIOTT LEFKO: Kory calls and says, "By tomorrow, I need you to find a road manager, and a rehearsal space in LA." Could everyone, including band

and crew, wear suits and hats? Done and done. For road manager, I called this punk rock guy—Joey Carenza, blue-green hair. Leonard thought he was kind of cool. I arranged to book SIR, a rehearsal space. And I got an immigration lawyer to get a visa for Javier Mas, a Spanish guitarist.

Addressing a meeting in Kory's office, Cohen said, "Friends, it's been fifteen years. I've stopped smoking and drinking. My voice isn't what it used to be. I'm afraid I can't sing these songs."

JOEY CARENZA: Everyone is trying to be helpful, make suggestions. "We'll arrange the songs in different keys." I said, "Leonard, why don't you take one for the team and start smoking and drinking again?" The room went dead silent. Leonard chuckled, patted my hand, and said, "He'll do." I was hired on the spot.

After Thanksgiving, Cohen flew to Austin. He had lunch with Roscoe Beck at El Sol y la Luna and asked him to assemble a band.

ROSCOE BECK: His only instructions were "Rossie, I only want the best band on the road this year." No pressure, then.

MITCH WATKINS: He talked in a matter-of-fact way about it. He was basically saying, "I gotta go back to work." He wasn't sure whether he'd have an audience.

BARRIE WEXLER: He knew he had to do it, but was nervous and wasn't sure anyone would show up after a fifteen-year absence. He said something about being a curiosity who might pull in a few people—at most. I predicted standing room only. "They'll be hanging from the rafters." He replied, "That's what I'll get—a suicidal audience."

RACHEL TERRY: He was very nervous. I was on a conference call with him and [Israeli songwriter] Haim Hefer, and he was scared to tour. I said, "It's like riding a bicycle. You'll be fine."

Auditions started in January, rehearsals in February. The Webb sisters, Charley and Hattie, were recommended by Sharon Robinson. They got the gig the next day.

CHARLEY WEBB: We worked on material as a three-piece. The blend of our voices seemed right.

HATTIE WEBB: Leonard was on the sofa with his eyes closed. Then he got us to do "Dance Me to the End of Love," "Anthem," and "Closing Time." He was a little resistant to having three musicians who were also going to sing in a ten-piece band, but we won him over. Or Sharon did. Leonard really respected her opinion.

Another backup singer, Montreal's Lhasa de Sela, was also considered. She was offered the role, but ended up rejecting it. Only a few days later, she learned that she had terminal breast cancer.

On percussion, Beck hired Rafael Gayol. Cohen had met him briefly in 1988 when, while on tour, he took then thirteen-year-old Lorca to see Gayol's band A-ha at Norway's Kalvøya festival.

WILLIE ARON: I heard guys [auditioning] were coming in with big drum kits. Neil Larsen said, "The thing drummers didn't understand is, Leonard's got a story to tell and it's not about the drums." Gayol came in with a cajón and a couple of shakers. Neil goes, "That guy's got the gig."

JOEY CARENZA: That gig was never his. He was hired to play while other people auditioned. And that man put in so much work. He's a rock drummer and he learned how to play softer, softer, and softer. We'd get there for rehearsal—he'd already been there for hours. And stay a few more hours afterward.

Finding a violinist proved more challenging.

BOBBY FURGO: He hired Raffi Hakopian. But Raffi was drunk and asleep in rehearsal. Then he hired a young Asian [classically trained Christine Wu].

She was formally announced as a band member but, by April, had been dismissed.

DINO SOLDO: He set her up for failure. I saw him do it to [Lorca] one time—her energy could be a little too much for him.

JOEY CARENZA: Leonard really liked Christine, thought she had amazing talent. It was just a vibe thing. She didn't have the greasiness to her playing, the darkness, the grief, necessary to convey the tone of his songs. It wasn't a technical or personal issue. It was a stylistic issue.

BOBBY FURGO: Then he wanted me to come in and remind him of where he came from. So I'm playing "Dance Me to the End of Love," and he leans over, looks me dead in the eye and says, "I dyed the brown shoes black yesterday." Hilarious. He knew I'd be right up to speed. [Furgo had pressured Cohen to buy a pair of brown shoes in 1993.] He couldn't wait to tell me, to make me laugh. I said, "Man, you're quite thin." He said, "All of us are beautiful."

Furgo was never told he didn't get the gig.

BOBBY FURGO: Roscoe thought he was going to hire me. Then nothing. It was hard for him to make decisions. I don't know if the decision was his or Roscoe's. They didn't want the old band. They wanted a complete change. I wanted to play on those tours. My ego did. But I had to learn how to deal with it. It was actually a gift. If my ego gets what it wants, I've learned nothing.

Then Cohen settled on Alex Bublitchi, a Moldavian violinist playing in Barcelona. He managed to secure a US work permit, but was denied visas for British Commonwealth countries that were part of the tour. Beck then hired multi-instrumentalist Dino Soldo—he played the violin parts—as well as Javier Mas, guitarist Bob Metzger, and keyboardist Neil Larsen. Cohen, Soldo said, was "very blue collar, as far as songwriting goes. He worked every day."

JOEY CARENZA: He never stopped working, the entire time. He was constantly writing, constantly rehearsing. He'd be at the venue thirty minutes before sound check, which was often an hour. The shows were over three hours, and he was seventy-two when we started. He'd listen to the same blues album for six hours. He was like an athlete, doing things until they became muscle memory. Then you can start to make art with it.

DINO SOLDO: He'd bounce ideas off you. There'd be no spirit of "What are we going to get out of this," no ulterior motive. He met you as an equal. Leonard was multifaceted, very gentle, very polished. He could listen very intently, but if he had a thought in his head, there was no getting through to him. Very stubborn. He was considerate of people, but you don't get to where he got by being too considerate. Even if he didn't know where he wanted to go, he had to keep searching. If you don't know where you're going, it doesn't mean you're not getting there.

Before rehearsals began, Cohen spent time alone, playing guitar and memorizing the songs.

JAVIER MAS: It was like he'd had a holiday from them—you come back with new energy. For him, it was good that we took so much time at the beginning, because he was getting into the songs very slowly, trying to get them to sound like he wanted. When we decided on instruments—bandurria, lute, archlute—he gave me absolute freedom. I adapted everything to his tone and voice. He let me express myself, a very free feeling.

ELLIOTT LEFKO: They rehearsed for months. Leonard rehearsed so much so he'd never had to worry about what to do or say. He never had teleprompters, like everyone [else]. Leonard had everything memorized.

JOEY CARENZA: We were doing six-hour rehearsals, six days a week, for three months. Sometimes, we'd do the same song for three hours. I never saw him get upset, never saw him single anyone out, never heard him say, "You played this the wrong way." He'd say, "That was great, friends. Let's try it again, just a little softer." Or, "Let's try it again with a little more energy in the bridge." It was never "You're fined fifty dollars." It was the complete antithesis of that.

DINO SOLDO: One day, we were doing this very slow country and western song, a downer, for three hours. He kept saying, "One more time, friends, one more time." It was not frustration—he didn't blow his top—it was almost there. People were falling into [musical] clichés.

Finally, Cohen was ready.

ROB HALLETT: A million dollars later, I get a phone call. "Come and see what you think." I fly to LA and they set up a sofa in front of the stage, just for me. Two and a half hours of bliss—my private Leonard Cohen concert. But I wasn't commercially driven on this [project]. It was me indulging myself and being able to work with my childhood hero. AEG indulged me—I was making them so much money—Beyoncé, Justin Bieber.

ROBERT FAGGEN: Hallett was putting him on tour for the prestige. He loved Leonard, but I don't think they saw this as the great moneymaker it became.

Cohen continued to voice doubt. "I don't know if anyone wants to see me," he said again. "I don't know if I can sell any tickets. I need you to book me a dozen shows in the Maritimes. Let's test it. If that works, we can go."

ROB HALLETT: I go, "Done." I walk out and go, "Where the hell are the Maritimes?" Good old Google. I booked my first tour of the Maritimes with [Montreal promoter] Rubin Fogel. I put key people in place—Mike Scoble, tour manager. Wade Perry, accounts guy. Those were the key positions, so I'd know what was going on and what was being spent.

RUBIN FOGEL: In addition to the Maritimes, we booked two nights in Saguenay. Leonard was more concerned about those dates than any others. He was blown away that he played to two sold-out houses there. Shows like that were really why he decided to tour worldwide.

ELLIOTT LEFKO: He wanted to start in small venues, get the kinks out. Canada was the baby steps. My role was to get him ready to go on to the big stage. But Leonard could not have done it without Hallett. He sold the vision and Leonard bought the vision. And Rob looked after Europe, which is really where all of the money was made.

DINO SOLDO: Hallett represented the corporate angle, but never turned it into a corporate affair. He really put a lot of money in this. If spending got out of control, Leonard would say, "Let's strip everything down and add things as needed." Which meant, nothing is changing. The things we had backstage—food and booze and candy and avocados and fresh things and flowers—[were] things you definitely can't refuse.

JOEY CARENZA: Leonard really went out of his way to look out for me. Initially, I was only hired to get through rehearsals. There was no plan for me to tour. At the final meeting, they divvied up the jobs and there was no job for me. Leonard said, "What's Joey going to do?" And Hallett said, "He can be the road manager."

For the tour, Cohen and Kory laid down some ground rules.

ELLIOTT LEFKO: We said, "You could have a private plane and not have to talk to people." He initially said, "I don't have to do that," but later agreed it was a good idea. He got a private plane.

ROBERT FAGGEN: Leonard made the terms very explicit. "I'll only do it if this, if that, the other." He enjoyed being on tour. He actually got more solitude on tour than at home. It was all very carefully orchestrated.

PICO IYER: "I love being on the road," he told me. "It's domestic arrangements I find impossible." He was ready to keep on touring for the rest of his life. But being in one place with one woman was a problem he'd never be able to solve. He was perfectly frank and self-deprecating about it, but women were the least of his concerns. His kids and Sasaki were the two poles of his life.

ANDREW COHEN: They say he didn't care about money, but he cared enough to say, "Two hundred and fifty thousand dollars a night. When you hear that, you prick up your ears."

JASON ROSENBLATT: He said, "There's still a lot of money to be made by an old fart like me." He said he still had his family to support, and mentioned [his] financial issues because of his former manager.

ROB HALLETT: Too much is made of the idea that he only went back on the road because Kelley stole his money. It's a nice story, but he wouldn't have gone on the road just for that.

JOHN SIMON: I don't think the very rigorous touring schedule was out of financial need. I imagine he might have felt a need to just get out there, stir people's thoughts and raise their consciousness.

PERLA BATALLA: He cared about money—oh yeah. But it wasn't about having money for himself. It was that you had something for your children. That's what that was about, because he lived in the same house with the same chipping paint for as long as I knew him.

Cohen and Anjani Thomas spent the evening of his seventy-third birthday at Rinzai-Ji with Sasaki Roshi and visiting vice-abbot, Sandy Stewart.

GENTEI SANDY STEWART: A lovely dinner of vegetarian curry and almonds and a bottle of tawny port, 1968. Leonard and Anjani sat on the couch. He called her "darling." She softly rested her head on his shoulder. We talked about how Jews and Buddhists know the primary importance of suffering, and of their mutual regard for oral and written traditions. Leonard offered a great gift from the profound ones: "Imagine how this universe might be created—some call it God, but it truly can't be named. Just imagine. We are free to imagine!" Roshi listened attentively, chin on hand, apparently asleep.

In October 2007, after summer shows in New York and South Carolina, Glass's *Book of Longing* was remounted at Stanford and at the Barbican, in

London. Cohen, with Glass, participated in a short, pre-concert talk. The next day, he returned for another Glass piece, a six-hour *Music in Twelve Parts*. While in London, he also attended a Patti Smith show dedicated to poet Allen Ginsberg, for which Glass wrote a piano accompaniment. The next month, in Montreal, Cohen took in a concert featuring Jason Rosenblatt and his band, Shtreiml.

JASON ROSENBLATT: We were only playing for forty people. I look down and see this old gentleman with a cap and a suit in the front row. "Oh, my God, Leonard Cohen." He [was] sitting with [singer] Basya Schechter. After, he congratulated us, and said, "Give me your number." You meet celebrities and nothing ever comes of the number exchange. But the next day he calls—"Would you like to get together?"

They soon met. After ordering pastry at a Greek bakery—Cohen spoke fluent Greek—they went to Vallières.

JASON ROSENBLATT: It looked like nothing had been touched since the 1960s, but it was immaculate. My wife, Rachel, came—we spent the day, ten a.m. until four o'clock, drinking coffee, talking about Mount Baldy. He had a tallis on one of the chairs. He played us a bunch of music, mouthing the words, and sat at his keyboard and played songs he was working on. He had a LA-based klezmer band on his iTunes library and Bruce Springsteen. I spent most of the day with my mouth shut.

Cohen had not yet decided on his band's final composition and told Rosenblatt he "was interested in our oud player."

JASON ROSENBLATT: I also think I'm the one who gave him the idea to work with the Shaar Hashomayim choir. I said, "Did you ever think of having the choir as backup singers?"

About this time, Cohen and Thomas hired a new personal assistant, Kezban Özcan, a young Turkish woman. Initially working part-time, Özcan would become an indispensable part of the Cohen operation—by turns, a secretary, gatekeeper, shopper, appointment maker, chauffeur, visitor greeter, and caterer. She would remain at his side until his death.

In January, Cohen came to Willie Aron's forty-fifth birthday party at Mordecai Finley's home.

WILLIE ARON: He gave me a signed bottle of wine. We were studying the Book of Job—Leonard, myself, Larry Klein, and a few friends, including [singer] Peter Himmelman, an Orthodox Jew, son-in-law of Bob Dylan. Rabbi Finley is reading the story and Leonard goes, "At this point, God is evil. God is a motherfucker." Peter was very upset with Leonard, physically shaking. He didn't say anything, but the next day I got an earful.

PETER HIMMELMAN: There was a circle of people worshipful of Leonard, who was on a high stool, being served grapes. Very theatrical. The rabbi parroted his line—"God is evil." Then a bass player of renown said, "God is evil." It shows the power of fame, the response to it.

On another occasion, Aron was booked to perform with Rebecca Pidgeon and singer Marvin Etzioni.

WILLIE ARON: Leonard used to come to every holiday at the Finley's. Passover. Break fast [after Yom Kippur], Thanksgiving, Chanukah. Marvin said to Leonard, "I've got to tell you, I'm really nervous." He goes, "I suggest drinking an entire bottle of wine."

Later, Anjani Thomas asked Aron to coproduce songs cowritten with Cohen, a prospective follow-up to *Blue Alert*. They met for preproduction at Anjani's Beverly Hills home.

WILLIE ARON: He's in a suit, bare feet, one of those big yarmulkes, and aviator shades, and he goes, "*As-salāmu alaykum.*" Then he starts eating salad with his hands, out of a bag. Then he opens the laptop, and starts playing songs. "These Arms of Mine," by Otis Redding. "I've Been Loving You Too Long" [Redding], Al Green's "Funny How Time Slips Away." Then he goes into

Mahler, Billie Holiday, and Nina Simone. He goes, "We're just trying to get a blessing." From the tower of song, as it were.

Later, Cohen sent other musical suggestions.

WILLIE ARON: He loved country music and said, "I love George Jones. Make it sound like George Jones."

BARRIE WEXLER: One afternoon on Tremaine, he played Jones's "He Stopped Loving Her Today" on a continuous loop over the computer.

WILLIE ARON: Anjani's a world-class pianist, and a great singer. She's intense—really intense. We did arrangements [and] were very pleased with them, everything from funk to country stuff. I sang lead, imitating Leonard. Anjani called me Willard—a combination of Willie and Leonard. Some were used later—"A Street" is one of them. When she sent him our mixes, he said, "It needs more vertical embroidery." What does that mean? I was trying as a producer to get away from his reliance on cheap modernity—synthesizers, Casios, etc. He didn't employ that approach on *Blue Alert.* We did other sessions in 2010 to '11—he was present and much happier with them. In a rare moment of chutzpah, I said he needed to be there—at Stagg Street Studio in Van Nuys. For those sessions, he'd say, "Make it sound like Otis Redding." He loved Otis. The songs remain unreleased.

In general, however, Cohen didn't talk about music the way other musicians do.

WILLIE ARON: He found musicians, and musician-talk, kind of boring. I don't think he saw the studio as the place where you experiment, as this huge canvas. It was "I'm putting a lyric across. The music's important, but nothing gets in the way of what I'm trying to say."

Similarly, except on tour, Cohen avoided teaser performances on late-night talk shows.

ROBERT FAGGEN: He had many, many offers, [but] he never wanted to perform a song separately. The concert was an entire experience.

It was Faggen who had introduced Cohen to several classical composers.

ROBERT FAGGEN: Schubert Lieder, Brahms, and Mahler song cycles. He wasn't easy to push, but he thought they were amazing. And I introduced him to an obscure French Jewish composer, [Charles-Valentin] Alkan, who wrote unbelievable piano music. I could really relax with him. He just understood things. He understood suffering, the complexities of relationships. I had my own issues—everybody does—and he was great to talk to. We were basically two Jewish guys talking about poetry, literature, music, and women.

As he prepared to begin his 2008 tour, Cohen ended his relationship with Anjani Thomas.

JOHN LISSAUER: It didn't end well. They often don't.

DAVID AMRAM: A damn good singer, Anjani, but on the make, angry at the world, at the music industry. I didn't feel the warmth and depth and spirituality that Leonard had.

ANN DIAMOND: Kelley says Anjani often complained about him and was in therapy, stemming from their relationship.

ANONYMOUS: There was the usual Sturm und Drang. She was not happy. She was making him miserable about it. Anjani was incredibly jealous of Leonard's past relationships. Anjani was jealous of *Anjani*. When Rebecca or Dominique would call, just to see how he was doing, Anjani would fly into a rage. An understandable emotion, but Rebecca had no designs on him. She wasn't after anything. Neither was Dominique. Kezban [Özcan], his assistant after 2007 or so, was jealous. There's a lot of jealousy flying around this whole story. Anjani got a lot of money from him. He wasn't too happy about this, believe me.

The impending tour likely played a part in the breakup. According to one insider, Thomas wanted to control how the band was run, and Cohen balked. Roscoe Beck and others essentially forced Cohen to make a decision, saying, "We won't work with her."

MORDECAI FINLEY: Leonard was a ladies' man. Anjani wanted to be the one lady.

NANCY BACAL: Anjani said I saved her life, because she was broken up by Leonard, over and over again. I took her aside one day and said, "Anjani, he can't do it. It's not you. He can't do it." And I told him. We were at the computer, looking at the eight thousand versions of everything he did, and we intuited each other. I didn't say who. I just said, "You're not a match." He paused and said, "Thank you." But he was torn, because he really cared about Anjani and knew she was a really good woman. He could not commit to a relationship. He needed his freedom, his space. He just couldn't do it.

AVIVA LAYTON: You wouldn't want to talk to Anjani about Leonard. Talk to his lovers. He's not husband material. Never was. You go there at your peril. You never want to rely on him emotionally, or rely on that intensity when Leonard looked at you. When he's there, he's really there. If I needed $50,000, it would be there the next minute. But rely on him on a daily basis? You could not depend on that. You had to take Leonard on his own terms.

KELLEY LYNCH: Part had to do with her being jealous. She became trouble between me and Cohen. She came in and took control, but it played into him, too. He was fine with it. He likes to keep people off-balance. It was a friendship of sorts, but these friendships fall apart. He orchestrates the falling apart.

JOEY CARENZA: This wasn't just about Anjani or even about the band. This was about how Leonard approached life and art. He had a vision of what the show could be, the standard he wanted it to be. Not an old guy singing for his supper, not a Leonard Cohen cover band, but a new take, a definitive thing. Leonard knew what it would take and, if Anjani was there, it couldn't be all about the work. And he was *all* about the work. He'd do the show, come back to the hotel and play his guitar all night, the same song for hours. Then travel, eat, walk around the city, and then go to bed. I don't think he could have done that if Anjani or any love interest were there. Originally, he didn't even want Sharon [Robinson]. She kind of auditioned for the part, worked her ass off, humbled herself, and changed the way she interacted with him. Same with Roscoe Beck. They earned that gig.

DINO SOLDO: Sharon had an amazing relationship with Leonard. She read him and knew how to have him read her. She knew not to say too much, how to make herself a little mysterious. I should have learned that.

In early March, Cohen took a break from rehearsals to fly to New York. On March 10, he was inducted into the Rock and Roll Hall of Fame at the Waldorf Astoria. Lou Reed introduced him, declaring, "We're so lucky to be alive at the same time Leonard Cohen is." Cohen's acceptance speech for the award again consisted almost entirely of the lyrics from "Tower of Song." At the event, he bumped into two friends, Sid McGinnis and John Miller, members of the evening's house band.

SID MCGINNIS: I went to congratulate him. He said, "Sid, they'll never get us." That's such a double thing—what do you mean? Years later, I told Lissauer the story. "He said that to everybody."

JOHN MILLER: We're rehearsing and, as soon as there's a break, Leonard makes a beeline for me. His opening line—after not seeing him for twenty years—"Comrade, how many times?" He meant how many times do I wake up in the night to take a piss.

For Hallett, the induction was deliciously ironic.

ROB HALLETT: Leonard quoted what [music critic] Jon Landau said in 1967— "I have seen the future of rock and roll and it's not Leonard Cohen."

How wrong he was. In 2018, Cohen won a best rock performance Grammy for "You Want It Darker."

The following Saturday, in shul in LA, Cohen was given an aliyah—in Judaism, an honour involving a reading from the Torah.

WILLIE ARON: He's there with his aviator shades. "*Shma Yisroel, Adonai, Eloheynu.*" Afterward, I said, "Mazel tov. What do you think about being elected [to the Hall of Fame with Madonna]?" He said, "What the hell. Let them all in. Who cares?" Ultimately, he didn't give a shit.

Rehearsals continued through April. In early May, after a full run-through, the band arrived in Fredericton, New Brunswick—the start of what would become an unprecedented journey.

ELLIOTT LEFKO: We rehearsed there for a week. We put it on sale and it sold out like crazy. The night before opening night, there was me, Rubin [Fogel], Hallett, and Kory—that's it. He did the whole set. It was beautiful.

And then at last, opening night, May 11, 2008, at the seven-hundred-seat Playhouse Theatre.

ROB HALLETT: Leonard's in the dressing room. He says, "Is there anyone out there? Is it full?"

Backstage, Cohen initiated what became a ritual for the band, a three-line vocal exercise, a chant sung in a round, while walking toward the stage, in Latin: *Ego sum pauper homo. Habeō nihil. Nihil opus est.* In English, "I'm a poor man. I have nothing. I need nothing." He won a standing ovation in Fredericton before he opened his mouth.

CHARLEY WEBB: Sharon, Hattie, and me walked on with him and, yeah, his hands behind his back were shaking. And the place just exploded. I was completely taken aback because I'd never experienced that sort of physical reaction before. Having hundreds of people immediately convulse with emotion. That feeling didn't go away. I just learned to manage it.

ROB HALLETT: It wasn't planned. We didn't ask for it. It just happened—naturally—every single night, from Fredericton to New Zealand. Really incredible.

WILFRED LANGMAID: Leonard was obviously nervous. We could see him pacing back and forth, backstage. He came on to a two-minute standing ovation. He looked out with that nervous, shy smile, and kept bowing and nodding his head. A sheepish grin, but loving every moment.

ROBERT FAGGEN: I don't think he was shocked by the response, but it kind of amazed him.

DINO SOLDO: He loved to be onstage. The audience reaction was damned impressive. It was impressive to give Bruce Springsteen a run for his money in terms of time onstage—three hours, one time four hours, with one tiny intermission.

On May 19, on a night off, Cohen and Hallett saw Bob Dylan perform in St. John.

ROB HALLETT: We didn't stay the whole show. He was mumbling, had his back to the audience, wasn't playing his sets. If Bob did a Leonard type show, he'd be bigger than Leonard. Dylan is the politics of politics. Cohen is the politics of the heart. I don't think they were rivals—not in Leonard's mind. In critics' minds.

If Hallett's AEG associates had doubted his vision, twenty-two sold-out gigs in Canada—dubbed "First we take Fredericton, then we take Moncton"—disabused them of the notion.

ROB HALLETT: About three million dollars and sixteen shows in, we knew we had a monster on our hands. I knew there was a market. Leonard's poetry has been translated into Polish, Greek, and so on. My American cousins really don't know what's going on in the rest of the world. Convincing Leonard was harder than convincing AEG.

ELLIOTT LEFKO: Kory made a deal with AEG to be Leonard's exclusive promoter. AEG didn't realize how big it was. So we guaranteed money—paid for all the touring, rehearsals. He earned back money from the draw and made considerably extra money. [AEG] did a contract with Leonard and then another contract. I promoted every single show in North America. Hallett did everything else.

To preserve energy, it was agreed that Cohen would operate in a carefully maintained bubble, and not have to greet well-wishers backstage after a show.

ELLIOTT LEFKO: Leonard, backstage, would talk to his guitar tech or his musicians. Just fun stuff. That's when he was happiest. There were no guests—ever. The bubble really worked. At the Sony Centre in Toronto, Kory called and said Leonard did not want Joni Mitchell backstage. I talked to her. She says, "Can I meet Leonard?" And I'm trying to stall. Finally, it's showtime and I escort her to her seat. At halftime, I took her to a little room for VIPs. She never got to meet him. He didn't have to worry about all that—the gracious persona—because it's a bit of an act, to be that person for everybody. He saved the brand for his performance.

CHRIS LORWAY: The following morning, I asked Joni how the concert was. She reflected on how, over the years, Leonard had grown into his voice, while she felt she had grown out of hers.

From Canada, the tour decamped for Dublin, playing three open-air shows at the Irish Museum of Modern Art.

ROB HALLETT: Dublin was Leonard's spiritual home. When the first two nights went on sale, they sold out in half an hour, so we added the third. We did thirty-six thousand tickets in Dublin. Amazing.

The first night, Bono, of U2 fame, asked Hallett if he could come backstage and say hello to Cohen.

ROB HALLETT: Leonard said, "I'm delighted he's here, but I'm going to have an early night." So I tell Bono, "Leonard's really tired. Long journey. Not tonight." He says, "How about you both come to my house for lunch tomorrow?" I call Leonard. "We're invited to Bono's for lunch." He says, "Thank you very much. I'm honoured, but I have a show to do." Then Bono suggested meeting after the second show. By this time, I'm starting to get it. "Ya know what, Bono? I don't think it's going to work out." From then on, it became policy.

RAFAEL GAYOL: Three nights in Dublin, 12,500 people a night. The only time you can make noise is in between the songs. It's so quiet you can almost hear dust collide.

PAT HARRIS: I've heard string quartets that were louder than that band.

It was during the next show, at the two-thousand-seat Manchester Opera House, that a light bulb went on for Hallett. During "Closing Time," he started dancing in the aisle, only to be reprimanded by the crowd.

ROB HALLETT: They're saying, "Shh! Sit down." What? In these small venues, it becomes too reverential. Fuck this. We're not here to worship in a church. We're here to celebrate his music. I said, "We should do an arena." Leonard said okay. His confidence was back. He looked ten years younger. The tour gave him a new lease on life. In the arenas, it became the party I had imagined. People were singing and dancing, as they had in Dublin.

From Manchester, the entourage returned to Montreal for three shows at Place des Arts. Inevitably, old friends came, including Patricia Nolin, former wife of his late friend Derek May, and their children.

PATRICIA NOLIN: We were transported. He was magnificent. This old man—so irresistible, such a good singer. I, as an actress, saw a magical performance, the best ever. It was one of the magic moments of our lives. Of course, we remembered Derek and cried and laughed, and Montreal was at his feet. So elegant, this old man, with his hat and chic. In my heart, I said, "You did it, Leonard. Bravo." I went backstage. Morton was there and his sister, Esther, but Leonard had already gone.

MICHEL ROBIDOUX: That show was awesome. His voice was fine, better than Zimmerman's [Dylan's] voice. He didn't force it. His strength was in the easiness. That—and the love of what he was doing and the sharing with the musicians. A guy with one knee down, listening to the guy doing solos with the oud. He always had a crush on these instruments.

DENNIS RUFFO: I saw him at an arena in Ottawa. I was curious to see how he'd pull that off. He was equally as charming in a big venue like that. He made it seem like a coffeehouse. When he came back from intermission, he had a line—"You're all still here. If it was me, I'd be home in bed by now."

Then it was back to Europe for nineteen shows, including at London's sixteen-thousand-seat O2 arena, arguably the biggest gamble of the tour.

ROB HALLETT: When I first put O2 on sale, everyone said, "Leonard Cohen in the O2?" We sold out in twenty-four hours and two subsequent shows in twenty-four hours.

LEIF BODNARCHUK: That first leg was pretty crazy. We crossed the Atlantic three times in sixteen days—long flights, unnecessarily epic bus journeys, and mountains of money wasted. We cursed the planners, while trying our best to keep sane and help Leonard deliver.

Busy as he was, Cohen was not too busy to help an old friend.

SANDRA ANDERSON: I'd been diagnosed with colon cancer. He had asked me my doctors' names and when I said Katz and Liberman, he approved. "Good Jewish names." A couple of days later, I had a phone call from Dr. Katz. He'd received a letter from Leonard. He read it to me. Leonard referred to me as his dear friend and said, "I thank you in advance for the excellent care I know you will take of her. Please treat her very well. She is a rare and bright shining spirit."

*　　*　　*

The first leg of Cohen's revival surpassed even its most optimistic projections. Some eighteen thousand turned up in Oslo's Bislett Stadium, twenty-one thousand for two dates at Copenhagen's Rosenborg Castle, eight thousand in Bruges. Seven thousand in Lucca, another seven thousand in Nice. At Benicàssim, in Spain, Cohen reconnected with Alberto Manzano.

ALBERTO MANZANO: Leonard's concert was just before Enrique Morente's [who recorded four Cohen songs on his 1996 album, *Omega*]. Morente had been trying to convince Leonard to sing "Hallelujah" with him onstage.

Cohen demurred. "Morente is one of the greatest singers in the world," he said. "I respect and admire him immensely. But I will be doing close to two hundred concerts this year. We are exhausted. If I stop to chat with friends or accept invitations to sing with other artists, I will die before this is over. Please ask Señor Morente to forgive me. Besides, Morente's mountain voice would bury my nightingale." However, the two singers did chat backstage for twenty minutes after Cohen's concert. A little more than a year later, Morente suffered a brain haemorrhage after surgery for oesophageal cancer and died, age sixty-seven.

After his August 3 show at Ledbury's Big Chill festival, Cohen spent most of August and September recuperating, then resumed the tour on his seventy-fourth birthday at Bucharest's Arcul de Triumf, performing for ten thousand people.

CHARLEY WEBB: The show was punctuated with the song "Happy Birthday" over and over. Then people came onstage with enormous cakes that were heavier than Leonard, which he held 'til we rescued him.

Literary critic Mircea Mihaies, who had written a book on Cohen's lyrics, was granted a rare backstage meeting, pre-concert. Cohen greeted him wearing "the facetious smile of an elderly prankster, his eyes shining with energy and charisma."

MIRCEA MIHAIES: He thanks me!—for the honour of writing a book about him. Slightly embarrassed, I try to disengage my hand, but he keeps holding it. . . . I wish him happy birthday, and give him the wine I brought as a present.

Mihaies started to leave, but Cohen insisted he stay. During the ensuing three-hour conversation, Cohen asked if the word "gypsy" had a derogatory connotation in Romanian, since it appeared in his songs and he didn't want to hurt anyone's feelings. Mihaies assured him it didn't and cited Romanian songs and poems about gypsies. Then Mihaies taught him the correct pronunciation of Bucureshti, as well as a few Romanian words, "*multumesc*" (thank you) and "*buna ziua*" (good day to you).

MIRCEA MIHAIES: It [was] a commonplace conversation, like between old acquaintances. Around me, ordinary people are going [about] their jobs . . . not revealing in any way that an exceptional human being is sitting among us.

Cohen's daughter, Lorca, orchestrated the birthday cake. After "Happy Birthday" was sung, Cohen blew out the candles and bowed, hands together, in the oriental custom.

MIRCEA MIHAIES: "There's something missing," he says, leaves the room, comes back with the bottle of wine I gave him. We drink to his health out of plastic cups.

Finally, as Mihaies prepared to leave, Robert Kory said, "Now you understand why I'm opposed to these meetings. Because Leonard is so gracious." A farewell photograph was taken. Mihaies has it still, in which "I see the lights in his eyes . . . alive, generous, and of a silky incandescence."

Then the marathon continued. Through November, he played thirty-three additional dates, including four more shows in London and three in Paris, where Cohen's isolation bubble was again broken.

ELLIOTT LEFKO: Carla Bruni got backstage because she was such a babe.

ROB HALLETT: [Nicolas] Sarkozy asked to say hi to Leonard. So we did the usual—"We're honoured, but . . ." I mention it to Leonard in passing—Sarkozy wants to come backstage. He says, "Really? Do you think he'd bring Carla Bruni?" I said, "I think that was the idea." He says, "Let's say yes." It turns out he wants to see if her ass was as magnificent as it looked in photos. After the show, everyone is there—band, crew, caterers—and she came in and everyone [is gawking]. There were probably other exceptions.

One had occurred at the O2 in London.

JEAN-MICHEL REUSSER: I had not seen him for four years. The guitar player was in the greenroom. I said, "Can you tell him Jean-Michel is here?" He says, "Leonard never sees anybody before the show." He left—I was kind of pissed—and suddenly, who do we see? Leonard. He looked at me from the other side of the room and came straight to me. I'll never forget that moment. He took me in his arms and hugged me and said, "Hey, my friend, how are you?" He passed me an incredible energy, very, very special. It got me high. Even talking about it now gives me shivers.

CHAPTER TEN

It's a Lovely, Lonely Life

It was like Lazarus, wasn't it? Those last five years. Started in small venues and, within six months, Glastonbury. It was Hallett's doing, but ultimately it was Leonard's doing. He finally realized what he was.

—Tony Bramwell

Who else, in their seventies, becomes bigger than they ever were in their career?

—Richard Zuckerman

Resting through December, Cohen's Unified Heart Touring Company flew to the South Pacific in January 2009 for eleven concerts. In response to devastating bushfires in Australia, which claimed 173 lives, he donated a portion of show revenues to relief; the full contribution from Cohen and others was $200,000. A major question remained, however: How would the reincarnation of Leonard Cohen play in the United States, a country previously impervious to his charms? It was about to be answered.

ELLIOTT LEFKO: Kory talked about one gig in New York, to test the waters. We put the Beacon Theatre on sale and it sold out. We realized this would be easy. I then started booking Austin, Phoenix, San Diego, Los Angeles, San Francisco. I wasn't surprised. In the years that had passed, he'd gained a lot of fans—older fans, plus new fans, through people like Nick Cave, Jeff Buckley. He did three-hour shows. And he didn't fuck with his songs.

PAUL MULDOON: I got into conversation with an usher, who said, "What sort of music is this?" A fascinating question, to which the answer might have been klezmer. But I said, "This is the best kind." Flip—but it was true and is true and will continue to be true.

LEON WIESELTIER: I ran into Esther there. Adorable—your central casting, upper-middle-class Manhattan Jewish woman, fur coats, bangles, the works. "Leon, that line in 'First We Take Manhattan'—'I don't like what's happening to my sister.' Do you think he means me?" I assured her he did not.

CHRISTINE JONES: The Beacon was incredible, the way he invokes the spirits. This was somebody who had absorbed all the lessons of his life and was laying it all out on the stage.

JOEY CARENZA: He was emptying the tank, so determined that every show be amazing. It was a grind.

Despite rare punctures, Cohen's bubble remained in effect. In New York, Paul Simon tried to see him.

DINO SOLDO: At breakfast, Leonard had said he had nag champa incense he could give me and to come to his room after the show. We're at the hotel and he's taking incense out of his bag—amazing how he packs, everything sectioned and rolled, really well packed. We hear a knock and [it's] Simon, who had been in the crowd. Leonard goes, "Be quiet, will you, Dino? Maybe if we don't say anything, he'll go away." So he goes to the door, gets on his toes to look through the keyhole, and nods his head—it's Paul. So there are the two greatest songwriters in the world, the door in between them, neither of them saying shit. And he doesn't open the door. *He never opens the door.* Paul goes away. Simon just wanted to talk to him. But that was the thing about Leonard—whatever he was doing, he just wanted to be in the moment.

In April, Cohen played back-to-back, sold-out dates at LA's Nokia Theatre.

BARRIE WEXLER: I sent him an email a week before, but didn't hear back, which was unusual. The day before the first show, I got a call—he'd left tickets at the box office. When we picked them up, they weren't marked with a row or seat numbers. We were led down the centre aisle, past the first row. Two stand-alone seats had been set up, practically rubbing the stage. Inside the ticket envelope was a handwritten note. "You were right, L"—which I took as a reference to my prediction that the audience would be hanging from the rafters.

JULIE CHRISTENSEN: I really was heartened to see him on the Nokia jumbotron, twinkling. I could see how happy he was. Roscoe Beck told me he'd leave before the houselights came up, without having to interact with anybody afterward. He really had found some happiness.

ROB HALLETT: The Americans still weren't quite getting it, and they never got it the way the rest of the world did, though he was the only artist to play Madison Square Garden, Radio City Music Hall, and the Beacon Theatre in the same cycle.

MOSES ZNAIMER: Americans want it fast and glitzy, cheap and disposable. Europeans were more inclined to listen to the words. The irony was that he was big in all the anti-Semitic European countries.

On the tour bus, Cohen often sat beside road manager Joey Carenza.

JOEY CARENZA: Leonard was the coolest, one of those people you're instantly comfortable with. Just an incredible vibe. The air is different. Nothing fantastical—he was just there, great, all the time, totally solid, super easy to be around. Completely unassuming. Endless energy. He always made it about other people. We had a very close connection. Most people reported to Mike Scoble, the tour manager. I reported directly to Leonard. That caused some friction. Over time, people got married, divorced, had kids, died. Every day, a new problem. He'd just sit there, listen intently and, at the end, whisper to me, "You should write this down and sell it." We spent a lot of time in comfortable silence.

The night before Cohen's one hundredth concert—June 4, 2009, in Morrison, Colorado—Lefko organized a celebration.

ELLIOTT LEFKO: I made the mistake of letting Bob Metzger, a noted oenophile, order the wine. I had a $10,000 bill. Leonard spoke. He was really modest. Then there was a terrible storm—the show was rescheduled. The first tour was bigger cities. Then we played Ohio, Louisville, New Orleans. He was selling out theatres there.

In earlier decades, Cohen had travelled with a handful of musicians and a few roadies. For these tours, he had an entourage of forty-five, including a stylist, a wardrobe assistant, and three caterers. Mostly, they got along.

ROB HALLETT: Leonard insisted that everyone working under his name was respectful, polite, no shouting, no arguing. A couple didn't respect those barriers. A bit too rock and roll.

ELLIOTT LEFKO: An English sound man, disliked by the crew—good at what he did, but bad attitude. Leonard was reluctant to fire anybody. Finally, he said okay. Robert flew Mark Vreeken to LA for a clandestine meeting. So we [hired] Mark. His sound was exquisite in an arena. How Leonard was able to take an arena and make it intimate—nobody's able to do that.

Cohen had never played large arenas in the past. Vreeken's magic formula involved placing measurement microphones around the room, and time aligning the sound to one source point.

MARK VREEKEN: Leonard doesn't like to hear the sound coming back, so I use lots of speakers and turn them down low. You get the same volume and tone everywhere and a more intimate experience. We use mono sound, so everyone hears exactly the same mix. It's all geared towards amplifying Leonard's very quiet vocal.

Very occasionally, there was band friction.

DINO SOLDO: Small rifts, not earth-shattering, more or less ego-based. Leonard said, "I found out a long time ago that maybe discord is the state of just what a band is." He was saying, "This is what it is and I'm content with that."

If anyone thought Cohen was too old to pay attention to the particulars, he soon disabused them of the notion.

ELLIOTT LEFKO: I was getting pressure to book bigger venues. But in Toronto, they did not sell out. One bad review [mentioned] empty seats. Leonard saw it and flipped. Onstage, the second night, he referenced the review. He was pissed. That was difficult. He held me accountable, for a long time. At a Christmas party in New York—Secret Santa, a jovial occasion at the hotel—Leonard got really mad—for these empty seats in Toronto. I just let him vent. I went to my room, but came back later and he again took me aside and said, "I'm really sorry. I really like you. I appreciate what you do." He got it off his chest and he was fine. But he definitely had a temper.

Lefko encountered Cohen's "dark side" again some time later, via an email.

ELLIOTT LEFKO: In the middle of the night. It had "WTF" in it. I turned to my wife and said, "I thought he was a Buddhist." One time, he called everyone to Kory's office—Leonard, Hallett, myself, the tour manager, and Ed Sanders, his right-hand man. He was pissed because there were too many shows in a row in North America. He was going to a party and was venting in a tuxedo. We said, "Leonard, we love you. We'll take care of it." Then there was a break, but he came back, really angry, right in your face. Again, I said, "We'll get it done to your satisfaction." He had to get mad at somebody.

DINO SOLDO: Leonard angry? Oh, heck, yeah. What would cause it? I don't know. I think he would get frustrated.

JOEY CARENZA: I [saw] the gloves off. Not yelling, but no pulling punches. That was eye-opening. Even if Leonard chooses to interact with graciousness or positivity, it's not because he's naive to what's happening. Robert would sometimes suggest things and Leonard would say to me, "Listen, I don't work for Robert Kory."

In Lefko's eyes, Cohen had rewritten the rule book for touring for older musicians.

ELLIOTT LEFKO: Everything was top-drawer—the songs, the look, the musicians. Go to the cool cities, don't go to the non-cool cities. Go on the edge states, nice theatres. Charge extra money and do the VIP thing. We guarded against speculating by taking the bulk of good seats and selling buyers his limited-edition art for two or three hundred dollars. He made all that extra money. Nobody ever complained.

Carefully looking after himself, Cohen—about to turn seventy-five—held up well. But on September 18, 2009, he collapsed at Valencia's Luis Puig stadium, mid-song ("Bird on a Wire"). He was rushed to the hospital, suffering from food poisoning, the result of a mayonnaise sandwich he ate.

JOEY CARENZA: We all—audience and band—thought it was curtains. He was the only person not freaking out. He wanted to finish the show, but whatever he ate earlier was determined to upstage him.

DINO SOLDO: There were other health issues, his back, gout. Someone would recommend a new fitness fad—he'd try it and fuck himself up. He was too old to be doing it. He wanted to be a trouper. "We can't let these people wait a minute longer." He'd always be onstage at the appropriate time. So goddamn inspiring—complete showmanship, old vaudeville. Leonard was that all the way. Massive integrity when it comes to his profession. Yet he'd also take the time to get to know the person frying his doughnut.

Recovering quickly, Cohen performed three days later, on his seventy-fifth birthday, in Barcelona. And then there was Israel. When it was announced that Cohen would play Tel Aviv's Ramat Gan Stadium, pro-Palestinian groups protested.

ROB HALLETT: At heart, he was a Zionist. However, he was absolutely disgusted with the government. Furious. We almost cancelled the show. At the same time, we had professors writing every day, telling him not to go. It got quite controversial.

At his July Weybridge concert in the UK, demonstrators had leafleted the crowd.

ROB HALLETT: There were about one hundred particularly nasty protesters, which steeled his resolve to go. "No one's telling me what I'm going to do or not going to do," [Cohen said]. "But I don't want the money. It's blood money."

To appease the Palestinians, Cohen proposed a second concert in the Ramallah Cultural Palace. The offer was declined.

ROB HALLETT: They said, "We don't want to be the token show after Tel Aviv." Not in an aggressive way, just in a matter-of-fact way. I said, "I understand, but if any Palestinians want to attend, we'll send buses from Ramallah to Ramat Gan." Six busloads came. Leonard actually acknowledged them from the stage.

After the Palestinian rejection, Cohen proposed that revenues from the Tel Aviv concert be donated to a new fund, for reconciliation, tolerance, and peace.

ROB HALLETT: Leonard met Yitzhak Frankenthal, who had a charity made up of families on both sides who had lost children—Parents' Circle. His son was murdered by Hamas. The idea was to fund projects that promoted coexistence.

ROBERT FAGGEN: He was very skeptical of both the right and the left. But I did help get Israeli novelist David Grossman to support the fund. Leonard read his work and was very impressed.

Cohen ended the Tel Aviv show, attended by some fifty-five thousand, saying, "May your life be as sweet as apples dipped in honey." He then recited a truncated version, in Hebrew, of the *Birkat Kohanim*, complete with out-stretched arms and hands—the *Nesi'at Kapayim,* through which divine blessings are bestowed. According to Judaic scholars, the arrangement of fingers during the prayer symbolizes windows through which God's blessing may flow.

ROBERT FAGGEN: He had creds for that—he's a *Kohen*. If he can't do it in Israel, who can? I don't think it was kitschy at all. He took it seriously.

JAMES DIAMOND: He drew more people closer to religion with that one gesture than the Lubavitch have.

MICHAEL LAWRENCE: I've come to see him as a contemporary rabbi, a wise person, fully realized as the great artist we all recognize. Attending a Cohen concert was like being brought into his synagogue. His presence remains with me.

CHRIS BYNUM: That concert was very stressful for everyone. A couple of months after, I had breakfast with Leonard. I got the feeling he wished more could have been achieved. The best part of that conversation was when Leonard said that a certain rock star known for activism was too much of a pussy to get involved in his charity. We both laughed really hard.

ROB HALLETT: We made a point. If we hadn't [played there], Israelis would have gone to see him in Germany. But inviting the Palestinians to come, and having [in effect] a Mass for peace, that made a difference. Leonard didn't like aggravation. Was he happy at the outcome? Yes. Was he mad that he had to go through it? Absolutely.

Ultimately, some $5 million was raised. Frankenthal, CEO of the fund, recruited twelve like-minded Israelis and Palestinians; Kory and Hallett sat on the board.

ROB HALLETT: It was uncomfortable, sitting like Solomon, because we weren't an active charity. We were a funding charity. We funded some great projects. Some crazy ones, we turned down. We funded a project to connect cell phones from East to West Jerusalem. Other monies were used to fund research into new approaches to peace. Eventually, the five million ran out. It came to its natural end.

Six years later, journalist Dovid Efune asked Cohen about the furor.

DOVID EFUNE: This was not a positive experience for him. He felt the money had gone to waste. The people he hoped would implement his vision weren't able to deliver.

For the most part, the Hallett-Kory relationship functioned reasonably well.

ROB HALLETT: We butted heads from time to time. We brought different skill sets to the table. He's not a touring guy and doesn't know the international [scene]. I'm not a tax guy. Robert got him out of his tax issues, kept the Kelley thing away, reinvented Leonard's life, gave him stability, made sure the money was properly spent, properly taxed, properly invested. I don't think either of us could have done it on our own.

According to Dino Soldo, Roscoe Beck had the toughest job.

DINO SOLDO: He's musical director, yet it was always Leonard's band. Anything Roscoe would say, Leonard might listen but, if it seemed that was the prevailing wind, Leonard would go the opposite way, just because he wants to. Sometimes, it would mess with Roscoe's head.

As in earlier tours, performance was an exercise in minimalism.

DINO SOLDO: You had ten musicians with this low bridge you had to pass under. Bob Metzger said, "I'm the Maytag repairman of guitar playing." A great guitarist. We did not see eye to eye, but only because we were on the same side of the stage and his amp faced my head. Roscoe had to turn down his bass so far, to avoid competing with Leonard. Rafi Gayol was almost playing brushes, to keep the sound down. Frustrating, but he pulled it off. The Webb sisters kept us laughing—hilarious girls, very creative. Javier [Mas] was a nut—he brought his entire Spanish self. We called it the Chasing the Sun tour—south in winter, Europe and North America in summer.

Even for crew technicians, Cohen was a figure of enormous respect.

LEIF BODNARCHUK: I never felt he was unapproachable. We had an in-joke we shared. Our hotel accommodations were usually so good that if the standard slipped, I'd say, "What a shithole this is." He paid us well. There were bonuses, even a profit-sharing deal. He just wanted everybody to be comfortable. He didn't want a lot of conflict. He was always of the mind that it could all come to a crashing end tomorrow. The less he worried about the band, the more he could focus on his own performance and give audiences what he wanted. He read two of my novels, said nice things and tried to get me into a publishing company. He was like no other employer I've ever had—a fine example of a man. Full stop.

When his schedule permitted, Faggen joined the tour for concerts in Poland, France, Italy, Israel, and various cities in the US, including Las Vegas for November 12, 2009.

ROBERT FAGGEN: He hated Vegas. He didn't want to come out of his room. He said something like "I never saw a place that tried so hard to be so unpleasant." But it was astounding that a seventy-five-year-old man could do three-and-a-half-hour concerts and skip off the stage.

ROB HALLETT: I came up with the idea of playing Vegas on Chanukah. Of course, he lit the candles.

BARRIE WEXLER: I had suggested he mount a comeback concert in Vegas in 2007. He swore he'd never set foot there, or go back on the road. Two years later, sold-out at Caesars Palace.

In Las Vegas, Cohen suggested that, during the next leg, the band wear white tuxedos.

DINO SOLDO: He was serious. "We're going to have a smoke machine, so there'll be clouds on the ground." I did say, "I don't see that as a good thing—a performance in which you die onstage." But I did not want it to end. I got so much mileage out of that. He was a major influence as a songwriter. He really encouraged me to go for the big Mount Everest ideas, not shy away.

The 2009 tour finished in San Jose in November. Cohen planned to resume in March 2010, but in February, during a Pilates class, he suffered a compression fracture in his lower back—a harbinger of more serious health problems. Recuperating in Montreal, he bumped into painter Erik Slutsky.

ERIK SLUTSKY: He looked horrible. I'd never seen him like that. I thought, "My goodness, he's sick." So thin and haggard-looking. I thought, "Does he have cancer?"

BILL FURY: I was heading out to the store and turned onto the Main, and heard a voice crying out from across the street, "Billy! Billy!" I looked over—Leonard. Late November, winter coat, cap, white grocery bags in his hands. I gave him a wave. "Billy," he said, "it's a lovely, lonely life."

Back in LA, Dianne Lawrence dropped by. She had joined a dating site.

DIANNE LAWRENCE: "Any success?" he asked. "Not really. All I get are bearded guys who live in the woods telling me I'm 'purty.'" Then I asked him how he'd describe himself if he joined a site. "I would never do that," he said. "But *if* you did, how would you describe yourself?" He became thoughtful and answered, "Handsome man available, lonely. Wanted: Everyone."

During his recovery, Cohen reached out to French producer Jean-Michel Reusser.

JEAN-MICHEL REUSSER: He said, "I've got this song. Do you think Jean-Philippe [Rykiel] would be available?" He sent me a demo, where, very frankly, he can barely sing, but which is so emotional, really, you cry when you hear it. I said, "If we work together, I insist we work [with] this vocal take."

He resisted that. I said, "I want that voice." . . . "No, it's not good, na, na, na." It was a waltz and a little too close to "Take This Waltz." Then I had no news. I knew it would go on the shelf. There were six or seven demos that never got the light of day, completely different versions, arrangements. Maybe I didn't insist enough.

When his health permitted, Cohen meditated at Rinzai-Ji, and encouraged friends to sit with him.

PERLA BATALLA: For Leonard, this [was] definitely a pilgrimage, a search for a very deep thing. Because Zen was so unglamorous. Julie [Christensen] and I went twice—all day, until five p.m. I said, "This is ridiculous. I have a kid. I'm going home." Leonard laughed hysterically. In our last conversation about Zen, I said, "I know it's good for me, but I just don't know if I'm feeling what I'm supposed to feel." He said, "Darling, ten minutes a day is all you have to do. I do it twice a day, but once a day is great." Then he says, "Let me tell you about this monk in India [Ramesh Balsekar]—ninety years old, been practicing forever. He said, 'I've been doing this for seventy years and every time I finish meditating, I ask myself, am I doing this right?'"

In March, on McGill University's 190th anniversary, sixty thousand graduates voted from among seven hundred alumni for the Greatest McGillian. Cohen came in second, behind Dr. Thomas Chang, inventor of the first artificial cell—forerunner of nanotechnology. Nobel Prize winner Ernest Rutherford finished third.

That same month, Cohen flew to New York to attend a NEeMA concert at Joe's Pub.

RALPH GIBSON: I saw him backstage. I'll never know why, but we had come to the end of our friendship—moved into different worlds. It's happened several times—great friendships that for no specific reason drift apart, fully intact. It's a by-product in part of living a long time.

Later that month, in Montreal, poet Asa Boxer came to visit, to discuss the new Montreal International Poetry Prize.

ASA BOXER: He didn't think poetry needed any help, but he took a liking to my poetry and said encouraging things. He said I was like Bezalel, who in the Bible supervised the building of the Ark of the Covenant. Leonard helped financially, anonymously, and substantially. A few grand here, a few grand there, but especially when we got started. Kabbalah came up. I said I found it helpful as a discipline, but it did not make one a moral being. He confirmed it. "These things don't change you," he said. "You are who you are."

In June, inducted into the American Songwriters Hall of Fame, Cohen sat at a table with Philip Glass, Leon Wieseltier, Robert Faggen, Robert Kory, and Michelle Rice. Kory was then promoting an ambitious new project, Broadway 4D, a venture envisaging 3D films of Broadway show tunes, sung by stars, with special effects, including scents.

ROBERT FAGGEN: Kory wanted Leonard to invest and Leonard wouldn't. He knew Kory was a good tax guy but not necessarily a good business guy. Kory lost a huge amount of money.

Kory had spent much of the 1990s immersed in another failed venture—the Wonderful World of Oz theme park in Kansas. State legislators initially backed the project but, as costs skyrocketed, support waned. Nothing came of it.

In mid-July, Cohen resumed the tour, playing thirty-five concerts in Europe, fourteen in Australia and New Zealand, and half a dozen in North America, finishing again in Las Vegas. According to *Billboard* Boxscore's incomplete tally, shows for just 60 percent of his itinerary grossed $85.7 million from 2008 to 2010. In 2010 alone, Cohen's revenues topped those earned by Elton John, Carrie Underwood, or Rod Stewart.

SEYMOUR MAYNE: It's an incredible story, a guy in his seventies going back on the road and becoming more famous and richer than ever. Leonard is a great inspiration because he went into the deepest hell of himself and the modern world—all the craziness, sexuality, everything—and came back out again, faced it and flourished. It's one of the great, affirming stories.

LEON WIESELTIER: He never ceased to be amazed at the magnitude of the love he found everywhere. Look at his eyes on those tours. He was lifted up by what he found on the road. And he discovered that he'd given the world its favourite song—"Hallelujah."

*   *   *

In June 2011, Spain's Prince of Asturias prize jury conferred its prestigious award for letters on Cohen—for "a body of literary work that has influenced three generations of people worldwide."

PAUL HUMPHREYS: I remember congratulating him. He said, "When they first called, I thought it was a mistake."

ALBERTO MANZANO: He made the most beautiful speech I've ever heard. He also showed his drawings and watercolours at the city's university, surrounded by students. He was very happy. I saw him crying, while a chorus of children sang "Hallelujah."

ROBERT FAGGEN: The Asturias speech is excellent, but those things were hard for him to write. It took a lot of energy and he didn't like doing it.

In his speech, Cohen expressed ambivalence about the award, since "poetry comes from a place that no one commands, that no one conquers." But inhaling the aroma of his forty-year-old Conde guitar, he seemed to hear a voice admonish him for not thanking "the soil and the soul of this land that has given me so much." Of course, he also saluted Lorca, the poet who had given him "permission to find a voice, to locate a voice . . . to locate a self, a self that is not fixed, a self that struggles for its own existence." Then Cohen retold the story of meeting—in the early 1960s in Montreal's Murray Hill Park—a young Spaniard playing flamenco guitar, who agreed to give Cohen guitar lessons. Over the next several days, he learned a six-chord progression which, Cohen insisted, formed the basis "of all my music. . . . So everything that you have found favourable in my songs and my poetry are inspired by this soil." The guitar teacher had failed to turn up for the final lesson.

LEONARD COHEN: When I phoned his boardinghouse, they told me he'd committed suicide. I don't know whether that was because of the progress with his student.

Cohen was certainly exaggerating when he claimed his entire oeuvre derived from six chords, but several songs do deploy flamenco progressions. According to some friends, Cohen may also have embellished the core anecdote, or even invented it.

DAVID LIEBER: What are the chances of a young gypsy guitarist hanging around Westmount [in that era]? He just happens to be suicidal, of course—a recurring theme. At the end of this incredibly self-conscious speech, Leonard says those chords are responsible for his whole career, and there's something distinctively Spanish about them, which they are not. No four chords form the basis of anybody's musical tradition. I call that bullshit.

GABRIELA VALENZUELA: Leonard didn't make it up. He told me he met him in a park. The guy was a lifeguard at a pool, where he'd go to swim. He found out he played the guitar and asked him to teach him. But Leonard didn't really have the rolling [flamenco style]. We used to laugh, because he was Leonard Cohen and he couldn't do this.

BARRIE WEXLER: The story is true, though there's no pool in Murray Hill. He was a Spaniard, not a gypsy. It wasn't four chords, it was six, part of a harmonic series that forms the basis of flamenco—a progression known as the Andalusian cadence. I guarantee you, Leonard Cohen did not lie to the king of Spain.

ROBERT COHEN: I know the story he told when he won the prize. I think [it's] a wonderful product of Leonard's imagination, a fabrication.

Filmmaker Tony Palmer saw Cohen in Spain. The reedited version of his 1972 documentary, *Bird on a Wire*, had recently won the Grierson Award—among the most prestigious awards in documentary film. The backstory is convoluted and contentious. Palmer's reedit was based on thirty-eight boxes of discarded outtakes from the original film, which Frank Zappa's manager, Herb Cohen, had found in a Hollywood warehouse. Palmer married almost three thousand fragments from 294 outtake reels to the original soundtrack, at a cost of about $100,000.

TONY PALMER: The [original] negative—that's still lost. But we had 70 percent of the sound mix. The cans were rusted solid. We had to hammer them open, extract the celluloid, then digitize it. I kept Leonard informed but didn't ask for his approval. The recent version is true to the original spirit of the film. I owed it to the feelings I had about him in 1972 to try to get it back to what it was. The songs are haunting. The poetry is extraordinary. But so is the man. I wanted the Tel Aviv riot scenes because they showed Cohen's power over an audience, not by shouting, but simply by his presence. Authority doesn't really describe it. Transparent goodness is closer. And a profound belief that it is the poet's responsibility to address the political problems of the world. My admiration for Cohen as a poet, singer, and man remains undiminished.

The following year, Palmer successfully screened the reedited film for Cohen-ophiles in Kraków. Cohen messaged him, saying, "I'm very glad the problem has been resolved." Ownership rights to the film remain what Palmer called "a thicket of confusion."

TONY PALMER: Everyone has attempted to claim ownership. But I paid for it, not Sony, not Steven, not the estate, nor Avril. The fact remains that had it not been for me, *Bird on a Wire* would not exist in its present form and would have been denied access to its legions of fans.

That fall, in 2011, the National Ballet of Canada's Karen Kain approached Cohen. To mark his eightieth birthday, she proposed to set his music to a new piece, choreographed by Wayne McGregor.

KAREN KAIN: Eventually, Leonard called me—I could barely breathe, I was so excited. He told me about his tour, that it would take every ounce of energy to complete. "I don't even have the energy for family or friends. I live like a monk. I don't see anyone. I recover, regroup, and do the next show." I was disappointed, as was Wayne. He was so lovely, and let me down in such a generous way. He told me that he loved me and remembered meeting me in the rain twenty years earlier.

When Willie Aron's father passed away in January 2012, Cohen attended the shiva in Hancock Park.

WILLIE ARON: He sat with me for at least two hours, asked me questions about my dad. There was a movie, an oral history, that my dad delivered about growing up in Poland before the war. Leonard was quite rapt. My dad started singing "The Partisan," a folk song every resistance movement sang. My dad sang it in English. Leonard sang it back to the screen, in Yiddish. I will never forget that moment as long as I live. He was a great, great person.

That month, Columbia released *Old Ideas*, Cohen's twelfth studio album. Although most of the work was his, the music for four tracks was written by Patrick Leonard, who had previously produced Adam Cohen. They had spent most of 2011 on the album. Cohen, as always, laboured over his songs.

NADINE NEEMEH: He wasn't happy with "Lullaby," but couldn't pinpoint why. He went on many walks, thinking about it. In the end, the only thing that remained was the chorus. The verses completely changed . . . and this new thing came up that was so much better. It's that nonstop search, uncovering after uncovering, digging and digging.

BARRIE WEXLER: He used to say you delve into work like a paleontologist. Dig deep, maybe come up with a rib, then a limb or two, if you're lucky, a jaw. It can take a while before you know what kind of creature you're dealing with.

Reflecting his resurgent popularity, *Old Ideas* became his bestselling American album, reaching number three on the Billboard 200, and topping charts in eleven other countries. Thematically, it saw Cohen wrestling with familiar motifs—fractured relationships ("Different Sides"), depression ("Darkness"), death—not imminent but approaching ("Going Home"), and God ("Amen"). The latter continued Cohen's "dialogue" with the Almighty—his uncertainty that God cared about the world he created. "I'm listening so hard that it hurts," Cohen sings, but his effort is unrewarded. Jan Swafford, writing in Slate, observed that the album's "valedictory quality is inescapable. . . . There's a kind of aura around every line, a sense of something said once and for all."

BARRIE WEXLER: He often alluded to his lifelong wrestling match with God, saying he got pinned every round.

The next month, in Boston, the New England chapter of PEN honoured Cohen and Chuck Berry for excellence in lyric writing. Eric Lerner joined him for the occasion. By now, Cohen was a certifiable celebrity, unable to leave his hotel without being recognized. "And to think," he said, "I owe it all to her." The her, of course, was Kelley Lynch, but for whose actions he might never have returned to the stage.

PAUL BURGER: The only thing we have Kelley to thank for is bringing him out of semi-retirement. He enjoyed the most successful tours of his life and rebuilt his financial position to way better than it had ever been.

SEYMOUR MAYNE: If Kelley hadn't done what she did, he would not have been the phoenix rising from the ashes.

BARRIE WEXLER: Talking about Kelley, he cited a principle espoused by the rabbinical ethicist, the Chofetz Chaim—the duty to thank someone who does you harm, if it turns out well.

Over dinner with Lerner, Cohen confessed: "I don't know what it all means. A kind of vindication, I suppose." In a reflective state of mind, he made an astonishing confession. Despite the parade of women to his bed, he told Lerner, "I've never really had what you had, that real thing with a woman, that psychosexual whatever. Love. And it's taken me a long time to come to terms with the fact that I'm never going to have it. . . . I never bumped into the right chick. Or if I did, had no idea who she was. I seem to be incapable. Or it's just not meant to be."

BARRIE WEXLER: It wasn't the right chick he never bumped into. He didn't want to bump into a different Leonard Cohen. That would have meant losing the thing that drove the work, which he protected at all costs. He was always acutely aware of exactly who he was meant to be.

RIFKAH ROTH: When he was with a lover, that's when he experienced connection with the universe. That's probably why he always had to have a woman on the go. It gave him an earthly resemblance to the connection he was looking for.

The new year found Cohen in Europe, promoting the new album. After interviews with journalists at Paris's Hôtel de Crillon, he met privately with singer Sandra Zemor.

SANDRA ZEMOR: Leonard was a mentor, something from my soul family. It was like meeting the Dalai Lama or [Hasidic thinker] Rabbi Nachman—the energy of a prophet, a high love, enveloping me. He was like a *passeur*. A transmitter of light, but also a soul awakener. He told me he read Nachman when his marriage was ending. For a week after [his visits], I couldn't go out. It was transforming me, to become closer to myself.

In February, Cohen's daughter, Lorca, gave birth to Viva Katherine Wainwright Cohen. Her childhood friend, Rufus Wainwright—married to arts administrator Jörn Weisbrodt—was the sperm donor. Whatever understandings they had arrived at soon led to friction. Indeed, according to one family friend, the parental custody agreement had failed to draw clear boundaries. Lorca was surprised when Rufus demanded more access to his daughter than had been bargained for.

ANONYMOUS: Lorca and Rufus were really close, for years. For a decade, she talked about having his sperm create a child. There was no contract, but it was understood that the child would be Lorca's. She'd be a single mom. She paid for everything—doctors, flights to follow Rufus on tour. There was one miscarriage—then she went through it all again, and it resulted in Viva. Rufus wanted to be part of raising Viva, but that was never Lorca's plan. There was a legal battle and a bunch of stressful shit. Leonard took the stance that Rufus should be allowed to be a father, especially since he was wanting it.

Protracted and bitter litigation ensued. Lorca kept losing. Cohen himself was said to be furious, maintaining that the couple were waging war in the little girl's heart. He felt Rufus had honourable intentions and it could be worked out. Lorca refused. Then she had a second child, also by a sperm donor, a gay interior designer in LA.

Cohen had also experienced friction with Adam. Touring his new album, *Like a Man*, Adam performed in Sutton, Quebec, at Salle Alec et Gérard Pelletier—named for the parents of Andrée Pelletier, his father's former lover. She went backstage to introduce herself.

ANDRÉE PELLETIER: I said, "I've met your father." He said, "Yeah, so have I." Not in a nice way. Like, not good things happening there.

BERNIE ROTHMAN: The boy resented his father, a lot.

LINDA GABORIAU: He and Adam were estranged for many years. I'm so glad they had a reconciliation.

By this time, Sasaki Roshi, 105, was in decline.

HAROLD ROTH: Roshi's epiglottis wouldn't close properly. He got lung infections from rotting food going to his lungs. He was going downhill.

SARAH KRAMER: Roshi used to say to Leonard, "Please forgive me for not dying."

MYOREN KUMIKO YASUKAWA: He had pneumonia. The acid reflux never stopped. He wasn't able to eat or drink. He needed IV. He was taken to Claremont

Hospital. I was Roshi's *inji*. The first person I called was Leonard. He came right away, a long drive. Then we moved Roshi to Cedars-Sinai. Leonard came every day to relieve me.

STEVE KRIEGER: I was helping Myoren, and Leonard became like his third caretaker. He and Roshi had a shared vision: Roshi taught it, Leonard sang it. I'd describe it as the union of contrary things, then their separation again, and the struggle in between.

BARRIE WEXLER: Leonard termed his vision the "orchestration of opposites."

RUTH COHEN: Esther told me Leonard paid all of Roshi's medical bills.

MYOREN KUMIKO YASUKAWA: [After] he was released, Leonard came every other day with lunch. Roshi was seeing the same doctor as Leonard—[Beverly Hills internist] Dr. Joshua Trabulus.

ROBERT FAGGEN: Rebecca De Mornay put Leonard together with Trabulus. Trabulus weighed in on Roshi's moral behaviour—in front of Rebecca. Leonard was none too happy.

HAROLD ROTH: After a week in Cedars-Sinai, they brought him back to Rinzai-Ji. Roshi had always been fond of smoked beef tongue. He was really weak, eating through a tube. They decided to blend the tongue and feed it through this tube into his stomach. They did it every day for two weeks. One day, he got out of bed, waddled into the kitchen, picked up a fistful, stuffed it into mouth, and said, "Roshi all better now." Then he revives, gets involved again in Rinzai-Ji, and basically fires the guy running it. He was teaching until he couldn't speak anymore.

MYOREN KUMIKO YASUKAWA: It was like a miracle. He was on three powerful antibiotics for two months. By May, he was able to talk.

In Canada, Max Layton was organizing a centenary celebration of his father, Irving.

MAX LAYTON: A beautiful thing. In every major town, from Newfoundland to Victoria, on March 12, 2012, people read his poems. It culminated in a ceremony [in Toronto]. Leonard couldn't come, but sent a video, reading one of my dad's poems. It was done perfectly.

Layton, then working on a new CD, sent sound files to Cohen for comment.

MAX LAYTON: This goes on for eleven or twelve songs. I never saw him, but went backstage after one of his [last] concerts. His eyes came to me—I had not seen him in thirty years—and, "Maxie! . . . How nice of you to come!" Instantaneous recognition.

Meanwhile, awards continued to be lavished on Cohen. In April, the Glenn Gould Foundation made him the ninth laureate of the Glenn Gould Prize. Its director, Brian Levine, had met him earlier in LA.

BRIAN LEVINE: As a gift, I brought him some really exquisite tea. He said, "I make tea for Roshi every day. This is what I'll make." He in turn handed me the pin for the Order of the Unified Heart and said he'd like to induct me. I struggled to insert the pin into my lapel and he said, "Brian, Brian, my father was a tailor, and he'd be horrified at the way you're mangling that fine piece of fabric. Let me do it for you." I may be the only person to be pinned by Leonard Cohen.

Cohen, Levine understood, "was noted for having a pretty serious temper, particularly in his [record] label dealings. But he'd crossed a Rubicon and become beloved. I found him gentle, humble, humorous, gracious, kind, appreciative, and very collaborative." Only one stipulation gave Cohen pause—that a Protégé Prize be awarded to a young artist of promise.

BRIAN LEVINE: He wasn't sure he could choose from so many deserving candidates. But after some explanation, he decided to award it to Sistema Toronto, an organization that provides free music training to disadvantaged children.

Cohen donated his own $50,000 award to the Canada Council for the Arts. The May 2012 ceremony at Massey Hall, featuring actor Alan Rickman reading Cohen's poetry, was followed by an after-party at Fran's Restaurant, a low-brow diner.

BRIAN LEVINE: We didn't know 'til the last minute if he'd come. Suddenly, we look out the window and there's a phalanx of people, minding Leonard as he crosses the street. He comes in and [the band] Lighthouse performs "Tower of Song" and he's totally into it, dancing. Then he ate sliders and fries with Adrienne Clarkson.

Meanwhile, preparing for the Old Ideas tour, Cohen made some band changes.

MITCH WATKINS: I replaced [Bob] Metzger. It was more people, higher stakes, more money, so it was less often you actually got to hang with him, though it did happen. Those were times I treasured because you never knew where a conversation was going to go, or what gem you'd pick up to take with you. Such a brilliant guy. Such a spiritual seeker.

Metzger had left of his own volition. Dino Soldo, replaced with violinist Alex Bublitchi, did not.

BOBBY FURGO: They fired Dino because he was showing off too much.

DINO SOLDO: We were going to start rehearsals in May but, in April, Leonard wanted to go through things, wanted new sounds. It seemed like he was doing to me that thing I'd seen him do to others. You could bring him a cake stuffed with a million dollars and he would not like it. You could have any idea—he was just not liking your contributions. I'd been featured on two live DVDs. It only made sense to let me go, feature Alex, and have a new show. I knew he wanted that, but he wasn't admitting it. I said, "Leonard, I'm happy. Do you want me here?" And he'd say, "Of course! I love you." But it never felt that way. It was a coldness.

Soldo sensed the axe descending.

DINO SOLDO: We both loved Louis Armstrong. We'd been working on a new song. He played the keyboard with horn sounds, but wanted your horn to sound like that sound—a plain, almost robotic sound. I said, "Why don't we forget all this and play like Louis?" He said, "Great idea." Ten minutes later, I'm playing like Louis and, out of the blue, I hear "No, no, no!" I'd never heard him raise his voice, ever. The whole band stops. It was, like, "Wow, something is going on here."

Other musicians told Soldo, "When he loves you, he loves you, and when he doesn't, he'll make a reason."

DINO SOLDO: Once [Leonard] has an emotion, everyone onstage cosigns to that emotion. It's the cult of Leonard Cohen. The greenroom would be a library—because he was in a mood to have quiet, everyone would be quiet. I'd never been in a band where people take their emotional cues off [the leader].

A week later, Soldo asked for a three-day leave to accompany his wife and newborn son to her native Germany.

DINO SOLDO: He said, "No problem." I said, "Are you sure?" . . . "No problem." I left Thursday night. He called everybody and booked [weekend] rehearsals without me. When I landed Sunday night, he [sent] an email saying please don't come to rehearsal. He behaved very poorly—let's just say that. He did the exact opposite of what he'd promised. Of course, it was his band. But he could have called me in Germany and said, "Stay with your family." It was just so weird. The email was about three sentences. It was generous financially because he kept me on the payroll at half salary through the end of the year. I can't take it personally. He wanted that, and I knew he wanted that, and I don't mind. He just didn't want to admit it.

JOEY CARENZA: It was awkward. It wasn't handled great. But those two paths had been diverging for a while. It was not about personality. Leonard *loved* Dino. That was one of his weak spots. He never wanted to fire anybody. It was gut-wrenching for him. Dino was maybe a bit bored with the show, wanted it to have more energy. Leonard was going another direction, and he gave everyone ample notice that was the direction the tour was going.

To this day, Soldo has not heard Cohen's final album. "I just can't listen to his music. His letting me go was the first and last time I was ever fired and I resented his not speaking the truth to me, just doing the hard thing. And the way he did it, making me fly back from Germany. In a way, he broke my heart. His music is very emotional for me and not in a good way."

By then, violinist Alex Bublitchi had secured a Romanian passport, allowing entry to Commonwealth countries. He improvised a series of violin riffs at the first rehearsal, and Cohen declared, "Friends, this will be something extraordinary." To one rehearsal, Cohen invited film producer Robert Lantos.

ROBERT LANTOS: I took [actress] Lucy Punch along, not knowing that we were in for the thrill of a lifetime. We sat there transfixed as Leonard performed the revamped two-and-a-half-hour show. At the end, he looked at me from the stage, and said, "This one is for Robert," and sang "Amen."

On Sunday, July 21, Cohen celebrated the fiftieth anniversary of Sasaki Roshi's arrival in the US. After a ceremony at Rinzai-Ji, almost three hundred people paraded across the road to the lawn of the Clark Memorial Library.

PAUL HUMPHREYS: We had it catered. Perla Batalla performed. We ran up quite a bill. Leonard was the go-to guy whenever the centre ran into trouble. At one point, I asked if he could help us out. Other people were pitching in a thousand dollars. He said, "Would five grand be okay?" He wrote the cheque right there. Leonard sat in front on the grass in his suit and his hat, knees up.

Soon after, Cohen dropped into Hollywood Hatters on Melrose Avenue, across the street from Lorca's antiques store. There, he met singer-songwriter Mark Huff.

MARK HUFF: I'm at the counter, looking at this hat and hear "Hey, man. That's the one." I turn and see this man in a suit, a hat, and sunglasses and thought, "What the hell is Dustin Hoffman doing here?" Then I realized who it was. I said, "Ya think?" He says, "Oh, yeah. Pay the man." So we started talking, about Nashville and songwriting. Rebecca De Mornay was there—she was driving him around. I told him I was having writer's block, and he said he had that, too, occasionally. He said, "Sometimes you just have to write shitty songs to get them out of the way, so the good ones can come. You have to stay with it." We talked for fifteen minutes, and when I went to leave, I said, "Mr. Cohen, it was nice to meet you." And I just felt this thing—and I hugged him. I got teary-eyed. Then he whispered in my ear, "Bless you, Mark." And I said, "Bless you, Leonard." It was destiny. I was supposed to meet him. My car had a parking ticket, like $75, and I didn't even care.

The next month, Cohen was briefly back in Montreal.

MARGIE GILLIS: That's the last time I saw him—in an alley, just off St.-Lawrence, leaning in the shadows, tucked into the alcove wall. I said, "Leonard, it's Margie." And he went, "Oh, Margie," and pulled his hat back. He said, "You've just got to keep going, Margie. There are so few of us left now. There's so few of us left." He looked and sounded like a sleepy, gravelly drug dealer. I was definitely buying what he had to sell. I still am.

The Old Ideas tour began August 12, 2012, in Ghent, Belgium, and continued into October. In Paris, Cohen played three concerts at the Olympia.

ANDREW SWEENY: That was the only time I saw Leonard live, at his final show in Paris. I'd been afraid I might be disappointed. I couldn't have been more wrong. After the first couple of minutes, tears began pouring from my eyes. I was struck by the fact that he was on his knees maybe half the time, as if in worshipful prayer. Those shows had the uncanny quality of a religious advent, as all great collective expressions of art should.

SHELDON TAYLOR: Going down on his knees—it was showmanship, but also smart. The rugs were there to protect his knees and give him a bit of a rest.

MAX LAYTON: A style adapted from the French chansonniers. He could easily have been Claude Léveillée, Jacques Brel. You go down on your knees for a love song. But he knows it's a theatrical moment.

AVIVA LAYTON: I said, "Leonard, the miracle isn't that you get down on your knees. The miracle is, you jump up again." The generosity—he gave the best concerts that anybody has ever given.

Cohen's personal assistant, Kezban Özcan, had joined the tour.

JOEY CARENZA: Without her, it would not have kept going. She freed up so much energy for him, taking care of the little things. She was absolutely essential to making sure he stayed in the game.

In October, in Madrid, Cohen granted another private pre-concert audience—to Pakistani writer Ahmed Rashid, a devotee since his days at Cambridge in the late 1960s. For decades, Cohen's music, almost exclusively, had accompanied his travels.

AHMED RASHID: I was bowled over—he'd read my book [*Descent into Chaos*] and given copies to the musicians. We were together two hours. We talked politics, Afghanistan, the Muslim world, Buddhism, Roshi, America. He was very engaged. I asked him if he was having an affair with Sharon [Robinson]. He said no. We discussed hats—his were Borsalinos, made in Italy. He was visibly older, frail, but then this old man was suddenly jumping around onstage with incredible energy.

RIFKAH ROTH: The hats were his self-imposed adherence to the Jewish call for a head covering.

That fall, Sylvie Simmons published her Cohen biography, *I'm Your Man*. Gabriela Valenzuela, his lover for six years in the 1980s, scanned the book in vain for her name.

GABRIELA VALENZUELA: One short line appeared about translating García Lorca's poems—"assisted by a Spanish speaking–Costa Rican girlfriend." I was disheartened, astonished by the erasure. In an attempt to heal, I reached Kory. He said Leonard was on tour, but I could visit him when he returned to LA.

In early November, Cohen again played LA's Nokia Theatre.

DON WAS: He infused every word with meaning. He was present the entire time. Nothing by rote. A very impressive performance. Leonard was ahead of just about everybody I know for distilling the truth out of a song. He didn't necessarily have the vocal gifts, but he had the intelligence, the focus, and the presence to inhabit every line. And the lines were brilliant.

YOSHIN DAVID RADIN: Even as a performer, he was a monk. He had the confidence and humour to expose the real nakedness of life.

The next month, an old summer-camp friend of Cohen's persuaded Kory to let her backstage at Boston's Wang Theatre.

CECILLE GOLD RAICHLEN: He was even more gracious than he'd been when we were unit heads in 1956. My memories of him are vivid. Almost every night, when the kids were in bed, he'd sing with his guitar. Mostly folk songs, some of his own as well. Even then he was a ladies' man. He was hitting on a young counsellor—Shulamit, eighteen, very attractive. I think he succeeded and she was crushed, because he didn't hang on very long. His girlfriend, Freda [Guttman], was around as well. Some days, I liked him. Other days, he was dark—like a vat of tar, black, solemn, and sticky. Freda put up with a lot.

Cohen was still on the road when the Sasaki Roshi bubble finally burst. Zen monk Eshu Martin—in an article on SweepingZen.com—publicly accused him of coercive sexual behaviour.

MATTHEW REMSKI: For decades, [Roshi] enticed, seduced, tricked, or forced dozens of his Western female acolytes into various forms of sexual service.

He'd tell them that to yield to him was to obey a cosmic harmony, that not yielding would keep their minds closed and dull. He interfered in marriages. He threatened noncompliers with mental darkness or social isolation.

Martin's allegations were based on interviews with forty-two women. One had called a crisis hotline. Another filed a police report. A third confronted Roshi in front of his wife, saying, "Try touching me now." Two women said their encounters with Roshi had healed sexual problems. Although five had rebuffed his advances, eleven others insisted he repeatedly grabbed at them, sometimes dozens of times in one day, over months, sometimes years. The Martin article triggered a tsunami of recrimination.

BRIAN LESAGE: Even though many knew about it, it hit a whole new level and completely disrupted the organization, which needed to happen.

CAROLE WILSON: Roshi would have private sessions with each student—sixty students, four times a day. Some of those sessions were to hit on women. Leonard wasn't really happy about [the revelations], because he wasn't only being asked about his music.

Interviewed by filmmakers Wilson and Don Farber, who were shooting a documentary about Sasaki Roshi, Cohen cited a petition to rein Roshi in.

DON FARBER: I asked what the petition was about. Leonard was vague, but alluded to Roshi's behaviour. It wasn't by accident.

Later, Farber posted a YouTube teaser for the film that included Cohen's comment.

CAROLE WILSON: Then the shit hit the fan.

DON FARBER: From then on, Leonard didn't want anything to do with the scandal. He didn't participate in the sangha meetings about it. But he kept supporting the film—he was the largest donor—though he knew we were going to deal with the scandal.

HAROLD ROTH: Leonard tried to keep away from all politics of Zen. He didn't like politics.

MATTHEW REMSKI: Who would believe that over a thirty-year-plus relationship, including five years as [Roshi's *inji*], and for years a director of the Rinzai-Ji board, that Cohen wasn't aware . . . of the oppressive predation tent-poling the old man's robes? If anything, I imagine he actually gravitated to someone who had managed to perfectly enshroud the most intimate sins in the stark beauty of the koan.

Another former *inji* told Remski that the old man had offered her sexually to Cohen. Embarrassed, he declined, telling her, "You think he's such a nice old man, but he's a monster."

SOHEYL DAHI: Roshi raped women, molested women. I confronted Leonard with it. How could he go along? He had to have known. He never said anything, never distanced himself. There was no excuse. Leonard didn't respond in a direct way. But he had this father-figure complex, all his life. Irving Layton was his first father [figure]. The ultimate father he found in Roshi. He didn't want to lose that, his last father, psychologically.

ARMELLE BRUSQ: Roshi is ninety when Leonard is sixty. There's a missing image of the father. And Leonard doesn't have friends, guys. He had disciples. At Baldy, Roshi would make some suggestion, and I'd say, "Are you joking?" He wasn't joking at all. Leonard once called it a bordello. There are many lost people there.

SUSAN RAY: Leonard had male friends—Steve Sanfield, Eric Lerner. Leonard was Roshi's friend, a role he took seriously. But remember his lyric, "Here's to the few / Who forgive what you do / And the fewer who don't even care." It's possible to pathologize Leonard's behaviour—father died young, mother unstable. But there's a flip side—these factors contributed to his awareness and other spiritual gifts. As the Old Man would say, "Don't attach human wisdom."

GRACE MORROW: I was aware that [Roshi] was using Leonard as a pimp, to bring women. I remember Leonard saying, "I'm done. He can find his own women."

BARRIE WEXLER: When Cohen was ordained, Roshi gave him the name "Jikan," which means "silent one." If you want to be darkly cynical, you could speculate he gave him that name for not calling him out. Keep in mind, Roshi's cult of personality was a lot like Leonard's. Leonard wasn't bothered by Roshi trying to get laid—that's how he knew he had the right teacher. Being the poster boy for Roshi's Zen centre when the scandal broke—that he resented.

BARBARA DODGE: It tells you a lot about Leonard because honestly, he's such a fraud himself. It doesn't matter that he was brilliant. The way he used words was a gift. It's called manipulation.

Within the sangha, reactions to the scandal spanned the gamut from damnation to guilty with an explanation.

SHINGETSU BILLY WHITE: If someone took the position that what he did was absolutely wrong, I don't think they understand Zen practice and the intimate experience with a teacher. He was one of the true Zen masters. He cut right to the core of your existence. He'd use anything, even sexuality, to push you off the cliff. Whatever you were trying to hide behind, he saw right through it.

SUSAN RAY: I once asked Roshi if his sexual behaviour toward me was teaching or something else. His answer, "Both."

MYOSHO GINNY MATTHEWS: I met Roshi at twenty-three and was with him for forty-one years. He does divinate this experience of the absolute. I cannot come up with the idea that he was a sexual predator. And the body—sexuality—can be a place of non-liberation. Was Roshi helping them to uncover that conditioning?

RICHARD COHEN: That strikes me as sentimental bullshit.

SUZANNE HYRNIW: Even in 1975, he'd gesture to sit on his lap. I was a different person then—shy, passive, obedient. And he'd just hug me. It was helpful. I didn't feel any sexual thing at all.

JUDY STEED: You hear the justification—Roshi opened up troubled women to their sexuality. What they don't say is that it's all about their sexual gratification. [You have] Roshi, using power to sexually exploit vulnerable women. [And] Leonard, wanting to do the opposite, because he'd done too much seduction, giving himself over to a master who was doing it.

As a senior nun, Matthews became the first point of response for women's complaints.

MYOSHO GINNY MATTHEWS: Another abbess said, "You need to focus on how it affected the community—the secrecy and lies, demonization of women who came forward, and unskilled responses." That, to me, was real damage.

MYOREN KUMIKO YASUKAWA: He hit on me, began to hug me a little longer. I myself had felt frustrated. It's not something you can understand logically—too many layers. A lot of women in this culture [are] very confused. Even I don't understand it, so how can anybody who has no context understand it?

For Ray Ronci, director of the Hokoku-An Zendo meditation centre in Columbia, Missouri, the scandal was "our collective koan—how do you proceed from the Master who fondled breasts? This is a huge dilemma."

SEIDO RAY RONCI: Sasaki Roshi was a great Zen Master, but not a worldly man. He was a Japanese greenhorn Zen Master. I often felt I was practicing with an eighteenth-century monk. I don't think he ever really knew this culture. Sometimes, I don't think he even knew this century. But I have no doubt about his enlightenment. Sasaki either ignored or refused to see the cultural boundaries of this particular time and place. He's a man with baggage. My teacher was flawed. So be it. I am flawed. My teacher made mistakes. I make mistakes.

CRISTOPHE LEBOLD: Leonard told me, "Roshi was not a little yoga teacher. He was a ball of fire, running down Mount Baldy. If you don't want to be charred, don't approach."

SUSAN RAY: Roshi could be a million things—a boorish peasant, a butterfly, the full moon, a horse. I did see what looked like compulsive behaviour. I don't think it was behaviour he could entirely control.

AVIVA LAYTON: Every time you surrender to a guru, there's going to be exploitation. I think he saved Leonard's life.

SUSAN RAY: I would say the same—he saved my life.

JULIANNA RAYE: Shinzen Young warned me. He said, "If he tries anything, tell him to fuck off." My own experience is that I always had agency to set boundaries. You swat away a gnat and I did. What I felt was, he was looking for me to have an authentic response and not fixating on being a victim. I got the best of him, because I was prepared. Otherwise, I would have been very confused.

MYOSHO GINNY MATTHEWS: Leonard called Roshi a rascal. Leonard himself, of course, could be a bit of a rascal.

PAUL HUMPHREYS: Leonard didn't lose sleep over it.

JACQUIE BELLON: Both Steve Sanfield and Leonard dismissed the scandal as Roshi being a bad boy and, being bad boys themselves, it was no big deal. My personal take is that women like to fuck power as much as power likes to fuck young women.

RICHARD COHEN: Leonard was bothered insofar as there was a scandal and he got sucked into the bureaucracy [of it]. Privately, his view was that

Roshi was a singular, weird [person] who didn't live by standards you and I would recognize.

DIANNE SEGHESIO: Leonard felt that people walk into that room as Zen practitioners. If you go in as a human being, you were at the wrong teacher.

CATHERINE INGRAM: Part of Leonard's greatness was his understanding of human possibilities, frailties, and complexities. You didn't get cancelled, basically, for behaviour that he might not approve of. He would have held it all in a huge cultural and historical context. He didn't paint people with one colour of the brush, even Kelley.

JOEY CARENZA: He could pragmatically take in positive and negative information about something and not let it sway his opinion. He knew the good and bad. He knew all your faults and he saw you as a human, the complete package.

PICO IYER: Leonard was impatient with explanations, reductions. He doesn't want to say anything glib and probably feels anything he says will be inadequate to the reality, so he brushes it off. People are offended because they think he's not taking it seriously. But what he's not taking seriously is the notion that he could explain very complicated, private transactions. He stressed to me, "This isn't Sunday school, this isn't about being a Boy Scout." I see Roshi as a surrogate partner and life's companion, more of a buddy in whom he could believe. A buddy and a mystery at the same time, a double whammy. Somebody he could be silent with, and someone who he didn't feel he could get to the bottom of. Suddenly, he couldn't reduce or explain.

YOSHIN DAVID RADIN: Roshi had an enormous will. It wasn't like he was subject to review. And Japan never intervened. He was already a scoundrel back in Japan. He has quite a few children floating around, I heard.

In the wake of the scandal, Cohen stepped down from Rinzai-Ji's board of directors; in fact, virtually the entire board resigned. Abbess Hosen Ranger wrote an open letter of apology to the community. And Koshin Christopher Cain, leader of the Puget Sound Zen Center, formally announced disaffiliation with Rinzai-Ji, Inc.

Against the backdrop of the scandal, the Old Ideas tour rolled on. In November, in Detroit, after decades with minimal contact, Cohen reconnected with his first cousin Robert Cohen.

ROBERT COHEN: It was like forty years had not passed, like we were teens again. We spent half an hour together, sang the old songs, spent time talking nonsense words, like a language from another planet. Many, many laughs. I recalled that he once [showed] me about a dozen black ink cartoons, much like *The Far Side*—funny social commentaries. And that he had read me a somewhat erotic short story, about a couple that didn't want body hair, and kept shaving off more and more, until the climax. They're in the bathtub, covered in Vaseline, head to toe, when they both slip and kill themselves by falling. The cartoons and the short story were burned in the [1959] fire on Stanley Street. *Qué lástima*.

MITCH WATKINS: On the last tour, I'd bring my guitar to his room and we'd veer off into conversation. One-on-one, it got to life and religion. He seemed to have so much knowledge in all of those areas. The Kabbalah, the Koran, the Bible—he'd interpret them. Occasionally, we'd go into personal matters. He had incredible insights. I can't be more specific than that. Insights into relationships, women, parents, life. It was so rewarding and I miss that. I miss just knowing he's alive.

JOEY CARENZA: He was also one of the funniest people I've ever been around. He knew every dirty joke, every backstage joke, and was quick with them. But it wasn't the line that was so hilarious. He had this graveyard humour, morbid, but [laced] with optimism. It showed his capacity to see all the levels of whatever was happening—how ridiculous and futile things were, but he would walk through it anyway.

One night in Montreal, Bill Fury saw lights on and rang his doorbell.

BILL FURY: He answered and said, "You won't believe this. We were just talking about you." He was with Morton Rosengarten, and a young girl, asleep in a chair. I said, "Who's that?" He said, "I don't know. She was there when I got here." I think she was someone in the band. It was the last time I saw him.

MORRIS FISH: I saw him twice in Ottawa. On both occasions, he arranged tickets. On the second occasion, he arranged backstage passes. I brought my three law clerks and his cousin, Susannah Cohen Dalfen. Backstage—a Friday—he had challah and wine. He waited for [us] and said the *brachot* [blessings] and made Shabbat. You can imagine the reaction of these young kids, the law clerks, two of them Jewish. They had bought Leonard's CDs and asked if he'd inscribe them, which he did.

After a short hiatus, the tour resumed in March 2013. Folk singer Andrew Calhoun, who had last seen Cohen thirty-eight years earlier, caught his Chicago show.

ANDREW CALHOUN: The greatest concert I ever saw—seven encores. He was seventy-eight and he skipped happily on and off the stage. When it was over, he took off his hat and called the entire crew onto the stage, thanking each. He said, "On a personal note, I'd like to thank you for keeping my songs alive all these years." It went right into my heart. I was one of those people, who sang his songs in small clubs and played them for friends. It was what his fame consisted of, and he knew it, and was grateful.

In April, Roscoe Beck experienced a brief crisis and it wasn't clear whether he'd be able to perform. Mitch Watkins found a bass player replacement from Austin.

PAT HARRIS: I went to the sound check and met Leonard—harrowing. Before they start, he says, "I want you all to meet Pat. He's here to help us out. Please make him feel welcome." I was very moved. He was the most gracious person. And that voice, like this deity coming from the centre of the Earth. I'm thinking he's going to ask, do I know his music? And he asks, "Do you have warm clothing? We're going to the Maritimes and it's going to be cold." That was his first concern. The vibe I got, a fly on the wall for thirty days, was "What can I say or do so that we could have genuine interaction?" Just as a person, he was really on a different plane. Demeanor, carriage, everything about him, the way he would speak. Never a word wasted. I'd overhear a question and, instead of just giving an immediate answer that might meander to the point, he'd pause and consider, then formulate and put it out there, and do it in five words.

After the Wallingford concert, Harris heard a knock at his hotel room door at about 1:00 a.m.

PAT HARRIS: The front-of-house engineer, with a flash drive. "Here's the Kentucky show. Leonard thought you might want to listen." The next morning we took the bus to New York. There, he sent me an email, "Dear Patrick, thank you so much for helping us out. If you need anything, please don't hesitate to let me know. Leonard." That spoke volumes.

Standing in the wings, Harris watched eleven shows, but never performed.

PAT HARRIS: It was closer to a Broadway pit gig than a rock and roll thing, nothing off-the-cuff. But everything about it was so tastefully done, with reverence for the material. That everyone was able to get behind that vision, and be egoless for three hours, says a lot about their ability as musicians. But it starts from the top down.

When the Canadian tour leg ended, Harris was excused.

PAT HARRIS: On my last day, I printed off the charts I'd made, bought a thank-you card, and mailed them with one of my own CDs, saying, "In case you're very bored." He wrote back, succinctly thanking me, saying, "These charts are gorgeous," and suggesting I push the vocal a bit north on my next project.

In May, after a sushi lunch with Sasaki Roshi, Cohen and Eric Lerner repaired to Tremaine to parse the universe in their favourite indoor uniform, underwear.

Over a bottle of scotch with roasted chicken, cheese, and crackers, they pondered the question that had obsessed them for forty years—what their attraction to Zen was fundamentally about. Cohen suggested it was about *sanzen*—the private sessions with Roshi. Nothing else mattered. Lerner maintained that something more was involved—namely, the ineluctable magic of Sasaki Roshi.

ERIC LERNER: In the presence of his radiance, your own pathetic-by-comparison limited self was obliterated. Zap. "That zap is better than anything I ever felt," Leonard noted dispassionately. It wasn't just about *sanzen*. It was about The Guy. It always had been.

But if enlightenment was found by freeing oneself of ego-driven desires, how then to reconcile the fact that The Guy himself "possessed all kinds of desires" he wasn't supposed to have. Ultimately, Cohen concluded, Sasaki Roshi "didn't give a shit about anything anyone else did, as long as he could do what he wanted to do. He liked giving *sanzen*. And he liked fondling girls. . . . Roshi was the only guy I ever met who got away with it. He put together a scene where he could do exactly what he wanted to do because everyone else wanted something from him. He was a total genius."

ERIC LERNER: Leonard was exuberant. It was as if he'd managed to keep this to himself all these years, waiting for the right moment to reveal it, and the right moment had finally come. "Roshi has no conscience." His eyes lit up. He loved saying it aloud. "He's one hundred percent Neanderthal. It's bullshit that Roshi was some kind of self-sacrificing holy man or whatever we want holy men to be. The rest of us try to pretend we don't want what we really want, or that we're acting for some greater good. Roshi never needed to soothe his conscience, because he doesn't have one."

For Lerner, the comment said as much about Cohen as about Roshi.

ERIC LERNER: After all, you are captivated by the master because . . . you want to be like him, possess what you perceive to be his extraordinariness, his spiritual understanding or power, which frees him from whatever you think ensnares you. What drew Leonard to Roshi from the start . . . was that Roshi didn't care. He has no conscience. But Leonard did. His conscience was woven so tightly into the fabric of his being that it was impossible for him to grab the thread and tug it out without the whole thing coming apart. Old Leo the Lion could only yearn and wonder what his life might be like—*if only I didn't have a heart.*

ROBERT FAGGEN: Whatever went on with Roshi, that's what needs to be unpacked. Roshi was very important to him, yet had the moral compass of a sociopath. Leonard and I also concluded that Roshi was an amoral maniac. But Leonard was very sensitive to people cutting up on Roshi.

BRIAN LESAGE: That's the key question—what was it about Roshi that could attract someone like Leonard Cohen? I can't emphasize this enough—in the same breath, he was an incredible Zen master and totally fucked up. He taught me through example what it is to love people. Leonard saw that power and it inspired him in some way. But it's illegal to harm women. It's a crime. That's the side I came down on. The power structure is horrible.

Later that evening, Cohen told Lerner that what Roshi had given him "more than anything else [was] encouragement. It wasn't just about the pleasure of his company, although that was the greatest pleasure of my life. He gave us confidence."

* * *

In June 2013, Cohen embarked on what would be the final legs of the tour. After a concert in Prague, he arrived in Ljubljana and had a few days off. By coincidence, gestalt therapist Jay Levin—brother-in-law of filmmaker Pierre and poet Phil Tétrault—was holding a training seminar in the hotel where Cohen was billeted.

JAY LEVIN: At these workshops, I show Pierre's film about Phil, which shows the impact of mental illness on the family. We approached Leonard's entourage and they said absolutely no. But I got one of Phil's books and delivered it with flowers to Leonard's room with a note explaining who we were. Would he join us? And he accepted.

With band members in tow, Cohen watched—for the first time—the ten-minute park bench outtake of Tétrault's film about his schizophrenic brother, and took questions from the audience.

JAY LEVIN: Incredibly gracious, incredibly generous. Such a gentle man, happy to share his knowledge, to talk about Phil. One person, from the ex-Soviet bloc, said Cohen's music had given him a sense of hope and freedom. Leonard was very touched—that his music had that political aspect. He *was* a little gaunt, but exuded a wonderful, clear energy. He was not a tired old man. One participant asked him if he ever used Phil's poetry in his music. He said, "Well, Phil's good, but not that good."

In early August, arriving in Pula, Croatia, Cohen invited Patrick Leonard and Dutch pianist Iris Hond to join him, Kezban Özcan, and Sharon Robinson for dinner.

IRIS HOND: The next night, at the concert, I cried. My grandmother and mother had loved his music. Afterward, it was Friday night, so Leonard lit the [Sabbath] candles.

JOEY CARENZA: That's where he fired me. It couldn't have been handled better. We sat down in a hotel room and came to a conclusion. Leonard became like a second father to me. I don't say that lightly. He profoundly affected my life, helped me become the kind of man I wanted to be. His strength of conviction. Very sure in his ideas, but that didn't preclude his being open to new ideas. So obviously intelligent, yet how much he delighted in new information. Constant feedback, in a way I'd never had from a male figure. He inspired me to want to work harder, be better. You know that thing with a parent—if they're mad, it's one thing. But if they're disappointed in you, it's heartbreaking? That's how it was with Leonard. A couple times, I totally dropped the ball and he was disappointed with me, and it *destroyed* me.

In Oslo, a few weeks later, Marianne Ihlen had front-row seats. "So Long, Marianne" was the first of the night's three encores. Afterward, she waited to see Cohen but, busy with a group that included Israel's ambassador to Norway, he never appeared. She told tour manager Mike Scoble to give Cohen her regards and a hug. Scoble conveyed the greetings, but opted to skip the hug. Cohen stamped his foot, saying, "I *insist* on having that hug." But Scoble fled the room.

The tour's last hurrah was in the South Pacific—fifteen concerts over five weeks. In Perth, longtime Cohenites Greg and Ann Ross deduced—from a Facebook photograph—that the band was staying at the Sheraton Hotel, and approached him the morning after the show.

GREG ROSS: He wasn't happy to see us. He was startled. I could see him trying to work out what our mission was. We were shocked at his physical condition. The ultra-cool rock god of the previous night had morphed into a small, frail, unfailingly courteous, but exhausted old guy. I established my bona fides as a fan, producing *Book of Longing* and a photo taken at his 2009 concert. He was gracious, in a resigned manner. Then Kezban said, "The bus is waiting." He smiled wanly and was gone. We were so concerned, we contacted the Cohen Forum. Jarkko Arjatsalo replied, saying the band was reporting travel sickness. We knew it was much more.

Cohen's final show was in Auckland on December 21, 2013. His final song was Doc Pomus's "Save the Last Dance for Me." By every possible metric, the tours had been a phenomenal success.

ROB HALLETT: How well did Leonard do financially? He replaced the money that he'd lost and then some. And then a lot some.

And then it was over.

MITCH WATKINS: Coming home from New Zealand, we got off the plane, and went to baggage claim. I suspected he was ill. He was much more frail [then]. I just had a feeling about it. I saw my bags and, when I came back, he was gone. He was never big on a long goodbye.

CHAPTER ELEVEN

Of Course, Life Is Terminal

The actual event I'm not sure about, one way or the other. But I sure don't like the preliminaries.

—Leonard Cohen

Contemporary writing, Leonard explained, comes in three waves. Guys who break down the walls—Henry Miller, Alan Ginsberg, Bob Dylan. Those who build from the toppled stones—Mailer, Roth, Updike, Bellow, others. After them, the ones who plant the flowers. I said he'd be among those in the initial wave. "I don't think so," he replied. "I'm still trying to put my hands on a gardening trowel."

—Barrie Wexler

Years of touring would have taken a toll on a performer half his age. It certainly took a toll on Leonard Cohen, septuagenarian. In 2013 alone, on the precipice of eighty, he played a gruelling fifty-two concerts in Europe and North America, then flew to the South Pacific for sixteen more. After his final European show, he complained to friends.

BARRIE WEXLER: He was upset about Europe—concerts in the rain and cold. His attitude was, Kory almost killed him.

But there were intimations of illness even earlier.

DIANNE SEGHESIO: Leonard was fighting illness for a long time. He had had throat things—[from] smoking.

STEVE ZIRKEL: In Austin [October 2012], I saw Leonard going into the elevator. He looked really different, small and hunched over and having back pain. Later, Mitch [Watkins] told me he was sick.

SARAH KRAMER: Neil Larsen told me they were on a plane and Leonard's tooth began to bleed, and wouldn't stop bleeding. That kind of thing can be systemic.

ROBERT FAGGEN: He had a root canal done in LA before he left, and it caused a massive infection. He had to be treated [with antibiotics] in Australia. But it took a huge toll on him.

Then, likely in 2013, he was diagnosed with immune thrombocytopenic purpura (ITP), a blood disorder; the immune system produces antibodies that inhibit platelet formation. The impaired clotting mechanism leaves ITP patients at risk of serious bleeding events.

ROBERT FAGGEN: The ITP came first. I think Leonard learned of this before the final leg of the 2013 tour.

More worrisome, ITP occurs in 40 to 65 percent of patients with myelodysplastic syndrome (MDS), cancers that inhibit the manufacture of mature blood cells.

ROBERT FAGGEN: They told him it would likely develop into MDS, a disorder that creates fracturing of the bones. I gulped and said, "That's a disease that can't be cured." And Leonard said, "We all have to go some way." The problem is that in 25 percent of all MDS patients, it morphs into leukaemia, which is what happened.

The median survival time from diagnosis is about thirty months. There was a certain irony in the diagnosis of faulty bone marrow machinery.

ROBERT FAGGEN: Leonard liked bone marrow. He'd let shank bones soak in salt water to get the blood out, then broil them so they were just right. Then we'd eat the marrow. In his last years, Leonard was interested in trying to maintain his strength. Certain rich foods were particularly good for his system. We'd go to places that served high-quality oysters. We had a particular fascination with steak. We watched a documentary—[*Steak (R)evolution*], about raising cattle for beef. We were constantly scoping out steak houses, as his health permitted. Musso and Frank [Grill] in Hollywood, the Grill on the Alley. Harvey Guss's Meats supplied the best houses in LA. I ordered two dry-aged rib eyes and we grilled them.

Back from New Zealand, Cohen attended Robert Kory's Christmas party.

ROBERT FAGGEN: He actually said, "Please come and protect me." We sat on the couch and talked about Lorca. Her relationship with Rufus [Wainwright] was blowing up. I can't tell you how much that troubled Leonard.

For a time, there was talk of another tour.

ELLIOTT LEFKO: Leonard wanted to do it. Robert wanted to. AEG wanted to. Because if I didn't do it, someone else would. Maybe just Montreal, New York, Europe. Maybe a residency in Ireland. Let the people come to him. There were rumours going out to the crew—get ready. Let's just wait 'til he gets better. I'd say, "Robert, what's going on?" . . . . "He's not well." He wouldn't state exactly what it was.

ROB HALLETT: We talked about potentially doing some dates, how to do it, easier. I knew about the leukaemia. I didn't know how serious. He kept it away from me. Always had a smile.

JAVIER MAS: He said, "I have many pains, especially in my back. I find it hard to get up and I'm tired. They are giving me tests." But he did not think it was so serious. He left the instruments in LA, thinking we'd tour again.

When Eric Lerner arrived in January 2014, Cohen joked about parking himself in a Las Vegas casino. "I could be the Wayne Newton of the introspective gambling set," he quipped.

ERIC LERNER: Then he received the diagnosis. "It's called MDS. Myelodys-plastic syndrome," he carefully enunciated.

ROBERT FAGGEN: He had fantastically low blood platelet counts. A normal count ranges from 150,000 to 350,000. His were in the thousands—way below anything resembling normal.

ERIC LERNER: His platelet count . . . became our closely watched Dow-Jones average for the next three years. He made me promise not to tell anyone, saying, "I can't deal with dying publicly."

Cohen's work ethic was already legendary; the diagnosis steeled his resolve. "He became slightly mesmerized by the grains of sand streaming through the narrow neck of the hourglass," Lerner recalled. "It's a race to the death." A bone marrow transplant was discussed, but Cohen, according to Faggen, was "not interested in extraordinary procedures." And, approaching eighty, Cohen was past the age when a transplant procedure was likely to be effective.

ERIC LERNER: In one of our first conversations after the diagnosis, he told me he'd already decided he wouldn't undergo any treatment that involved a significant degree of discomfort or hassle in order to extend his life. He ruled out transplants . . . and also took chemotherapy off the table. He was not, however, naive. He took the soothing prediction that he'd end up painlessly in bed, very tired until he quietly slipped away, to be just one possible scenario.

ROBERT FAGGEN: We discussed how he'd likely die—that there could be severe haemorrhaging. Pretty much what happened. But he went to extraordinary lengths to ensure that he not be resuscitated. He made a video. He wore a vial around his neck which carried DNR instructions.

Cohen's former assistant Sarah Kramer wrote to him in March; she was raising funds to start a toddlers' playgroup. Cohen replied, saying he was a "bit under the weather . . . but always ready to throw in a few grand, books, lithographs, etc." Cohen eventually donated about $5,000 and said, "There'll be more down the line." Kramer, unmarried, had long wanted to have a child. Cohen twice offered—without being asked—to pay for procedures that might lead to motherhood.

SARAH KRAMER: Not his sperm, but either paying for sperm or, if I became pregnant, to help me financially for up to two years. He wanted to give me that gift. It never felt right. Same thing with community college. I didn't ask, but he offered to pay, and I took classes. He was always there for me. A friend of Lorca's was in my playgroup. There was a vibe. Something was up with Leonard, but she couldn't talk about it. Later, I asked Adam and he said, "He's ageing."

That same month, Gabriela Valenzuela was in LA for a friend's funeral. Still seeking closure of the Cohen relationship, she called Kory.

GABRIELA VALENZUELA: I said, "Would you please tell Leonard I am in LA. I'd like to have a brief visit." He said he would, and to call him in a day. I was preparing for the funeral when we got word of a family tragedy. We spent the following days grieving with loved ones. I never called Robert and never saw Leonard.

Meanwhile, driven by a sense of urgency, Cohen was collaborating on *Popular Problems*, his thirteenth studio album. Patrick Leonard composed music for seven of the nine tracks. Dutch pianist Iris Hond was simultaneously working with Patrick on her own new album.

IRIS HOND: Leonard always asked me, "Are you hungry?" The Jewish mother. The first time, I was sitting in the garden and he walked towards me, stopped and picked this jasmine flower, took his hat off, bowed, and gave me the flower. I keep it in my diary. One Shabbas dinner, at a Greek restaurant, we talked about music. He said something like "If you haven't written [a work like] *Moonlight Sonata*, you're not really a composer." It felt judgmental, like he thought I was an amateur. Then Patrick showed him my music and he totally changed.

Cohen told her, "I never give quotes, but you're very dear to me, so I'll give you this quote." His blurb—"A great spirit revealed"—appeared on Hond's next album.

IRIS HOND: Leonard gave you the impression that you were very special. He connected very deeply, the most gentlemanly guy you could imagine. There was never a mistake. At the same time, there was so much pain. I felt it. I wondered—when nobody is around, is he really such a nice guy? Or does he have a [negative] thing in his character, and he's trying to do the opposite?

Later, back in Holland, Hond maintained an email relationship with Cohen. "I opened my heart to him, and he responded with so much love—short, sweet, perfectly written, balanced, beautiful lines. I think about him every day." She also wrote a piano and violin piece for Cohen, "A Letter To You."

Although Cohen had fired tour manager Joey Carenza in 2013, he continued to give him work.

JOEY CARENZA: Leonard never stopped reaching out, never stopped trying to help. He'd buy photographs off me, just so I'd have money, throw me jobs here and there. He never stopped trying to be in my life.

Largely confined to his Tremaine Avenue home, Cohen received a steady stream of visitors, including his dharma brother Sandy Stewart.

GENTEI SANDY STEWART: He was in pain. He had a Turkish girlfriend [Kezban]. She served us in his kitchen. They were so familiar and comfortable with each other. I assumed they were lovers.

Another day, he welcomed Barrie Wexler, and reminisced about various Hydriot characters, including Cap'n Yannis.

BARRIE WEXLER: About forty. Completely mad. Child-like, brush-cut, baggy pants, held up by suspenders. He walked around in circles, making engine noises with outstretched arms, like an airplane. I said, "He belonged in an institution." Leonard grinned. "Barrie, he was the only free man on the island."

Their conversation turned to Samye Ling, a Tibetan Buddhist monastery in Scotland, cofounded by Chögyam Rinpoche. Cohen had visited in 1969, and had complained about the broken shutters, which opened only a few inches for ventilation. Chögyam told him, "The cracks is how the light gets in."

In June, Eric Lerner accompanied Cohen to Cedars-Sinai for his weekly infusion of romiplostim (Nplate)—designed to boost platelet production. The old friends discussed the illness "the way we talked about all important matters, not about our feelings, but what it felt like."

ERIC LERNER: None of that "I'll beat the big C" chest-thumping. But a carefree pose wasn't difficult to hold at this early stage, when the symptoms were still relatively mild. [But] he couldn't miss his appointments or bad things would happen.

The use of Nplate was not uncontroversial. Nplate literature specifically cautions against its use in patients with pre-cancerous myelodysplastic syndromes. Cohen had considered going to Montreal for the treatment—he consulted with his friend Dr. Michael Malus—but no hospital there could provide the infusion drug. He researched taking it with him to Canada, but it wasn't possible.

ROBERT FAGGEN: I remember Leonard describing the risks, the potential morphing into leukaemia. He was well informed and made decisions about treatment carefully. They did get the platelets up and they started to stay up, over 100,000. Barry Rosenbloom, a hematologist, was the main doctor.

Some days, Cohen insisted on seeing Roshi. One afternoon, the old man, 106 years old and incontinent, had an accident in his diapers.

STEVE KRIEGER: Jikan [Cohen] filled a basin with warm water, removed his suit coat and cuff links, and rolled up his crisp white sleeves. "Jikan, I can do that part," I said. "I wouldn't think of it," he said. I helped Roshi stand while Jikan knelt behind him and gently wiped him clean. Watching Jikan serve our teacher, with intelligence, care, and respect, a great artist humbling himself, you learn that there is something greater than artistic success.

There was, briefly, talk of a diversionary road trip—up the coast road or to the desert; they never managed to pull it off. Lerner did manage to drag Cohen to a pitch meeting with director Norman Jewison—yet another stab at making a movie of *Beautiful Losers*. Jewison turned him down; he already had "an Indian film" in development. On Tremaine, Cohen showed Lerner his vast collection of photos, recently digitized. "He wanted me to know everything about his pet dog and his trip to Cuba at twenty [twenty-six, actually]. He wanted . . . to fill in the blanks in my version of his life." That night, they visited Roshi, who was only weeks away from death.

ERIC LERNER: I don't know if Leonard was thinking about what his life would be like without Roshi. I had yet to start thinking about what my life would be without Leonard, but I felt terrible and Leonard felt terrible and Roshi felt terrible. Roshi was the only one who had no inhibition about letting all of us know how terrible he felt. After the visit, Leonard didn't have to say it—that's not the way I want to go.

Sick as Roshi was, he had Myoren Kumiko Yasukawa drive him to Phoenix. He spent the weekend tending to a dying friend, Sokei, lying in bed with him, holding his hand.

HAROLD ROTH: With the last ounce of his life energy, he wanted to be with Sokei.

Soon after, Roshi himself was hospitalized for the final time.

STEVE KRIEGER: Leonard went to visit every day. Then he went to New York, because his sister [Esther, who had been ill for many years with leukaemia] was dying.

PICO IYER: The last time I saw Leonard was the day before Sasaki died. The only thing occupying him was Roshi, getting hourly reports. He was veiled about his own illness, but said it was terminal and in characteristic style added, "Of course, life is terminal." He showed me medications he was taking and said the one result was that he felt exhausted. So I said, "Well, I should leave." And he said, "No, no. Let's have lunch." He was so eager to be the perfect host.

In Cohen's study, they listened to *Popular Problems*, then adjourned to a Turkish café.

PICO IYER: At one point, he looked at me with passion and said, "That's what this practice, this whole life, is about—cleaning the bottom of a 107-year-old man, helping him go to the bathroom when he can't do it himself, changing his diapers."

STEVE KRIEGER: The last time I saw him—he looked epiphanic and light, as if he were disappearing. There was great pain in his eyes, and his breath was heavy. But he said, "Somehow everything I've been doing all these years comes down to the work I did with Roshi." He played his new album. He sat in silence, this aged, tiny, impeccably dressed poet, black fedora tilted lightly on his head, his voice booming all around us.

Joshu Sasaki Roshi died July 27, 2014, at Cedars-Sinai Hospital.

MYOREN KUMIKO YASUKAWA: Leonard wasn't there when Roshi passed. We had a funeral service and he came for that. I was breaking down and Leonard was beside me and said, "Darling, let's go upstairs." He stayed with me for over an hour.

KOSHIN CHRIS CAIN: I saw him for the last time at the funeral. I sat with him, Steve [Sanfield], and Hal [Roth] through dinner. He was just so gracious, telling me how much he enjoyed the newsletter we [Cain's Puget Sound Zen Center] put out, and keeping up with our scene. Those were things he didn't have to do. I felt this very strongly about Leonard—he did not care about the politics of the moment. That was true when he dedicated his last album to the Roshi and when he talked to me, an apostate to some degree. I really admired him for that. And he was our major donor, including after we formally left Rinzai-Ji.

YOSHIN DAVID RADIN: The service was formal—horns, clappers, chanting, a Japanese form, plucked down. At one point, I went outside. Leonard and my wife, Marcia, were there. We all said, "This isn't for us." I noticed Leonard was starting to get thin and weak.

Cohen outlined his final battle plan for Lerner. Drug infusions had prolonged his life and elevated his mood. But if his condition deteriorated, he would stop taking drugs and die. "All I have to do is not show up at the hospital one Monday morning and it's sayonara." He had already investigated leasing a flat in Oregon, which had legalized assisted suicide for state residents.

Cohen's sister, Esther, passed away in New York on September 7. Cohen was already there to promote the launch of *Popular Problems*. One night, Cohen, Issermann, Lerner, Kory, Özcan, Lorca, and a friend of hers met for dinner at an Italian restaurant. They had gathered to celebrate the album, but, says Lerner, "Esther's absence was too insistent a reminder of Leonard's own precarious state of health. He was particularly fond of the adjective 'diabolical.' He used it several times to describe Esther's demise." The cancer's final manifestation had left her with an extremely painful skin condition. Cohen had shouted at her doctors on the phone to give her pain medication. "The disturbing confluence of their illnesses," Lerner writes, "was not lost on him." At the dinner, the group raised several toasts to Esther with glasses of Barolo. "Dominique kept glancing at Leonard and he at her, like an old married couple out with the kids."

BRIAN CULLMAN: I spoke to him in New York. He told me how much he liked a song I'd sent him and wanted me to send more. I asked for a blurb, but he said, "I don't do that. If I did that for one, I'd be doing it for the rest of my life."

Among the songs on the new album was "A Street." Part of the lyric had been written decades earlier.

CHARMAINE DUNN: Leonard was always singing country and western songs to me. One day, walking, he's singing "Lucille" by Kenny Rogers. "You picked a fine time to leave me, Lucille / With four hungry children and a crop in the field." He says, "What a brilliant line." Then I see him go into his head and he's thinking, and a little while later says, " 'You left me with the dishes / And a baby in the bath.' That works."

BARRIE WEXLER: He'd thumb through old notebooks looking for odd lines to fill in a lyric. It never mattered to him when the words were written.

A week after Esther's passing, Cohen flew to London, where the High Commission of Canada hosted a press event for *Popular Problems.* His next album, he quipped, would be titled *Unpopular Solutions.* In fact, he added, it would be marked by a mood of "despair and melancholy." It played like a joke, but wasn't.

ROB HALLETT: A doctor [in London] gave him a certain painkiller that worked. When he got back to America, he couldn't get it. I went to my doctor and got him to prescribe it for me.

By then, Cohen had begun to receive eightieth birthday greetings.

GALE ZOE GARNETT: I emailed him, in Greek. He wrote back, in Greek, "my little heart. thank you very, very much for your birthday day wishes. leontis."

Barrie Wexler sent him a congratulatory poem, "If I Make It to Eighty," which referenced his brief liaison with Suzanne Elrod. "If I get that far, Leonard / I'll come clean about that night in New York / hoping you'll put it down to youthful indiscretion / even though I was almost forty / I'll abandon your style / stop pretending I like seaweed snacks and yoga / scrape the rust off the promise I showed / and publish chapbooks of erotic dotage / to tempt beautiful women / without dropping your name."

Through the offices of Cohen archivist Dominique Boile, Brigitte Bardot also sent birthday wishes, including a photograph from her halcyon days. The card contained a note reading "Happy birthday, My dear Leonard, I give you 80 kisses of love." She also wrote, "We are twins"—her eightieth birthday was exactly one week later. Cohen asked Boile for Bardot's address so he could send her "a little something." In response to well-wisher Sandra Anderson, Cohen wrote, "How beautiful we were! (and didn't believe it)."

RACHEL TERRY: I sent him a collector's item that belonged to Scatman John—a tie with a fedora hat on it. Then I called him. He never said cancer. He said fractures in his lower back. He hired a woman to help him. He finally told me on October 10. An email. "I'm a little under the weather these days and much of my time is consumed with doctors and medical procedures. I hope you understand. Love, Eliezer."

On September 26, Cohen sent an email to Kelley Lynch—still seeking to overturn the multimillion-dollar default judgment issued against her seven years earlier. Its entire message was contained in the subject line: "How are you?" She did not respond.

KELLEY LYNCH: I think he thought maybe we could be friends again, if I would just stop what I was doing. He didn't think I would fight the default judgment.

Cohen had stayed in touch with Steve Sanfield and his ex-wife, Jacquie Bellon, for decades. When, in 2014, their daughter-in-law developed breast cancer and saw her insurance premiums double, Bellon wrote to him.

JACQUIE BELLON: He'd given Steve and I three hundred dollars to go to Mexico in 1973, but I'd never asked him for money [until then]. He immediately offered to give them ten thousand dollars. Steve found it an affront to his pride and put pressure on [their son] Aaron not to accept it. But Leonard kept saying, "Give me the bank number. I want to wire these funds." Steve eventually accepted it—a huge gift. She recovered after a double mastectomy.

Cohen also lent support, financial and otherwise, to others.

YOSHIN DAVID RADIN: Leonard heard a version of my album—ten songs and three spoken poems. He said, "I'd like to produce it, but just spoken."

I sent ten tracks, including one dedicated to Roshi that Leonard really liked. Patrick Leonard wrote classical string quartets. Cohen paid for the whole thing, maybe $15,000. Later, we all sat on couches in his listening room. Nobody opened an eye for the whole thing. That kept us close, because I was also in LA three or four times a year and we'd hang out, talking about life. There aren't so many people who you feel you're heart-to-heart with. An openhearted, suffering Buddhist Jew. He was something. We had a lot in common, Roshi, poetry, Zen, Judaism—or kichel or gefilte fish. Leonard would serve this crazy stuff I would never eat—salami and cheese sandwiches. He'd keep it around just for people who came over.

JULIE FELIX: We were in touch by email when [an old Hydra friend] Chuck Hulse died. He said, "Yes, all the old friends are leaving, one by one."

MAX LAYTON: I'd email him and it would come back—"Sorry, I won't be available until September." I emailed back—"My guess is you're not well. Next September is a long time from now or did you not like the songs [I sent?]" . . . "I'm hanging with the doctors." Then I knew it was something not good. I gave Aviva his email and she went to see him.

AVIVA LAYTON: He was in a special medical chair and couldn't even walk across the room. It was terrible to see him like that. Although he was in excruciating pain, the first thing he said was "What can I get for you, Avivarooney?"

LEIF BODNARCHUK: I got my final email in November 2014. A Slovenian poet wanted to send Leonard a book. Leonard thanked me for playing buffer and said, "The Tired Old Guy just can't keep up with it all." He included a picture of himself smiling contentedly in an apron, surrounded by kids, carved pumpkins, and floating soap bubbles.

MALKA MAROM: I was coming to LA and wanted to meet him. He said something like "The car is getting old, it's leaking and needs to be taken to the garage." I figured he was ill. Afterwards, he sent me a photo. He was dressed to kill—tie, jacket, hat—in full dignity.

BARRIE WEXLER: He used the same words in his last email to me. "The old vehicle has sprung a few more leaks. In and out of the shop these days. But still scratching away. See you down the road."

In February 2015, Cohen, plagued with osteoporosis, suffered a compression fracture in his back.

ROBERT FAGGEN: First one fracture, then a second one—mind-bogglingly painful. There was a point early on when the back pain seemed utterly inexplicable [and] frustration with that. The osteoporosis, the fragility of the skeleton was related to MDS, the underlying problem.

AVIVA LAYTON: He was in agony—*agony.* He was allergic to opiates. He tried acupuncture, massage, and couldn't relieve the pain. Can you imagine your spine crumbling?

The idea for a final volume of poetry was born about the same time.

ROBERT FAGGEN: The idea was both of ours. If there had been more time, it might have morphed into something with dialogue between us, taped. An eclectic, oddball book. His books are all oddball books. That's what brilliant people do—they write oddball books. There's a fiction that he wrote these poems in the last months. He'd been working on some of them for years. His notebooks are voluminous and contain basically drafts of lyrics at various stages.

Some of the final poems reflect on past relationships. In "G-d Wants His Song" he mentions a "Vanessa," who called him from Toronto to offer support. Later, he played the six-finger flute she had given him and cried, remembering her extraordinary beauty.

CHARMAINE DUNN: I did make the telephone call and did give him a six-finger African flute.

In another poem, Cohen recalls the deaths of old friends, Robert [Hershorn] and Derek [May]; his brother-in-law, Victor Cohen; a high school teacher,

Mr. Waring; and an old flame, Sheila. Like his lyrics, the poems were stripped to their essence, consisting almost entirely of one- and two-syllable words.

BARRIE WEXLER: I once asked if there was a magic number for words in a line of poetry. He said four. One of his favourite devices was to use the second person singular when writing about himself, which has distance built in. "You" could be himself, or someone he's referring to, or the person listening to the song.

Another poem, almost three pages long, was clearly written for Gabriela Valenzuela. It contains coded clues so that she, at least, would know it was intended for her. These include the line, "The little silence whose name is Abishag," his pet name for her, and references moments they had shared—picking muguets and Russian jasmine flowers for his mother's grave in Montreal ("all the jasmine in Moscow"); shopping for shoes at Bloomingdale's in New York; telephone calls between Manhattan and Long Island, where she spent weekends; and an otherwise obscure allusion to "the blue in Istanbul." The last—an indication of the sharp memory that Cohen often professed not to have—is a line from a song by Spain's Joan Manuel Serrat, whom she had once met.

GABRIELA VALENZUELA: Serrat was the Spanish Leonard Cohen. I had told Leonard about him and shared his songs.

There's also a reference to an evening at the Royalton Hotel when they ordered pizza that was never delivered. Cohen's line is "and the pizza never came." The passage also riffs on the familiar phrase "Not for all the tea in China." Here, Cohen suggests that, not for the entire world—Moscow, Istanbul, New York—would he relinquish the memory of her. The poem also contains an abject apology, delivered not once, but twice, and two allusions to "a voice that cries out from the dead," perhaps referring to their lost child.

ROBERT FAGGEN: He may well have decided that this was the last moment when he could send her a message. But it is absolutely against Leonard's nature to talk about his poetry in terms of the personal relationships that may have been behind it. It was always about how to turn the monkey and the plywood violin into metaphor. If it didn't work on some larger visceral level, he didn't want to get too personal.

Steve Sanfield—Sasaki Roshi's first American student—had passed away, age eighty-eight, from heart failure in January 2014. On March 29, a memorial service was held at Rinzai-Ji in LA.

DIANNE SEGHESIO: Leonard's relationship with Steve was beautiful—one of his treasures. Steve and Sarah [Sparks]—both were gifts to him—decent, loving, kind, generous people. Old souls. Leonard was always there whenever Steve had health problems. When his friends were sick, he'd be the first one at their hospital bed. He'd go out of his way to help people. He had people's backs, ya know?

JOHN BRANDI: Steve said he honoured Cohen because he wasn't a suspicious man. He had a trust in humanity based on insight, and he had the poet's eye. Of course, they had a lot of fun. They sat in *sesshins* with Roshi, very intense. That was one reality—the *zendo*. But afterward, they would sit in the car, sharing a bucket of Kentucky Fried Chicken wings, watching women on the street. Probably not saying a lot, but chuckling. That, too, was a reality.

PAUL HUMPHREYS: Leonard spoke at the very end. He seemed more infirm every time I saw him, although he sat cross-legged for the ceremony.

After lighting incense, Cohen said he had neglected to install his hearing aid that morning and had missed most of the other remarks. Recalling their nearly fifty-five-year friendship, he noted that it was Sanfield who had introduced him to Roshi. Sanfield's conversation, he said, "was an education, filled with parables and fables and stories."

LEONARD COHEN: He operated on a very, very high moral plain. He was filled with judgments. When he was young, he would not hesitate to apply his judgments to your behaviour. As he grew older, that moral sense was tempered by his practice. He exemplified that kind of flourishing of the spirit because he was a tough guy to hang out with at a certain point, because not only could he out-drink, out-smoke, and out-talk you, but he could out-ethic you. I just wanted to invoke his spirit, which was judgmental, forgiving, transcendent, funny. He was a real friend, a guy you could count on. And that's all Steve would want me to say.

In May, Lerner returned. Cohen, by then, had invoked alternative medical treatments, including regular massages, which helped; apple cider vinegar baths; and, though he said he never enjoyed pot, various forms of cannabis.

ERIC LERNER: We stayed stoned pretty much for the week, [using] vape pipes, candies, and cookies, some for daytime and some for beddy-bye. It was the craziest week we ever spent together. We were on a bender. Nothing hurt.

They went to the movies. They went for a steak dinner. They went for an oyster dinner, and passed the vape pipe around, inducing a spasm of giggles. Then Cohen suffered another compression fracture, leaving him in agony. Their lingua franca had once been women or "chicks," as Cohen called them. Now it was pain. Richard Cohen quoted J. M. Coetzee. "Pain is truth; all else is subject to doubt."

Rob Hallett saw him for the last time that summer at the Peninsula Hotel.

ROB HALLETT: He was quite frail. We sat in the tearoom and had tea. We were half hopeful we might be able to do [something]. I'd done twenty-one nights in London with Prince, and made everyone come to him. I said, "So maybe not twenty-one, maybe three or four [nights], make a couple of mil." His eyes lit, but it became clear it could never happen. Most of the meeting he was showing me videos of FKA Twigs, a British recording artist. He found her online and fell in love with her. I said, "Maybe she could open for you."

In June, Cohen spent three hours with Dovid Efune, editor of the *Algemeiner*, an online newspaper. Sipping Turkish coffee and munching on kosher cookies outdoors, they ranged over various topics, including the politics of the Middle East. Cohen wore his trademark attire—hat, suit, tie.

DOVID EFUNE: I remember being bowled over by his knowledge of the [Syrian war]. The various alliances are not straightforward. Very few people could discuss it at that level. At least with respect to that conflict, his perspective was primarily driven by humanitarian concerns, areas where populations were undergoing tribulation.

Cohen was equally conversant with Israeli politics. Efune was surprised when, after asking him to name an Israeli politician whose ideas he admired, Cohen cited Moshe Feiglin, former leader of the Manhigut Yehudit faction of the governing Likud party. Feiglin had long suggested that Israel assist any Arab who wished to emigrate to other countries.

DOVID EFUNE: Leonard's line was that separation should be encouraged and incentivized, as opposed to enforced, and done in the most humane possible fashion.

PAUL MULDOON: Most of the time, he talked about politics. He was a very political person.

ROBERT FAGGEN: Leonard loved politics. The same forces that kept him interested in debate in college kept him interested in politics. He was fascinated by the way politicians argued with each other. He was very involved in what was going on in the world, especially the Middle East. He was fundamentally pro-Zionist, no question. At the same time, he was tormented by what was happening on the West Bank.

LEON WIESELTIER: His favourite Israeli politician most certainly was not the lunatic Feiglin. He loved the idea of Israel and most of its reality. He hated the anti-Zionist piling on, of the left—not so much a political matter as an expression of his steadfastness as a Jew. He detested Netanyahu and the settlers, and ardently wanted a just settlement between Israelis and Palestinians, which implied territorial compromise. But he didn't believe that the occupation is all you need to know about Israel. And he knew a lot of history—knew that the moral story is complicated.

BARRIE WEXLER: Leonard told me the reason he was elected president of McGill's Debating Union was that he was equally comfortable arguing either side of any controversy. That held true throughout his life, no matter what the subject was.

It's indicative of how chameleonic Cohen could be that others found him strongly apolitical.

VIOLET ROSENGARTEN: He refused to take a stand on issues in order to protect his persona.

PICO IYER: He told me that, once he began his [Zen] practice, he regarded thinking about one side or the other, right and left, as absurd. His concern about Israel and the threat to Israel was unquestionably a huge and a genuine concern.

The only time the subject was raised in Iyer's presence was during a Chanukah celebration, when Cohen took delight in explaining the history of the holiday, comparing the ancient adversaries of the Jews to Israel's modern-day enemies, Hamas and Hezbollah. What Iyer did recognize was Cohen's enduring attachment to Judaism.

PICO IYER: His commitment to Judaism was probably the one thing that was there from his opening breath to his final breath. And his final breath was an embrace of that.

LINDA GABORIAU: I [found] him moderately Zionistic. He actually forwarded me a piece [that argued] radical Islam was a very serious threat. A friend of his had written it. He truly did believe it, he said.

RACHEL TERRY: Deep inside, he was quite on the right side. But he was conflicted, and also because of his profession. I told him, "Don't deal with politics. It's a poison for you." He adopted the politics of Leon Wieseltier, more centre left. He changed.

WILLIE ARON: He was pro-Israel, absolutely, staunchly. He was much more conservative than the public at large would like him to be, and he absolutely knew it. He was a proud National Rifle Association member. He showed Mordecai [Finley] and I his card a few times.

ROBERT FAGGEN: Leonard was a life member of the NRA. He'd send Finley's blog postings on the subject to me, Adam, Lorca, and Rebecca, and we'd discuss them. Finley strongly favoured gun control, but argued that no legislation can prevent mass shootings, short of a complete ban and confiscation of all firearms. Leonard was pro-gun. One time, we discussed our mutual attraction to the military and he said, "Let's go join."

KELLEY LYNCH: Cohen told me he put [NRA] stickers on his car, in case the police ever pulled him over.

During a long afternoon with Cohen, Steve Krieger—discussing how to revitalize the monastery, now that Roshi was dead—suggested installing a rifle range.

STEVE KRIEGER: Jikan said, "Man, if I were fifteen minutes younger, I'd join you." For all the self-satisfied liberals who want to claim him as one of their own, I'm sorry—Leonard Cohen belongs to everyone. Once, when we were waiting at the doctor's office, he said, "My NRA hat came in the mail today." I said, "You're an NRA member?" He kept staring straight ahead. "Let's keep that between us," he said.

Later, during an email exchange, Efune asked Cohen if the *Algemeiner* might honour him as a Warrior for Truth, at a fundraising gala. He declined. "May I be frank? I have never been comfortable in the world of honours and rewards. These designations seem to compromise the heart-to-heart intimacy on which my line of work depends. . . . I can't whisper in anyone's ear as the Warrior for Truth. As far as possible, in this celebrity culture, I prefer to operate undercover. There is no room for victory in this curious realm of fragile healing. I seem to be one to whom the scriptural cautions apply: avoid the company of princes and the powerful. I hope you will forgive me."

As his health declined, Cohen consulted LA lawyer Reeve Chudd to draft a will. One issue concerned his literary estate.

ROBERT FAGGEN: Leonard was a person who said things very deliberately, once. He said what he meant, and he meant what he said, and he wasn't going to say it again. He said to me very clearly [that] Kory had to hire me as literary executor. I said, "Is this definitive?" He said, "He has to hire you." I didn't ask more questions. I didn't want to engage in the ghoulish enterprise of how his will was structured. But I did say, "Has to?" But the language [later] shown to me by Kory and Chudd [was] if the executor deems that a literary executor shall be necessary, then it is the preference of Cohen that it be Robert Faggen.

The wording, in short, gave Kory, as executor, discretion about appointing Faggen. In the end, Faggen won coeditor credit, with Canadian scholar Alexandra Pleshoyano, on *The Flame*, but was frozen out of other decision-making. Pleshoyano was subsequently named literary adviser to the estate. The relationship between Cohen and Kory was friendly, but never particularly close.

ROBERT FAGGEN: Kory running around with the fedora annoyed the shit out of him. He said about Kory, "My success has gone to his head." And he did say to him, "If you steal from me, so help me I'll haunt you."

JOEY CARENZA: Leonard would say that to Robert's face. He had this thing— all managers over time think they're the reason for success. But that's the thing about Leonard—he can see that [flaw] in a person, but that doesn't sour or end the relationship. He understands that it's just a component of how humans work.

By then, Cohen was working on an instrumental, spoken-word collaboration with Patrick Leonard—the album that became *You Want It Darker*. When Joan Buck came to visit, he played her one of the songs.

JOAN BUCK: I doubted he'd ever finish the album. He gave me Turkish coffee and sweet cakes. He'd been ill but, as ever, wore a dark suit and a good shirt.

The mood on Tremaine was not always grim.

PATRICK LEONARD: Sometimes we'd laugh ourselves sick about just about anything. There was a very light heart there. He said a couple of times how lucky he felt. I have recordings as real and raw as anything I'd ever heard. Live versions with Bill Bottrell playing guitar, me playing piano and bass, and Leonard singing. They were messy and noisy. By then, he wasn't really playing guitar.

Still, Cohen continued to seek the perfect lyric.

PATRICK LEONARD: We used to talk about "Treaty: The Movie," as I did no less than twenty-five versions. Ultimately, it was about the line that he didn't have. There were many variations of the chorus, and until he found what he wanted it to say, we just kept trying it.

ANONYMOUS: Patrick wrote these tunes. Some Leonard liked and some, he just said, "I have a different artistic vision." An amicable rift. Creative differences. But at one point, Leonard said, "They're yours." In other words, he was giving the tunes back to Patrick. When Leonard died, Kory insisted they belonged to the estate. Leonard always spoke of Patrick in the most reverential terms.

At that point, Cohen's son, Adam, took over the album's production. Adam later described the ensuing months as "one last father and son bonding experience. That last fishing trip. Even though he was wearing a suit and sitting in his own living room, he was an old, frail man and didn't want to contend with a stranger while completing his work." But there was tension, too, with Adam.

PATRICK LEONARD: There was father-son stuff I wasn't about to get in the middle of. You could see that he couldn't keep going much longer. It was just a matter of when something was going to happen. I don't like the "tragic end" thing, because it wasn't. This was a beautiful man.

ANONYMOUS: It's a complicated story, production of the album. Adam said at one point, "Why don't you just record this poem to a metronome?" That irritated him. He accused Adam of trying to cannibalize him. He was annoyed whenever Adam talked about "the family business." That drove him crazy. He hated that and hated phrases that Adam used, like "mytho-romantic."

ERIC LERNER: He told me Adam had saved his ass. Of course, working together drove them slightly bonkers, but it was an unexpected late gift for both of them . . . the last gift Leonard would receive.

Three years later, Sony Music released *Thanks for the Dance*, an album of Cohen songs produced by Adam Cohen and recorded before his father's death. In interviews, Adam maintained that, before he passed, his father had "charged" him with creating the new record.

ANONYMOUS: That's what had made him angry, because he detected that Adam was trying to pull out of him a posthumous album. It's why he said Adam was engaged in patricide. Rebecca was a witness, too. He never said a word about Adam pulling together another album. He would never have approved an album he didn't have full control over, especially when it came to using his voice for music he didn't write. He did not have an album conceived. It's just wrong.

In September, returning from the East Coast, Lerner found Cohen thinner, frailer. They left the house once, for the platelet infusion. One night, at the kitchen table, Cohen confided, "I don't want to die. I know. I'm as surprised as you are to find this out. This won't go on forever. But I'm not going to end it." In October, he was hospitalized for a week at Cedar-Sinai, treated for pain. He wrote "Steer Your Way" there.

ERIC LERNER: He sent me a selfie from his bed, his doctor beside him. In the caption, he wondered why his doctor looked so happy.

ROBERT COHEN: He said he was having his plumbing fixed. He did not want to discuss the details, because I asked.

LEON WIESELTIER: I arrived on a Friday afternoon. He was in the hospital bed. We lit Shabbat candles. I was shocked. He was thinner than I'd ever seen him, all tubed up. His deterioration was clear in the things he [later] sent me to listen to. I asked Adam and Lorca for updates.

For the album, Adam reached out to his father's former collaborator Jeff Fisher.

JEFF FISHER: It was Leonard's request that we do three songs. I started with one and did about three permutations—I had no contact with him—just a voice and a 4/4 bass drum and a nine-minute, almost, monologue. It never appeared on the album. The only way to work with Leonard was to have him close by, so he could approve it. With him in LA, it was hard. There was also a story about this particular song that I wasn't given the whole truth to. His son loved all the versions, but Leonard had the final say.

Despite his frailty, Cohen that month welcomed French academic Christophe Lebold, whom he'd met in Liverpool in 2009. Lebold had written his PhD thesis on Cohen and, in 2013, sent him his remarkable French-language biography of Cohen, *The Man Who Saw the Angels Fall*. When there was no response, Lebold wrote to ask if he'd given offence.

CHRISTOPHE LEBOLD: Then he said, "I'm really sorry, man. I'm not feeling well. Keep this to yourself. Leukaemia."

When Lebold arrived, Cohen was "not well—not at all."

CHRISTOPHE LEBOLD: He was cooking for me. I said, "Leonard, I'll do it." He said, "No, no. I'll do it." I could see how frail he was, but what blew me away was the power, the power. I felt I was under the wings of an archangel. I felt his protection and love. His spirit was so strong. I felt compassion, because he was in so much pain, but not pity. He was so much more powerful than I. And the voice—he made the room vibrate, but with complete relaxation. That changed my life. He took a burden off.

They enjoyed a Friday night dinner, then sat down for a conversation that touched on everything from "LA to *Starsky and Hutch* to girlfriends, mothers, death, *Hamlet*, his pain."

CHRISTOPHE LEBOLD: He really wanted to know my relationship with my girlfriend, how I was manifesting love. He was interested in my relationship to women and his own—why he'd done all this. He told me he wasn't sure he'd ever truly loved a woman. He was thinking about his childhood, his mother. He talked about Roshi every twenty minutes. He was having problems with the album. He talked about Rebecca [De Mornay] with a beaming face. We talked about Nashville and the farm he had rented [in 1969].

Cantor Gideon Zelermyer, of Montreal's Congregation Shaar Hashomayim, had for some years been exchanging greetings with Cohen on major holidays. One Rosh Hashanah, Cohen wrote him, "May your voice reach that Place and bring down the blessings." In 2015, Cohen again emailed seasonal greetings, including the blessing of the Kohanim: May the Lord bless you and preserve you. A few months later, Zelermyer had another email from Cohen. "I'm looking for the sonorities of the cantor and choir of my youth. Would you be interested in collaborating on a new record?"

GIDEON ZELERMYER: I opened my phone at about six in the morning and shouted something that nobody should shout. At first I thought it was a joke. So I wrote him back and said, "I have two responses—Hallelujah and I'm your man."

Cohen put Zelermyer in touch with his son, Adam.

GIDEON ZELERMYER: Adam sent us lyrics and raw tracks, just Leonard's voice and sparse instruments in the back, and said, "See what you make of it." He wanted something solemn, sacred, mysterious—a more spiritual album, incorporating verses and prayers from Judaism, such as *Yitgadal V'yitkadash* [the *Kaddish* prayer] and *hineni*. Adam said it was probably the last album, that Leonard wanted to close a circle. We came up with three or four different options for each section. Leonard wrote back, "I have so many fond memories of that [synagogue]. It means so much to me that you are involved."

Cohen had initially hoped to record in Montreal but, shortly before the studio sessions, acknowledged that "health problems" would keep him in LA.

SARAH KRAMER: It was a chore just to get dressed and, once dressed, to walk to the front and sit on the porch.

YOSHIN DAVID RADIN: He was using marijuana oil, consumed orally. He said it was like tripping. He took a certain dosage and could not even get up to go to the bathroom, and lay in bed for eighteen hours in a trance state. Then he couldn't take it anymore, because he was way too out of it. Eventually, he gave up on all the things and it was time to go.

In December 2015, Adam Cohen arrived in Montreal to work with Zelermyer and the Shaar choir, at Howard Bilerman's Hotel2tango studio. Bilerman had already established a relationship with Cohen.

HOWARD BILERMAN: If you had asked me the one person I would have liked to work with, it was Leonard. Just a wonderful, funny, intelligent, accommodating man. He was just like his work, incredibly poetic and economical with language. It was the craft that he mined, how to say the most with the least. He was so incredibly welcoming and never made anybody feel less than him. It really did feel like talking to your grandfather or one of the wise elders. Never arrogant, never stuffy. He took the piss out of himself a lot. He taught me so much about dealing with people. Treat people as you would want to be treated. He was a very present and connected man, way more than I imagined he could be.

The choir ultimately sang on two tracks, "You Want It Darker" and "It Seemed the Better Way."

GIDEON ZELERMYER: He almost didn't want us to do the second one. There are stronger Christian allusions in that song. He said, "Are you okay with the words?" I passed them by a rabbi friend. But if anything, the song is almost a Christian repudiation—"It's much too late to turn the other cheek."

Zelermyer proposed bookending the song with a *nigun*, the wordless melody of the ancient priestly benediction. "They thought it was an amazing homage to the legacy and the family history. They kept it on the record." He took no payment, although choir members were compensated for their time. He asked for only one thing—to have a cup of tea with Cohen.

ISRAEL CHARNEY: The final album is brilliant, but *hineni* and bringing in the chazan [cantor]—it's still lying to yourself, somehow. These are gestures. It's part of his search, his chance at redemption. All those years at Mount Baldy—was that "If I do this often enough, maybe I'll find peace?"

Lebold, meanwhile, had flown to Tennessee to see where Cohen and Suzanne Elrod had once lived. "When I returned to LA in December, Leonard wanted to know if the creek and the cabin were still there. The cabin was gone, but I had recorded the creek, and played him the recording."

*   *   *

Trying to complete *The Flame*—then titled *Happens to the Heart*—Faggen worked through Cohen's notebooks, scanning, archiving, and transcribing thousands of pages.

ROBERT FAGGEN: His attitude toward the notebooks was that they were not finished material, but worthy material. He went through them very carefully and together we said, "These are the choices, passages." Later, people tried to suggest that Leonard was burning with single-minded purpose to finish the book. He was working with me on it but, if I were to be fair to Leonard, I was goading him as much to pull it together as he was goading himself. I feel I get an asshole pin for that. Leonard wanted me to push him.

406   LEONARD COHEN, UNTOLD STORIES: THAT'S HOW THE LIGHT GETS IN

BARRIE WEXLER: On the back of his first album is a religious picture of a woman surrounded, but not consumed, by flames. The cover of *The Flame* is another religious emblem, the burning bush, surrounded but not consumed by fire. Almost like graphic bookends to a lifetime's work. But Leonard could never tell if he'd nailed something until he'd seen it on the page. No matter what confidence he had in his editors—or in himself—had he seen these galleys, he would not have been satisfied. The book's reviews and its bestselling status—none of that would have made a difference.

To Lerner, Cohen confessed that he was trying to finish the book "mostly out of boredom."

ERIC LERNER: He described to me the experience of waiting to die. . . . He described the brutal details of his deterioration more graphically than ever. The ironic tough guy faltered momentarily.

Still, it was the work that was keeping Cohen alive.

GALE ZOE GARNETT: He was getting progressively sicker. I heard it from Ellen Seligman, his editor. "He's not well." . . . "Is he working?" . . . "That's what's holding him together."

PATRICK LEONARD: He never stopped. No matter what, he worked. I know he was still looking for something else—looking for better.

ROBERT FAGGEN: Right until the end, he was working in his notebooks. We often talked about how, in a way, everything in life conspires against getting work done. Not a new thought, but it's not easy to have that level of commitment day in and day out. That's what it was for him. He'd work on a lyric for years. Sometimes, it was just a matter of finding the right rhymes. When he sent poems, I might say, "I wonder about this phrase," and sometimes he'd give very strong pushback. That was a good enough exercise. Making him defend it was all he needed. Or he'd say, "Come to think of it, yes, the whole thing needs to be reworked." But he was no pushover. He had a very strong sense of what he wanted to say and how he wanted to say it. One of the things that impressed me was his extraordinary integrity. He really admired people who didn't sell out—very hard to do, especially when you have to make a living. He insisted upon doing it his way.

CHAPTER TWELVE

In Love We Disappear

What did he live—the life of ten men, twenty men, thirty men? He was ready to go anyway. I think you get tired. *La comedia finita.* Once the body fails, no matter how philosophical or wise you are, you don't see the point.

—Ralph Gibson

He said the years of his practice were his resource, to be in pain but not in pain, not rejecting it and not fighting it. It took all his spiritual training to be able to do that.

—Yoshin David Radin

The new year dawned; Leonard Cohen's prognosis did not improve. In January 2016, Dominique Issermann flew in from Paris and stayed a few weeks. On one outing, she shot an iPhone video of him—"A very nice moment in a restaurant," she later said. "We always think we have time, but it catches up with us."

Anjani Thomas had also dropped by. She had a request—that Cohen continue to pay her money for the rest of her life.

ANONYMOUS: He had supported her quite a bit, even after they were no longer together. He was particularly incensed about this, because he'd bought her not one, but two houses. At this point Leonard is like, "What the fuck?" In the condition he was in, she asked him to keep her on a revenue stream.

And she had remarried by then. He said, "No way." He was very angry. If she didn't know when she came that he was desperately ill, the minute she saw him, any other person would have said, "Is there anything I can do for you?"

ANJANI THOMAS: I did visit Leonard in July, but I absolutely refute [this] claim.

Although Cohen typically declined requests for promotional blurbs, he made an exception for Brandon Ayre's book-in-progress, *Edward's Animals*. "He said, 'Sure, man,'" Ayre recalls. "He knew I was asking, 'before you kick off.'" Cohen wrote, "I haven't read the book, but know the work of Brandon Ayre and I know that this has to be good." Earlier, Cohen had emailed Bobby Furgo—"How about playing some fiddle for an old friend?" The notion was to put him on the album, still in production.

BOBBY FURGO: As I walked up to the duplex, I hear him yell out, "Bobby Furgo!" Like I'm his good buddy. He says, "Forgive me that I can't stand up to greet you." One of the first things he said was, "Are you still in your faith?" [The Church of Jesus Christ of Latter-day Saints.] He was really sweet and kind about that, deeply involved in the human condition. He was looking for answers. I don't think anyone has any answers. I was extremely nervous, musically. But the real gift was the visit. He really opened up. He spoke of [guitarist Bob] Metzger—Leonard had a lot of love for him. He was really open, in prime emotional form, leaning into his life with eagerness. He sang along with the playback, 110 percent into it—a huge energy. He was extremely sick, bone-thin—it was alarming. He could barely stand, barely walk, almost completely broken. But he was lighthearted, [at once] funny and serious. I felt he was at [his] peak, mentally. He said the pain was ferocious, [but] he was allergic to opium and couldn't take pain pills. Edible marijuana didn't take pain away, but softened his mind to deal with it. He said it was horrible. He said he greatly missed the ability to go places, was bored out of his mind, was hating the way it was going. He didn't admit to cancer. He figured I could put the dots together. I had tears driving home. I knew it would be the last time I'd see him.

Furgo was recorded, but his work was not used on the album.

On February 7, Cohen emailed Jacquie Bellon, saying cannabis was part of his medicinal arsenal, but that it really didn't ease his discomfort. Most days, he said, he just "white-knuckled" it. A mini-studio was set up in his living room, and he sang from an adjustable medical chair. His work helped him forget "how fucked-up the old vehicle has become." Cohen promised to send chocolate that had produced what he called "interesting mental activity, though not much relief from pain."

ROBERT FAGGEN: Medical marijuana? He was taking painkillers that would have wiped out herds of elephants.

Cohen spent the afternoon and evening of March 31 with Rabbi Mordecai Finley.

MORDECAI FINLEY: He was very formal about it. He said he needed half a day, had a lot of questions. I went over and he said, "Well, Reb, I'm getting ready to shuffle off my mortal coil." It was a high-level conversation—what happens to the soul when you die. He says, "Do you know? How do you know? Tell me." I said, "The soul survives the death of the body. I believe the personality stays intact. Your soul is going to be around for a while." Leonard reminded me of the pre-Socratic Greeks. Nothing is real. Everything is an illusion. It's all fated, all in the stars. There's nothing we can do. I'm 180 degrees from that. I do think we have free will. That's one reason he sought me out, because I gave him pushback. This was one of our most recurring conversations—as if he wanted me to testify that free will is real. We create the destiny of God. You can't repair the broken vessels if you don't believe in free will. We live in a realm ruled by a demiurge that we have to fight. He said, "Are you sure?" I said, "Absolutely." He took great solace in it.

BARRIE WEXLER: We talked about free will when discussing Maimonides's idea that God knows what will happen but doesn't control it. I said individual agency—in Torah terms, *bechirah chofshit*—was the whole basis for accountability in Judaism. But he still had this romantic, if not Christian, notion that on some level it was all preordained.

Cohen had more practical questions for Finley.

MORDECAI FINLEY: "What happens when they find my body? What exactly happens when you call 911?" He wanted all the details. He thought it was pretty efficient. He approached his own death with great philosophical equanimity, like Socrates.

Finley stayed four or five hours. "We took a walk around the block. I held him up. Rebecca De Mornay dropped in to visit. He tried to convince her to come to synagogue."

In the spring, Henry Zemel saw him for the first time in years.

HENRY ZEMEL: It was like old times. I was there maybe three times a week for several weeks. The first day, he stood up—he had shrunk five or six inches. It was like his whole backbone had melted away. He was down to 105 pounds, though he said he was doing better. But his mind? Perfect. We talked about the Tower of Babel, stuff we were interested in. Of course, he played me the new album. I remember telling him—because I'd never seen signs of it earlier—that after all these years, I believed that he had depression. Leonard made me change my mind.

On June 7, Cohen sent Cantor Zelermyer a self-portrait in charcoal, captioned "Just to be one of the [angels], even on the lowest rung," a reference to Jacob's ladder. Under it, he printed the verse, "To blessed God, we offer pleasantries," from the morning prayer service.

JARKKO ARJATSALO: Leonard kept me updated with his health issues. On June 24, he sent me a new poem—"Happens to the Heart"—and asked me to post it. He hoped it would be on the next record as a song, but wanted the community to see it in case that record never happened.

YAKOV LEIB HAKOHAIN: He wrote to me—he was down to 104 pounds and could not eat.

PETER DALE SCOTT: My wife, Ronna, and I saw him in June. He was approaching the end, and he knew that—in such pain he could hardly move. We wanted to go again before Rosh Hashanah, but he was not well enough. But he was in good spirits. He played *You Want It Darker* for us. I cried.

In June, Irwin Cotler called. President Barack Obama, planning a visit to Ottawa, asked if Cohen might perform. The prime minister's office deputized Cotler to make the inquiry.

IRWIN COTLER: Leonard was tempted. He said no, but there was a long pause. He was thinking about it. I think he'd have loved to do it, but it was not possible.

Soon after, Dominique Issermann returned, staying several weeks.

ROBERT FAGGEN: She was very helpful. We'd all go out and talk about things. He remained very good friends with Rebecca, as well. It wasn't Leonard's way to get into fights with people. He was very courtly—it doesn't mean he was a pushover. I rarely saw him interested in being vindictive, even toward Kelley. And she was torturing him. Leonard in his work was persistent and focused, but not demonically charged about people.

In July, Norwegian filmmaker Jan Christian Mollestad received a text from Marianne Ihlen saying she was dying of leukaemia, with days to live.

MARIA COHEN VIANA: It was very sudden. She was not feeling very well, went to the doctor, and died in two weeks.

At Ihlen's request, Mollestad relayed the news to Cohen. Within hours, he sent a letter. It read "I'm just a little behind you, close enough to take your hand. This old body has given up, just as yours has too, and the eviction notice is on its way any day now. I've never forgotten your love and your beauty. But you know that. I don't have to say any more. Safe travels old friend. See you down the road. Love and gratitude. Leonard."

JULIE FELIX: He told me he called her, moments before she died.

In a subsequent radio interview, Mollestad paraphrased—and embellished—Cohen's message. That version was hailed as a declaration of eternal love. Two days later, on July 28, 2016, Marianne Ihlen Jensen Stang passed away, age eighty-one.

ROBERT FAGGEN: When that letter went viral, he made it very clear that the representation of Marianne as his ultimate muse was distorted, way overblown. We had a number of conversations about that. Mollestad wanted to suggest there was a special place for her, that he was thinking about her at the end. I just don't think that's true. She may have felt that way more than him.

Hearing about Ihlen, another old friend, Don Johnston, reconnected. In the ensuing email exchange, Johnston offered Cohen the formula he was using to battle pancreatic cancer—an experimental vaccine, an acid pill, and massive doses of vitamin C. Nothing came of it, though Johnston survived another six years.

In August, Irish poet Paul Muldoon, poetry editor of the *New Yorker*, arrived "on an errand, as we say in Ireland, with the express purpose of seeing him."

ROBERT FAGGEN: The three of us were going to go out to eat, but Leonard couldn't make it. So Paul and I ate, then went to Leonard's to listen to *You Want It Darker*.

PAUL MULDOON: He was gracious as ever, moving very slowly. I said, "Are you a fan of Époisses de Bourgogne [from France's Côte-d'Or]?" He didn't know it or it had slipped his mind. I later sent him époisses, through Murray's cheese store [in New York]—a fabulous cheese. He said, "It's all I want to eat now." I'd asked him if there was a particular incense he liked—he said Superior. I sent him some of that, too.

The three men were conversing in the kitchen when Lorca Cohen arrived. Later, Muldoon wondered if he had offended her—her manner had been cold. An irate Cohen later berated Lorca for her rudeness and, despite his illness, at least temporarily ordered her not to visit him (she was still living downstairs).

MITCH WATKINS: I sent him an email on my birthday, in August, reminiscing about how fast time goes by. "I was twenty-eight on your first tour and I'm about to turn sixty-four. What happened?" He said something like "My g-g-generation"—he wrote the stutter—"is dropping like flies. It's up to you youngsters to continue." Which I thought was hilarious.

Cohen also heard from Suzanne Elrod.

ROBERT FAGGEN: She wrote him—not a warm letter. He was a little amused because she was forgiving him. He may have seen that maybe the forgiveness should have been coming from the other direction.

BARRIE WEXLER: Children aside, that's what they still had in common—an equal amount to atone for.

In September, *New Yorker* editor David Remnick arrived to do an in-depth profile.

ROBERT FAGGEN: For the second round of interviews, David [Remnick] and I misunderstood the timing and arrived two hours late. Leonard was furious, as David recounted in his article. What Remnick did not know was that there was a two-hour window of mental clarity and relatively less pain. The interview had been scheduled taking that window into account. Leonard did not tell him why he was upset.

YOSHIN DAVID RADIN: He had to time his two hours [of] energy with this drug, which also left him more depleted. He did the vocals then.

In the article, published the following month, Cohen acknowledged his imminent death. He told Remnick that he was hearing the *Bat Kol*, the divine voice.

"I hear it saying, 'Leonard, just get on with the things you have to do.' . . . More than at any time of my life, I no longer have that voice that says, 'You're fucking up.' That's a tremendous blessing, really." Cohen disclosed details of his illness, but asked that they not be published. A podcast of the interview, however, included a discussion of the illness.

DEB FILLER: I read the *New Yorker* article and remember thinking, "He's going to go soon and he's ready." I wrote and wished him Godspeed. I needed to say goodbye. When I heard he'd passed, I didn't feel any grief. He's resting now.

For the profile, Remnick scored an interview with Bob Dylan, who made a point rarely made about Cohen's work.

BOB DYLAN: When people talk about Leonard, they fail to mention his melodies, which to me, along with his lyrics, are his greatest genius. Even the counterpoint lines—they give a celestial character and melodic lift to every one of his songs. As far as I know, no one else comes close to this in modern music.

When Radin arrived, Cohen "told me I looked worse than he did."

YOSHIN DAVID RADIN: I said, "The race isn't over yet." He said, "I still have some tricks up my sleeve." We spent three or four hours [together]. We were laughing about dying, really. That's been the whole purpose of my training—preparing for the loss of the thinking faculty. In Zen, there is no reincarnation. You're just absorbed back into that Prior to Individual [state]. All you have to do is relax and disappear. People take the totality of their existence to be their individuality. If you're embedded in that, you will struggle and be terrified, at death. Leonard was not struggling, but he had a lot of pain—bone pain, I think. He didn't want medication because the dullness was worse than the pain. But it was all in the context of humour, not in the context of something significant. That's what made our time together so beautiful. "Let's have coffee and kichels."

JOAN BUCK: In September, I wrote to him: "I wish I'd gone to Greece with you in 1972." He wrote back, "We still can go, later." When *You Want It Darker* was released, I thought, "He did it. He beat all the odds."

DON FARBER: We wrote back and forth until September 17. A lot of it deals with the film [I was making on Roshi]. He asked Kory to give us the final cheque, which he did.

RON GETMAN: On his last birthday, I wrote him a happy birthday note and said, "I hope you're well and I'm sure you are." As it turned out, he wasn't, but he didn't tell me, though he did respond.

SHARON WEISZ: The last email—around Rosh Hashanah—I thought it was strange. Later, I realized—he was saying goodbye.

In early October, Cohen heard from Ruth Wisse. Reminding him of her critical 1995 essay, she confessed that, over time, she had come to see that, for all his flirtations with other faiths and ideologies, "Jews had made Leonard Cohen their own." In response, Cohen wrote that he was so happy to hear her voice. "The years collapsed, the questions evaporated, and once again we were friends walking down the campus to the streets of the city of Montreal, that curious incubator of faith and longing. Thank you for your work in the world on behalf of our people, now as before, under siege. You have always been on the front line." Cohen ended the email with his trademark logo and the priestly benediction from the Book of Numbers.

RUTH WISSE: It was as though he had assumed the priestly role I had once tried to assign him. Or maybe he knew he was saying his goodbyes and that is how he signed off to everyone.

BARRIE WEXLER: Before Robert Hershorn went to Hong Kong and overdosed in 1972, he went around and made peace with the people in his life. To some extent, Leonard was doing the same.

In those final weeks, Cohen exchanged emails with many others, among them Wayne Liquorman, Linda Gaboriau, and Sarah Kramer.

PETER DALE SCOTT: I had a new book of poems, *Walking on Darkness*. I inscribed his copy, "If you want it darker, this book is not for you. I've always wanted it lighter and I think God does too." That produced an email from Leonard, saying, "Who says 'I' want it darker? Who says the 'you' is 'me'?"

Cohen's email included a poem with the lines "he will make it darker / he will make it light / according to his torah / which leonard did not write."

PETER DALE SCOTT: It was slightly nettled, not as jocular as mine. So I wrote a poem in response, and that produced another response—"Well, that was great fun. . . . Be well, dear friends. Much love, Eliezer."

Cohen wrote to Harold Roth on October 11, thanking him for "all you've done out of love for our ever-present Roshi, and for the righteous man you are in this landscape of thickening shadows." His body, he confided, was lingering on against his will. Some pain had abated, but he was "comically weakened." He thought Roth would be among the few who would understand that he had "never felt better." Roth responded. "Please now imagine that I—and all the young students sitting with me at this moment—are there with you . . . surrounding you with just a fraction of the love and affection your generous soul has given to others. I will never forget the email you sent when [our compassionate and mischievous teacher, Roshi] passed: 'Weren't we lucky?' Indeed, old friend: the same can be said of those of us who knew you. Weren't we lucky!"

Richard Cohen came by shortly before the new album's release.

RICHARD COHEN: He talked about dying. He was pretty stoic about it. He'd joke about the medication and how it made him constipated. He was sardonic about the doctors, [but] grateful they gave him really good medical marijuana that helped a lot. The people he wanted to come around, came around, and he was very attentive. He wanted to make sure you had tea or beer. It wasn't striking, because that's just how he was. But in retrospect, it *is* striking, because even when he was dying, he was the same. The antithesis of a prima donna.

On October 12, Cohen sent an email to Robert Lantos.

ROBERT LANTOS: He usually signed off with "See you down the road." This time, he ended with "Much love, old friend."

By the time *You Want It Darker* was finished, Cohen's pain had become nearly unendurable.

ERIC LERNER: The longer he endured it, the worse it got. His mood darkened in a way I'd never known before. He drew away, as if sensing how poisonous his mind had become, and he didn't want to infect me.

The next evening, October 13, Cohen and his son, Adam, appeared at the residence of the Canadian consul general to play the album for reporters and guests.

GIDEON ZELERMYER: It was the day after Yom Kippur. You can imagine: On Yom Kippur, I fast for twenty-five hours and sing for about thirteen of them. I woke up at four the next morning and flew to LA. I brought something—an old Yom Kippur prayer book given by the congregation [in] about 1940—to his sister, Esther, in recognition of her achievement in religious school. At the press conference, they played the album from beginning to end. Then Leonard appeared. Everyone rose. It was like the rebbe walked in. He was very frail.

HOWARD BILERMAN: His eyes were so alive, and his smile was mischievous as always.

Interviewed by KCRW's Chris Douridas, Cohen was asked about the choir featured on the album, and said, "Perhaps Gideon could speak to that."

GIDEON ZELERMYER: I died a thousand deaths. I was in abject shock. I said, "If you want me to." He looked at me and said, "Oh, there you are. Friends, we haven't met yet." Afterward, I gave him the prayer book. He said, "Thank you, this gift is meaningful to me, especially since I read this book only yesterday." And added, "I can't believe you came after what you did yesterday."

SHEILA FISCHMAN: He was speaking as beautifully as always. But his suit jacket just hung on him and he looked gaunt. They played "You Want It Darker" and it came to the line "Magnified, sanctified," and I thought, "My God, he's saying *Kaddish*." By the time he got to *hineni*—"I'm ready, Lord"—it was explicit.

PICO IYER: The beauty of that record is his saying, "I've hung out with this wise man [Roshi] for forty-five years and it's not helping me at all. I've got this pain. What he says sounded great, but it doesn't fly." Zen practice is all about cutting though projection, even if that means staring right into the void.

In his own remarks—the last he would deliver publicly—Cohen revoked a statement he had made to David Remnick: that he was ready to die. "I think I was exaggerating," he said. "One is given to self-dramatization from time to time. I intend to live forever." His message that day was consistent with everything he had said before about his work.

LEONARD COHEN: You don't write the songs, anyhow. If you're lucky, you can keep the vehicle healthy and responsive. . . . Your own intentions have very little to do with this. . . . Whether you're actually going to be able to go for the long haul is really not your own choice. Nothing in this racket makes any sense to me, to tell you the truth. . . . My mind was always very cluttered, so I took great pains to simplify my environment, because if my environment were half as cluttered as my mind, I wouldn't be able to make it from room to room.

BARRIE WEXLER: It's like Kahlil Gibran's famous quote—"Your children are not your children . . . they come through you, but not from you." That was Leonard's attitude. The songs came through him, not from him.

Asked about the album's religious allusions, he said, "There's a deep tribal aspect to my own nature."

LEONARD COHEN: I've never thought of myself as a religious person. I don't have any spiritual strategy, [but] this is a vocabulary that I grew up with. This biblical landscape is very familiar to me, and it's natural that I use those landmarks as references. . . . I try to make sure that they're not too obscure.

October 13, as it happened, was also the day on which Bob Dylan was awarded the Nobel Prize for Literature—"A recognition," said Christophe Lebold, "that a literary experience can be something you listen to, which was the original literary experience." Cohen was characteristically gracious, saying that [the award] was "like pinning a medal on Mount Everest for being the highest mountain."

BOBBY FURGO: I was resentful. I felt Leonard deserved it. His works on the human condition were unprecedented.

LINDA BOOK: It pissed me off. If you were going to give it to anyone, it had to be Leonard. Except Dylan made more money. They were trying to make the Nobel Prize more popular.

PETE CUMMINS: Without any aspersions on Leonard, I thought Bob deserved the Nobel. He's the greatest songwriter—maybe not the greatest poet—of our era. His output is phenomenal. In the pantheon, Leonard is right there with Dylan. My wife says Leonard is for the heart and Dylan is for the head.

MICHAEL HARRIS: There could have been a Bob Dylan without Leonard Cohen. I don't think there could have been a Leonard Cohen without a Bob Dylan.

STEVE ZIRKEL: I wouldn't take Dylan's albums to a desert island. I'd take Leonard's.

PICO IYER: I don't think either of them deserves it over the great, full-time writers. Dylan's songs will always last as songs. Leonard's poems will always last as poems. The ten years he spent chiseling those lyrics were not wasted. There are no shortcuts in his poetic work. I would put him midway between George Herbert and Emily Dickinson. He worked so hard on them so that they would last a long, long time—and they will.

AVIVA LAYTON: Although Dylan is one of the great songwriters, and a hugely important cultural figure, awarding him the Nobel for Literature was a travesty. No Nobel to Philip Roth, who was alive at the time? Julian Barnes? Not to mention so many other European, Asian, and South American writers. Gimme a break.

MALKA MAROM: Dylan didn't want it or think he deserved it. Leonard did want it and thought he deserved it. Joni Mitchell deserves it more than them. Dylan was the voice of a generation, all social classes, all ages. Joni gave voice to women of her generation. And she took it a step further, to experimental poetry and music. Leonard is the voice of the twentieth century.

JUDY COLLINS: Honest to God, I completely object. It's a violation of trust in writers in general. They should make a special category for singer-songwriters and leave the [literature] prize for writers.

BARRIE WEXLER: Dylan travelled a horizontal line. Leonard traversed a vertical one. The difference had less to do with mould-breaking than with what Cohen might have called "sifting the ashes" of his own experience. Leonard may not have shaped the culture as directly as Dylan, but his sensibilities touched a lot of people who did. He was an artist's artist and, in that sense, did help to inform an era.

LINDA CLARK: Leonard had a babysitter who knew Dylan. She told me Dylan said there was only one songwriter he'd trade places with—Leonard Cohen.

*   *   *

Only weeks before he died, Cohen also exchanged emails with Judaic studies professor James Diamond.

JAMES DIAMOND: With [the album], it was pretty clear this was his goodbye. Others said the *hineni* [in "You Want It Darker"] related to the binding of Isaac, but other people in the Bible used that word, too. I mentioned Moses at the burning bush, for whom it was the start of a new career. And he wrote this pretty long email, which just blew my mind, basically telling me, not in a bad way, but putting me straight—that he's accepted this, he can't even capture how happy he is. And in response to my Moses spiel, he wrote—this is really genius—"Jim, as I recall, after [Moses] said *hineni*, didn't God sneak into his tent and try to kill him?" And there is a very cryptic passage [Exodus 4:24–26] in which an angel comes [to kill Moses]. That really put me in my place, saying that he didn't really need consolation.

PICO IYER: The last email exchange was after his album came out. I wrote saying how moved I was. He wrote back instantly, saying something like "That really restores me." It was a very different voice than any I had heard before. I knew he was fading. I replied with a poem by Basho—"This road / No one on it / As autumn ends." For once, I never heard back.

AVIVA LAYTON: I saw Leonard three weeks before he died. I thanked him for giving me Greece. I never would have had it without him. He said, "I've got six weeks to live. But I don't believe the doctor." He did, he didn't—you can't know. How can you believe in your own death? It's impossible. He played me his entire album and sang along. I really loved him. I'd known him since he was twenty-one. It still makes me cry, because there's nobody like him in the world.

ADRIENNE CLARKSON: My last email came with a selfie and the text "I'm not looking too good these days." I replied, "You always look good to me."

BARBARA LAPCEK: His last email said, "You were always beautiful."

CHRISTOPHE LEBOLD: With his illness, he always seemed to be treating it like a little joke. "Body sincerely insisting on gravitational rights, but I should be up and running soon."

After hearing the new album, Steve Machat sent a congratulatory note. Cohen responded, and apologized for the brevity of his note, saying, "It's a little tricky to write these days. We have been on the same path for a long time. . . . Love and blessings, Your old comrade, Leonard."

MORDECAI FINLEY: I received a flurry of emails in those final weeks. Until then, our correspondence had been about my teaching. He was listening to my online talks—we'd discuss those. But then I got one poem after another, an outpouring of creativity. He apologized—"I'm sorry I'm barraging you." I said, "Are you kidding. I'm so honoured." I felt like Mozart's rabbi.

AVIVA LAYTON: Before he died, Leonard sent me something a Zen Buddhist had written about grace and transcendence. Since I consider myself the most unspiritual person you can imagine, I replied that I'd never experienced grace or transcendence or even wanted it. He wrote back, "Nobody's any good at it, but you've failed over the years with exceptional grace and humour." It's one of the most treasured emails I've ever received. Precious.

ALAN GOLDEN: We were corresponding. I was saying, "You got me my second star [in Cub Scouts, in 1947]. We should get together as soon as possible." He wrote back, "Colette [Golden's wife] is your only star today. I'd love to have a drink with you, but I can't make it." This was very close to the end, but I didn't know.

On October 20, Jacquie Bellon wrote to suggest a nerve-deadening shot in the spine, a treatment that had worked for her. Cohen replied the same day: "Happy to hear of your relief . . . let's go dancing . . . compression fractures in this old body seem to be healing slowly, and the worst of the pain punishing me less and less frequently . . . for your eyes only, now dealing with the final stages of acute myeloid leukaemia, which has its own delightful challenges . . . much love, dearest Jacquie." Bellon wrote back immediately: "I'm so sorry you are going through AML and I'm so sad to learn this, but I'll go dancing with you, to the end of love if need be."

DIANNE LAWRENCE: He emailed to say that I'd been a good friend, but he was going to have to withdraw. He was shutting down a lot of functions, fading. The email was basically saying we can't communicate. He signed it not "love, Leonard," but "like, Leonard," which was curious but appropriate, because he really liked me, liked who I was. And I liked him. He was a good soul.

On October 26, after Simchat Torah, Zelermyer had his last exchange with Cohen.

GIDEON ZELERMYER: It's a day when you let your hair down in synagogue and we traditionally sing the last hymn, "Adon Olom," as a satire. That year, I suggested we do it to "Tower of Song." I sent it to Leonard and said, "I hope it will bring a smile to your face." He wrote back in Hebrew, "Be strong, be strong and let us strengthen one another." It's a phrase you say when one of the Five Books of Moses is completed, a major empowering moment in synagogue. He knew that it's said on Simchat Torah—that blew me away. He meant those words as a compliment. I wrote back, "I'm glad you liked it. I don't know if [your grandfather] Lyon and [your great-grandfather] Lazarus would have liked it. The Shaar was too serious in those days." He wrote back, "I just asked Lazarus. He liked it too. He's dead, but we're in touch." He knew that he'd soon be gathered to Lazarus and the rest of his family.

Only days before he passed, Jennifer Warnes came to visit. Inevitably, he dressed in a suit for the occasion.

JENNIFER WARNES: Looking me in the eyes, saying almost a prepared speech, he wanted to say thank you [for her *Famous Blue Raincoat* album]. But the truth is we didn't want to get into the goodbye conversation. It was clear as a bell that everything he was doing in the last days was goodbye stuff. He did say thank you so much. It was why he dressed up.

Cohen and Eric Lerner continued to communicate, frequently by phone. Cohen was still writing—often in the night, when the pain somehow eased, his notebook at his bedside. When talking became too difficult for Cohen, they resorted to email, a medium in which it was harder to maintain their ironic tone. Cohen kept him apprised of his deterioration, including a third spinal fracture, a regimen of nerve-blocking drugs, and a procedure—kyphoplasty—that injected cement into his vertebrae. On November 2, Lerner wished him a happy Day of the Dead, the annual Mexican ritual honouring those who have passed. In response, Cohen said he was now without appetite for food, unable to stand for very long, and had almost no desire to get out of bed.

ALBERTO MANZANO: I tried to reach him on the sixth. I think the day was drawing to a close. I wrote, "My tears are feathers flying with you."

JARKKO ARJATSALO: My last email from him came Sunday evening, just hours before the accident.

PETER DALE SCOTT: Our last contact came [when] Rebecca De Mornay came to visit her daughter [Sophia] at college [in Berkeley]. At breakfast, she took a picture of me with her daughter. We texted it to Leonard. He texted back, "Blessed are the peacemakers, for they shall be called the children of God," from the Sermon on the Mount. I linked that to our earlier exchange [of dueling poems] thinking he was saying, "No hard feelings."

On Sunday evening, Cohen invited Robert Faggen to join him for dinner.

ROBERT FAGGEN: He made corn and we ordered pizza. Mentally, he was one hundred percent until the end. I didn't have any idea that he was losing it. He was in great pain, great discomfort. But the degree to which he bore that pain and his humour were extraordinary. I was partly there to distract him. That's what a friend does. But it wasn't that he one day fell asleep and didn't wake up. He was sick.

At 3:30 a.m. LA time, Lerner emailed, saying he planned to retire to Italy. Cohen replied, quoting Dante:"Through me the way into the suffering city / Through me the way to the eternal pain / Through me the way among the lost."

Later in the exchange, Cohen told Lerner he had fainted, fallen, and hit his head on the floor. Lerner made "a useless stab at humour," asking him if the back door was open so he could get there and jump.

MARCIA RADIN: He got up to go to the bathroom and fell and was in excruciating pain.

DIANNE LAWRENCE: Eric suggested he go to the hospital, but Leonard said no. He thought he'd be okay.

In another email to Lerner, Cohen described "how sweet it was to be back in his bed . . . the waves of sweetness felt overwhelming." And then another, saying it had been "quite a little excursion," and he'd been glad Lerner had been there with him.

MARCIA RADIN: Then he called Kezban. She said, "I'm coming," and told him the doctor was coming.

YOSHIN DAVID RADIN: Kezban and her sister were giving him twenty-four-hour coverage.

There was one last email to Lerner; the full effects of the fall had finally hit him.

ERIC LERNER: I wrote back quickly, desperately, several times, but there was no reply. Our long conversation had finally come to an end.

What happened next is unclear. Cohen's internist, Dr. Joshua Trabulus, was summoned and raced to the house. He found Cohen still alive, in bed, vomiting. Only afterward did he fall into a coma; he never regained consciousness. Cohen passed on Monday, November 7, 2016, age eighty-two, a great light extinguished.

The prevailing medical assumption—no autopsy was performed—is that Cohen died from an internal haemorrhage, caused by the fall, and his body's inability to arrest the bleeding.

AVIVA LAYTON: He didn't die because he fell. He fell because he was dying.

But questions remain. Trabulus later voiced doubt about the precise cause of death. More puzzling, he reported, was the presence in the house of two women he had never seen before—not Kezban Özcan or her sister. In private conversations, Trabulus apparently raised the possibility that Cohen had consumed poison—hence the vomiting. How and by whom it was administered—if it was—remain uncertain.

DR. JOSHUA TRABULUS: I'm not going to talk about vomiting. He didn't die from the fall. He was so ill. It's amazing he lived so long. That last record— extraordinary. He was dying at that stage. He got himself through it— mind-boggling. When he finished, he was ready. He was an extraordinary man who decided to make one more artistic thing. He was ready to die, and he died. I really miss him.

MARCIA RADIN: David and I were going on vacation and I got up at five a.m. and said—I got this really strongly—"We have to send Leonard flowers. Now."

RICHARD COHEN: Eric phoned me a few hours after their email exchange to tell me he had passed.

IRIS HOND: Patrick Leonard called and said, "You can't tell *anyone*." I locked myself up in my house. That was very difficult.

ANNE RAMIS: I had a dream about him the night he died. He was saying goodbye to me.

ROBERT FAGGEN: The next afternoon, I was about to go to his house. Dominique sent me a text—"My heart touches yours." I thought, "Isn't that sweet?" It didn't occur to me that anything had happened. I drive over about four or five p.m. and the door was open, which is extremely rare, and Lorca and Kezban are crying. I realized then. The body had just been removed. They're frantically trying to book flights to Montreal for the funeral. I didn't know whether to go—I had to teach. I knew Leonard would say, "Teach. Don't come to my burial." That would be Leonard. So I didn't go.

AVIVA LAYTON: Nancy Bacal called—"Leonard's gone and you mustn't tell anybody until the family buries him in Montreal."

MORDECAI FINLEY: I was at a dinner. Adam texted me. There was a question about where the burial would be—in LA or [Montreal]. It was still in the air. Adam and his wife, Jessica, came [to the shul]. Leonard [had] wanted me to officiate, but Adam said we're just going to do the liturgy, put him in the ground, which is what I recommended, and then plan a memorial service.

To prevent news of his death from being publicized, the body was flown back to Montreal under the name Eliezer Cohen.

PETER DALE SCOTT: Rebecca, Ronna, and I drove to Oliveto for dinner. We were waiting for a table. The phone rang. It was Bob [Faggen]. He said, "I need to speak to Rebecca." Ronna handed the phone to her, and we went upstairs and waited and waited. When Rebecca came up, she was sobbing. She didn't have to break the news. . . . This is the first I've actually sobbed about [it]. We had the dinner, but it was so different from what it could have been.

HOWARD BILERMAN: Adam texted me Tuesday morning, in complete secrecy. It was the saddest and worst secret to have to keep.

LARRY SLOMAN: I got a call from Hal Willner, maybe Tuesday, saying there's a rumour Leonard has died. So I emailed him. Usually, five minutes later, you'd hear from him. This time, nothing. I thought, "This isn't good."

GIDEON ZELERMYER: I was in my office around five o'clock. The phone rings and it's Kory. He said, "Something's happened and I don't know what to do." He told me Leonard had had a fall and hadn't woken up. I told him that a few months earlier Leonard had asked to verify the status of his cemetery plot and, as per the tradition, to visit his parents' graves before the Jewish New Year. I did—and sent him a picture. He'd written back saying, "That means a lot to me."

ERIC LERNER: He sent me a photo of the neatly tended graves of his forebears that he entitled "Family Gathering."

GIDEON ZELERMYER: Kory and I talked for about twenty minutes and I hung up. Thirty seconds later, I got an email from him saying Leonard just passed. I called back to start moving on logistics for the funeral. Leonard had asked in his will that the rabbi [Adam Scheier] and I conduct the ceremony in a traditional style, and that he be buried in the family's burial plot. When I got off the phone, I went in to tell the rabbi, and burst into tears.

ROB HALLETT: I got a call from Kory. He said, "A great soul has been lost." I started crying. He said, "Don't tell anyone 'til after the funeral." Then he called and said I should let certain people know before they read about it in the press. So I started calling tour promoters, Marcel Avram, the ones he liked. Another day of grief. Then it was in the press and my phone started going mad.

NADINE NEEMEH: He was sick, everybody knew. It didn't make news of his death land any more softly. It reminds me of a story he told. He was playing the Isle of Wight and a man backstage said, "Mr. Cohen, are you ready?" He said, "No." The man said, "You're never ready for the big things in life—being born, getting married, or dying."

On Thursday, the day of the funeral, Shaar Hashomayim was hosting an evening symphony concert with the McGill Chamber Orchestra.

GIDEON ZELERMYER: I had to leave the dress rehearsal to officiate at the funeral and couldn't say why. No one knew.

Cohen's funeral was held Thursday afternoon, at graveside. Fourteen people were present—Rabbi Scheier; Cantor Zelermyer; Lorca with her two children, Viva and Lyon; Adam, his wife, Jessica, and their son, Cassius; Dominique

Issermann; Kezban Özcan; Morton Rosengarten; Hazel Field; Eric Lerner; and Robert Kory.

RUTH COHEN: He was buried in the orthodox tradition in a plain pine coffin with just a wrapping.

GIDEON ZELERMYER: It was grey—cool, but not cold—and wet. He wanted no fanfare, no speeches. The rabbi only gave explanations. Kory spoke for about sixty seconds and said how much Leonard had meant to him. Eric basically addressed Adam and Lorca, saying that when he and Leonard sometimes turned to the end of things, Leonard would say, "I want one thing written on my tombstone—Father." And that Leonard was proud of them and their young families and it had meant so much to be close to them in his final years.

ERIC LERNER: Throughout his ordeal . . . Leonard had maintained his impeccable posture as the father who was always there for his kids. . . . Of course, it was a brilliant defensive posture as well, a bulwark against the profound disappointment of not receiving what you might ask for from your children. . . . He was determined to play his role until the very end and never had to ask his children—let me go.

GIDEON ZELERMYER: I sang Psalm 23 to begin, and the Memorial Prayer (*El Malei Rachamim*) at the end. It was very plain, very understated. It was over in fifteen minutes. The whole time, I was looking over my shoulder expecting a CBC television truck to pull up. I had known that I'd eventually do his funeral, but that connection changed my life—the sense of meaning I got from the interactions. It was validating for me—as we fight against the tide of assimilation, budgets and the "Kumbaya" culture that is most religious music these days—to see him say in print that [shul music] was a sonority it was important for him to be attached to.

The official announcement, issued by Robert Kory on Thursday, at about 8:00 p.m., said that Cohen had died in his sleep following a fall in the night. "The death was sudden, unexpected and peaceful."

REGINA SOLOMON: I went to the synagogue concert. Gideon was singing. Driving home, my son texted me—Leonard Cohen has passed away.

GIDEON ZELERMYER: As soon as I got off the stage, people were hugging me, crying on my shoulder. I had to act surprised and shaken.

LENNY LIGHTER: His close friends convened that night [at Moishes steak house]—Lerner, Rosengarten, Hazel, Lorca, his grandson. They had not spoken about his death and [the news] popped up on my phone. Hazel came over and told me.

ERIC LERNER: We kept looking over our shoulders at the door, wondering when he was going to join us. We drank Barolo, of course.

BRANDON AYRE: I hope he told St. Peter that he's the guy who wrote "Priests."

PICO IYER: I was closing a story with the *Walrus*—eleven p.m. in Toronto—a review of his final album. Literally two minutes later, [the editor] sent an email: "We've just heard the news. We're going to have to change all the tenses." I spent the next month grieving. No death has ever hit me so hard.

ROBERT FAGGEN: I was contacted by the BBC. They wanted to know what Leonard and I talked about. I started to talk about steak and could almost hear at the other end, "What about heaven, hell, nature, time, and space?" I said, "The steaks first."

JULIE FELIX: I was in Mexico and saw it on the news. Then the BBC called. I was so devastated. I couldn't talk. When Marianne died, I felt cheated. When Leonard died, I felt abandoned. They're up there together now.

BARRIE WEXLER: When Leonard passed, it was as if someone had taken away one of the walls. I sat glued to my front step, wondering how I'd ever had such a friend. I kept thinking of that line from *Hamlet*—"I shall not look upon his like again."

ANONYMOUS: I cried when I heard the news. I played Leonard Cohen music for the day. Then I called Suzanne. This is not a good memory, because I was talking about the loss and her answer was "Well, what about me?"

IRINI MOLFESSI: After he died, I was talking to an old Greek lady in Athens who knows nothing of music. She'd never heard of Leonard. She said, "I was listening to the news and they were talking about this man who died and, for some reason, all I was thinking about was you. I see his picture and hear his voice and he looks like he is made of the fibre of your hair." That is how I felt. He was family.

JUDY COLLINS: I was in my apartment in New York when I heard and was thinking, "My God, he's the smartest person I know," because he died the morning before the election, leaving us with *You Want It Darker*. And we got it darker.

AVIVA LAYTON: Some people said, "Thank God Leonard died before knowing that Trump was elected." In my opinion, he wouldn't have given a tinker's fuck. That wasn't the plane on which he moved. He was above politics— above it, below it, to one side of it. He was more likely to have thought Trump's election an act of deliciously perverse absurdity.

In fact, Cohen had predicted Trump's victory.

BARRIE WEXLER: Not only predicted it. Based on his fondness for contrarian views, I suspect Cohen wanted him to win. He'd read Sabbatai Sevi and was familiar with his idea—that one must confront one's demons before they can be exorcised. In the US, that was the need to confront white nationalism and other scourges, which Trump represented.

PETER KATOUNTAS: They announced his death and I went over to Morton's house. We toasted Leonard in the Greek fashion. I said, "When are you going to bury him?" He says, "We buried him this morning. We did it like that—otherwise it would have been a zoo."

LINDA BOOK: It really was like a light had gone out in a part of my life. That surprised me, because he was this big celebrity and I was just a passing moment in his career. It felt like a profound loss.

When she heard the news, Cohen's former lover Felicity Buirski posted a Facebook tribute. "Darling Leonard . . . You kept us poised on the right side of madness. By salvaging beauty from so much sadness. Your perfect offering will continue to honour our wounds and bind them, now and for many generations to come. Thank you . . . and I salute you Field Commander Cohen . . . a true and faithful servant of the light."

WILLIE ARON: I was about to go into the supermarket and saw on Facebook that he had died. I went into the car and burst out crying. I'd sent him an email that morning, not knowing.

Aron's email complimented Cohen on the album, calling it "a towering achievement. . . . I understand you are facing some health challenges. I assume you have an abundance of care, but if you ever need anything, I would be honoured to be of service. May you go from strength to strength." Cohen's reply was automated. "Unable to read. Apologies."

LESLEY ST. NICHOLAS: Leonard used to say, "They'll never catch us alive, my beauty." And I'd say, "No, they won't, Leotard"—my pet name for him. After he passed, I called his number in Montreal and said, "No, they didn't, Leotard," told him I loved him, and said, "See you on the other side."

The week Cohen died, Perla Batalla had completed a recording session in Ojai, California, and flew to Europe.

PERLA BATALLA: I get to Paris, check in, go to sleep. In the morning, I had two hundred texts and emails. I was in absolute shock. I wrote Adam and Lorca right away. [At] newsstands, Leonard was on every cover. I had such a hard time processing the information. But I was in the right place and I knew it. Everything was Leonard connected. On a train from Paris to Barcelona, I get up to grab my bag and the dad [of the family near me] says, "You're Perla Batalla. I'm really sorry about your loss," and gives me a big hug. It was such an odd moment. Everyone there felt it.

ERICA POMERANCE: I was coming out of a film when Ina Fichman said, "Did you hear? Leonard died." I nearly fell down. All night they played his music on Radio-Canada. We went to his house and a group congregated with candles, and sang his songs, Francophones, Anglophones, of different generations and cultural origins. He has such a universal message.

NOAH ZACHARIN: I was on the train to Montreal, and it exploded on the internet. I wept and then wept some more. The next morning, we walked past his house—heaps of flowers and Manischewitz wine, as if he would drink that.

GALE ZOE GARNETT: I heard he had passed on the thing that runs across the bottom of the TV set. And I wept.

DIANNE SEGHESIO: When Roshi died, when Leonard died—you don't really lose these people. On some level, I was sad. But I was just so grateful that he's so deep in me. I still use him as my muse, still feel like he's here and I can call him up. I miss not being able to call or email him, but I have a bunch of his stuff, a leather jacket from *The Future* tour. We used to read and cry at each other's poetry. I miss that. We had deep stuff.

JULIE CHRISTENSEN: After he passed, I was playing phone tag with Jenn [Warnes]. I was leaving a message for her, driving to my house. In my neighbourhood, there are lots of animals, and a big buck stopped in front of my car just as I was saying, "I love you, Jenny." I hung up and the deer stopped and looked at me. I said, "Well, hello, Leonard."

JOEY CARENZA: He's still in my life. He's in my dreams all the time. We have conversations. He gives advice.

DIANNE LAWRENCE: I am sad I won't ever see him again, [but] I can't miss him, because the moment I remember him, I feel him, and see that smile of small delight, and remember him asking, "Can I make you a grilled cheese, darling?" He came to me in a dream after he passed. I was in a trailer park. Leonard showed up and said, "I'd like to take you for dinner." He pulled me away from the crowd and we engaged in a long discussion. Then he said, "I have to go back now. Let me walk with you." Suddenly, we were walking along the path and at the end is a beautiful green meadow. We kept talking until it was time to let him go. That dream was my goodbye. Oddly enough, I did a painting years ago—a silhouette of a man in a long cloak and hat going down a road in a forest towards this light. And years later, he did an album cover—a man in robes and a hat—except the light he is going toward is the stage. I would say we had a golden thread.

From Japan, Pico Iyer flew over with his wife to attend both memorial services, at Rinzai-Ji—Sunday, December 11, 2016—and then at the shul.

PICO IYER: I thought Joni Mitchell would be there or Bob Dylan, but it was just everyday friends, musicians, and his kids. What always shocked me about Leonard was that although he was a figure of global fascination, he had made such a tiny, homemade, unpretentious life for himself. Again, this is about being invisible, as if he were a nobody, living in the middle of nowhere. It's an extraordinary thing to be a person of such prominence and also to cut away that prominence, so that you're just a regular person, living, it seems, more modestly than everyone else. He was an ancient soul from the beginning. It's a cliché, but he had a unique air of agelessness.

HAL ROTH: Paul Humphreys and I organized the memorial at Rinzai-Ji. Julie Christensen and Perla Batalla sang. Then a pickup band played a half dozen Leonard songs. It was *very* moving.

David Radin spoke at the Zen centre. When Cohen was only months away from death, Radin had asked him why he was using the last ounces of his energy to produce yet another CD.

YOSHIN DAVID RADIN: He said, "There are hundreds of thousands of people who have been so kind as to listen to my music. This is my last chance to thank them." Who says something like that? Only someone who had himself poured his heart into countless poems and songs and was so touched that his heart had been received. Leonard was my . . . dear friend. We had made many of the same mistakes. We grew up in similar Jewish communities. He was a comrade in the world of words and music and a comrade in the world of silence. I felt he was my brother and, at the same time, while there is sadness at his passing, there is also a deep, poignant, sweet memory—a gentle crack—that's how the light gets in.

GIDEON ZELERMYER: The shul service was intimate—a hundred to a hundred and twenty people, in the sanctuary, a room with no windows, stage lighting, a piano, and velvety purple cloth. Eric read their final email exchange. Surreal. Kory spoke. Adam Cohen chose the music. The choir and I did two songs, Patrick Leonard at the piano, no words, only backing vocals. Leonard's voice was deliberately missing. We did a reading of the 23rd Psalm, another song, and then *Kaddish* to end it. There was a reception afterward.

BOBBY FURGO: Leonard made a list of who he wanted to invite to the memorial, a very small number. I was invited and I was shocked. Alex Bublitchi came from Spain.

DIANNE SEGHESIO: I wasn't invited. I was surprised. I was hurt. I should have been. It would have been nice to be thought of.

AVIVA LAYTON: The memorial was so intense. I'd never met Dominique Issermann until then. I'd never heard of Eric Lerner. The memorial was like a jigsaw puzzle of Leonard's life and all the different pieces flew in to form a portrait of Leonard. It was small, maybe forty people. Peter Dale Scott came—I had no idea he and Leonard were friendly. Total compartmentalization. There was so much I didn't know about him, that he withheld. But he did that with everybody. There was no point in being hurt, although many were. You were close to Leonard on his terms and his terms only.

RACHEL TERRY: I met Lorca and Adam only at the memorial. The kids were strange. Lorca is an introvert in some ways, pained in some ways. It was a little weird. The kids said nothing.

Leon Wieseltier could not attend, but sent a powerful eulogy that included these words: "Leonard . . . has been portrayed as a sage, a rebbe, a Kabbalist, an exegete, a kind of troubadour theologian. There is some truth to these descriptions. . . . [But] my brother was also, and more primarily, a poet, a lover, a voluptuary, a worshipper of beauty, a man who lived as much for women as for God, a man who lived for women because he lived for God, a man who lived for God because he lived for women, a servant of the senses, a student of pleasure and pain, an explorer whose only avenue of access to the invisible was the visible, a sinner and a singer about sin, a body and a soul preternaturally aware of the explosive implications of the duality."

ROB HALLETT: I was leaving the synagogue and the cab stopped at a traffic light, opposite a tattoo parlour. I've never had a tattoo in my life. I said, "Stop here. I'm going in." I said, "Tell me where it'll hurt the least and put it there." He happened to be a Leonard fan. They put on the album and I sat there with my eyes closed.

The tattoo was Cohen's unified heart logo. Rabbi Finley and others said *Kaddish* for Cohen for thirty days.

NANCY BACAL: Sandra, his housekeeper . . . he left her something in his will and she didn't get it—not a penny. He promised her—he told me. I called Robert [Kory] to ask him and he said Leonard's income was impossible to sort out. It was so complicated.

ROBERT FAGGEN: His old car, the Pathfinder. When it was obvious he wouldn't be driving anymore, he gave it to the man who did repair work on his house.

BARRIE WEXLER: After he died, I planted an almond tree to remember him by. The Hebrew word for almond is *shaked*, meaning "watcher." Allegorically, almond trees represent God's watchfulness over his people. In fact, God linked the almond branch to His creation of the *Kohenim*, the priestly class to which Leonard belonged. On Hydra, one of his neighbours had a large almond tree. Leonard loved the way its shadows played on the walls of his own house. Now, in the early morning light, the fledgling leaves of my little tree shadow dance on my whitewashed exterior and it gives me the feeling that Leonard is watching over me.

GABRIELA VALENZUELA: I had been meditating and noticed that the tree outside my bedroom was filled with hummingbirds. I was taking a selfie with the tree behind me when the sad news of his death was delivered.

CHAPTER THIRTEEN

The Man Who Never Died

One day I said, "Cohen, you're going to go down like Jacques Brel as one of the great balladeers and poets." His response was to pull out an eight-hundred-page book, *The Oxford Book of English Verse*, the entire arc of English poetry. "Here," he says, "I want you to see something." And he began flipping pages. "Alfred, Lord Tennyson—three pages. William Butler Yeats—two and a half pages. Shakespeare—fourteen pages. I'll be lucky if I'm a footnote."

—Barrie Wexler

I could never locate that appetite for posterity within myself. . . . You're up against some heavy competition. King David, Homer . . . Shakespeare, Dante, Donne . . . Whitman. It's like going up against Muhammad Ali, if you're a pretty good neighbourhood boxer. That's what I think of myself as. I'm just a pretty good neighbourhood boxer. Legacy? I never thought that it would mean anything to me when I'm dead. I'm going to be busy.

—Leonard Cohen

The word "legacy" conventionally refers to an estate—property, money, or gifts bequeathed in a last will and testament. More broadly, it might also embrace aspects of reputation. But originally it meant something else—a papal or state envoy, dispatched on a specific mission. All of those meanings would apply to any consideration of the legacy of Leonard Norman Cohen. To his work—the novels, poems, songs, and art. To his good character—attested, with few exceptions, by the people he met, befriended, and loved. And to his mission, recognized and embraced at an early age, to "address the world" in some way. It therefore seemed fitting to ask those who knew him to assess that legacy and how he will be remembered.

SANDRA ANDERSON: Before I met Leonard, Irving Layton told me Leonard had taken his bodhisattva vow. Supposedly this meant he was to keep returning to Earth until all sentient beings were liberated. So he may be back.

JARKKO ARJATSALO: His work—both music and poetry—is both timeless and universal. He covers the whole course of a human's life, from a young man searching for his role, to a serene old man looking back. His texts are multilayered. We can always find something new, because our own point of view changes when the years are passing. He will be a classic in both poetry and music, and will be there for new generations to find.

WILLIE ARON: The fact that I could say I was Leonard Cohen's cantor is not a small thing. He called me friend. I don't think I'd have wanted to be in a relationship with him, but to be his friend was a great treat. He was humble, cordial, gracious, loyal, [showed] a great sense of decency to the people around him. Sometimes I wondered, "Is this guy snowing me, by being so gracious?" But I knew nobody to say a bad word about him. He could be a hip motherfucker and yet he had gentility, old manners, civility. He was from a different time. He'll be regarded as possibly the greatest pure poet that popular music has ever encountered—I include Dylan in that—and absolutely one of the greatest artists that popular music has ever produced. Leonard wasn't shooting for peer group approval. He was reaching for something older, deeper, higher—King David, the Upanishads, the Kabbalah.

FRAN AVNI: His legacy is a love of humanity. His most significant phrase is "There's a crack in anything, that's how the light gets in." It helps people get through their days. He was never without grace and kindness when he met people. There was an elegance to him, an old-world charm, and a profundity, even as a nasty young man.

BRANDON AYRE: What I want to say is what a lovely man Leonard was, what a *great* guy he was. Generous. Supportive. I was one of probably hundreds of young friends who he kept in touch with, giving a boost here, offering his prodigious intelligence. There is a certain kind of drive that forces one to write. Very few consciously abandon ship to pursue it, let the demon of creativity rule their lives. Very, very few are good enough to make a living at it. When fame—the devil!—steps into the equation—"the equation" would be a very Leonard way of discussing it—things really change. Leonard handled that devil—and the narcissistic drive required—well. He produced into his eighties. This was yet another aspect of his immense intelligence. And, I suppose, heart. I will always love him. He taught me how to be a mensch. He was a very smart, compassionate cookie, and by far the most perceptive man I've ever met.

HOWARD BILERMAN: To say that he was one of the greats is a huge understatement. He was special to be around, not because he was a celebrity, but because he was always the smartest, wittiest, and most profoundly insightful person in the room.

LINDA BOOK: Leonard had a difficult psychology. He was narcissistic and egocentric. To be emotionally committed was an intense experience for him. It was all or nothing, and all was either never enough or it was too much. Relationships became problematic and, when he could not say what he wanted, he had sex. Relating physically took the pressure off his need for words. His interest in words was such that it would bother him if he could not find the exact word. He'd refine words all the time. He did that in conversation, too.

JOHN BRANDI: My wife, Renee, and I were travelling in the Pindus Mountains, south of Albania. As we walked into the tavern, "Dance Me to the End of Love" was playing. When we expressed awe that here, in the middle of nowhere, Leonard Cohen was in the air, Dimitrios, the owner, smiled. "Of course! Everybody knows Leonard Cohen. He was of our people." We took our coffees outside in the warm mountain sun, and sat with such happiness to once more hear Leonard Cohen filling the air.

FELICITY BUIRSKI: I feel Leonard was always part of the plan, for the evolution of consciousness for many in the world. I cannot imagine my own life without him in it, or being in a world he had not infused with his honesty, wisdom, wit, and insight. His poetic lyrics were wrapped up and caressed in the exquisite melodies that accompanied them and wonderfully embellished by virtuoso musicians and angelic female voices that helped to carry them deep into our hearts and souls.

RICHARD COHEN: For me, the legacy is more about grief. I lost a very dear friend. I'll never have a friend like that again. I miss him, his smile, his emails, his insights, our talks.

PIERRE COUPEY: Virtually everything he did will endure. But like his beloved García Lorca, like all great creators, he will remain an enduring inspiration and challenge to anyone who wants to understand how this world works. He, as few others have, was able to achieve genuine popularity without any diminishment of his intellectual and spiritual search. And so, finally, his voice. Its integrity, dignity, and beauty. Hallelujah.

BRIAN CULLMAN: I would hope this legacy would be that he created an atmosphere of real kindness and compassion in the world. It's rare, especially in the performing arts, to encounter someone who is genuinely kind, genuinely respectful, takes other people into account, and is sensitive to their lives and feelings.

CHRIS DARROW: I don't know whether "Hallelujah" is his best song, but if there's going to be a legacy, that's going to be the one.

REBECCA DE MORNAY: Leonard Cohen was one of the greatest poets, but for me, he was also one of the most important people in my life, and losing him is like losing a limb. He was my ground, he was my aerial. I really cannot fathom what life will be like without him in it. . . . There was no one like him, and there never will be.

JAMES DI SALVIO: My Leonard is a superhero, the beautiful old man that he is. My dad, a true, true fan of Leonard's [and his friend], saw Leonard's legacy more than anybody. He used to tell me as a kid, "Not now, but later, he'll be seen as one of the greatest of all time."

SANDRA DJWA: His legacy is probably the international pop singer who had enormous influence especially in Europe. I can't see people reading *Beautiful Losers*. Cohen offered a lot to young people—a sense of love, love that originated in the physical, but maybe had some relationship to the spiritual, and this is a very non-spiritual age. Cohen never moved too far from his roots. He grew up in a Jewish household with a sense of Jehovah and a desire to create art that had some transcendent meaning. Later, transcendent came to mean something different, but every now and then it pokes through—the "Forever wilt thou love and she be fair" vision, which he never quite abandoned.

BARBARA DODGE: Had we all lived at a more enlightened stage of our evolution, Leonard would have been a light, an incredible force for change, which deep down is what he wanted to be. The path he took, to serve his own purposes, unfortunately took him into some real darkness. He was a true seeker, but he indulged himself, so that he could experience everything. He missed his true calling. I believe he was a rabbi who couldn't see his way through the chaos he created. He craved the fame, but eschewed the game that came with it. At the end, he came back to his real spiritual home with his childhood rabbis. That was the value that bore fruit.

JOE D'URSO: Leonard was always an artist I put on when I was feeling blue and he'd make me feel better. I always joked that the reason he made me feel better was that someone else in the room felt worse than I did. By walking that path, he helped a lot of people. He was a poet and a songwriter—I would never call him a musician. The guitar was there to serve his words, not the other way around. The work will definitely last.

JULIE FELIX: His songs come out of longing, a place where you feel loss. His legacy is a man who touched our souls very deeply, in a way that popular music doesn't do to that extent. But there's always a mystery about Leonard. He was a mystery to himself in many ways. Maybe it's the mystery we follow. We don't know where we're being taken, but we go there with Leonard, places we would not go on our own. All his work, even the humour, comes out of a place of trying to fit into a crazy, hostile world. For someone as sensitive as Leonard, [that] causes pain. Which is why so many people felt the loss of Leonard, because the music is intimate. I was so crushed when he died, but so were others who did not know him. People felt a personal loss. He was unique. He has this duality, which is Virgonian—very tender and then absolutely "You want it darker." Jewish and Buddhist.

DEB FILLER: He was my rabbi. I'm a Buddhist, too, and I don't believe in God, but I felt like he was a shepherd—with his love. He's the only person I've ever met who I felt that with—this unbelievably high spiritual state that he had, of generosity and calm, something peaceful within himself. He was so open in his mind, to everything. It was extraordinary.

MORDECAI FINLEY: He saw himself as a liturgist and his songs were like the sacraments he offered up. The *Kohenim* worked in the *mishkan* [sanctuary] to offer the sacrifice, and the Levites sang. He took that stuff seriously—that he was a channel. He was endowed with divine charisma. He had prophetic stature. God's word flowed through to him. He felt it possessed him. He didn't know where it came from. On the other hand, he knew it was a charismatic gift. People will be reading his stuff a thousand years from now. Part of it, like Maimonides, is because what he wrote was so simple. The fact that he wrote understandable poetry is almost a guarantee of his longevity.

MORRIS FISH: Will Leonard's work be remembered? In twenty-five years, I think it will be. In fifty years, perhaps. In one hundred, who knows?

RUBIN FOGEL: His legacy will be eternal. There are literally millions and millions whose lives have been touched by him. He was a man whose aura was just so infectious. He was such a mensch, one hundred percent sensitive to the people around him. He will go down as one of the greatest artists, poets, novelists in the English language.

SYLVIA FRASER: A man of many masks, he will manifest a magical travelling show in many acts, staged in a maze of mirrors, some of them distorting.

GALE ZOE GARNETT: There's a song by Gilbert Bécaud: "*Quand il est mort le poète / Quand il est mort le poète / Le monde entier / Le monde entier / Le monde entier pleurait.*" I sang it when I heard Leonard had died. Anybody who engaged with Leonard's music belongs to that group of mourners. So many things combine in him. I told you when I came, I was a stranger. So if you've got a problem, it's because you didn't want to look at what was right in front of you. His loyalty, his generosity, his kindness—extraordinary.

MARGIE GILLIS: His legacy is his remarkable kindness, his astonishing poetry, his honesty, as well as being a Buddhist, a very devout person. He was honest about failing, extremely talented, a gifted, gifted writer, a man who loved us well.

IRA GLADNICK: He came across as deeply humble, despite his fame, as someone who lived with one hundred percent sincerity, and was truly in the moment.

YOAV GOREN: His legacy as a songwriter is well secured. On the recording side—possibly. But his musical persona—he's there with Dylan, though he didn't achieve the same commercial success. You immediately know who Leonard Cohen is. On the musical side, it's weighty, intelligent, poetry and music that represents a certain art form that is not really in music much anymore. No one ever can rise to that level again. His legacy is the poetry, the lyrics. It's deep. It's not just on the surface. It's a truth that comes from experience and it resonates. *You Want It Darker*—even with his own demise, he seems to be above everything, the thirty-thousand-foot approach.

BARBARA GOWDY: What I can't get over is that all his songs are in the minor key. They're all a kind of dirge, have a Jewish sound. . . . It's a narrow range, but he never repeats himself. That was partly his genius, that he could mine this vein and always find something new and catchy. I don't think his legacy is the novels or even his poetry, but his lyrics. He liked to say he was just a songwriter and put them down. But as he said, you have to subject yourself to the "anvil of rhyme." The word exists that you need, but it has to seem like the inevitable word and you have to feel—what a coincidence. The exact word you needed happens to rhyme. He always gave you that feeling. He's one of the great lyricists of all time.

MICHAEL HARRIS: It's going to be an active enjoyment of the work he did. If that's a legacy, that's the legacy. I can't imagine it won't survive. The songs are so seductive and the poetry is so accessible. It's memorable and if stuff is memorable, it will survive.

PAT HARRIS: If society doesn't implode on itself, I fail to see a world in which he will not be studied. Not in the sense of being ahead of his time, but as someone who had all the pieces of the puzzle.

MARK HUFF: There are only two kinds of singers—the ones you believe and the ones you don't. Cohen, Dylan, Waits—those are the greatest singers. To be a writer, you need honesty and discipline. I don't think anyone's been more disciplined than Leonard Cohen.

PAUL HUMPHREYS: It was extraordinary the way he could turn depression into redemption, laying all his faults bare so that the light gets in.

JANIS IAN: Everybody I know aspires to be as good a songwriter as Leonard Cohen. *Leonard* aspired to be as good a songwriter as Leonard Cohen. Fuck, he's the best songwriter since Johnny Mercer. Start with that. I would put him and Dylan as peers. Dylan changed the form, like the Beatles did. Leonard didn't change the form. But Leonard set a standard and maintained it. He kept his edge. Any songwriter worth his salt studies Leonard—his economy with words, chiselling away to find the [essence]. He managed to reinvent himself. There is a fierceness to his writing and also an acceptance in his later writing that calls to mind Brecht and Weill and that school. Later, it calls to mind the writing of Thomas Merton. I have ten Grammy nominations and three Grammys, but the things that mean the most to me are things like Leonard Cohen saying he loved my work. When I moved down here [to Florida], I had room for only one hundred CDs. Maybe fifteen or sixteen of those are Leonard's. Another ten are Dylan's. Leonard and Billie Holiday are where I go when I feel lost as a writer or a singer. That's my book.

PICO IYER: I have many friends who are writers, but I have never met one as articulate as he, so beautifully able to put everything into this high-toned diction, spiked with irony, his classic signature sound. I always think of him as the rare grown-up in our entertainment world, and the rare Old Testament figure in our midst. As a person, as a poet, in his temperament, he was so rooted and so restless at the same time. He will take a verse from 1960, record it forty years later with extraordinary consistency, and yet from moment to moment you don't know if he's in Montreal, or LA, or on Mount Baldy. Everyone aspires to write lucidly about mystery, but none have succeeded where he has.

PETER KATOUNTAS: Never mind the work. The real accolade should be that he fought depression his whole life. That's one of the significant honours—he fought this monster and survived.

STEVE KRIEGER: I don't like to think about his legacy as a public figure, because eventually those legacies disappear. I like to think of him as a really unique guy who could write powerful, sad, melancholic music, yet not defeated by life, humbling himself before his teacher, not afraid of death.

STEPHEN LACK: Leonard's legacy began fifteen years ago when "Hallelujah" was captured by John Cale and then Tim Buckley. That moment reinvigorated the entire catalogue.

CÉLINE LA FRENIÈRE: His work continues to resonate with men and women of all ages and cultures. He will be remembered long after we have gone. Leonard was a gift. He was definitely not a saint by any stretch of the imagination. He took his sins very seriously and recycled them in all their beauty and ugliness for everyone to witness. His appeal is universal because we are all imperfect creatures longing to rise above the mediocrity of our daily lives.

K.D. LANG: He imparted so much wisdom. He was a translator between the gods and humans.

BARBARA LAPCEK: I was at a Cohen concert, sitting next to a beautiful young woman and her boyfriend. At some point, she grabbed my hand and we held hands. That's his legacy.

AVIVA LAYTON: I don't think he'll ever go out of fashion. Where he is now, which is as high as you can possibly get, he will stay.

CHRISTOPHE LEBOLD: I don't know where he'll be in fifty years. This is a technological dark age we're going into. Our interest in language is deteriorating. I know he'll survive somehow, because he has expressed something there was a deep hunger for, a form of spiritual literature that was subversive and sexy, as it should be. And he did it in song. Even on the cusp of death, you can still be subversive, ironic, funny. You can talk to God as the head of the Mafia. It comes from language—logos. In the beginning was the word and the word was with God. When you manifest that dimension, when you take language seriously, it centres you. We are language and language is God and it connects you to everything and everyone. At the same time, [he was] so humble, so simple, so nice. He was *so nice* and yet so incredibly powerful.

DENNIS LEE: The best songs will definitely last, a half dozen or so. If they don't, it will be a real miscarriage. To me, his best poems are at the beginning and towards the end, some of the effortless lyrics in *Spice Box* particularly. His work certainly belongs in the canon of Canadian poetry, but I'm not sure I'd use the word "great." His finest work is in the songs.

ELLIOTT LEFKO: He wasn't just from the past. He showed people you can be an older musician and still be relevant.

PATRICK LEONARD: If you want to be a poet . . . an archer or whatever, you want to look up at what you think is the best and move in that direction. The difference between Leonard and everybody else I worked with is, he was the star everybody wanted to move towards, whether they knew it or not.

STEVE LINDSEY: Will his music last? Oh, yeah. Leonard, Dylan, Joni Mitchell. They're dealing on a much bigger terrain, saying things you have inside you, but don't know how to articulate. And he does it with humour.

JOHN LISSAUER: He was just the easiest artist to work with—no neurosis, no self-indulgence, no play drama. He was so clear with his vision of the song and how he wanted to sound—very generous, open-minded, nonjudgmental, and brave, willing to try things out of his comfort zone, with no defensiveness. He was very funny, compassionate, warm, touching. He left a dozen spectacular, ageless songs for the world. And he was an amazing performer. He never was onstage for less than two hours forty-five minutes, and he always had complete focus and concentration. He never phoned it in. He could mesmerize you with sincerity.

ELLIOT MAJERCZYK: In some people, talent and character are separate. This is a man where character was just as impressive as his output. Some people don't get him, but when you do get him, he goes very, very, very, very deep. He embodied the word *mensch*. He always gave the other person their dignity. He'd use the phrase "I can sympathize with their position." The Talmud says you can learn from a rabbi by the way he ties his shoes. Watching Leonard was along those lines. Only years later did I fully realize the depth, insight, spirituality, and compassion of the person. It resonates more as I grow older. His work touches me to the core. His work sets you straight. He spoke right to the heart of the matter—and the heart of the person.

MENDL MALKIN: There have been three people that I didn't know how much they meant to me, until they died. Leonard was one. Watching him become a wise old man, a spiritual person, a gentle, caring person, with his Jewishness newly out front, no longer really singing, almost whispering, while the music, in a sense, kept getting better and better . . . getting his shit together over the last years after being cheated out of his nest egg. . . . He was really impressive.

NICK MANCUSO: The thing that was so wonderful about Leonard was the *humility* he manifested. There was absolutely no ego in this guy. A pure artist— kind, tolerant, compassionate, helpful. Truly a human being—a mensch. He had an affability and a kindness of soul that is incredibly rare. I think he was truly a luminary. And he was Canadian, which meant something to him.

SEYMOUR MAYNE: He went through a gauntlet of doubt and a sense of failure and came out with songs that are haunting, not just because of the music—the language itself puts them at a very high level of expression. Haunting in its simplicity and its power. It's a simplicity that touches the deepest experience that defines us as human beings. I consider him to be the greatest lyricist in the twentieth century in English. The poetry and songs will not disappear. Some of the lyrics not only move people—they have the texture and intensity of poetry. You hear it once and it's not over. You go back.

CLAUDIA MOORE: Ah, Leonard—we were so young when you first moved into our hearts, gently slicing us open to teach us about love and loss and other essential aspects of life. He aged so magnificently, older and reckless. He had the courage to follow personal impulses, and creative and romantic ones. When he was writing, we were young, falling in love. Now, listening to those songs, that whole period is evoked and deep memories stirred. For him to come back in his late years was a great gift for us all. His legacy? Follow your heart, even though it hurts.

PAUL MULDOON: For me, there was no distinction between his collected poems and his collected songs. There's no need for a song to have the density his songs do. The pressure per square inch doesn't have to be as high as it is in Leonard's case for it to be effective. But the quality of the work really holds up on the page in a way that is remarkable.

KEN NORRIS: Leonard had the fame gene. If he'd stayed in the clothing business, there'd be a line of suits we'd all be wearing. Whatever he did, he would have been famous at. What I'm more impressed with is his success. First he did poetry—he'll be in Canadian poetry anthologies 'til the end of time. Then he turns to novels. *Beautiful Losers* still stands tall fifty years after it was written, one of the greatest novels ever published in Canada, though it could not be written today because of cultural appropriation. He was out to write the most outrageous book that he could that would offend everybody. And then there's the song writing. Does the music last? Who can say?

RONNIE OPPENHEIMER: I judge an artist by longevity. Everything else is subjective. He was a real class act. I consider him one of the all-time great artists.

PAUL OSTERMAYER: His legacy, besides being a great artist, will be his spiritual side. Some of those songs are prophetic. He saw it all coming—the big picture, in terms of democracy, the spiritual trends—where things were headed. He was a prophet. That's probably what will be recognized.

KEZBAN ÖZCAN: What he taught me was that when you think you are really too good, you are just beginning to be good enough.

ANDRÉE PELLETIER: For people who knew him, a very profound legacy of wisdom.

LOU POMANTI: His music lasts—absolutely. Neil [Young], Joni [Mitchell], and Leonard—those three will be part of world music forever. With Leonard, they're just simply great songs, almost like Rodgers and Hart, songs that can be done as jazz, as rock, as folk. Most of his songs are interpretable in many ways, the mark of a good song.

ERICA POMERANCE: He always had a certain magic to him. He was a timeless soul, a true poet, and is still around somewhere, and his spirit will grow.

ROSEMARY RADCLIFFE: There was a hunger in Leonard to be famous. He turned down that job as a CBC interviewer [in 1966] because he wanted to become a songwriter. He had a vision of what he should be. He was never afraid. I don't think he ever let anybody subvert his own particular vision of himself. That was what was special about him.

YOSHIN DAVID RADIN: Our dear friend Leonard made it easy for us. He arranged words and music with such elegance, he could express emotion with such utter sincerity, that minds and hearts stopped to listen. He could even mesmerize six hundred thousand cold, angry, nearly rioting people, in the middle of the night, on a small island off the coast of England, simply by the power of his humility, the purity of his heart, the authenticity of his presence. And forty years later, he could skip and sing and fall to his knees and into the hearts of fans around the world, turning crowds of concertgoers into a spiritual community, and music into prayer and worship. Worship of what? Worship of the deep bond we all ultimately share—crossing the sea of life in our fragile little boats.

HARRY RASKY: Leonard Cohen has become part of our language and we don't really know it yet. He will be regarded as the best Canadian poet, without question. I don't think he has any peers.

SUSAN RAY: There's a word in Tibetan—*dakini*—it literally translates as "skywalker." It's an enlightened feminine energy. Descriptors of *dakini* go from bad to worse—ugly, mean, bad-tempered, and yet they bear the energy of enlightenment. He was a big soul. I believe he was intended to reach a lot of people. It's unequivocally in his songs. That was his service. And he was in service, no question about it. And he did it with less bullshit than pretty well anybody else.

JEAN-MICHEL REUSSER: He was a great man who taught me a lot, without teaching. He taught me to be who you are. He taught me exigency, about what you put down in words, and how to be Zen and no Zen at the same time. A shrink would probably say I'm talking about a father figure. That may be true, but totally unconsciously. He was a strong person, rooted.

Even onstage, his presence was magnetic. He was a seigneur of truth, no fake, no business. He was a very simple man. That always struck me. And one of the best songwriters, ever. There's absolutely no equivalent—this mix of sexuality, mysticism, humour, sadness, guilt, everything. And the lyrics stand without the music. You can't compare him to whoever. Leonard is a universe, a universe unto himself.

MICHEL ROBIDOUX: Leonard's music is eternal. The proof is you can listen to it now and never get tired of it. It will stay forever. It's like the Beatles. It's that quality, that talent. And his humility—ordinary and humble, but bigger than life.

BERNIE ROTHMAN: I don't know anyone who uses the English language more beautifully. No poet captures the human spirit or describes the psychic landscape better than Cohen. No one's writing has ever warmed my romantic heart like Cohen's has. Not Shelley's, not Byron's, not Tennyson's. No one's.

BUFFY SAINTE-MARIE: I think of him as one of the great poets, like Rumi, Baudelaire, Rimbaud. He's a real classic. I don't think he'll be forgotten. There are things a combination brain can do with poetry and music and philosophy. Leonard had that kind of brain, and we'll profit from it, not just because of the poetry, but the songs, the philosophy, and the humour behind the content.

PAUL SALTZMAN: He was one of the most conscious people I've ever met, a beacon. When you're with him, you're not blabbing. "How's the weather?" If you're going to talk, let's talk about what's real, and let's do it with precision, with depth. He's one of my heroes, in the stunning creativity and depth of heart and soul he brought to the rest of us. He was a gift—to me, to so many, an emotional gift, a spiritual gift. He impacted my life in a big way.

DIANNE SEGHESIO: His house was empty. He wasn't into material things. It's not so surprising that he gave away all of his family heritage. He lived a very Spartan existence. I think his most cherished possessions were his two little kitchen chairs and that 1950s yellow, linoleum-covered table.

Just sit in the chair and look out that window at the concrete and over the telephone wires. All the birds would land and he'd watch those birds sitting there. It was such a simple life. He just had what he needed to eat for two days. He was in the moment. He really enjoyed living the simple monk's life and it didn't matter who his teacher was—it could've been the garbageman. That's who he was. He was a student and he was proud of it. He didn't need to be the teacher, but he wanted to be the best student he could be.

ERIK SLUTSKY: In some ways, he never really died. His physical body died, but his work is so powerful. His work is the legacy. It will last a very long time.

KIM SOLEZ: Leonard understands life better than the rest of us. His choice of words is better than ours so, ultimately, though he's no longer here, there are clues in the words and in the lyrics to the deep abiding questions that most of us have. I don't feel that way about anybody else.

NIC SUROVY: Leonard once told me that Joni Mitchell was the Bach of contemporary music. But Leonard was like an old *tanguero*, a tango dancer who, though old, is still a great dancer of the tango. Because you don't have to be young to be a great dancer of tango. All you have to do is know the dance, and just be yourself. He was that. Without doubt, one of the most interesting, complicated, *myterioso* people I've ever met.

TERESA TUDURY: Leonard filled a space that young men and young women long for—a matriculated male voice, not a hyper-extended cartoon of masculinity, which our culture foists on us, like Arnold Schwarzenegger. Leonard, with his deep, profound, testosterone-drenched voice and this magnificent ability to be strong in his vulnerability, able to be clawed and in thrall to ineffable, unattainable love, and to make mistakes and shake his fist at God, and then be so tender and loving. This full masculine life, lived on a stage for everyone, fulfills that longing for the healthy, conscious loving archetype of the male in our culture. He transcended all culture. I don't know anybody else who holds that position. He spoke to all of us. He was the father—the great flawed, human human.

ALAN TWIGG: I remember him saying one day, after he's dead, someone might find one of his books on the bottom shelf of a used bookstore. Just do the work, put it out there, don't hope for anything big. His work will last. I found him more inspirational and intriguing than Dylan. His legacy, like Joni Mitchell's, amounts to entirely original songs. Some of the poetry will survive, but the songs will last longer.

GABRIELA VALENZUELA: My body is vibrating, echoing my thoughts. Our paths would never cross again. It is too painful to bear. Ladies and gentlemen, Mr. Leonard Cohen! Grand, quirky, funny, kind, horny, foodie, generous, wordy, unforgetful, kid-tonic, yes indeed! If he showed you something, he would explain it in such a gentle, naive, shy kind of way. He came to you like winter wind. If you wanted him, you had to withstand the force. . . . So long, my friend, I see you in my dreams, holding hands now with our beautiful September.

JENNIFER WARNES: What I'm going to remember are a few tones of voice and the look in the eyes and his impeccable timing when you were in pain— those kinds of things. I'll remember that I woke up from a surgery to see him there, sleeping in the hospital, and I'll remember him at my mother's funeral. If we make it to another century, his songs will be spoken of and still referenced. I firmly believe that. He sacrificed his personal needs for that body of work to exist. It's the greatest gift of an artist, just to leave all of this. The deep humanity in it is going to be missed. . . . I can think of no more beautiful job than to have loved him and supported him and known him. That to me is like a very fulfilling feeling. There's no emptiness when I think of him.

MITCH WATKINS: The songs and the writings are pretty much undeniable. He's left a legacy among his sidemen who became better musicians and better artists because of being around him. Without question. It's like an unspoken club.

LEON WIESELTIER: Leonard was not so much a wise man as a man in search of wisdom. He found it, he lost it, he found it again, he tested it, he lost it, he found it again. The seeking was his calling. He was never certain, never done, never daunted, never saved.

HOWIE WISEMAN: His legacy is beyond our ability to say, so soon. This is not the normal passing of a singer-songwriter, artist. He has a depth and a visionary quality that puts him in the category of *the* great poets, observers of humanity. I don't want to say William Blake—he was a visionary of another kind. But Leonard was the embodiment of so much of what he sang about, in a way that we will see our society move towards, on a spiritual level, to handle the future. He was at the forefront of that. I see him as a profound influence on our times, on my times anyway.

MOSES ZNAIMER: Of all the singer-songwriters, he's the one who will last. He can be your soundtrack. Whatever you're thinking, experiencing, suffering, Leonard's done a song for that.

Afterword

One or two evenings a year, a group of some thirty hard-core Leonard Cohen fans gather in a home in Sydney, Australia, to play his music and sing his praises. As one of the group's principal organizers, Stephen Katz, explains, "Not only have I listened to more of Leonard's music than everyone else's, collectively, but he's had a greater influence over my persona than any teacher, rabbi, or lecturer. His music goes right through me, right to my inner core. I never get bored." The Aussie assembly, which continued to meet via Zoom during the recent pandemic, is just one of many such amateur groups, in cities around the world, dedicated to keeping Cohen's work and memory alive.

Field Commander Cohen's cadres are not limited to amateurs. Rarely a month goes by without the Cohen songbook being featured in pub concerts in cities as diverse as Kraków, Glasgow, Liege, and Copenhagen. Many professional performers routinely feature songs from his repertoire in their acts, or cover them on albums. Cohen's former backup singer, the luminous Perla Batalla, has created *House of Cohen*, a cabaret show based exclusively on his jukebox. Pre-COVID-19, she played to sold-out houses in Europe; and she returned to the road in Spring 2022, playing dates in six European countries. Sharon Robinson, both a backup singer and collaborator, followed suit, launching her own tribute show, *My Time with Leonard Cohen*, in June 2022. Irish musician Paddy McQuaile's Leonard Cohen tribute band toured Finland in April 2022 with six concerts. In 2018, Toronto's Art of Time ensemble mounted *A Singer Must Die*, an evening of Cohen music and poetry, sung and recited by notable Canadian performers and writers. And in the past several years, more than two dozen tribute albums have been released by artists in Croatia, the Netherlands, the United States, Poland, Germany, and Denmark. In 2021, the Swedish folk duo First Aid Kit released *Who by Fire*, based on a live concert in Stockholm. And in November 2022, Blue Note Records was scheduled to release *Here It Is: A Tribute to Leonard Cohen*, featuring Sarah McLachlan, James Taylor, Norah Jones, Peter Gabriel, Mavis Staples, Iggy Pop, and David Gray.

Cohen's appeal stretches to other artistic genres as well. To his voice, the Montreal dance company Ballet Jazz choreographed *Dance Me*, an eighty-eight-minute homage. *A Crack in Everything*, an exhibition examining diverse aspects of Cohen's life and curated by Montreal's Museum of Contemporary Art, has drawn huge crowds in several cities around the globe. And, scheduled to open in December 2022, is the Art Gallery of Ontario's *Everybody Knows*, an exhibit of never-before-seen treasures from the Cohen archive, including original art, concert footage, musical instruments, notebooks, lyrics, and letters.

In 2017, Montreal artist Kevin Ledo painted a vast mural of Cohen on a building in the city's Plateau neighbourhood. It was soon joined by *Tower of Song*, an even more ambitious effort, a ten-thousand-square-foot replica of a photograph of Cohen—originally taken by his daughter, Lorca Cohen—painted on a building on downtown Crescent Street. Now a permanent fixture, it has since become an urban landmark—the secular saint of Montreal, as the *New York Times* dubbed him, gazing down on his disciples beneficently, fedora cocked. A team project led by Montreal artist Gene Pendon and American street portrait artist El Mac, the mural is located only steps away from some of Cohen's favourite haunts, including the legendary Bistro on whose wall, in the early 1960s, he scribbled a famous graffiti plaint of unrequited love to a woman he was fruitlessly pursuing: "Marita, please find me. I am almost 30."

Feature-length documentary filmmakers have long been interested in Cohen's work, beginning with the National Film Board of Canada's *Ladies and Gentlemen, Mr. Leonard Cohen* (1965). It was followed by Tony Palmer's *Bird on a Wire* (1972), Harry Rasky's *Song of Leonard Cohen* (1980), and Lian Lunson's *I'm Your Man* (2005). More recent films include Nick Broomfield's *Marianne and Leonard—Words of Love* (2019); Daniel Geller and Dayna Goldfine's *Hallelujah: Leonard Cohen, A Journey, A Song* (2021);

and Fabien Greenberg and Bård Kjøge Rønning's *Little Axel*, which chronicles the troubled life of Marianne Ihlen's son, Axel Jensen, who Cohen helped raise. More documentaries are now in development. In time, one expects, there will be a biopic.

Then there are the Cohen books—five new ones in 2021, alone—a cottage industry of biographers, explicators, and analyzers, popular and academic. Other volumes were issued in 2022, including Cohen's first, previously unpublished novel, *A Ballet for Lepers*, and ten short stories written during the 1950s. This burgeoning library of Coheniana can be reliably predicted to grow, especially after his vast archive of notebooks, journals, and correspondence—now in the hands of his estate—is acquired by one or more institutions, and made available to researchers.

Scores of Cohenites have made private pilgrimages to Montreal to visit his various homes and his grave on Mount Royal. Many more have boarded the ferry to Hydra, the Greek island where he resided for parts of four decades, or turned up there, and in other towns and cities, for the Leonard Cohen Event—a celebratory weekend of all things Cohen. There have been twelve of these Cohen-ventions since 2005.

But perhaps the most meaningful metric of how vital Cohen's work remains six years after his death are the tens of thousands of members of Cohen fan sites, set up on Facebook, Instagram, and other social-media platforms. Virtually every day, they post clips from his concert videos, photographs, quotes, excerpts from interviews, and memories of encounters with the man himself—posts that are then met with cascades of enthusiastic GIFs and emojis, in one form or another shouting, "Hallelujah."

In Cohen's autobiographical first novel, *The Favourite Game*, Lawrence Breavman, the central character, at one point confesses his ambition: "I want to touch people like a magician . . . leave my brand."

And so he has. And so he will, it's a safe bet, for a long time to come.

—Michael Posner
Toronto, Ontario
May 2022

Acknowledgements

In my former life—an ink-stained wretch, in the shrinking world of daily journalism—it was my custom to walk to work each morning.

On one such morning, I was stopped in my tracks by a sharp pain in my chest. It passed, but returned the next day, and the one after that. Hypochondriacal at the best of times, I seized the opportunity of an audience with one of Canada's leading internists, Dr. Herbert Ho Ping Kong, to voice my concerns.

It was the end of December 2012. Toronto Western Hospital was already deep into holiday mode, but Dr. Ho Ping Kong persuaded a senior cardiologist, Dr. John Janevski, to see me the very next day. Blood work, stress test, echocardiogram—I failed them all. The ensuing angiogram reported a 99 percent blockage in the main artery, 80 percent in two others. I remember another cardiologist, Dr. Matthew Sibbald, gently conceding that I was very close to suffering a catastrophic cardiac event.

Two days later, I underwent triple bypass surgery at Toronto General Hospital, under a team led by cardiac surgeon Dr. Terence Yau. It is to these remarkable individuals—and the fleets of nurses in prep, the OR, and the ICU—that I owe these last ten years. No mere acknowledgement could ever fully express my gratitude, but let it be known that, without their care, wisdom, and skill, this series of Leonard Cohen oral biographies would surely not exist. And nor would I. I owe them my very life.

Both for this volume and its predecessors, I must of course thank the 560-plus people who freely (or with a little coaxing) surrendered some of their most precious memories—their stories and observations of Leonard. They constitute the real, collective biographers; I merely served as amanuensis. To some extent, I hope, it's their biography as much as his, a tableau spanning almost a century, a stage set on which some characters are mere walk-ons, while others take a seat for ten or twenty or fifty years.

Among the many extraordinary things about Leonard Cohen was that he seemed to take an interest in, and leave a lasting impression on, virtually everyone he met, even the commis chef buttering his bagel. I am indebted to them all: friends, family members, bandmates and backup singers, other professional associates, Hydriots, Los Angelinos, Montrealers, Parisiennes, Mount Baldians, New Yorkers, journalists, photographers, rabbis and cantors, Zen dharma brothers and sisters, lovers and, yes, the occasional metaphoric bagel butterer. Among these were several who have produced their own books and articles on Leonard, and kindly granted me permission to quote from their writing—most notably, the brilliant scholar Ruth Wisse and the incisively droll Eric Lerner.

Always technically challenged, I have depended on the patience and talents of my old friend David Groskind, and never been disappointed. And I owe a debt of thanks and service to my indefatigable researchers, Maria Cohen Viana, of Porto, and Dominique Boile, of Normandy.

I have likewise been fortunate to be counselled on this six-year journey by two very wise literary agents, the late Arnold Gosewich and—thanks to the assistance of an old writer friend, David Hayes—Hilary McMahon at Westwood Creative Artists. Along the way, I have also been the grateful beneficiary of the vision and unflagging support of the editorial team at Simon & Schuster Canada—President and Publisher Kevin Hanson; Senior Editor Justin Stoller; and Director of Publicity Adria Iwasutiak.

Although the time invested in this endeavour might suggest otherwise, my precious children—Lauren and Dany, Susan, Sam and Erin, and grandchildren (Gabriel, Deborah, Joseph, Matan, Max, Nathan, June, Mariana, and Alice)—were never far from my thoughts.

Finally, of course, there is Leonard himself, sui generis—a glorious, late-life gift to me, as he and his work have been to so many millions.

—Michael Posner
Toronto, Ontario
May 2022

Dramatis Personae

DAVID AMRAM: American singer-songwriter, friend
ERIC ANDERSEN: American singer-songwriter, friend
SANDRA ANDERSON: Montreal psychologist, friend
JARKKO ARJATSALO: Finnish accountant, Cohen webmaster, friend
WILLIE ARON: American singer, cantor, arranger, friend
HOWARD ASTER: Canadian publisher, friend
BRANDON AYRE: Physician, folk singer, friend
TONY BABINSKI: Canadian screenwriter, acquaintance
NANCY BACAL: Canadian filmmaker, friend for more than seventy years
PERLA BATALLA: American singer, backup singer 1988, 1993, friend
ROSCOE BECK: American musician, band member, friend after 1979
MARILYN BEKER: Canadian journalist, acquaintance
JACQUIE BELLON: Friend, former wife of Steve Sanfield
ROLOFF BENY: Canadian photographer, acquaintance
DINAH BERLAND: American acquaintance
HARRIET BERNSTEIN: Fourth wife of Irving Layton, friend
MARILYN BIDERMAN: Canadian publishing executive, friend
HOWARD BILERMAN: Canadian music producer, friend
BILL BISSETT: Canadian poet, acquaintance
MATT BISSONNETTE: Canadian film director, acquaintance
DAVID BLUE: American singer-songwriter, friend, died 1982
LEIF BODNARCHUK: Irish-Canadian writer/musician, friend
LINDA BOOK: Art gallery manager, friend
ASA BOXER: Montreal poet, friend
LIONA BOYD: Canadian singer, guitarist, friend

DAWN BRAMADAT: Canadian spiritualist, acquaintance

TONY BRAMWELL: British music producer/promoter, friend

JOHN BRANDI: American poet, friend

LAURIE BROWN: Canadian journalist, acquaintance

LINDA BRUMBACH: American arts producer, friend

ARMELLE BRUSQ: French documentary filmmaker, friend after the mid-1990s

JOAN BUCK: American writer, friend after 1972

FELICITY BUIRSKI: British actress, singer-songwriter, lover

PAUL BURGER: Former Sony music executive, friend

CHRIS BYNUM: American roadie, friend

KOSHIN CHRIS CAIN: Zen Buddhist monk, dharma brother, friend

JORGE CALDERÓN: American musician, composer, band member 1993, friend

ANDREW CALHOUN: American folk singer, fan

JOEY CARENZA: American tour manager, friend

ANDY CHARD: Tour truck driver 1988, friend

ISRAEL CHARNEY: Canadian artist, friend during the 1960s and '70s

JULIE CHRISTENSEN: American singer, backup singer 1988, 1993, friend

LINDA CLARK: Lover 1988–89, 1993–94

ADRIENNE CLARKSON: Canadian writer, editor, former governor general, friend
    for fifty years

ADAM COHEN: Canadian-American singer-songwriter, producer, son

ANDREW COHEN: Canadian journalist, author, cousin

ESTHER COHEN: Sister, died 2014

LORCA COHEN: Business proprietor, daughter

MASHA COHEN: Mother, died 1978

RICHARD COHEN: American business executive, Zen dharma brother, friend

ROBERT COHEN: Canadian psychotherapist, cousin

RUTH COHEN: Wife of Cohen's cousin, Edgar

JUDY COLLINS: American singer-songwriter, friend

IRWIN COTLER: Canadian lawyer, politician, friend

PIERRE COUPEY: Canadian artist, writer, friend

BRIAN CULLMAN: American writer/songwriter, friend

PETE CUMMINS: Irish musician, acquaintance

BILL CUNLIFFE: British barkeeper on Hydra, friend, died 2011

SOHEYL DAHI: American writer, poet, publisher, friend

CHRIS DARROW: American musician, friend, died 2020
REBECCA DE MORNAY: American actress, lover
ANN DIAMOND: Canadian writer, lover, friend
JAMES DIAMOND: Canadian Judaic scholar, acquaintance
JAMES DI SALVIO: Canadian producer, friend
SANDRA DJWA: Canadian literary critic, acquaintance
BARBARA DODGE: Artist, friend after the late 1960s
BILL DODGE: Canadian bookstore proprietor, friend
DENISE DONLON: Canadian music executive, friend
JAY DOVER: American acquaintance
CHARMAINE DUNN: Canadian model, lover, friend
JOE D'URSO: American musician, acquaintance
BOB DYLAN: American singer-songwriter, friend
DOVID EFUNE: American journalist, acquaintance
JULIE EISENBERG: American acquaintance
SUZANNE ELROD: Girlfriend and "wife" 1969–78, mother of Adam and Lorca
DAVID FAGAN: British writer, Hydriot friend
ROBERT FAGGEN: American professor of literature, writer, friend from 1995 on
DON FARBER: American photographer, filmmaker, friend
SAM FELDMAN: Canadian artist manager, friend
JULIE FELIX: American-British folk singer, lover, friend, died 2020
HAZEL FIELD: Montreal photographer, friend
DEB FILLER: Canadian comedienne, friend
MORDECAI FINLEY: American rabbi, friend
SHEILA FISCHMAN: Canadian translator, friend
MORRIS FISH: Canadian jurist, friend
JEFF FISHER: Canadian composer, friend
GERRY FLAHIVE: Canadian film producer, acquaintance
RUBIN FOGEL: Canadian concert promoter, friend
SYLVIA FRASER: Canadian novelist, acquaintance
BUNNY FREIDUS: American music executive, friend
YAN CALMEYER FRIIS: Norwegian journalist, friend
LEWIS FUREY: Canadian singer-songwriter, collaborator on *Night Magic*, friend after 1966
BOBBY FURGO: American musician, band member 1988, 1993, friend

BILL FURY: Canadian poet/writer, archivist, friend

LINDA GABORIAU: Canadian dramaturge, translator, friend

MICHEL GARNEAU: French-Canadian writer, friend, translator of Cohen's work, died 2021

GALE ZOE GARNETT: Canadian actress, singer, lover, friend

RAFAEL GAYOL: Mexican-American musician, friend, band member 2008–13

NAHUM NOOKIE GELBER: Lawyer, friend from the 1950s

RON GETMAN: American musician, band member 1985, died 2021

GISELA GETTY: German film director, friend

AVRIL GIACOBBI: Scottish public relations executive, lover, girlfriend of Marty Machat

RALPH GIBSON: American photographer, friend after the late 1960s

MARGIE GILLIS: Canadian dancer, choreographer, friend

ALLEN GINSBERG: American poet, friend after the late 1950s, died 1997

IRA GLADNICK: American dharma brother

BOB GLAUB: American musician, friend

ALAN GOLDEN: Montreal lawyer, cousin, friend

RICHARD GOODALL: British art gallery owner, friend

LEX GORE: Daughter of Cohen's girlfriend, Eva LaPierre, died 2020

YOAV GOREN: American composer, producer, friend

BARBARA GOWDY: Canadian novelist, acquaintance

KATE GRANT: Canadian photographer, acquaintance

ROGER GREEN: British writer, Hydriot friend

NEAL GREENBERG: American investment manager, acquaintance

JOHN GRIERSON: Canadian cinematographer, acquaintance

ROGER GUERIN: Canadian music engineer, friend

CHARLIE GURD: Canadian architect, writer, friend after 1971

DON GUY: American filmmaker, friend

NOAH GUY: American designer, son of Don Guy and Yafa Lerner

ROB HALLETT: British concert promoter, friend

MICHAEL HARRIS: Canadian poet, friend

PAT HARRIS: American musician, acquaintance

KARI HESTHAMAR: Norwegian journalist, biographer of Marianne Ihlen, acquaintance

PETER HIMMELMAN: American musician, acquaintance

CELIA HIRSCHMAN: American music executive, daughter of Jack

JACK HIRSCHMAN: American poet, friend after 1965, died 2021

IRIS HOND: Dutch composer, friend

MARK HUFF: American musician, acquaintance

PAUL HUMPHREYS: Zen dharma brother

SUZANNE HYRNIW: Zen dharma sister

JANIS IAN: American singer-songwriter, backup singer on one album

DON IENNER: American music executive, friend

MARIANNE IHLEN: Girlfriend, 1960–68, friend for life, died 2016

CATHERINE INGRAM: American writer, teacher, healer, friend

ALBERT INSINGER: Dutch singer, doppelgänger, friend

DOMINIQUE ISSERMANN: French photographer, lover 1981–91, friend

PICO IYER: British essayist and novelist, friend after 1995

SIMON JACOBSON: American rabbi, friend

ELTON JOHN: British singer-songwriter, friend

DON JOHNSTON: Canadian politician, diplomat, friend, died 2022

JUDE JOHNSTONE: American singer, composer, acquaintance

CHRISTINE JONES: Canadian-American stage designer, friend

JANIS JOPLIN: American singer, died 1970

KAREN KAIN: Canadian ballerina, ballet director, friend

PETER KATOUNTAS: Montreal friend, after 1977

SANGYE KHANDRO: American Tibetan Buddhist, friend

ANTHONY KINGSMILL: British painter, close Hydriot friend, died 1993

GEORGE KLAUS: Canadian music producer, acquaintance

DR. HERBERT HO PING KONG: Canadian internist

ROBERT KORY: American tax lawyer, artist manager, friend

SARAH KRAMER: American musician, friend

STEVE KRIEGER: Zen Buddhist monk, dharma brother, friend

HARVEY KUBERNIK: American music journalist, author, friend

STEPHEN LACK: Canadian-American painter, cousin

CÉLINE LA FRENIÈRE: Canadian-American screenwriter, lover 1977–79

K.D. LANG: Canadian singer-songwriter, friend

WILFRED LANGMAID: Canadian journalist

ROBERT LANTOS: Canadian film producer, friend

BARBARA LAPCEK: American artist, Hydriot friend

CAROLE LAURE: Canadian actress, friend

DIANNE LAWRENCE: Canadian-American artist, lover 1979–80, friend

MICHAEL LAWRENCE: American painter, Hydriot friend, died 2021

AVIVA LAYTON: Writer, friend for sixty years, "wife" of Irving

IRVING LAYTON: Canadian poet, friend for sixty years, died 2006

MAX LAYTON: Canadian poet, singer-songwriter, friend, son of Irving

CHRISTOPHE LEBOLD: French professor, Cohen biographer, friend

DENNIS LEE: Canadian poet, editor, friend

ELLIOTT LEFKO: Canadian-American concert promoter, friend

YAKOV LEIB HAKOHAIN: American Kabbalist, friend, died 2017

PATRICK LEONARD: American songwriter, producer, collaborator, friend

ERIC LERNER: American screenwriter, Zen brother, friend for forty years

YAFA LERNER: Canadian-American therapist, friend from the 1950s on, died 2003

BRIAN LESAGE: Zen monk, friend

JAY LEVIN: American therapist, acquaintance

BRIAN LEVINE: Canadian arts executive, acquaintance

GEORGE LIALIOS: Greek musician, spiritual seeker, friend, died 2011

DAVID LIEBER: Montreal writer, friend

LENNY LIGHTER: Canadian restaurateur, friend

PETER LINDFORSS: Swedish writer, friend, died 2015

STEVE LINDSEY: American music producer, friend, ex-husband of Kelley Lynch

JONATHAN LIPSIN: Canadian record store proprietor, acquaintance

WAYNE LIQUORMAN: American Advaita teacher, friend

JOHN LISSAUER: American producer, composer, arranger, friend

DON LOWE: British writer, Hydriot friend

PAUL LOWENSTEIN: Canadian businessman, fraternity brother

KELLEY LYNCH: Personal manager 1988–2004

CHERYL (DORSKIND) MACHAT: Daughter of Marty, friend

MARTY MACHAT: American lawyer, Cohen's business manager 1970–88, died 1988

MICHAEL MACHAT: American lawyer, son of Marty Machat

STEVE MACHAT: American music and film producer, writer, son of Marty, friend

DEBORAH MAGERMAN: Acquaintance, daughter of Cohen's friend from youth, Alfie Magerman

AL MAIR: Canadian music producer, distributor, acquaintance

ELLIOT MAJERCZYK: Canadian-American music broadcaster, friend

MENDL MALKIN: Canadian fan

SEIJU BOB MAMMOSER: Zen dharma brother, friend

NICK MANCUSO: Canadian actor, friend

ALBERTO MANZANO: Spanish writer, translator, friend

HELEN MARDEN: American painter, friend

MALKA MAROM: Israeli-Canadian folk singer, journalist, author, lover, friend

SUSAN MARSHALL: American director, friend

LINDSEY MARTIN: Zen dharma sister, friend

MICHELLE MARTIN: Zen dharma sister, friend

JAVIER MAS: Spanish musician, friend, band member 2008–13

RATNESH MATHUR: Indian businessman, friend

MYOSHO GINNY MATTHEWS: Zen dharma sister

SEYMOUR MAYNE: Canadian poet, friend after 1961

CASSIDY A. MAZE: American writer, friend

ANDY MCCLELLAND: Canadian musician, acquaintance

KEVIN MCGRATH: American scholar, Hydriot friend

TOM MCMORRAN: American musician, band member 1988, friend

STEVE MEADOR: American drummer, band member 1988, 1993, friend

BOB METZGER: American musician, band member 1988, 1993, 2008–11, friend

MIRCEA MIHAIES: Romanian writer, friend

DORIAN MILLER: Canadian poet, friend

JOHN MILLER: American musician, band member 1974–76, friend

JONI MITCHELL: Canadian folk singer, lover 1967–68, friend

IRINI MOLFESSI: Greek-French animal rights advocate, friend

CLAUDIA MOORE: Canadian dancer/choreographer, acquaintance

GRACE MORROW: American girlfriend, 1983

HENRY MOSCOVITCH: Canadian poet, friend, died 2004

ALLAN MOYLE: Canadian film director, friend

PAUL MULDOON: Irish poet, friend

FRANK MUTTER: German fan, acquaintance

LORI NAFSHUN: American music producer, acquaintance

NADINE NEEMEH: Canadian singer-songwriter, friend

PATRICIA NOLIN: French-Canadian actress, friend

KEN NORRIS: Canadian poet, friend

RONNIE OPPENHEIMER: British businessman, acquaintance

PAUL OSTERMAYER: American saxophonist, band member 1979, 1993, friend

KEZBAN ÖZCAN: Friend, Turkish-American assistant to Cohen for the last decade of his life

DIANNA PALAMAREK: Canadian caregiver, acquaintance

TONY PALMER: British filmmaker, friend

EVANGELIA PAPAIOANNOU: American consultant, friend

PINA PEIRCE: Zen dharma sister, friend

ANDRÉE PELLETIER: French-Canadian actress, lover 1976, 1978

DAVID PELOQUIN: American writer, artist, Cohen scholar

DOUGLAS PENICK: American writer, acquaintance, ex-husband of Kelley Lynch

SEPPO PIETIKÄINEN: Finnish writer, translator, friend

MAURICE PODBREY: South African–Canadian theatre director, acquaintance

LOU POMANTI: Canadian musician, band leader, friend

ERICA POMERANCE: Canadian filmmaker, lover mid-1960s

JACOB POTASHNIK: Canadian screenwriter, acquaintance

ANNA POTTIER: Friend, fifth wife of Irving Layton

BILL POWNALL: British painter, Hydriot friend

DEVA PREMAL: German singer, healer, acquaintance

MORGANA PRITCHARD: Welsh poet/artist, friend

DAVID PULLMAN: American investor, friend

JACK RABINOVITCH: Canadian businessman, acquaintance, died 2017

ROSEMARY RADCLIFFE: Canadian actress, friend

MARCIA RADIN: Zen dharma sister, friend, wife of David

YOSHIN DAVID RADIN: Zen dharma brother, friend

CECILLE GOLD RAICHLEN: Canadian summer camp counsellor from Cohen's youth

ANNE RAMIS: Hydriot friend

HOSEN CHRISTIANE RANGER: Zen dharma sister, friend

AHMED RASHID: Pakistani writer, acquaintance

SUSAN RAY: American writer, editor, lover, Dharma sister

JULIANNA RAYE: American mindfulness teacher, friend

ALISA REGAS: American arts producer, friend

MATTHEW REMSKI: American yoga teacher, writer

JEAN-MICHEL REUSSER: French music producer, friend from the mid-1980s

BRIAN ROBERTSON: Canadian producer, acquaintance

VICTORIA ROBERTSON: American teacher, Advaita student, friend

MICHEL ROBIDOUX: French-Canadian composer/arranger, friend, died 2021

SHARON ROBINSON: American singer, songwriter, collaborator, friend

MICHIKO JANE ROLEK: American writer, life coach, acquaintance

SONNY ROLLINS: American musician, acquaintance

SEIDO RAY RONCI: American professor, Rinzai Buddhist monk

JASON ROSENBLATT: Canadian musician, friend

MORTON ROSENGARTEN: Canadian sculptor, friend from the 1940s on

VIOLET ROSENGARTEN: Canadian artist, ex-wife of Morton Rosengarten, friend

GREG ROSS: New Zealand fan

HAROLD ROTH: American professor, Zen dharma brother, friend

RIFKAH ROTH: Swiss-Canadian healer, friend

BERNIE ROTHMAN: Canadian TV writer, producer, friend for sixty years, died 2020

GIKO DAVID RUBIN: Zen dharma brother

DENNIS RUFFO: Canadian concert promoter, acquaintance

BUFFY SAINT-MARIE: Canadian singer-songwriter, friend

PAUL SALTZMAN: Canadian filmmaker, friend

STEVE SANFIELD: American writer, friend after 1961, died 2015

MALAVIKA SANGGHVI: Indian journalist, acquaintance

KYOZAN JOSHU SASAKI: Rinzai-Ji Zen master, friend, died 2014

MUSIA SCHWARTZ: Canadian cultural figure, friend after 1950s, died 2021

PETER DALE SCOTT: Canadian professor, poet, friend after 1954

DIANNE SEGHESIO: Zen dharma sister, friend

RUTH SEYMOUR: American broadcast executive, friend

RUTH BROYDE SHARONE: American acquaintance

BRIAN SIDAWAY: Boat captain, Hydriot friend

VALERIE LLOYD SIDAWAY: Hydriot friend, wife of Brian

WIN SIEMERLING: Canadian scholar, acquaintance

FLORIA SIGISMONDI: Canadian TV director, friend

MICHAEL SIMMONS: American music journalist

JOHN SIMON: American record producer, friend

EDWARD SINGER: Canadian businessman, fan

LARRY SLOMAN: American music journalist, friend

ERIK SLUTSKY: Canadian artist, friend

NORMAN SNIDER: Canadian screenwriter, acquaintance, died 2020

DINO SOLDO: American musician, friend, band member 2008–11

KIM SOLEZ: Canadian pathologist, friend

MEL SOLMAN: Canadian journalist, friend

REGINA SOLOMON: Canadian acquaintance

DAVID SOLWAY: Canadian poet, singer-songwriter, friend

NANCY SOUTHAM: Canadian writer, friend

SHIRLEY SPENCER: Canadian fan

LESLEY ST. NICHOLAS: Canadian model, lover, friend

JUDY STEED: Canadian writer, acquaintance

PATSY STEWART: Canadian broadcast executive, lover, friend

GENTEI SANDY STEWART: Zen dharma brother, friend

OLIVER STONE: American film director, friend

BARBARA SUMNER: New Zealand writer, filmmaker

BETSY SUPERFON: American businesswoman, poker player, acquaintance

NIC SUROVY: American actor, friend

CRAIG SUSSMAN: American music producer, acquaintance

ANDREW SWEENY: American writer, fan

SHELDON TAYLOR: Canadian summer camper from Cohen's youth

RACHEL TERRY: Israeli-American model, Olympian, lover, friend

PHIL TÉTRAULT: Canadian poet, friend

PIERRE TÉTRAULT: Canadian writer, filmmaker, friend, brother of Phil

ANJANI THOMAS: American singer-songwriter, collaborator, lover

DR. JOSHUA TRABULUS: Cohen's LA internist, friend

JAMES TRUMAN: American writer, acquaintance

TERESA TUDURY: American singer, friend

ALAN TWIGG: Canadian writer, friend

LEANNE UNGAR: American recording engineer, friend

GABRIELA VALENZUELA: Costa Rican artist, model, friend, lover 1982–86

PETER VAN TOORN: Canadian poet, friend, died 2021

SUZANNE VERDAL: Canadian dancer, inspiration for the song "Suzanne"

MARIA COHEN VIANA: Portuguese researcher, fan

MARK VREEKEN: Canadian sound engineer, friend

CLYDE WAGNER: Canadian arts executive, acquaintance

JENNIFER WARNES: American singer, backup singer 1972, 1979, lover, friend

DAVID WAS: American musician, acquaintance

DON WAS: American musician, music executive, friend

MITCH WATKINS: American musician, band member 1979–80, 1985, 2011–13

CHARLEY WEBB: British singer-songwriter, friend, band member 2008–13

HATTIE WEBB: British singer-songwriter, harpist, friend, band member 2008–13

PHYLLIS WEBB: Canadian poet, friend, died 2021

SHARON WEISZ: American publicist, friend

RICHARD WESTIN: American tax lawyer, acquaintance

BARRIE WEXLER: Canadian writer and producer, friend for fifty years

SHINGETSU BILLY WHITE: American composer, healer, friend

LEON WIESELTIER: American writer, editor, friend

HAL WILLNER: American music producer, friend, died 2020

CAROLE WILSON: American filmmaker, friend

HOWIE WISEMAN: Canadian screenwriter, acquaintance

RUTH WISSE: Canadian-American scholar, college friend

MYOREN KUMIKO YASUKAWA: Canadian Zen dharma sister, friend

SHINZEN YOUNG: American Zen Buddhist, scholar, teacher, friend

NOAH ZACHARIN: Canadian poet, musician, friend

GIDEON ZELERMYER: Canadian cantor, friend

CAROL ZEMEL: Canadian professor of art, friend from the 1960s, died 2021

HENRY ZEMEL: Canadian filmmaker, physicist, friend from the 1960s on

SANDRA ZEMOR: French musician, artist, friend

MATT ZIMBEL: Canadian musician, acquaintance

STEVE ZIRKEL: Texan musician, band member 1988, friend

MOSES ZNAIMER: Canadian broadcast executive, friend

RICHARD ZUCKERMAN: Scottish-Canadian record executive, friend